Rick Steves

BEST OF

SCOTLAND

Rick Steves with Cameron Hewitt

Contents

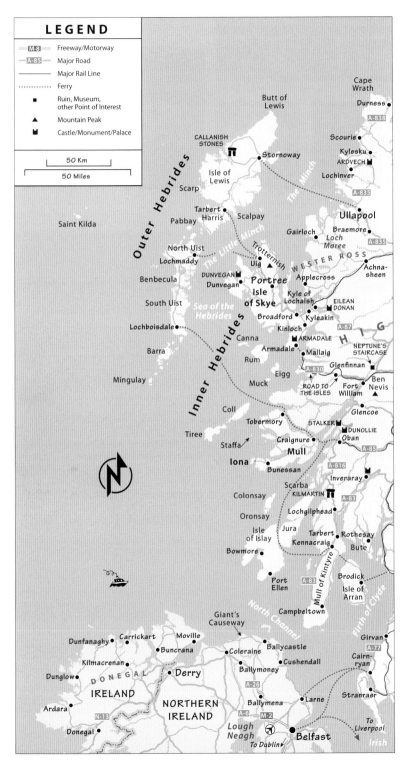

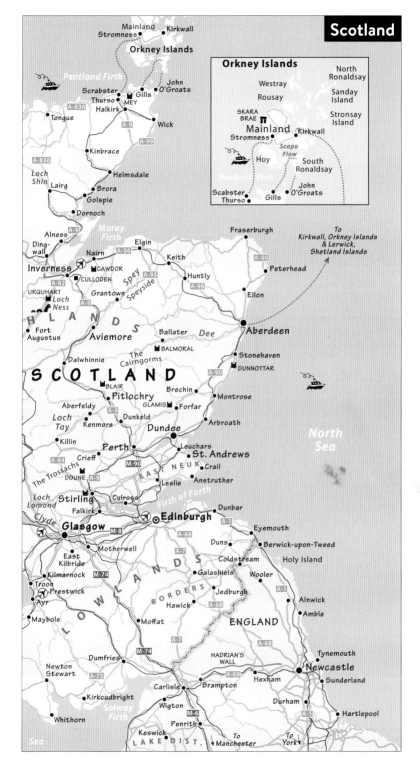

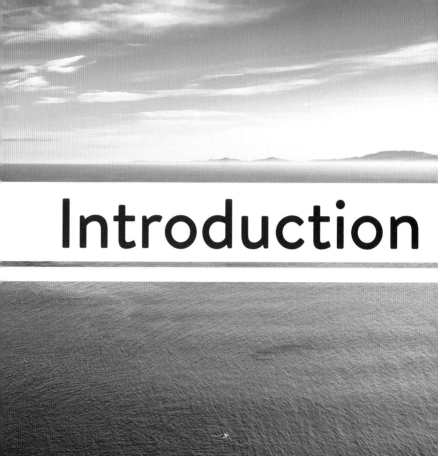

Introduction

One of the three countries that make up the island of Great Britain, Scotland is the most feisty and colorful, from its laid-back people and poetic heritage to its rugged landscape.

Scotland encompasses about a third of Britain's geographical area (30,400 square miles), but has less than a tenth of its population (about 5.4 million).

The southern part of Scotland, called the Lowlands, is relatively flat and urbanized. The northern area—the Highlands—has a hilly terrain dotted with lochs (lakes) and fringed by sea lochs (inlets) and islands.

Scotland's iconic symbols—bagpipes, moody glens, whisky distilleries, golf links, kilts, and yes, even haggis (organ-meat sausage)—seem at first like touristic clichés, but they're an authentic part of the cultural heritage of this engaging country.

The proud Scots are enjoying some recent political autonomy from England. The Scottish parliament, though limited in power, convened in Edinburgh in 1999 for the first time in nearly 300 years. The Scots appreciate the refreshing breeze of increased self-governance, and the question of independence is likely to remain a pivotal issue for years to come.

Whether you're toasting with beer, whisky, or Scotland's favorite soft drink, Irn-Bru, enjoy meeting the Scottish people. It's easy to fall in love with the irrepressible spirit and striking scenery of this faraway land.

THE BEST OF SCOTLAND

This book focuses on Scotland's top destinations, from its lively cities and Highland towns to its sleepy islands. The top cities in the Lowlands are vibrant Edinburgh, up-and-coming Glasgow, and medieval-but-youthful St. Andrews. The Highlands offer a rural, craggy contrast, with port-town Oban (island excursions), pleasant Inverness (near Loch Ness and an historic battlefield), and the inviting Isle of Skye.

Beyond the major destinations, I'll cover the Best of the Rest—great destinations that don't quite make my top cut, but are worthwhile: Stirling, Glencoe, Pitlochry, and Balmoral Castle.

When there are interesting sights near my top destinations, I cover these briefly (as "Near" sights), to help you fill out a free day or a longer stay.

To link the major destinations, I've designed a two-week itinerary (see page 26) with tips to help you tailor it to your interests and time.

THE BEST OF EDINBURGH

Nestled by bluffs and studded with a skyline of spires and towers, Scotland's showpiece capital boasts excellent museums and lively culture. The attraction-studded Royal Mile, lined with medieval buildings, connects the grand castle and stately palace in a wonderful way. The city's exuberance is enjoyable year-round and nonstop during August's festivals.

❶ *Edinburgh's famous street, the **Royal Mile,** offers a pleasing array of attractions, pubs, shops, and historic churches.*

❷ ***Highland dancers** stepping over crossed swords practice the Sword Dance.*

❸ *Some shops make **custom kilts** using woven (not cheaply printed) tartan material.*

❹ *A **bagpiper** in full regalia plays Scotland's national instrument.*

❺ *The **Fringe Festival** brings out people's Inner Wild.*

❻ *Try a few drams of **whisky** at a tasting.*

❼ *Edinburgh's **formidable castle** repelled foes long ago and attracts visitors today.*

THE BEST OF GLASGOW

Glasgow, once a mighty ship-building center, is now a cosmopolitan destination, with an unpretentious friendliness, an energetic dining and nightlife scene, top-notch museums (most of them free), and a flair for art and design. Its famous home-town architect, Charles Rennie Mackintosh, left his mark all over Glasgow at the turn of the 20th century.

❶ Glasgow's **cathedral**—a rare Scottish cathedral that survived the Reformation

❷ A **bagpiper** plays to a captive audience.

❸ **Charles Rennie Mackintosh** designed the **Willow Tea Rooms**— even the lights, furniture, and silverware.

❹ The **Mural Trail** offers **street art** on a grand scale.

❺ Visiting the **Gallery of Modern Art** is a heady experience.

❻ Rocco's **Empire Coffee Box** is open for caffeination.

❼ Glasgow's **pedestrian-only streets** are lively thoroughfares.

THE BEST OF ST. ANDREWS

This coastal town hosts Scotland's top university and the world's most famous golf course. With a medieval Old Town, evocative ruins of its castle and cathedral, sandy beaches (with activities), and a student vibe, St. Andrews attracts visitors of all ages, whether they prefer tee time, tea time, or just a fun time.

❶ *St. Andrews Cathedral* was destroyed during the Scottish Reformation.

❷ *Golfers* get their game on at St. Andrews.

❸ Quaint *shop-lined streets* invite browsing.

❹ *Locals* are as photogenic as the town.

❺ *Students* wear their robes for special events—and always on Sunday for the *Pier Walk.*

THE BEST OF OBAN & THE INNER HEBRIDES

Midway between the Lowlands and Highlands, the handy home-base of Oban hosts a fine distillery tour and boat excursions. As a "gateway to the isles," the charming port offers a fascinating day-trip to the nearby islands of the Inner Hebrides: rugged Mull, spiritual Iona, and remote Staffa, populated only by sea birds.

❶ *Nightlife* *in Oban comes with a bagpipe soundtrack.*

❷ *A* *fisherman* *displays the catch of the day.*

❸ *The port town of* *Oban* *clusters around its harbor.*

❹ *The island of* *Iona,* *with its historic abbey, makes an* *easy day trip.*

❺ *At Oban's* *fish-and-chips joints*, *the fish is very fresh.*

❻ *A* ceilidh—*music and dancing*—*is fun on summer evenings.*

❼ *Puffins* *populate the island of* *Staffa,* *just off Iona.*

❽ *The* *ferry* *takes visitors throughout the Inner Hebrides.*

THE BEST OF THE ISLE OF SKYE

The dramatically scenic island, the best of the Inner Hebrides, offers a concentrated dose of the Highlands, featuring craggy Cuillin Hills, the jagged Trotternish Peninsula, castles, a distillery, dynamic clan history, and the colorful harbor town of Portree.

❶ A **hairy coo**'s thick hair keeps it warm during cold, wet winters.

❷ **Eilean Donan Castle** greets visitors coming and going from the island.

❸ **Portree** is Skye's leading town.

❹ Happy graduates of **Talisker Distillery**'s tour make a toast.

❺ The **falls near Kilt Rock** drop precipitously to the sea.

❻ Portree's **peaceful harbor** is protected by peninsulas.

❼ Skye's sweeping **green vistas** are sprinkled with sheep.

THE BEST OF INVERNESS & LOCH NESS

The regional capital of Inverness has easy access to more Highland sights, including the historic Culloden Battlefield (where Bonnie Prince Charlie was defeated), beautiful Cawdor Castle, monster-spotting at the famous Loch Ness, Urquhart Castle, and the impressive Caledonian Canal.

❶ *On the shores of Loch Ness,* **Urquhart Castle** *crumbles away.*

❷ *Who says the* **Loch Ness monster** *doesn't exist?*

❸ **Inverness** *makes a* **good home base** *for day trips.*

❹ *The* **old town** *of Inverness invites* **strolling.**

❺ *The* **Leault sheepdog demonstration** *wows visitors.*

❻ *Inverness has a range of appealing,* **cosmopolitan eateries.**

❼ **Cawdor Castle,** *near Inverness, is surrounded by lovely* **gardens.**

THE BEST OF THE REST

With extra time, splice any of these destinations into your trip. Stirling is one of Scotland's top castles, with interesting sights nearby—from giant horse heads to a Ferris wheel for boats at Falkirk. The stirring "Weeping Glen" of Glencoe offers some of the Highlands' best scenery and hikes. Pitlochry is awash with whisky distilleries and laced with hiking trails. Balmoral Castle, the Queen's Scottish retreat, is yours to visit when she's away.

❶ *Glencoe* offers an easy, refreshing look at the Highlands.

❷ Of historic **Stirling Castle,** it's been said: "He who holds Stirling, holds Scotland."

❸ The **Falkirk Wheel** ingeniously lifts boats between locks.

❹ **Balmoral Castle** is the Queen's go-to spot in Scotland.

❺ With moors and mountains, **Glencoe Valley** attracts nature lovers.

❻ **Pitlochry distilleries** stock ample whisky for their popular tours.

❼ The **Kelpies** pay homage to **sprites of Scottish lore** who took the shape of horses.

TRAVEL SMART

Approach Scotland like a veteran traveler, even if it's your first trip. Design your itinerary, get a handle on your budget, make advance arrangements, and follow my travel strategies on the road.

For my best advice on sightseeing, accommodations, restaurants, and transportation, see the Practicalities chapter.

Designing Your Itinerary

Decide when to go. July and August are peak season for good reason: very long days, the best weather, and the busiest schedule of tourist fun. Edinburgh is abuzz throughout August with festivals.

Travel during "shoulder season"— May, early June, September, and early October—offers better room availability and prices. In May and June, the full range of sights and tourist fun spots are open— not so much in fall.

In winter, tourists are few and room prices are soft, but the weather is reliably bad. City sightseeing is fine, but rural sights may be open only on weekends or may close entirely.

Whenever you go, your B&B host will warn you to prepare for "four seasons in one day," though the weather is rarely extreme. Bring a jacket, dress in layers, and take full advantage of bright spells.

Choose your top destinations. My itinerary (on page 26) gives you an idea of how much you can reasonably see in 14 days, but you can adapt it to fit your own interests and timeframe.

If you enjoy all that big cities have to offer, you could easily spend a week in Edinburgh, even outside of festival time. For nightlife, Edinburgh and Glasgow are tops.

Historians find much to study in Scotland. Royalists tour Scotland's many castles (Edinburgh's Castle and Palace of Holyroodhouse, Stirling, Balmoral, Dunvegan, and more), while clansmen gather at Glencoe's Weeping Glen, the Culloden Battlefield, and the Isle of Skye. Architects are drawn to Glasgow, and engineers are intrigued by the Caledonian Canal and Falkirk Wheel.

Hikers love to go a 'wandering in the Highlands, particularly around Glencoe and the Isle of Skye. Golfers head to St. Andrews, of course. Photographers want to go everywhere.

For countryside fun in summer, be sure to see if any Highland Games coincide with your visit (check www.shga.co.uk).

Highland Games, held in many towns, offer authentic Scottish culture.

These quintessentially Scottish competitions—day-long events held in various towns throughout summer—celebrate Highland dancing, footraces, and feats of strength. They're well worth a day of your trip.

Draft a rough itinerary. Figure out how many destinations you can comfortably fit in the time you have. Don't overdo it— few travelers wish they'd hurried more. Allow enough days per stop: Figure on two days for most destinations and more for Edinburgh. Staying in a home base— like Oban or Inverness—and making day trips can be more time-efficient than changing locations and hotels. Minimize one-night stands, especially consecutive ones; it can be worth taking a late-afternoon drive or train ride to get settled into a town for two nights.

Connect the dots. Link your destinations into a logical route.

Instead of spending the first few days of your trip in busy Edinburgh, you could start in less-touristy, more laid-back Glasgow and save Edinburgh—with its heavy-duty sightseeing—for the grand finale. Going from Edinburgh's airport to Glasgow takes under an hour by train. You'll be more rested and ready to tackle Scotland's greatest city at the end of your trip.

Decide if you'll travel in Scotland by car or public transportation or a combination. I prefer a car for exploring the Highlands, but it's useless in Edinburgh and Glasgow (pick up your car as you leave Glasgow and drop it upon arrival in Edinburgh). Some travelers rent a car on site for a day or two (the Isle of Skye is a good candidate for this), and use public transportation for the rest of their trip.

If relying on public transportation, you'll likely use a mix of trains and buses. Buses are slower than trains but cheaper, and go many places that trains don't. In the mountainous Highlands, buses are often your only option (note that they run less frequently on Sundays). If you

have limited time, consider taking minibus tours of the Highlands, offered from Inverness, Glasgow, and even Edinburgh. But with more time, everything is workable by public transportation.

To determine approximate transportation times, check driving distances (see the "Driving" map in Practicalities), train schedules (www.nationalrail.co.uk or www.bahn.com), or this route-planning site that includes train and bus options: www.traveline.info.

If your plans extend beyond Scotland, determine which cities in Europe you'll fly into and out of—for instance, into Edinburgh and out of Amsterdam. Begin your search for flights at Kayak.com; for budget flights within Europe, try Skyscanner.com.

Plan your days. Fine-tune your trip; write out a day-by-day plan of where you'll be and what you want to see. To help you make the most of your time, I've suggested day plans for destinations. But check the opening hours of sights; avoid visiting a town on the one day a week that your must-see sight is closed. Research whether any holidays or festivals will fall during your trip—these attract crowds and can close sights (for the latest, check Scotland's website, www.visitscotland.com).

Give yourself some slack. Nonstop sightseeing can turn a vacation into a blur. Every trip, and every traveler, needs downtime for doing laundry, picnic shopping, relaxing, people-watching, and so on. Pace yourself. Assume you will return.

Ready, set... You've designed the perfect itinerary for the trip of a lifetime.

Trip Costs

Run a reality check on your dream trip. You'll have major transportation costs in addition to daily expenses.

Flight: A round-trip flight from the US to Edinburgh costs about $1,000-2,000.

Car Rental: Figure on a minimum of $250 per week, not including tolls, gas,

BEST OF SCOTLAND IN 2 WEEKS

This unforgettable trip will show you the very best that Scotland has to offer. While this itinerary is geared for drivers (who pick up their rental car when leaving Glasgow), most connections can be done by train or bus, though allow extra time, and consider a bus tour from Inverness for Highland day-tripping.

DAY	PLAN	SLEEP IN
	Fly into Edinburgh, train (50 minutes) to Glasgow	Glasgow
1	Sightsee Glasgow	Glasgow
2	Glasgow	Glasgow
3	Pick up car, drive to Oban (or 3-hour train ride)	Oban
4	Day-trip to islands of Mull, Iona, and maybe Staffa	Oban
5	Drive to Glencoe in morning, then to Isle of Skye (or 6-hour bus ride)	Portree
6	Explore the Isle of Skye by car or minibus tour. Hikers will want to spend another day.	Portree
7	Drive along the Caledonian Canal and Loch Ness to Inverness (or 3.5-hour bus ride)	Inverness
8	Inverness and side-trip to Culloden Battlefield	Inverness
9	Head south to Pitlochry (1.5 hours by train), then St. Andrews (2 hours by train and bus)	St. Andrews
10	Sightsee St. Andrews	St. Andrews
11	Visit Stirling Castle and nearby sights, then drop car in Edinburgh. Nondrivers head straight to Edinburgh (1.5 hours by bus and train) and save Stirling for a day trip from Edinburgh.	Edinburgh
12	Sightsee Edinburgh	Edinburgh
13	Edinburgh	Edinburgh
14	Edinburgh	Edinburgh
	Fly home	

Atlantic
Ocean

Orkney
Islands

SCOTLAND

H I G H L A N D S

Isle of
Skye

Portree ②

② **Inverness**

Loch
Ness

Balmoral

Glencoe

Pitlochry

Mull

Iona

Oban ②

Stirling

St. Andrews ②

Glasgow ③

④ **Edinburgh**

Irish
Sea

North
Sea

L O W L A N D S

ENGLAND

50 Kilometers

50 Miles

L E G E N D
② Number of
Overnights
• Other Stops

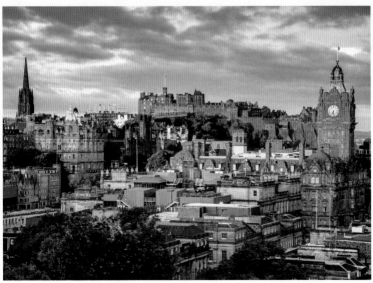

Average Daily Expenses per Person: $160 in Scotland ($200 in Edinburgh)

Cost	Category	Notes
$70	Lodging	Based on two people splitting the cost of a $140 double room that includes breakfast
$50	Meals	$15 for lunch and $35 for dinner
$30	Sights and Entertainment	This daily average works for most people.
$10	City Transit	Buses and trams
$160	**Total**	Figure on $200 for Edinburgh

parking, and insurance. Rentals and leases (an economical way to go if you need a car for at least three weeks) are cheaper if arranged from the US.

Public Transportation: For a two-week trip, you'd spend about $250 to cover train and bus tickets. To reduce train costs, you can get discounted advance-purchase tickets online, though you'll be locked into the travel time you choose. A Spirit of Scotland pass, which covers trains, buses, and ferries, could be worth it for the convenience.

Budget Tips: Cut your daily expenses by taking advantage of the deals you'll find throughout Scotland and mentioned in this book.

City transit passes for all-day usage keep your costs down in Edinburgh and Glasgow.

Avid sightseers consider Scotland's country-wide sightseeing passes and memberships (see page 256). If you don't get a pass, see only the sights you most want to see, and seek out free sights—especially easy to do in Glasgow.

Some businesses—especially hotels and walking-tour companies—offer discounts to my readers (look for the RS% symbol in the listings in this book).

Book your rooms directly with the hotel. Some hotels offer a discount if you pay in cash and/or stay three or more nights; check online or ask. And even seniors can sleep cheap in hostels (some have double rooms) for as little as $30 per person. Or check Airbnb-type sites for deals. (But don't expect any deals in Edinburgh during festival-filled August when hotel prices often soar; your best bet is booking well in advance.)

It's easy to eat cheap in Scotland. You can get tasty, inexpensive meals at pubs, cafeterias, cheap chain restaurants, fish-and-chips joints, and ethnic eateries. Some upscale restaurants offer early-bird dinner specials. Bakeries and groceries sell sandwiches; cultivate the art of picnicking in atmospheric settings.

When you splurge, choose an experience you'll always remember, such as a musical event or an island day-trip. Minimize souvenir shopping. Focus instead on collecting vivid memories, wonderful stories, and new friends.

Before You Go

You'll have a smoother trip if you tackle a few things ahead of time. For more information on these topics, see the Practicalities chapter and check www.ricksteves.com for book updates, more travel tips, and travel talks.

Make sure your passport is valid. If it's

due to expire within six months of your ticketed date of return, you need to renew it. Allow up to six weeks to renew or get a passport (www.travel.state.gov).

Arrange your transportation. Book your international flights. Figure out your main form of transportation within Scotland, whether you're renting a car, ordering discounted train tickets online in advance, getting a rail pass, or buying tickets as you go. If traveling beyond Scotland, think about booking cheap European flights. (You can wing it once you're there, but it may cost more.)

Book rooms well in advance, particularly if your trip falls during summer or any major holidays or festivals; those visiting Edinburgh in August or the Isle of Skye in summer should book especially early.

Book ahead for major sights, experiences, or guides. If you'll be in Edinburgh in August, check the festival schedule for theater and music in advance; if there's something you just have to see, consider buying tickets before your trip. Tickets to Edinburgh's Military Tattoo (also in Aug) sell out early—book as far ahead as possible. To golf at St. Andrews' famous Old Course, reserve the previous fall, or put your name in for the "ballot" two days before. If you plan to hire a **local guide,** book ahead by email. Specifics on making reservations are in the chapters.

Consider travel insurance. Compare the cost of the insurance to the cost of your potential loss. Check whether your existing insurance (health, homeowners, or renters) covers you and your possessions overseas.

Call your bank. Alert your bank that you'll be using your debit and credit cards in Europe. Ask about transaction fees, and get the PIN number for your credit card. You don't need to bring pounds for your trip; you can withdraw pounds from cash machines in Scotland.

Use your smartphone smartly. Sign up for an international service plan to reduce your costs, or rely on Wi-Fi in Europe instead. Download any apps you'll want on the road, such as maps, transit schedules, and Rick Steves Audio Europe (see sidebar).

Pack light. You'll walk with your luggage more than you think. Bring a single carry-on bag and a daypack. Use the packing checklist in the Practicalities chapter as a guide.

Travel Strategies on the Road

If you have a positive attitude, equip yourself with good information (this book), and expect to travel smart, you will.

Read—and reread—this book. To have an "A" trip, be an "A" student. Note opening hours of sights, closed days, crowd-beating tips, and whether reservations are required or advisable. Check for any changes at www.ricksteves.com/update.

Be your own tour guide. As you travel, get up-to-date info on sights, reserve

∩ Stick This Guidebook in Your Ear!

My free Rick Steves Audio Europe app makes it easy for you to download my audio tours of many of Europe's top attractions and listen to them offline during your travels. For Scotland, this includes my Edinburgh Royal Mile Walk, which is marked with this symbol: ∩. The app also offers insightful travel interviews from my public radio show with experts from Scotland and around the globe. It's all free! You can download the app via Apple's App Store, Google Play, or Amazon's Appstore. For more info, see www.ricksteves.com/audioeurope.

tickets and tours, reconfirm hotels and travel arrangements, and check transit connections. Find out the latest from tourist-information offices (TIs), your hoteliers, checking online, or phoning ahead. Upon arrival in a new town, lay the groundwork for a smooth departure; confirm the train, bus, or road you'll take when you leave.

Give local tours a spin. Your appreciation of a city or region and its history can increase dramatically if you take a walking tour in any big city or at a museum (some offer live or audio tours), or even hire a private guide (some will drive you around). If you want to learn more about any aspect of Scotland, you're in the right place with experts happy to teach you.

Outsmart thieves. Pickpockets abound in crowded places where tourists congregate. Treat commotions as smokescreens for theft. Keep your cash, credit cards, and passport secure in a money belt tucked under your clothes; carry only a day's spending money in your front pocket. Don't set valuable items down on counters or café tabletops, where they can be quickly stolen or easily forgotten.

To reduce potential loss, keep expensive gear to a minimum. Bring photocopies or take photos of important documents (passport and cards) to aid in replacement if they're lost or stolen.

Guard your time and energy. Taking a minibus tour can be a good value if it saves you a long day of waiting for bus connections. A taxi can be worthwhile when you're tired. To avoid long lines at sights, follow my crowd-beating tips, such as making advance reservations, or sightseeing early or late.

Be flexible. Even if you have a well-planned itinerary, expect changes, closures, sore feet, drizzly days, and so on. Your Plan B could turn out to be even better. And when problems arise (a bad meal or a noisy hotel room), keep things in perspective. You're on vacation in a beautiful country.

Connect with the culture. Interacting with locals carbonates your experience. Enjoy the friendliness of the Scottish people. Ask questions; most locals are happy to point you in their idea of the right direction. Set up your own quest for the best hike, castle viewpoint, or whisky tasting. Dare to try haggis. When an opportunity pops up, make it a habit to say "yes."

Hear the trill of the bagpipes? Taste a wee dram of whisky? Feel the winds of history blowing through the glens?

Your next stop...Scotland!

Welcome to Rick Steves' Europe

Travel is intensified living—maximum thrills per minute and one of the last great sources of legal adventure. Travel is freedom. It's recess, and we need it.

I discovered a passion for European travel as a teen and have been sharing it ever since—through tours, my public television and radio shows, and travel guidebooks. Over the years, I've taught thousands of travelers how to best enjoy Europe's blockbuster sights—and experience "Back Door" discoveries that most tourists miss.

This book offers a balanced mix of Scotland's rich cultural heritage and the rugged beauty of its countryside. It's selective: Scotland has more than 790 islands, but I recommend only the best—Skye, Mull, Iona, and Staffa. And it's in-depth: My self-guided city walks and driving tours give insight into the country's vibrant history and today's living, breathing culture.

I advocate traveling simply and smartly. Take advantage of my money- and time-saving tips on sightseeing, transportation, and more. Try local, characteristic alternatives to expensive hotels and restaurants. In many ways, spending more money only builds a thicker wall between you and what you traveled so far to see.

We visit Scotland to experience it—to become temporary locals. Thoughtful travel engages us with the world, as we learn to appreciate other cultures and new ways to measure quality of life.

Judging from the positive feedback I receive from my readers, this book will help you enjoy a fun, affordable, and rewarding vacation—whether it's your first trip or your tenth.

Happy travels!

Edinburgh

Edinburgh (ED-in-burah—only tourists pronounce it like "Pittsburgh") is the historical, cultural, and political capital of Scotland. For nearly a thousand years, Scotland's kings, parliaments, writers, thinkers, and bankers have called Edinburgh home. Today, it remains Scotland's most sophisticated city.

Edinburgh feels like two cities in one. The Old Town stretches along the Royal Mile, from the grand castle on top to the palace on the bottom. Along this colorful labyrinth of cobbled streets and narrow lanes, medieval skyscrapers stand shoulder to shoulder, hiding peaceful courtyards.

A few hundred yards north of the Old Town lies the New Town. It's a magnificent planned neighborhood (from the 1700s). Here, you'll enjoy upscale shops, broad boulevards, straight streets, and Georgian mansions decked out in Greek-style columns and statues.

Since 1999, when Scotland regained a measure of self-rule, Edinburgh reassumed its place as home of the Scottish Parliament. The city hums with life. Students and professionals pack the pubs and art galleries. It's especially lively in August, when the Edinburgh Festival takes over the town. Historic, monumental, fun, and well-organized, Edinburgh is a tourist's delight.

EDINBURGH IN 3 DAYS

Day 1: Tour the castle. Then, you could hop on the city bus tour (departing from a block below the castle at the Hub/Tolbooth Church). Or you could dive into my self-guided Royal Mile walk, stopping in at shops, churches, and museums that interest you (Gladstone's Land is tops but you can only visit it by booking a tour). At the bottom of the Mile, consider visiting the Scottish Parliament, the Palace of Holyroodhouse, or both. If the weather's good, you could hike back to your B&B along the Salisbury Crags.

On any evening: Options include various "haunted Edinburgh" walks, literary pub crawls, theater, live music in pubs, or a touristy Scottish folk evening.

Day 2: Visit the National Museum of Scotland. After lunch, stroll through the Princes Street Gardens and the Scottish National Gallery. Then follow my self-guided walk through the New Town, visiting the Scottish National Portrait Gallery and the Georgian House.

Day 3: Choose among these appealing

options—Tour the good ship *Britannia* (just outside of town; allow a half-day). Visit any museums you didn't get to on Days 1 and 2. Go hiking for great city views: up Calton Hill or above the Salisbury Crags to Arthur's Seat. Browse the shopping streets, try a whisky tasting, and stroll the Royal Mile again, this time without a sightseeing agenda, simply to enjoy this grand city.

ORIENTATION

With 490,000 people (835,000 in the metro area), Edinburgh is Scotland's second-biggest city (after Glasgow). But the tourist's Edinburgh is compact: Old Town, New Town, and the B&B area south of the city center.

Edinburgh's **Old Town** stretches across a ridgeline slung between two bluffs. From west to east, this "Royal Mile" runs from the Castle Rock—which is visible from anywhere—to the base of the 822-foot extinct volcano called Arthur's Seat. For visitors, this east-west axis is the center of the action. Just south of the Royal Mile is

Edinburgh's Old Town

the National Museum of Scotland; farther to the south is a handy B&B neighborhood that lines up along **Dalkeith Road.** North of the Royal Mile ridge is the **New Town,** a neighborhood of grid-planned streets and elegant Georgian buildings.

In the center of it all—in a drained lake bed between the Old and New Towns—sit the Princes Street Gardens park and Waverley Bridge, where you'll find the Waverley train station, TI, Waverley Mall, bus info office (starting point for most city bus tours), Scottish National Gallery, and a covered dance-and-music pavilion.

Tourist Information

The crowded TI is as central as can be, on the rooftop of the Waverley Mall and Waverley train station (Mon-Sat 9:00-17:00, Sun from 10:00, June daily until 18:00, July-Aug daily until 19:00; tel. 0131-473-3868, www.visitscotland.com).

For more information than what's included in the TI's free map, buy the excellent *Collins Discovering Edinburgh* map (which comes with opinionated commentary and locates almost every major sight). If you're interested in evening music, ask for the comprehensive entertainment listing, *The List.*

Tours
Royal Mile Walking Tours

Walking tours are an Edinburgh specialty; you'll see groups trailing entertaining guides all over town. Below I've listed good all-purpose walks; for **literary pub crawls** and **ghost tours,** see "Night Walks" on page 78.

Edinburgh Tour Guides offers a good historical walk (without all the ghosts and goblins). Their Royal Mile tour is a gentle two-hour downhill stroll from the castle to the palace (£16.50; daily at 9:30 and 19:00; meet outside Gladstone's Land, near the top of the Royal Mile, must reserve ahead, mobile 0785-888-0072, www.edinburghtourguides.com, info@edinburghtourguides.com).

EDINBURGH AT A GLANCE

▲▲▲**Royal Mile** Historic road—good for strolling—stretching from the castle down to the palace, lined with museums, pubs, and shops. **Hours:** Always open, but best during business hours, with walking tours daily. See page 35.

▲▲▲**Edinburgh Castle** Iconic hilltop fort and royal residence complete with crown jewels, Romanesque chapel, memorial, and fine military museum. **Hours:** Daily 9:30-18:00, Oct-March until 17:00. See page 54.

▲▲▲**National Museum of Scotland** Intriguing, well-displayed artifacts from prehistoric times to the 20th century. **Hours:** Daily 10:00-17:00. See page 64.

▲▲**Gladstone's Land** Seventeenth-century Royal Mile merchant's residence. **Hours:** Daily 10:30-16:00 by tour only, closed Nov-March. See page 59.

▲▲**St. Giles' Cathedral** Preaching grounds of Scottish Reformer John Knox, with spectacular organ, Neo-Gothic chapel, and distinctive crown spire. **Hours:** Mon-Fri 9:00-19:00, Sat until 17:00; Oct-April Mon-Sat 9:00-17:00; Sun 13:00-17:00 year-round. See page 61.

▲▲**Scottish Parliament Building** Striking headquarters for parliament, which returned to Scotland in 1999. **Hours:** Mon-Sat 10:00-17:00, longer hours Tue-Thu when parliament is in session (Sept-June), closed Sun year-round. See page 62.

▲▲**Palace of Holyroodhouse** The Queen's splendid official residence in Scotland, with lavish rooms, 12th-century abbey, and gallery with rotating exhibits. **Hours:** Daily 9:30-18:00, Nov-March until 16:30, closed during royal visits. See page 63.

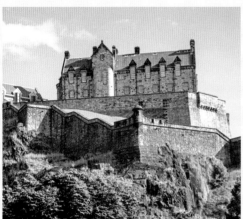

▲▲**Scottish National Gallery** Choice sampling of European masters and Scotland's finest. **Hours:** Daily 10:00-17:00, Thu until 19:00; longer hours in Aug. See page 67.

▲▲**Scottish National Portrait Gallery** Beautifully displayed Who's Who of Scottish history. **Hours:** Daily 10:00-17:00. See page 70.

▲▲**Georgian House** Intimate peek at upper-crust life in the late 1700s. **Hours:** Daily 10:00-17:00, March and Nov 11:00-16:00, closed Dec-Feb. See page 72.

▲▲**Royal Yacht *Britannia*** Ship for the royal family with a history of distinguished passengers, a 15-minute trip out of town. **Hours:** Daily 9:30-16:30, Oct until 16:00, Nov-March 10:00-15:30 (these are last entry times). See page 72.

▲**Scotch Whisky Experience** Gimmicky but fun and educational introduction to Scotland's most famous beverage. **Hours:** Generally daily 10:00-18:00. See page 59.

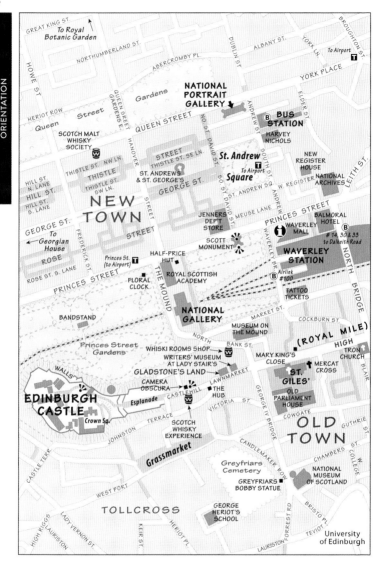

Mercat Tours offers a 1.5-hour "Secrets of the Royal Mile" walk that's more entertaining than intellectual (£13; £30 includes optional, 45-minute guided Edinburgh Castle visit; daily at 10:00 and 13:00, leaves from Mercat Cross on the Royal Mile, tel. 0131/225-5445, www.mercattours.com). They also offer a variety of other tours (check their website).

Rick's Tip: *Sunday is a good day to* **take a guided walking tour** *along the Royal Mile or a city bus tour (buses go faster in light traffic). Although many Royal Mile sights are closed on Sunday (except in Aug), other major sights and shops are open.*

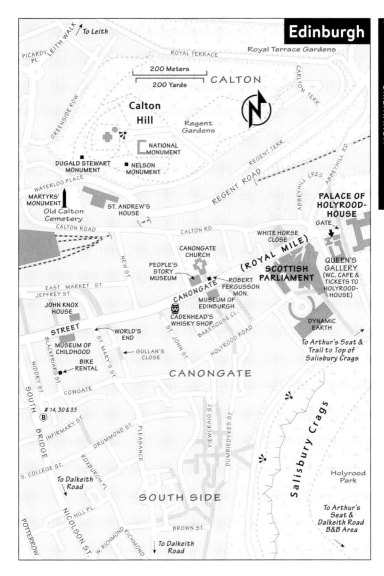

Blue Badge Local Guides

The following guides charge similar prices and offer half-day and full-day tours: **Jean Blair** (a delightful teacher and guide, £190/day without car, £430/day with car, mobile 0798-957-0287, www.travelthroughscotland.com, scotguide7@gmail.com) and **Ken Hanley** (who wears his kilt as if pants don't exist, £130/half-day, £250/day, extra charge if he uses his car—seats up to six, tel. 0131/666-1944, mobile 0771-034-2044, www.small-world-tours.co.uk, kennethhanley@me.com).

Hop-On, Hop-Off Bus Tours

The following one-hour hop-on, hop-off bus tour routes, all run by the same company, circle the town center, stopping at

the major sights. **Edinburgh Tour** (green buses) focuses on the city center, with live guides. **City Sightseeing** (red buses, focuses on Old Town) has recorded commentary, as does the **Majestic Tour** (blue-and-yellow buses, includes a stop at the *Britannia* and Royal Botanic Garden). You can pay for just one tour (£15/24 hours), but most people pay a few pounds more for a ticket covering all buses (£20; buses run April-Oct roughly 9:00-19:00, shorter hours off-season; every 10-15 minutes, buy tickets on board, tel. 0131/220-0770, www.edinburghtour.com). On sunny days the buses go topless, but come with increased traffic noise and exhaust fumes. For £52, the Royal Edinburgh Ticket covers two days of unlimited travel on all three buses, as well as admission (and line-skipping privileges) at Edinburgh Castle, the Palace of Holyroodhouse, and *Britannia* (www.royaledinburghticket.co.uk).

Day Trips from Edinburgh

Many companies run a variety of day trips to regional sights, as well as multiday and themed itineraries. (Several of the local guides listed earlier have cars, too.)

The most popular tour is the all-day **Highlands trip** (about £50, roughly 8:00-20:00). Itineraries vary but you'll generally visit/pass through the Trossachs, Rannoch Moor, Glencoe, Fort William, Fort Augustus on Loch Ness (some tours offer an optional boat ride), and Pitlochry. To save time, look for a tour that gives you a short glimpse of Loch Ness rather than driving its entire length or doing a boat trip. (Once you've seen a little of it, you've seen it all.)

Larger outfits, typically using bigger buses, include **Timberbush Highland Tours** (tel. 0131/226-6066, www.timberbushtours.com), **Gray Line** (tel. 0131/555-5558, www.graylinescotland.com), **Highland Experience** (tel. 0131/226-1414, www.highlandexperience.com), **Highland Explorer** (tel. 0131/558-3738, www.highlandexplorertours.com), and **Scotline** (tel. 0131/557-0162, www.scotlinetours.co.uk). Most of these companies run similar tours from Glasgow.

Other companies pride themselves on keeping group sizes small, with 16-seat minibuses; these include **Rabbie's** (tel. 0131/212-5005, www.rabbies.com) and **Heart of Scotland Tours: The Wee Red Bus** (10 percent Rick Steves discount on full-price day tours—mention when booking, does not apply to overnight tours or senior/student rates, occasionally canceled off-season if too few sign up—leave a contact number, tel. 0131/228-2888, www.heartofscotlandtours.co.uk).

Rick's Tip: *If visiting in festival-filled* **August, book ahead** *for your must-see events, hotels, and fancy restaurant dinners. Expect hotel prices to jump.*

Helpful Hints

Baggage Storage: At the train station, you'll find pricey, high-security luggage storage near platform 2 (daily 7:00-23:00). There are also lockers at the bus station on St. Andrew Square, just two blocks north of the train station.

Laundry: The **Ace Cleaning Centre** launderette is located near my recommended B&Bs south of town (Mon-Fri

8:00-20:00, Sat 9:00-17:00, Sun 10:00-16:00, along bus route to city center at 13 South Clerk Street, opposite Queens Hall, tel. 0131/667-0549).

Bike Rental and Tours: The laid-back crew at **Cycle Scotland** happily recommends good bike routes with your rental (prices starting at £20/3 hours or £30/day, electric bikes available for extra fee, daily 10:00-18:00, may close for a couple of months in winter, just off Royal Mile at 29 Blackfriars Street, tel. 0131/556-5560, mobile 07796-886-899, www.cyclescotland.co.uk, Peter). They also run guided three-hour bike tours daily (£45/person, extra fee for e-bike, book ahead).

EDINBURGH WALKS

I've outlined two walks in Edinburgh: along the Royal Mile, and through the New Town. Many of the sights we'll pass on these walks are described in more detail later, under "Sights."

➲ The Royal Mile

The Royal Mile is one of Europe's most interesting historic walks—it's easily

worth ▲▲▲. The following self-guided stroll is also available as a 🎧 downloadable Rick Steves audio tour; see page 29.

Overview

Start at Edinburgh Castle at the top and amble down to the Palace of Holyroodhouse. Along the way, the street changes names—Castlehill, Lawnmarket, High Street, and Canongate—but it's a straight, downhill shot totaling just over one mile. And nearly every step is packed with shops, cafés, and lanes leading to tiny squares.

As you walk, you'll be tracing the growth of the city—its birth atop Castle Hill, its Old Town heyday in the 1600s, its expansion in the 1700s into the Georgian New Town (leaving the old quarter an overcrowded, disease-ridden Victorian slum), and on to the 21st century at the modern Scottish parliament building (2004). Despite the drizzle, be sure to look up—spires, carvings, and towering Gothic "skyscrapers" give this city its unique urban identity.

This walk covers the Royal Mile's landmarks, but skips the many museums and indoor attractions along the way. Most of

The Royal Mile

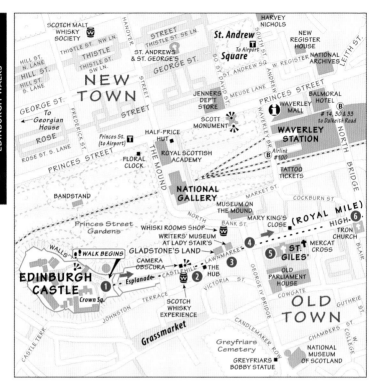

these sights are described in more detail under "Sights," later in this chapter. You can stay focused on the walk (which takes about 1.5 hours, without entering sights), then return later to visit the various indoor attractions; or review the sight descriptions beforehand and pop into those that interest you as you pass them.

• *We'll start at the Castle Esplanade, the big parking lot at the entrance to...*

❶ EDINBURGH CASTLE

Edinburgh was born on the bluff—a big rock—where the castle now stands. Since before recorded history, people have lived on this strategic, easily defended perch.

The **castle** is an imposing symbol of Scottish independence. Flanking the entryway are statues of the fierce warriors who battled English invaders, William Wallace (on the right) and Robert the Bruce (left). Between them is the Scottish

motto, *Nemo me impune lacessit*—roughly, "No one messes with me and gets away with it." (For a self-guided tour of Edinburgh Castle, see page 54.)

The esplanade—built as a military parade ground (1816)—is now the site of the annual Military Tattoo. This spectacular massing of regimental bands fills the square nightly for most of August. There

Edinburgh Castle's esplanade

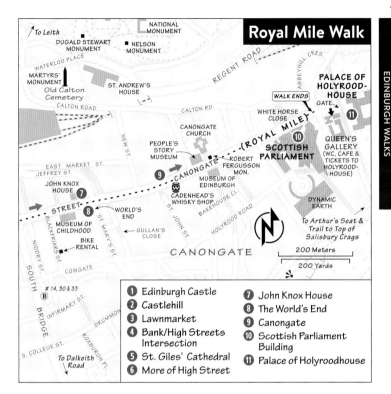

Royal Mile Walk

1 Edinburgh Castle
2 Castlehill
3 Lawnmarket
4 Bank/High Streets Intersection
5 St. Giles' Cathedral
6 More of High Street
7 John Knox House
8 The World's End
9 Canongate
10 Scottish Parliament Building
11 Palace of Holyroodhouse

are fine views in both directions from the esplanade. Facing north, you'll see the body of water called the Firth of Forth, and Fife beyond that. (The Firth of Forth is the estuary where the River Forth flows into the North Sea.) Still facing north, find the lacy spire of the Scott Monument and two Neoclassical buildings housing art galleries. Beyond them, the stately buildings of Edinburgh's New Town rise. Panning to the right, find the Nelson Monument and some faux Greek ruins atop Calton Hill.

• *Start walking down the Royal Mile. The first block is a street called…*

❷ CASTLEHILL

You're immediately in the tourist hub-bub. The big tank-like building on your left was the Old Town's **reservoir.** You'll see the wellheads it served all along this walk. While it once held 1.5 million gallons

of water, today it's filled with the touristy Tartan Weaving Mill and Exhibition.

The black-and-white tower ahead on the left has entertained visitors since the 1850s with its **camera obscura,** a darkened room where a mirror and a series of lenses capture live images of the city surroundings outside. (Giggle at the funny mirrors as you walk fatly by.) Across the street, filling the old Castlehill Primary School, is a gimmicky-if-intoxicating whisky-sampling exhibit called the **Scotch Whisky Experience** (a.k.a. "Malt Disney"; described later).

• *Just ahead, in front of the church with the tall, lacy spire, is the old market square known as…*

❸ LAWNMARKET

During the Royal Mile's heyday, in the 1600s, this intersection was bigger and served as a market for fabric (especially "lawn," a linen-like cloth).

Towering above Lawnmarket, with the tallest spire in the city, is the former **Tolbooth Church.** This impressive Neo-Gothic structure (1844) is now home to the Hub, Edinburgh's festival-ticket and information center. The world-famous Edinburgh Festival fills the month of August with cultural action. The various festivals feature classical music, traditional and fringe theater (especially comedy), art, books, and more. Drop inside the building to get festival info. This is a handy stop for its WC, café, and free Wi-Fi.

In the 1600s, this—along with the next stretch, called High Street—was the city's main street. At that time, Edinburgh was bursting with breweries, printing presses, and banks. Tens of thousands of citizens were squeezed into the narrow confines of the Old Town. Here on this ridge, they built **tenements** (multiple-unit residences) similar to the more recent ones you see today. These tenements, rising 10 stories and more, were some of the tallest domestic buildings in Europe.

• *Continue a half-block down the Mile.*

Gladstone's Land (at #477b, on the left), a surviving original tenement, was acquired by a wealthy merchant in 1617. Stand in front of the building and look up at this centuries-old skyscraper. This design was standard for its time: a shop or shops on the ground floor, with columns and an arcade, and residences on the floors above. Because window glass was expensive, the lower halves of window openings were made of cheaper wood, which swung out like shutters for ventilation—and were convenient for tossing out garbage. (Gladstone's Land can be seen by tour only and is closed Nov-March—consider dropping in and booking ahead for a spot. For details, see listing later.) Out front, you may also see trainers with live birds of prey. While this is mostly just a fun way to show off for tourists (and raise donations for the Just Falconry center), docents explain the connection: The building's owner was named Thomas

Gledstanes—and "gled" is the Scots word for "hawk."

Branching off the spine of the Royal Mile are a number of narrow alleyways that go by various local names. A "wynd" (rhymes with "kind") is a narrow, winding lane. A "pend" is an arched gateway. "Gate" is from an Old Norse word for street. And a "close" is a tiny alley between two buildings (originally with a door that "closed" at night). A "close" usually leads to a "court," or courtyard.

Opposite Gladstone's Land (at #322), a close leads to **Riddle's Court.** Wander through here and imagine Edinburgh in the 17th and 18th centuries, when tourists came here to marvel at its skyscrapers. Some 40,000 people were jammed into the few blocks between here and the World's End pub (which we'll reach soon). Visualize the labyrinthine maze of the old city, with people scurrying through these back alleyways, buying and selling, and popping into taverns.

No city in Europe was as densely populated—or perhaps as filthy. The dirt streets were soiled with sewage from bedpans emptied out windows. By the 1700s, the Old Town was rife with poverty and cholera outbreaks. The smoky home fires rising from tenements and the infamous smell (or "reek" in Scottish) that wafted across the city gave it a nickname that sticks today: "Auld Reekie."

• Return to the Royal Mile and continue down it a few steps to take in some sights at the...

❹ BANK/HIGH STREETS INTERSECTION

A number of sights cluster here, where Lawnmarket changes its name to High Street and intersects with Bank Street and George IV Bridge.

Begin with **Deacon Brodie's Tavern.** Read the "Doctor Jekyll and Mr. Hyde" story of this pub's notorious namesake on the wall facing Bank Street. Then, to see his spooky split personality, check out both sides of the hanging signpost. Brodie—a pillar of the community by day but a burglar by night—epitomizes the divided personality of 1700s Edinburgh. It was a rich, productive city—home to great philosophers and scientists, who actively contributed to the Enlightenment. Meanwhile, the Old Town was riddled with crime and squalor. (In the next century, in the late 1800s, novelist Robert Louis Stevenson would capture the dichotomy of Edinburgh's rich-poor society in his *Strange Case of Dr. Jekyll and Mr. Hyde.*)

In the late 1700s, Edinburgh's upper class moved out of the Old Town into a planned community called the New Town (a quarter-mile north of here). Eventually, most tenements were torn down and replaced with newer **Victorian buildings.** You'll see some at this intersection.

Look left down Bank Street to the green-domed **Bank of Scotland.** This was the headquarters of the bank, which had practiced modern capitalist financing since 1695.

If you detour left down Bank Street toward the bank, you'll find the recommended **Whiski Rooms Shop.** If you head in the opposite direction, down George IV Bridge, you'll reach the excellent **National Museum of Scotland,** restaurant-lined Forrest Road, and photogenic Victoria Street, which leads to the pub-lined Grassmarket square (all described later in this chapter).

Otherwise, continue along the Royal Mile. As you walk, be careful crossing the streets along the Mile. Edinburgh drivers—especially cabbies—have a reputation for being impatient with jaywalking tourists. Notice and heed the pedestrian crossing signals, which don't always turn at the same time as the car signals.

Across the street from Deacon Brodie's Tavern is a seated green statue of hometown boy **David Hume** (1711-1776)—one of the most influential thinkers not only of Scotland, but in all of Western philosophy. The atheistic Hume was one of the towering figures of the Scottish Enlightenment of the mid-1700s.

Follow David Hume's gaze to the opposite corner, where a **brass H** in the pavement marks the site of the last public execution in Edinburgh in 1864. Deacon Brodie himself would have been hung about here (in 1788, on a gallows which had a design he had helped to improve—smart guy).

• From the brass H, continue down the Royal Mile, pausing just before the church square at a stone wellhead with the pyramid cap.

All along the Royal Mile, **wellheads** like this (from 1835) provided townsfolk with water in the days before buildings had plumbing. This neighborhood well was served by the reservoir up at the castle.

• *Ahead of you (past the Victorian statue of some duke), embedded in the pavement near the street, is a big heart.*

The **Heart of Midlothian** marks the spot of the city's 15th-century municipal building and jail. In times past, in a nearby open space, criminals were hanged, traitors were decapitated, and witches were burned.

• *Make your way to the entrance of the church.*

❺ ST. GILES' CATHEDRAL

This is the flagship of the Church of Scotland (Scotland's largest denomination)—called the "Mother Church of Presbyterianism." The interior serves as a kind of Scottish Westminster Abbey, filled with monuments, statues, plaques, and stained-glass windows dedicated to great Scots and moments in history.

The reformer John Knox (1514-1572) was the preacher here. His fiery sermons helped turn once-Catholic Edinburgh into a bastion of Protestantism. During the Scottish Reformation, St. Giles' was transformed from a Catholic cathedral to a Presbyterian church. The spacious interior is well worth a visit (described later in "Sights").

• *Facing the church entrance, curl around its right side, into a parking lot.*

SIGHTS AROUND ST. GILES'

The grand building across the parking lot from St. Giles' is the **Old Parliament House.** From the early 1600s until 1707, this building evolved to become the seat of a true parliament of elected officials. That came to an end in 1707, when Scotland signed an Act of Union, joining what's known today as the United Kingdom and giving up their right to self-rule. (More on that later in the walk.)

The great reformer **John Knox** is buried—with appropriate austerity—under parking lot spot #23. The statue among the cars shows King Charles II riding to a toga party back in 1685.

• *Continue on through the parking lot, around the back end of the church.*

Every Scottish burgh (town licensed by the king to trade) had three standard features: a "tolbooth" (basically a town hall, with a courthouse, meeting room, and jail); a "tron" (official weighing scale); and a "mercat" (or market) cross. The **mercat cross** standing just behind St. Giles' Cathedral has a slender column decorated with a unicorn holding a flag with the cross of St. Andrew. Royal proclamations have been read at this mercat cross since the 14th century. In 1952, a town crier heralded the news that Britain had a new queen—three days after the actual event (traditionally the time it took for a horse to speed here from London). Today, Mercat Cross is the meeting point for many of Edinburgh's walking tours—both historic and ghostly.

• *Circle around to the street side of the church.*

The statue to **Adam Smith** honors the Edinburgh author of the pioneering Wealth of Nations (1776), in which he laid out the economics of free market capitalism. Smith theorized that an "invisible hand" wisely guides the unregulated free market.

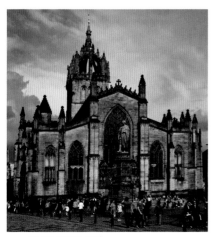
St. Giles' Cathedral

❻ MORE OF HIGH STREET

Continuing down this stretch of the Royal Mile, which is traffic-free most of the day (notice the bollards that raise and lower for permitted traffic), you'll see the Fringe Festival office (at #180), street musicians, and another wellhead (with horse "sippies," dating from 1675).

Notice those **three red boxes.** In the 20th century, people used these to make telephone calls to each other. (Imagine that!)

At the next intersection, on the left is **Cockburn Street** (pronounced "COE-burn"). This street has a reputation for its eclectic independent shops and string of trendy bars and eateries.

• *When you reach the **Tron Church** (17th century, currently housing shops), you're at the intersection of **North and South Bridge streets.** These major streets lead left to Waverley Station and right to the Dalkeith Road B&Bs. Several handy bus lines run along here.*

This is the halfway point of this walk. Stand on the corner diagonally across from the church. Look up to the top of the Royal Mile at the Hub and its 240-foot spire. Notwithstanding its turret and 16th-century charm, the **Radisson Blu Hotel** just across the street is entirely new construction (1990), built to fit in. The city is protecting its historic look.

In the next block downhill are three **characteristic pubs,** side by side, that offer free traditional Scottish and folk music in the evenings.

• *Go down High Street another block, passing near the **Museum of Childhood** (on the right, at #42) and a fragrant fudge shop a few doors down, where you can sample various flavors (tempting you to buy a slab).*

Directly across the street, just below another wellhead, is the...

❼ JOHN KNOX HOUSE

Remember that Knox was a towering figure in Edinburgh's history, converting Scotland to a Calvinist style of Protes-

tantism. His religious bent was "Presbyterianism," in which parishes are governed by elected officials rather than appointed bishops. This more democratic brand of Christianity also spurred Scotland toward political democracy. Full disclosure: It's not certain that Knox ever actually lived here. Attached to the Knox House is the Scottish Storytelling Centre, where locals with the gift of gab perform regularly; check the posted schedule.

• *A few steps farther down High Street, at the intersection with St. Mary's and Jeffrey streets, you'll reach...*

❽ THE WORLD'S END

For centuries, a wall stood here, marking the end of the burgh of Edinburgh. For residents within the protective walls of the city, this must have felt like the "world's end," indeed. At the intersection, find the brass bricks in the street that trace the gate (demolished in 1764).

• *Continue down the Royal Mile—leaving old Edinburgh—as High Street changes names to...*

❾ CANONGATE

About 10 steps down Canongate, look left down Cranston Street (past the train tracks) to a good view of the Calton Cemetery up on **Calton Hill.** The obelisk, called

Calton Hill

Martyrs' Monument, remembers a group of 18th-century patriots exiled by London to Australia for their reform politics. The round building to the left is the grave of philosopher David Hume. And the big, turreted building to the right was the jail master's house. Today, the main reason to go up Calton Hill is for the fine views.

• *A couple of hundred yards farther along the Royal Mile (on the right at #172) you reach Cadenhead's, a serious place to learn about and buy whisky. About 30 yards farther along, you'll pass two free museums, the People's Story Museum (on the left, in the old tollhouse at #163) and Museum of Edinburgh (on the right, at #142). But our next stop is the church just across from the Museum of Edinburgh.*

The 1688 **Canongate Kirk** (Church)—located not far from the royal residence of Holyroodhouse—is where Queen Elizabeth II and her family worship whenever they're in town. (So don't sit in the front pew, marked with her crown.) The gilded emblem at the top of the roof, high above the door, has the antlers of a stag from the royal estate of Balmoral. The Queen's granddaughter married here in 2011.

The church is open only when volunteers have signed up to welcome visitors (and closed in winter). Chat them up and borrow the description of the place. Then step inside the lofty blue and red interior, renovated with royal money; the church is filled with light and the flags of various Scottish regiments. In the narthex, peruse the photos of royal family events here, and find the list of priests and ministers of this parish—it goes back to 1143 (with a clear break with the Reformation in 1561).

• *After leaving the church, walk about 300 yards farther along the Royal Mile. In the distance you can see the Palace of Holyroodhouse (the end of this walk) and soon, on the right, you'll come to the modern Scottish parliament building.*

Just opposite the parliament building is **White Horse Close** (on the left, in the white arcade). Step into this 17th-century courtyard. It was from here that the Edinburgh stagecoach left for London. Eight days later, the horse-drawn carriage would pull into its destination: Scotland Yard. Note that bus #35 leaves in two directions from here—downhill for the Royal Yacht *Britannia,* and uphill along the Royal Mile (as far as South Bridge) and on to the National Museum of Scotland.

• *Now walk up around the corner to the flagpoles (flying the flags of Europe, Britain, and Scotland) in front of the...*

❿ SCOTTISH PARLIAMENT BUILDING

Finally, after centuries of history, we reach the 21st century. And finally, after three centuries of London rule, Scotland has a parliament building...in Scotland. When Scotland united with England in 1707, its parliament was dissolved. But in 1999, the Scottish parliament was reestablished, and in 2004, it moved into this striking

Canongate Kirk

White Horse Close

new home. Notice how the eco-friendly building, by the Catalan architect Enric Miralles, mixes wild angles, lots of light, bold windows, oak, and native stone into a startling complex.

Since it celebrates Scottish democracy, the architecture is not a statement of authority. There are no statues of old heroes. There's not even a grand entry. You feel like you're entering an office park. Given its neighborhood, the media often calls the Scottish Parliament "Holyrood" for short (similar to calling the US Congress "Capitol Hill"). For details on touring the building and seeing parliament in action, see page 62.

• *Across the street is the* **Queen's Gallery,** *where she shares part of her amazing personal art collection in excellent revolving exhibits. Finally, walk to the end of the road (Abbey Strand), and step up to the impressive wrought-iron gate of the Queen's palace. Look up at the stag with its holy cross, or "holy rood," on its forehead, and peer into the palace grounds. (The ticket office and palace entryway, a fine café, and a handy WC are just through the arch on the right.)*

⓫ **PALACE OF HOLYROODHOUSE**

Since the 16th century, this palace has marked the end of the Royal Mile. Because Scotland's royalty preferred living at Holyroodhouse to the blustery castle on the rock, the palace grew over time. If the Queen's not visiting, the palace welcomes visitors.

• *Your walk—from the castle to the palace, with so much Scottish history packed in between—is complete. Enjoy the rest of Edinburgh.*

⮕ Bonnie Wee New Town Walk

With some of the city's finest Georgian architecture (from its 18th-century boom period), the New Town has a completely different character than the Old Town. This self-guided walk—worth ▲▲—gives you a quick orientation in about one hour.

• *Begin on Waverley Bridge, span—— gully between the Old and New tow—— there from the Royal Mile, just head do—— the curved Cockburn Street near the Tron Church (or cut down any of the "close" lanes opposite St. Giles' Cathedral). Stand on the bridge overlooking the train tracks, facing the castle.*

View from Waverley Bridge: From this vantage point, you can enjoy fine views of medieval Edinburgh, with its 10-story-plus "skyscrapers." It's easy to imagine how miserably crowded this area was, prompting the expansion of the city during the Georgian period. Pick out landmarks along the Royal Mile, most notably the openwork steeple of St. Giles'.

A big lake called the **Nor' Loch** once was to the north (nor') of the Old Town; now it's a valley between Edinburgh's two towns. The lake was drained around 1800 as part of the expansion. Before that, the lake was the town's water reservoir... and its sewer. Much has been written about the town's infamous stink (a.k.a. the "flowers of Edinburgh"). The town's nickname, "Auld Reekie," referred to both the smoke of its industry and the stench of its squalor.

The long-gone loch was also a handy place for drowning witches. With their thumbs tied to their ankles, they'd be lashed to dunking stools. Those who survived the ordeal were considered "aided by the devil" and burned as witches. If they

View from Waverley Bridge

New Town Walk

❶ Princes Street Gardens
❷ Scott Monument
❸ Jenners Department Store
❹ St. Andrew Square
❺ George Street
❻ St. Andrew's & St. George's Church
❼ The Dome Restaurant
❽ King George IV Statue
❾ Thistle Street
❿ William Pitt Statue
⓫ Rose Street
⓬ Charlotte Square
⓭ Georgian House

died, they were innocent and given a good Christian burial. Edinburgh was Europe's witch-burning mecca—any perceived "sign," including a small birthmark, could condemn you. Scotland burned more witches per capita than any other country—17,000 souls between 1479 and 1722.

Visually trace the train tracks as they disappear into a tunnel below the **Scottish National Gallery** (with lesser-known paintings by great European artists; you can visit it during this walk—see "Sights," later).

Turning 180 degrees (and facing the ramps down into the train station), notice the huge, turreted building with the clock tower. **The Balmoral** was one of the city's two grand hotels during its glory days (its opposite bookend, the **Waldorf Astoria Edinburgh,** sits at the far end of the former lakebed—near the end of this walk). Today The Balmoral is known mostly as the place where J. K. Rowling completed the final Harry Potter book.

• *Now walk across the bridge toward the New Town. Before the corner, enter the gated*

gardens on the left, and head toward the big, pointy monument. You're at the edge of...

❶ **Princes Street Gardens:** This grassy park, filling the former lakebed, offers a wonderful escape from the bustle of the city. Once the private domain of the wealthy, it was opened to the public around 1870—not as a democratic gesture, but in hopes of increasing sales at the Princes Street department stores. Join the office workers for a picnic lunch break.

• *Take a seat on the bench indicated by the Livingstone (Dr. Livingstone, I presume?) statue. (The Victorian explorer is well equipped with a guidebook, but is hardly packing light—his lion skin doesn't even fit in his rucksack carry-on.)*

Look up at the towering...

❷ **Scott Monument:** Built in the early 1840s, this elaborate Neo-Gothic monument honors the great author Sir Walter Scott, one of Edinburgh's many illustrious sons. When Scott died in 1832, it was said that "Scotland never owed so much to one man." Scott almost singlehandedly

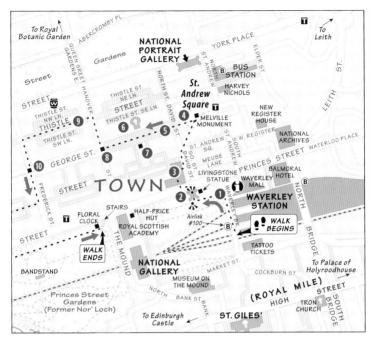

created the Scotland we know. Just as the country was in danger of being assimilated into England, Scott celebrated traditional songs, legends, myths, architecture, and kilts, thereby reviving the Highland culture and cementing a national identity. And, as the father of the Romantic historical novel, he contributed to Western literature in general. The 200-foot monument shelters a marble statue of Scott and his favorite pet, Maida, a deerhound who was one of 30 canines this dog lover owned during his lifetime. They're surrounded by busts of 16 great Scottish poets and 64 characters from his books. Climbing the tight, stony spiral staircase of 287 steps earns you a peek at a tiny museum midway, a fine city view at the top, and intimate encounters going up and down (£5, daily 10:00-19:00, Oct-March until 16:00, tel. 0131/529-4068).

• *Exit the gate near Livingstone and head across busy Princes Street to the venerable...*

❸ **Jenners Department Store:** As you wait for the light to change (and wait...

Scott Monument

Jenners Department Store

St. Andrew Square

and wait…), notice how statues of women support the building—just as real women support the business.

Step inside and head upstairs into the grand, skylit atrium. The central space—filled with a towering tree at Christmas—is classic Industrial Age architecture. The Queen's coat of arms high on the wall indicates she shops here.

• *From the atrium, turn right and exit onto South St. David Street. Turn left and follow this street uphill one block up to…*

❹ **St. Andrew Square:** This green space is dedicated to the patron saint of Scotland. In the early 19th century, there were no shops around here—just fine residences; this was a private garden for the fancy people living here. Now open to the public, the square is a popular lunch hangout for workers.

One block up from the top of the park is the excellent **Scottish National Portrait Gallery,** which introduces you to all of the biggest names in Scottish history (described later, under "Sights").

• *Follow the Melville Monument's gaze straight ahead out of the park. Cross the street and stand at the top of…*

❺ **George Street:** This is the main drag of Edinburgh's grid-planned New Town. Laid out in 1776, when King George III was busy putting down a revolution in a troublesome overseas colony, the New Town was a model of urban planning in its day. The architectural style is "Georgian"—

British for "Neoclassical."

St. Andrew Square (patron saint of Scotland) and Charlotte Square (George III's queen) bookend the New Town, with its three main streets named for the royal family of the time (George, Queen, and Princes). Thistle and Rose streets—which we'll see near the end of this walk—are named for the national flowers of Scotland and England.

• *Halfway down the first block of George Street, on the right, is…*

❻ **St. Andrew's and St. George's Church:** Designed as part of the New Town plan in the 1780s, the church is a product of the Scottish Enlightenment. It has an elliptical plan (the first in Britain) so that all can focus on the pulpit. If it's open, step inside. A fine leaflet tells the story of the church, and a handy cafeteria downstairs serves cheap and cheery lunches.

Directly across the street from the church is another temple, this one devoted to money. This former bank building (now housing the recommended restaurant ❼ **The Dome**) has a pediment filled with figures demonstrating various ways to make money, which they do with all the nobility of classical gods. Consider scurrying across the street and ducking inside to view the stunning domed atrium.

Continue down George Street to the intersection with a ❽ statue commemorating the visit by **King George IV.**

Charlotte Square

Scottish National Gallery

• *Turn right on Hanover Street; after just one (short) block, cross over and go down...*

❾ Thistle Street: This street seems sleepy, but holds characteristic boutiques and good restaurants. Halfway down the street on the left, Howie Nicholsby's shop 21st Century Kilt updates traditional Scottish menswear.

You'll pop out at Frederick Street. Turning left, you'll see a **❿** statue of **William Pitt,** prime minister under King George III. (Pitt's father gave his name to the American city of Pittsburgh—which Scots pronounce as "Pitts-burrah"...I assume.)

• *For an interesting contrast, we'll continue down another side street. Pass the statue of Pitt (heading toward Edinburgh Castle), and turn right onto brash, boisterous...*

⓫ Rose Street: This stretch of Rose Street feels commercialized, jammed with chain stores; the second block is packed with pubs and restaurants. As you walk, keep an eye out for the cobbled Tudor rose embedded in the brick sidewalk. When you cross the aptly named Castle Street, linger over the grand views to Edinburgh Castle. It's almost as if they planned it this way...just for the views.

• *Popping out at the far end of Rose Street, across the street and to your right is...*

⓬ Charlotte Square: The building of the New Town started cheap with St. Andrew Square, but finished well with this stately space, designed by Scottish Robert Adam in 1791. Adam's design, which raised the standard of New Town architecture to "international class," created Edinburgh's finest Georgian square.

• *Along the right side of Charlotte Square, at #7 (just left of the pointy pediment), you can visit the ⓭ Georgian House, which gives you a great peek behind all of these harmonious Neoclassical facades (described later).*

Return Through Princes Street Gardens: From Charlotte Square, drop down to busy Princes Street (noticing the red building to the right—the grand Waldorf Astoria Hotel and twin sister of The Balmoral at the start of our walk). But rather than walking along the busy bus-and-tram-lined shopping drag, head into **Princes Street Gardens** (cross Princes Street and enter the gate on the left). With the castle looming overhead, you'll pass a playground, a fanciful Victorian fountain, more monuments to great Scots, war memorials, and a bandstand. Finally you'll reach a staircase up to the **Scottish National Gallery;** notice the oldest **floral clock** in the world on your left as you climb up.

• *Our walk is over. From here, you can tour the gallery; head up Bank Street just behind it to reach the Royal Mile; hop on a bus along Princes Street to your next stop (or B&B); or continue through another stretch of the Princes Street Gardens to the Scott Monument and our starting point.*

SIGHTS

▲▲▲EDINBURGH CASTLE

The fortified birthplace of the city 1,300 years ago, this imposing symbol of Edinburgh sits proudly on a rock high above you. The home of Scotland's kings and queens for centuries, the castle has witnessed royal births, medieval pageantry, and bloody sieges. Today it's a complex of various buildings, the oldest dating from the 12th century, linked by cobbled roads that survive from its more recent use as a military garrison. The castle—with expansive views, plenty of history, and the stunning crown jewels of Scotland—is a fascinating and multifaceted sight that deserves several hours of your time.

Cost and Hours: £17, daily 9:30-18:00, Oct-March until 17:00, last entry one hour before closing, tel. 0131/225-9846, www.edinburghcastle.gov.uk.

Rick's Tip: *To* **avoid the castle's ticket lines** *(worst in Aug),* **book online** *in advance. You can print your ticket at home, or pick it up at machines just inside the entrance or at the Visitor Information desk a few steps uphill on the right.*

Avoiding Lines: The castle is usually less crowded after 14:00 or so; if planning a morning visit, the earlier the better.

Getting There: Simply walk up the Royal Mile (if arriving by bus from the B&B area south of the city, get off at South Bridge and huff up the Mile for about 15 minutes). Taxis get you closer, dropping you a block below the esplanade at the Hub/Tolbooth Church.

Tours: Thirty-minute introductory **guided tours** are free with admission (2-4/hour, depart from Argyle Battery, see clock for next departure; fewer off-season). The informative **audioguide** provides four hours of descriptions, including the National War Museum Scotland (£3 if you purchase with your ticket; £3.50 if you rent it once inside, pick up inside Portcullis Gate).

Eating: You have two choices within the castle. The **$ Redcoat Café**—just past the Argyle Battery—is a big, bright, efficient cafeteria with great views. The **$$ Tea Rooms** in Crown Square serves sit-down meals and afternoon tea. A **Whisky Shop,** with tastings, is just through Foog's Gate.

◑ SELF-GUIDED TOUR

From the ❶ **entry gate,** start winding your way uphill toward the main sights—the crown jewels and the Royal Palace—located near the summit. Since the castle was protected on three sides by sheer cliffs, the main defense had to be here at the entrance. During the castle's heyday in the 1500s, a 100-foot tower loomed overhead, facing the city.

• *Passing through the portcullis gate, you reach the...*

❷ **Argyle (Six-Gun) Battery, with View:** These front-loading, cast-iron cannons are from the Napoleonic era (c. 1800), when the castle was still a force to be reckoned with.

From here, look north across the valley to the grid of the New Town. The valley sits where the Nor' Loch once was; this lake was drained and filled in when the New Town was built in the late 1700s, its

Edinburgh Castle

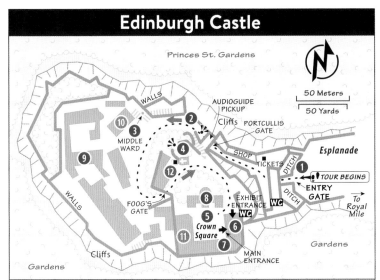

Tour

1. Entry Gate
2. Argyle Battery
3. One O'Clock Gun
4. St. Margaret's Chapel, Mons Meg & Dog Cemetery
5. Crown Square
6. Scottish Crown Jewels (Honours of Scotland)
7. Royal Apartments
8. Scottish National War Memorial
9. National War Museum Scotland

Eateries & Other

10. Redcoat Café
11. Tea Rooms
12. Whisky Shop

swamps replaced with gardens. Later the land provided sites for the Greek-temple-esque Scottish National Gallery and Waverley Station.

Now look down. The sheer north precipice looks impregnable. But on the night of March 14, 1314, 30 armed men silently scaled this rock face. They were loyal to Robert the Bruce and determined to recapture the castle, which had fallen into English hands. They caught the English by surprise, took the castle, and—three months later—Bruce defeated the English at the Battle of Bannockburn.

• *A little farther along, near the café, is the...*

❸ **One O'Clock Gun:** Crowds gather for the 13:00 gun blast, a tradition that gives ships in the bay something to set their navigational devices by. Before the gun, sailors

set their clocks with help from the Nelson Monument—that's the tall pillar in the distance on Calton Hill. The monument has a "time ball" affixed to the cross on top, which drops precisely at the top of the hour. But on foggy days, ships couldn't see the ball, so the cannon shot was instituted instead (1861). The tradition stuck, every day at 13:00. (Locals joke that the frugal Scots don't fire it at high noon, as that would cost 11 extra rounds a day.)

• *Continue uphill, winding to the left and passing through Foog's Gate. At the very top of the hill, on your left, is...*

❹ **St. Margaret's Chapel:** This tiny stone chapel is Edinburgh's oldest building (around 1120) and sits atop its highest point (440 feet). It represents the birth of the city.

St. Margaret's Chapel

Crown Square

In 1057, Malcolm III murdered King Macbeth (of Shakespeare fame) and assumed the Scottish throne. Later, he married Princess Margaret, and the family settled atop this hill. Their marriage united Malcolm's Highland Scots with Margaret's Lowland Anglo-Saxons—the cultural mix that would define Edinburgh.

Step inside the tiny, unadorned church—a testament to Margaret's reputed piety. The style is Romanesque. The nave is wonderfully simple, with classic Norman zigzags decorating the round arch that separates the tiny nave from the sacristy. You'll see a facsimile of St. Margaret's 11th-century gospel book. The small (modern) stained-glass windows feature St. Margaret herself, St. Columba, and St. Ninian (who brought Christianity to Scotland in AD 397), St. Andrew (Scotland's patron saint), and William Wallace (the defender of Scotland). These days, the place is popular for weddings. (As it seats only 20, it's particularly popular with brides' parents.)

Margaret died at the castle in 1093, and her son King David I built this chapel in her honor (she was sainted in 1250). David expanded the castle and also founded Holyrood Abbey, across town. These two structures were soon linked by a Royal Mile of buildings, and Edinburgh was born.

Mons Meg, in front of the church, is a huge and once-upon-a-time frightening 15th-century siege cannon that fired 330-pound stones nearly two miles. Imagine.

Nearby, belly up to the banister and look down to find the **Dog Cemetery,** a tiny patch of grass with a sweet little line of doggie tombstones, marking the graves of soldiers' faithful canines in arms.

• *Continue on, curving downhill into...*

❺ **Crown Square:** This courtyard is the center of today's Royal Castle complex. Get oriented. You're surrounded by the crown jewels, the Royal Palace (with its Great Hall), and the Scottish National War Memorial.

• *We'll tour the buildings around Crown Square. First up: the crown jewels. Look for two entrances. The one on Crown Square, only open in peak season, deposits you straight into the room with the crown jewels but usually comes with a line. The other entry, around the side (near the WCs), takes you—often at a shuffle—through the interesting, Disney-esque "Honours of Scotland" exhibition, which tells the story of the crown jewels and how they survived the harrowing centuries, but lacks any actual artifacts.*

❻ **Scottish Crown Jewels (Honours of Scotland):** For centuries, Scotland's monarchs were crowned in elaborate rituals involving three wondrous objects: a jewel-studded crown, scepter, and sword. These objects—along with the ceremonial Stone of Scone (pronounced "skoon")—are known as the "Honours of Scotland." Scotland's crown jewels may not be as impressive as England's, but they're treasured by locals as a symbol of Scottish nationalism. They're also older than England's; while Oliver Cromwell destroyed England's jewels, the Scots managed to hide theirs.

History of the Jewels: The Honours of Scotland exhibit that leads up to the Crown Room traces the evolution of the jewels, the ceremony, and the often turbulent journey of this precious regalia. Here's the SparkNotes version:

In 1306, Robert the Bruce was crowned with a "circlet of gold" in a ceremony at Scone—a town 40 miles north of Edinburgh, which Scotland's earliest kings had claimed as their capital. Around 1500, King James IV added two new items to the coronation ceremony—a scepter (a gift from the pope) and a huge sword (a gift from another pope). In 1540, James V had the original crown augmented by an Edinburgh goldsmith, giving it the imperial-crown shape it has today.

These Honours were used to crown every monarch: nine-month-old Mary, Queen of Scots (she cried); her one-year-old son James VI (future king of England);

and Charles I and II. But the days of divine-right rulers were numbered.

In 1649, the parliament had Charles I (king of both England and Scotland) beheaded. Soon Cromwell's rabid English antiroyalists were marching on Edinburgh.

When the monarchy was restored, the regalia were used to crown Scotland's last king, Charles II (1660). Then, in 1707, the Treaty of Union with England ended Scotland's independence. The Honours came out for a ceremony to bless the treaty.

The crown's most recent official appearance was in 1999, when it was taken across town to the grand opening of the reinstated parliament, marking a new chapter in the Scottish nation. As it represents the monarchy, the crown is present whenever a new session of parliament opens. (And if Scotland ever secedes, you can be sure that crown will be in the front row.)

The Honours: Finally, you enter the Crown Room to see the regalia itself. The four-foot steel **sword** was made in Italy under orders of Pope Julius II (the man who also commissioned Michelangelo's Sistine Chapel and St. Peter's Basilica). The **scepter** is made of silver, covered with gold,

Diorama in the Honours of Scotland *exhibit*

Laich Hall

Great Hall

and topped with a rock crystal and a pearl. The gem- and pearl-encrusted **crown** has an imperial arch topped with a cross. Legend says the band of gold in the center is the original crown that once adorned the head of Robert the Bruce.

The **Stone of Scone** (a.k.a. the "Stone of Destiny") sits plain and strong next to the jewels. It's a rough-hewn gray slab of sandstone, about 26 by 17 by 10 inches. As far back as the ninth century, Scotland's kings were crowned atop this stone, when it stood at the medieval capital of Scone. But in 1296, the invading army of Edward I of England carried the stone off to Westminster Abbey. For the next seven centuries, English (and subsequently British) kings and queens were crowned sitting on a coronation chair with the Stone of Scone tucked in a compartment underneath.

In 1996, in recognition of increased Scottish autonomy, Queen Elizabeth II agreed to let the stone go home, on one condition: that it be returned to Westminster Abbey for all British coronations. One day, the next monarch of the United Kingdom—Prince Charles is first in line—will sit atop it, re-enacting a coronation ritual that dates back a thousand years.

• *Exit the crown jewel display, heading down the stairs. But just before exiting into the courtyard, turn left through a door that leads into the...*

❼ **Royal Apartments:** Scottish royalty lived in the Royal Palace only when safety

or protocol required it (they preferred the Palace of Holyroodhouse at the bottom of the Royal Mile). Here you can see several historic but unimpressive rooms. The first one, labeled **Queen Mary's Chamber,** is where Mary, Queen of Scots (1542-1587), gave birth to James VI of Scotland, who later became King James I of England. Nearby **Laich Hall** (Lower Hall) was the dining room of the royal family.

The **Great Hall** (through a separate entrance on Crown Square) was built by James IV to host the castle's official banquets and meetings. It's still used for such purposes today. Most of the interior—its fireplace, carved walls, pikes, and armor—is Victorian. But the well-constructed wood ceiling is original. This hammer-beam roof (constructed like the hull of a ship) is self-supporting.

• *Across the Crown Square courtyard is the...*

❽ **Scottish National War Memorial:** This commemorates the 149,000 Scottish soldiers lost in World War I, the 58,000 who died in World War II, and the nearly 800 (and counting) lost in British battles since. This is a somber spot (no photos). To appreciate how important this place is, consider that Scottish soldiers died at twice the rate of other British soldiers in World War I.

• *Our final stop is worth the five-minute walk to get there. Backtrack to the café (and One O'Clock Gun), then head downhill to the War Museum.*

❾ National War Museum Scotland:
This thoughtful museum covers four centuries of Scottish military history. Instead of the usual musty, dusty displays of endless armor, there's a compelling mix of videos, uniforms, weapons, medals, mementos, and eloquent excerpts from soldiers' letters.

Here you'll learn the story of how the fierce and courageous Scottish warrior changed from being a symbol of resistance against Britain to being a champion of that same empire.

This museum shows the human side of war as well as the cleverness of government-sponsored ad campaigns that kept the lads enlisting. Two centuries of recruiting posters make the same pitch that still works today: a hefty signing bonus, steady pay, and job security with the promise of a manly and adventurous life—all spiked with a mix of pride and patriotism.

Stepping outside the museum, you're surrounded by cannons that no longer fire, dramatic views of this grand city, and the clatter of tourists (rather than soldiers) on cobbles. Consider for a moment all the bloody history and valiant struggles, along with British power and Scottish pride, that have shaped the city over which you are perched.

Sights on and near the Royal Mile

▲THE SCOTCH WHISKY EXPERIENCE
This attraction seems designed to distill money out of your pocket. The 50-minute experience consists of a "Malt Disney" whisky-barrel ride through the production process followed by an explanation and movie about Scotland's five main whisky regions. Though gimmicky, it does succeed in providing an entertaining yet informative orientation to the creation of Scottish firewater (things get pretty psychedelic when you hit the yeast stage). Your ticket also includes sampling a wee dram and the chance to stand amid the world's largest Scotch whisky collec-

tion (almost 3,500 bottles). At the end, you'll find yourself in the bar, with a fascinating wall of unusually shaped whisky bottles. Serious connoisseurs should stick with the more substantial shops in town, but this place can be worthwhile for beginners.

Cost and Hours: £15 "silver tour" includes one sample, £26 "gold tour" includes samples from each main region, generally daily 10:00-18:00, tel. 0131/220-0441, www.scotchwhiskyexperience.co.uk.

▲▲GLADSTONE'S LAND
This is a typical 16th- to 17th-century merchant's "land," or tenement building. These multistory structures—in which merchants ran their shops on the ground floor and lived upstairs—were typical of the time (the word "tenement" didn't have the slum connotation then that it has today). At six stories, this one was still just half the height of the tallest "skyscrapers."

Gladstone's Land, which you'll visit via one-hour guided tour, comes complete with an almost-lived-in, furnished interior and 400-year-old Renaissance painted

Gladstone's Land

Scotland's Literary Greats

Edinburgh was home to Scotland's three greatest literary figures, pictured above: Robert Burns (left), Robert Louis Stevenson (center), and Sir Walter Scott (right).

Robert Burns (1759-1796), known as "Rabbie" in Scotland and quite possibly the most famous and beloved Scot of all time, moved to Edinburgh after achieving overnight celebrity with his first volume of poetry (staying in a house on the spot where Deacon Brodie's Tavern now stands). Even though he wrote in the rough Scots dialect and dared to attack social rank, he was a favorite of Edinburgh's high society.

One hundred years later, **Robert Louis Stevenson** (1850-1894) also stirred the Scottish soul with his pen. Traveling through Scotland, Europe, and around the world, he distilled his adventures into Romantic classics, including *Kidnapped* and *Treasure Island* (as well as *The Strange Case of Dr. Jekyll and Mr. Hyde*).

Sir Walter Scott (1771-1832) wrote the *Waverley* novels, including *Ivanhoe* and *Rob Roy*. He's considered the father of the Romantic historical novel. Through his writing, he generated a worldwide interest in Scotland, and reawakened his fellow countrymen's pride in their heritage.

The best way to learn about and experience these literary greats is to take Edinburgh's Literary Pub Tour (see page 78).

Consider also the other great writers with Edinburgh connections: J. K. Rowling (who captures the "Gothic" spirit of Edinburgh with her Harry Potter series); current resident Ian Rankin (with his "tartan noir" novels); J. M. Barrie (who attended University of Edinburgh and later created Peter Pan); Sir Arthur Conan Doyle (who was born in Edinburgh and is best known for inventing Sherlock Holmes); and James Boswell (who lived in Edinburgh and is revered for his biography of Samuel Johnson).

Stained-glass window in St. Giles' Cathedral

ceiling. The downstairs cloth shop and upstairs kitchen and living quarters are brought to life by your guide.

Cost and Hours: £7, tours run daily 10:30-16:00, 3-8 tours/day, must book ahead by phone or in person; closed Nov-March, tel. 0131/226-5856, www.nts.org.uk/Visit/Gladstones-Land.

▲▲ST. GILES' CATHEDRAL

This is Scotland's most important church. Its ornate spire—the Scottish crown steeple from 1495—is a proud part of Edinburgh's skyline. The fascinating interior contains nearly 200 memorials honoring distinguished Scots through the ages.

Cost and Hours: Free but £3 donation encouraged; Mon-Fri 9:00-19:00, Sat until 17:00; Oct-April Mon-Sat 9:00-17:00; Sun 13:00-17:00 year-round; info sheet-£1, guidebook-£6, tel. 0131/225-9442, www.stgilescathedral.org.uk.

Concerts: St. Giles' busy concert schedule includes free organ recitals and visiting choirs (frequent events at 12:15 and concerts Sun at 18:00, also sometimes Wed, Thu, or Fri at 20:00, see schedule or ask for Music at St. Giles' pamphlet at welcome desk or gift shop).

○ Self-Guided Tour: Today's facade is 19th-century Neo-Gothic, but most of what you'll see inside is from the 14th and 15th centuries. Engage the cathedral guides in conversation; you'll be glad you did.

Just inside the entrance, turn around to see the modern stained-glass Robert Burns window, which celebrates Scotland's favorite poet. The top is a rosy red sunburst of creativity, reminding Scots of Burns' famous line, "My love is like a red, red rose"—part of a song near and dear to every Scottish heart.

To the right of the Burns window is a fine **Pre-Raphaelite window.** Like most in the church, it's a memorial to an important patron (in this case, John Marshall). From here stretches a great swath of war memorials.

As you walk along the north wall, find **John Knox's statue** (standing like a six-foot-tall bronze chess piece). Knox, the great religious reformer and founder of austere Scottish Presbyterianism, first preached here in 1559. His insistence that every person should be able to personally read the word of God—notice that he's pointing to a book—gave Scotland an educational system 300 years ahead of the rest of Europe.

Knox preached Calvinism. Consider that the Dutch and the Scots both embraced this creed of hard work, frugality, and strict ethics. This helps explain why the Scots are so different from the English (and why the Dutch and the Scots—both famous for their thriftiness and industriousness—are so much alike).

The oldest parts of the cathedral—the **four massive central pillars**—are Norman and date from the 12th century.

Cross over to the **organ** (1992, Austrian-built, one of Europe's finest) and take in its sheer might. (To light it up, find the button behind the organ to the right of the glass.)

Immediately to the right of the organ (as you're facing it) is a tiny chapel for silence and prayer. The dramatic **stained-glass window** above shows the commotion that surrounded Knox when he preached. The bearded, fiery-eyed Knox had a huge impact on this community. Notice how there were no pews back then.

Head toward the east (back) end of the church, and turn right to see the Neo-Gothic **Thistle Chapel** (£3 donation requested, volunteer guide is a wealth of information). The interior is filled with intricate wood carving. Built in two years (1910-1911), entirely with Scottish materials and labor, it is the private chapel of the Order of the Thistle, the only Scottish chivalric order. Are there bagpipes in heaven? Find the tooting stone angel at the top of a window to the left of the altar, and the wooden one to the right of the doorway you came in.

Downstairs you'll find handy public WCs and an inviting **$ café**—a good place for paupers to munch prayerfully (simple, light lunches, coffee and cakes; Mon-Sat 9:00-17:00, Sun from 11:00, in basement on back side of church, tel. 0131/225-5147).

▲▲SCOTTISH PARLIAMENT BUILDING

Scotland's parliament originated in 1293 and was dissolved when Scotland united with England in 1707. But after the Scottish electorate and the British parliament gave their consent, in 1997 it was decided that there should again be "a Scottish parliament guided by justice, wisdom, integrity, and compassion." Formally reconvened by Queen Elizabeth II in 1999, the Scottish parliament now enjoys self-rule in many areas (except for matters of defense, foreign policy, immigration, and taxation). The current government, run by the Scottish Nationalist Party (SNP), is pushing for even more independence.

The innovative building, opened in 2004, brought together all the functions of the fledgling parliament in one complex. It's a people-oriented structure, conceived by Catalan architect Enric Miralles. Signs are written in both English and Gaelic (the Scots' Celtic tongue).

For a peek at the building and a lesson in how the Scottish parliament works,

Scottish Parliament exterior

Scottish Parliament interior

drop in, pass through security, and find the visitors' desk. You're welcome in the public parts of the building, including a small ground-floor exhibit on the parliament's history and function and, up several flights of stairs, a viewing gallery overlooking the impressive Debating Chambers.

Cost and Hours: Free; Mon-Sat 10:00-17:00, Tue-Thu 9:00-18:30 when parliament is in session (Sept-June), closed Sun year-round. For a complete list of recess dates or to book tickets for debates, check their website or call their visitor services line, tel. 0131/348-5200, www.parliament.scot.

Tours: Free worthwhile hour-long tours covering history, architecture, parliamentary processes, and other topics are offered by proud locals. Tours generally run throughout the day Mon and Fri-Sat in session (Sept-June) and Mon-Sat in recess (July-Aug). While you can try dropping in, these tours can book up—it's best to book ahead online or over the phone.

Seeing Parliament in Session: The public can witness the Scottish parliament's hugely popular debates (usually Tue-Thu 14:00-18:00; book ahead online, over the phone, or at the info desk).

On Thursdays from 11:40 to 12:45 the First Minister is on the hot seat and has to field questions from members across all parties (reserve ahead for this popular session over the phone a week in advance; spots book up quickly—call at 9:00 sharp on Thu for the following week).

▲▲PALACE OF HOLYROODHOUSE

Built on the site of the abbey/monastery founded in 1128 by King David I, this palace was the true home, birthplace, and coronation spot of Scotland's Stuart kings in their heyday (James IV; Mary, Queen of Scots; and Charles I). It's particularly memorable as the site of some dramatic moments from the short reign of Mary, Queen of Scots—including the murder of her personal secretary, David Rizzio, by agents of her jealous husband. Today, it's one of Queen Elizabeth II's official residences. She usually manages her Scottish affairs here during Holyrood Week, from late June to early July (and generally stays at Balmoral in August). Holyrood is open to the public outside of the Queen's visits. The one-way audioguide route leads you through the fine apartments and tells some of the notable stories that played out here.

Cost: £12.50, includes quality one-hour audioguide; £17.50 combo-ticket includes

Palace of Holyroodhouse

Ruined abbey

Queen's Gallery

the Queen's Gallery; £21.50 combo-ticket adds guided tour of palace gardens (April-Oct only); tickets sold in Queen's Gallery to the right of the castle entrance (see next listing).

Hours: Daily 9:30-18:00, Nov-March until 16:30, last entry 1.5 hours before closing, tel. 0131/556-5100, www.royalcollection.org.uk. It's still a working palace, so it's closed when the Queen or other VIPs are in residence.

Visiting the Palace: The building, rich in history and decor, is filled with elegantly furnished Victorian rooms and a few darker, older rooms with glass cases of historic bits and Scottish pieces that locals find fascinating. Bring the palace to life with the audioguide. The tour route leads you into the grassy inner courtyard, then up to the royal apartments: dining rooms, Downton Abbey-style drawing rooms, and royal bedchambers, including the private chambers of Mary, Queen of Scots, where conspirators stormed in and stabbed her secretary 56 times.

After exiting the palace, you're free to stroll through the evocative **ruined abbey** (destroyed by the English during the time of Mary, Queen of Scots, in the 16th century) and the **palace gardens** (closed Nov-March except some weekends).

Nearby: Hikers, note that the wonderful trail up Arthur's Seat starts just across the street from the gardens (see "Urban Hikes," later for details).

QUEEN'S GALLERY

This small museum features rotating exhibits of artwork from the royal collection. Though the gallery occupies just a few rooms, its displays can be exquisite. The entry fee includes an excellent audioguide, written and read by the curator.

Cost and Hours: £7, £17.50 combo-ticket includes Palace of Holyroodhouse, daily 9:30-18:00, Nov-March until 16:30, last entry one hour before closing, café, on the palace grounds, to the right of the palace entrance, www.royalcollection.org.uk. Buses #35 and #36 stop outside, saving you a walk to or from Princes Street/North Bridge.

South of the Royal Mile

▲▲▲NATIONAL MUSEUM OF SCOTLAND

This huge museum has amassed more historic artifacts than every other place I've seen in Scotland combined. It's all wonderfully displayed, with fine descriptions offering a best-anywhere hike through the history of Scotland.

Cost and Hours: Free, daily 10:00-17:00; two long blocks south of St. Giles' Cathedral and the Royal Mile, on Chambers Street off George IV Bridge, tel. 0131/247-4422, www.nms.ac.uk.

Tours: Free one-hour general tours are offered daily at 11:00 and 13:00; themed tours at 15:00 (confirm tour schedule at info desk or on TV screens). The National

Museum of Scotland Highlights app provides thin coverage of select items but is free and downloadable using their free Wi-Fi.

Eating: A **$$ brasserie** is on the ground floor near the information desks, and a **$ café** with coffee, tea, cakes, and snacks is on the level 3 balcony overlooking the Grand Gallery. On the museum's fifth floor, the dressy and upscale **$$$ Tower restaurant** serves good food with a castle view (lunch/early bird special, afternoon tea, three-course dinner specials; daily 10:00-22:00—use Tower entry if eating after museum closes, reservations recommended, tel. 0131/225-3003, www.tower-restaurant.com). A number of good eating options are within a couple of blocks of the museum (see "Eating," later).

Overview: The place gives you two museums in one. One wing houses the Natural World galleries (T. Rex skeletons and other animals), the Science and Technology galleries, and more. But we'll focus on the other wing, which sweeps you through Scottish history covering Roman and Viking times, Edinburgh's witch-burning craze and clan massacres, the struggle for Scottish independence, the Industrial Revolution, and right up to Scotland in the 21st century.

◑ Self-Guided Tour: Get oriented on level 1, in the impressive glass-roofed Grand Gallery right above the entrance hall. Just outside the Grand Gallery is the millennium clock, a 30-foot high clock with figures that move to a Bach concerto on the hour from 11:00 to 16:00. The clock has four parts (crypt, nave, belfry, and spire) and represents the turmoil of the 20th century, with a pietà at the top.

• *To reach the Scottish history wing, exit the Grand Gallery at the far right end, under the clock and past the statue of James Watt.*

On the way, you'll pass through the science and technology wing. While walking through, look for Dolly the sheep—the world's first cloned mammal—born in Edinburgh and now stuffed and on display. Continue into Hawthornden Court (level 1), where our tour begins. (It's possible to detour downstairs from here to level -1 for Scotland's prehistoric origins—geologic formation, Celts, Romans, Vikings.)

• *Enter the door marked...*

Kingdom of the Scots (c. 1300-1700): From its very start, Scotland was determined to be free. You're greeted with proud quotes from what's been called the Scottish Declaration of Independence—the Declaration of Arbroath, a defiant letter written to the pope in 1320. As early as the ninth century, Scotland's patron saint, Andrew (see the small statue in the next room), had—according to legend—miraculously intervened to help the Picts and Scots of Scotland remain free by defeating the Angles of England. Andrew's X-shaped cross still decorates the Scottish flag today.

National Museum of Scotland

Replica tomb of Mary, Queen of Scots

Enter the first room on your right, with imposing swords and other objects related to Scotland's most famous patriots—William Wallace and Robert the Bruce. Bruce's descendants, the Stuarts, went on to rule Scotland for the next 300 years. Eventually, James VI of Scotland (see his baby cradle) came to rule England as well (as King James I of England).

In the next room, a big guillotine recalls the harsh justice meted out to criminals, witches, and "Covenanters" (17th-century political activists who opposed interference of the Stuart kings in affairs of the Presbyterian Church of Scotland). Nearby, also check out the tomb (a copy) of Mary, Queen of Scots, the 16th-century Stuart monarch who opposed the Presbyterian Church of Scotland. Educated and raised in Renaissance France, Mary brought refinement to the Scottish throne. After she was imprisoned and then executed by Elizabeth I of England in 1587, her supporters rallied each other by invoking her memory. Pendants and coins with her portrait stoked the irrepressible Scottish spirit (see display case near tomb).

Newcomen steam-engine water pump

Browse the rest of level 1 to see everyday objects from that age: carved panels, cookware, and clothes.
• *Backtrack to Hawthornden Court and head up to level 3.*

Scotland Transformed (1700s): You'll see artifacts related to Bonnie Prince Charlie and the Jacobite rebellions as well as the ornate Treaty of Union document, signed in 1707 by the Scottish parliament. This act voluntarily united Scotland with England under the single parliament of the United Kingdom. For some Scots, this move was an inevitable step in connecting to the wider world, but for others it symbolized the end of Scotland's existence.

Union with England brought stability and investment to Scotland. In this same era, the advances of the Industrial Revolution were making a big impact on Scottish life. Mechanized textile looms (on display) replaced hand craftsmanship. The huge Newcomen steam-engine water pump helped the mining industry to develop sites with tricky drainage. Nearby is a model of a coal mine (or "colliery"); coal-rich Scotland exploited this natural resource to fuel its textile factories.
• *Journey up to level 5.*

Industry and Empire (1800s): Turn right and do a counterclockwise spin around this floor to survey Scottish life in the 19th century. Industry had transformed the country. Highland farmers left their land to find work in Lowland factories and foundries. Modern inventions—the phonograph, the steam-powered train, the kitchen range—revolutionized everyday life. In Glasgow near the turn of the century, architect Charles Rennie Mackintosh helped to define Scottish Art Nouveau. Scotland was at the forefront of literature (Robert Burns, Sir Walter Scott, Robert Louis Stevenson), science (Lord Kelvin, James Watt, Alexander Graham Bell...he was born here, anyway!), world exploration (John Kirk in Africa, Sir Alexander Mackenzie in Canada), and whisky production.
• *Climb the stairs to level 6.*

Scotland: A Changing Nation (1900s): Turn left and do a clockwise spin through this floor to bring the story to the present day. The two world wars decimated the population of this already wee nation. In addition, hundreds of thousands emigrated, especially to Canada (where one in eight Canadians has Scottish origins). Other exhibits include Scots in the world of entertainment (from early boy-band Bay City Rollers to actor-comedian Billy Connolly); a look at the recent trend of devolution from the United Kingdom (1999 opening of Scotland's own parliament and the landmark 2014 referendum on Scottish independence); and a sports Hall of Fame (from golfer Tom Morris to auto racers Jackie Stewart and Jim Clark). • *Finish your visit on level 7, the rooftop.*

Garden Terrace: The well-described roof garden features grasses and heathers from every corner of Scotland and spectacular views of the city.

Museums in the New Town

These sights are linked by the "Bonnie Wee New Town Walk" on page 49.

▲▲**SCOTTISH NATIONAL GALLERY**
This delightful, small museum has Scotland's best collection of paintings. In a short visit, you can admire well-described works by Old Masters (Raphael, Rem-brandt, Rubens), Impressionists (Monet, Degas, Gauguin), and a few underrated Scottish painters. (Scottish art is better at the National Portrait Gallery, described next.) Although there are no iconic masterpieces, it's a surprisingly enjoyable collection that's truly world-class.

Cost and Hours: Free; daily 10:00-17:00, Thu until 19:00, longer hours in Aug; café downstairs, The Mound (between Princes and Market streets), tel. 0131/624-6200, www.nationalgalleries.org.

Expect Changes: The museum is undergoing major renovation to increase the space of its Scottish collection and build a grand main entrance from Princes Street Gardens.

Visiting the Museum: Start at the gallery entrance (at the north end of the building). Climb the stairs to the upper level (north end), and take a left. You'll run right into...

Van der Goes, *The Trinity Panels,* c. 1473-1479: For more than five centuries, these two double-sided panels have remained here—first in a church, then (when the church was leveled to build Waverley train station) in this museum. The panels likely were the wings of a triptych, flanking a central scene of the Virgin Mary that was destroyed by Protestant vandals during the Reformation.

In one panel is the Trinity: God the Father, in a rich red robe, cradles a

Van der Goes, The Trinity Panels

Scottish National Gallery

spindly, just-crucified Christ, while the dove of the Holy Spirit hovers between them. (This is what would have been seen when the triptych was closed.) The flip side of the Christ panel depicts Scotland's king and queen, who are best known to history as the parents of the boy kneeling alongside them. He grew up to become James IV, the Renaissance king who made Edinburgh a cultural capital. On the other panel, the church's director (the man who commissioned the painting from the well-known Flemish painter) kneels and looks on while an angel plays a hymn on the church organ. On the opposite side is Margaret of Denmark, Queen of Scots, being presented by a saint.

In a typical medieval fashion, the details are meticulous—expressive faces, intricate folds in the robes, Christ's pallid skin, observant angels. The donor's face is a remarkable portrait, with realistic skin tone and a five-o'clock shadow. But the painting lacks true 3-D realism—God's gold throne is overly exaggerated, and Christ's cardboard-cutout body hovers weightlessly.

• *Go back across the top of the skylight, to a room where the next two paintings hang.*

Botticelli, *The Virgin Adoring the Sleeping Christ Child,* c. 1485: Mary looks

down at her baby, peacefully sleeping in a flower-filled garden. It's easy to appreciate Botticelli's masterful style: the precisely drawn outlines, the Virgin's pristine skin, the translucent glow. Botticelli creates a serene world in which no shadows are cast. The scene is painted on canvas—unusual at a time when wood panels were the norm. For the Virgin's rich cloak, Botticelli used ground-up lapis lazuli (a very pricey semiprecious stone), and her hem is decorated with gold leaf.

Raphael, *Holy Family with a Palm Tree,* 1506-1507: Mary, Joseph, and the Christ Child fit snugly within a round frame (a tondo), their pose symbolizing geometric perfection and the perfect family unit. Joseph kneels to offer Jesus flowers. Mary curves toward him. Baby Jesus dangles in between, linking the family together. Raphael also connects the figures through eye contact: Mary eyes Joseph, who locks onto Jesus, who gazes precociously back. Like in a cameo, we see the faces incised in profile, while their bodies bulge out toward us.

• *Back downstairs at ground level is the main gallery space. Circle around the collection chronologically, watching for works by Bellini, Titian, Velázquez, and El Greco. In*

Gainsborough, The Honorable Mrs. Graham

hand, staring off to the side (Thoughtfully? Determinedly? Haughtily?). Her faultless face and smooth neck stand out from the elaborately ruffled dress and background foliage. This 18th-century woman wears a silvery dress that echoes 17th-century style—Gainsborough's way of showing how, though she was young, she was classy. Thomas ("Blue Boy") Gainsborough—the product of a clothes-making father and a flower-painting mother—uses aspects of both in this lush portrait. The ruby brooch on her bodice marks the center of this harmonious composition.

• *Climb the stairs to the upper level (south end, opposite from where you entered) and turn right for the Impressionists and Post-Impressionists.*

Impressionist Collection: The gallery has a smattering of (mostly smaller-scale) works from all the main artists of the Impressionist and Post-Impressionist eras. You'll see Degas' ballet scenes, Renoir's pastel-colored family scenes, Van Gogh's peasants, and Seurat's pointillism.

• *Keep an eye out for these three paintings.*

Monet's *Poplars on the River Epte* (1891) was part of the artist's famous "series" paintings. He set up several canvases in a floating studio near his home in Giverny. He'd start on one canvas in the morning (to catch the morning light), then move to the next as the light changed. This particular canvas captures a perfect summer day, showing both the poplars on the riverbank and their mirror image in the still water. The subject matter begins to dissolve into a pure pattern of color, anticipating abstract art.

Gauguin's *Vision of the Sermon* (1888) shows French peasant women imagining the miraculous event they've just heard preached about in church—when Jacob wrestles with an angel. The painting is a watershed in art history, as Gauguin throws out the rules of "realism" that had reigned since the Renaissance. The colors are surreal, there are no shadows, the figures are arranged almost randomly, and

Room 7, look for the next two paintings.

Rubens, *Feast of Herod,* c. 1635-1638: All eyes turn to watch the dramatic culmination of the story of John the Baptist. Salome (standing in center) presents John's severed head on a platter to a horrified King Herod, who clutches the tablecloth and buries his hand in his beard to stifle a gag. Meanwhile, Herod's wife—who cooked up the nasty plot—pokes spitefully at John's head with a fork. A dog tugs at Herod's foot like a nasty conscience. The canvas—big, colorful, full of motion and drama—is totally Baroque.

Rembrandt, *Self-Portrait, Aged 51,* c. 1657: It's 1657, and 51-year-old Rembrandt has just declared bankruptcy. Besides financial hardship and the auctioning-off of his personal belongings, he's also facing social stigma and behind-his-back ridicule. Once Holland's most renowned painter, he's begun a slow decline into poverty and obscurity. His face says it all.

• *In Room 11, find...*

Gainsborough, *The Honorable Mrs. Graham,* 1775-1777: The slender, elegant, lavishly dressed woman was the teenage bride of a wealthy Scottish landowner. She leans on a column, ostrich feather in

Sargent's Lady Agnew of Lochnaw

Mary, Queen of Scots

there's no attempt to make the wrestlers appear distant. The diagonal tree branch is the only thing separating the everyday world from the miraculous. Later, when Gauguin moved to Tahiti (see his *Three Tahitians* nearby), he painted a similar world, where the everyday and magical coexist, with symbolic power.

Sargent's *Lady Agnew of Lochnaw* (1892) is the work that launched the career of this American-born portrait artist. Lady Agnew—the young wife of a wealthy old Scotsman—lounges back languidly and gazes out self-assuredly. The Impressionistic smudges of paint on her dress and the chair contrast with her clear skin and luminous eyeballs. Her relaxed pose (one arm hanging down the side) contrasts with her intensity: head tilted slightly down while she gazes up, a corner of her mouth askew, and an eyebrow cocked seductively.

▲▲SCOTTISH NATIONAL PORTRAIT GALLERY

Put a face on Scotland's history by enjoying these portraits of famous Scots from the earliest times until today. From its Neo-Gothic facade to a grand entry hall featuring a *Who's Who* of Scotland, to galleries highlighting the great Scots of each age, this impressive museum will fascinate anyone interested in Scottish culture. The gallery also hosts temporary exhibits highlighting the work of more contemporary Scots. Because of its purely Scottish focus, many travelers prefer this to the (pan-European) main branch of the National Gallery.

Cost and Hours: Free, daily 10:00-17:00, good **$** cafeteria serving healthy meals, 1 Queen Street, tel. 0131/624-6490, www.nationalgalleries.org.

Visiting the Gallery: In the stirring **entrance hall** you'll find busts of great Scots and a full-body statue of Robbie "Rabbie" Burns, as well as (up above) a glorious frieze showing a parade of historical figures and murals depicting important events in Scottish history. (These are better viewed from the first floor and its mezzanine—described later.) We'll start on the **second floor,** right into the thick of the struggle between Scotland and England over who should rule this land.

Reformation to Revolution (gallery 1): The collection starts with a portrait of **Mary, Queen of Scots** (1542-1587), her cross and rosary prominent. This controversial ruler set off two centuries

Central atrium of Scottish National Portrait Gallery

of strife. Mary was born with both Stuart blood (the ruling family of Scotland) and the Tudor blood of England's monarchs (Queen Elizabeth I was her cousin). Catholic and French-educated, Mary felt alienated from her own increasingly Protestant homeland. Her tense conversations with the reformer John Knox must have been epic. Then came a series of scandals: She married unpopular Lord Darnley, then (possibly) cheated on him, causing Darnley to (possibly) murder her lover, causing Mary to (possibly) murder Darnley, then (possibly) run off with another man, and (possibly) plot against Queen Elizabeth.

Amid all that drama, Mary was forced by her own people to relinquish her throne to her infant son, **James VI.** Find his portraits as a child and as a grown-up. James grew up to rule Scotland, and when Queen Elizabeth (the "virgin queen") died without an heir, he also became king of England (James I). But James' son, **Charles I,** after a bitter civil war, was arrested and executed in 1649: See the large *Execution of Charles I* painting high on the far wall, his blood-dripping head displayed to the crowd; nearby is a portrait of Charles in happier times, as a 12-year-old boy. His son, Charles II, restored the

Stuarts to power. He was then succeeded by his Catholic brother James VII of Scotland (II of England), who was sent into exile in France. There the Stuarts stewed, planning a return to power, waiting for someone to lead them in what would come to be known as the Jacobite rebellions.

The Jacobite Cause (gallery 4): One of the biggest paintings in the room is *The Baptism of Prince Charles Edward Stuart.* Born in 1720, this Stuart heir to the thrones of Great Britain and Ireland is better known to history as "Bonnie Prince Charlie." (See his bonnie features in various portraits nearby, as a child, young man, and grown man.) Charismatic Charles convinced France to invade Scotland and put him back on the throne there. In 1745, he entered Edinburgh in triumph. But he was defeated at the tide-turning Battle of Culloden (1746). The Stuart cause died forever, and Bonnie Prince Charlie went into exile, eventually dying drunk and wasted in Rome, far from the land he nearly ruled.

• *The next few rooms (galleries 5-6) contain special exhibits that swap out every year or two—they're worth a browse.*

The Age of Improvement (gallery 7): The faces portrayed here belonged to a new society whose hard work and public spirit achieved progress with a Scottish accent. Social equality and the Industrial Revolution "transformed" Scotland— you'll see portraits of the great poet Robert Burns, the son of a farmer (Burns was heralded as a "heaven-taught ploughman" when his poems were first published), and the man who perfected the steam engine, James Watt.

• *Check out the remaining galleries, with more special exhibits, then head back down to the first floor for a good look at the...*

Central Atrium (first floor): Great Scots! The atrium is decorated in a parade of late 19th-century Romantic Historicism. The **frieze** (working counterclockwise) is a visual encyclopedia, from an ax-wielding Stone Age man and a druid, to the early legendary monarchs (Macbeth), to warriors William Wallace and Robert the Bruce, to many kings (James I, II, III, and so on), to great thinkers, inventors, and artists (Allan Ramsay, Flora MacDonald, David Hume, Adam Smith, James Boswell, James Watt), the three greatest Scottish writers (Robert Burns, Sir Walter Scott, Robert Louis Stevenson), and culminating with the historian Thomas Carlyle, who was the driving spirit (powered by the fortune of a local newspaper baron) behind creating this portrait gallery.

Around the first-floor mezzanine are large-scale **murals** depicting great events in Scottish history, including the landing of St. Margaret at Queensferry in 1068, the Battle of Stirling Bridge in 1297, the Battle of Bannockburn in 1314, and the marriage procession of James IV and Margaret Tudor through the streets of Edinburgh in 1503.

• *Also on this floor you'll find the...*

Modern Portrait Gallery: This space is dedicated to rotating art and photographs highlighting Scots who are making an impact in the world today, such as Annie Lennox, Alan Cumming, and physicist Peter Higgs (theorizer of the Higgs boson, the so-called God particle).

▲▲GEORGIAN HOUSE

This refurbished Neoclassical house, set on Charlotte Square, is a trip back to 1796. It recounts the era when a newly gentrified and well-educated Edinburgh was nicknamed the "Athens of the North." Begin on the second floor, where you'll watch an interesting 16-minute video dramatizing the upstairs/downstairs lifestyles of the aristocrats and servants who lived here. Try on some Georgian outfits, then head downstairs to tour period rooms and even peek into the fully stocked medicine cabinet. Info sheets are available in each room, along with volunteer guides who share stories and trivia, such as why Georgian bigwigs had to sit behind a screen while enjoying a fire. A walk down George Street after your visit here can be fun for the imagination.

Cost and Hours: £7.50, daily 10:00-17:00, March and Nov 11:00-16:00, closed Dec-Feb, last entry 45 minutes before closing; 7 Charlotte Square, tel. 0131/226-3318, www.nts.org.uk.

Near Edinburgh

▲▲ROYAL YACHT *BRITANNIA*

This much-revered vessel, which transported Britain's royal family for more than 40 years on 900 voyages (an average of once around the world per year) before being retired in 1997, is permanently moored in Edinburgh's port of Leith. Queen Elizabeth II said of the ship, "This is the only place I can truly relax." Today it's open to the curious public, who have access to its many decks— from engine rooms to drawing rooms— and offers a fascinating time-warp look into the late-20th-century lifestyles of the rich and royal. It's worth the 20-minute bus or taxi ride from the center; figure on spending about 2.5 hours total on the outing.

Cost and Hours: £15.50, includes 1.5-hour audioguide, daily 9:30-16:30, Oct until 16:00, Nov-March 10:00-15:30, these are last entry times, tearoom; at the

Royal Yacht Britannia

The yacht's dining room

Ocean Terminal Shopping Mall, on Ocean Drive in Leith; tel. 0131/555-5566, www. royalyachtbritannia.co.uk.

Getting There: From central Edinburgh, catch Lothian bus #11 or #22 from Princes Street (just above Waverley Station), or #35 from the bottom of the Royal Mile (alongside the parliament building) to Ocean Terminal (last stop). From the B&B neighborhood, you can either bus to the city center and transfer to one of the buses listed earlier, or take bus #14 from Dalkeith Road to Mill Lane, then walk about 10 minutes. The Majestic Tour hop-on, hop-off bus stops here as well. Drivers can park free in the blue parking garage. Take the shopping center elevator to level E, then follow the signs.

Visiting the Ship: First, explore the museum, filled with engrossing royal-family-afloat history. You'll see lots of family photos that evoke the fine times the Windsors enjoyed on the *Britannia*, as well as some nautical equipment and uniforms. Then, armed with your audioguide, you're welcome aboard.

This was the last in a line of royal yachts that stretches back to 1660. With all its royal functions, the ship required a crew of more than 200. Begin in the captain's bridge, which feels like it's been preserved from the day it was launched in 1953. Then head down a deck to see the officers' quarters, then the garage, where a Rolls Royce was hoisted aboard to use in places where the local transportation wasn't up to royal standards. The Veranda Deck at the back of the ship was the favorite place for outdoor entertainment. Ronald Reagan, Boris Yeltsin, Bill Clinton, and Nelson Mandela all sipped champagne here. The Sun Lounge, just off the back Veranda Deck, was the Queen's favorite, with Burmese teak and the same phone system she was used to in Buckingham Palace. When she wasn't entertaining, the Queen liked it quiet. The crew wore sneakers, communicated in hand signals, and (at least near the Queen's quarters) had to be finished with all their work by 8:00 in the morning.

Take a peek into the adjoining his-and-hers bedrooms of the Queen and the Duke of Edinburgh (check out the spartan twin beds), and the honeymoon suite where Prince Charles and Lady Di began their wedded bliss.

Heading down another deck, walk through the officers' lounge (and learn about the rowdy games they played) and

Mountain skyline of Holyrood Park

Hiking along the Salisbury Crags

past the galleys (including custom cabinetry for the fine china and silver) on your way to the biggest room on the yacht, the state dining room. Now decorated with gifts given by the ship's many noteworthy guests, this space enabled the Queen to entertain a good-size crowd. The drawing room, while rather simple (the Queen specifically requested "country house comfort"), was perfect for casual relaxing among royals. Princess Diana played the piano, which is bolted to the deck. Note the contrast to the decidedly less plush crew's quarters, mail room, sick bay, laundry, and engine room.

EXPERIENCES

Urban Hikes
▲▲HOLYROOD PARK

Rising up from the heart of Edinburgh, Holyrood Park is a lush green mountain squeezed between the parliament/Holyroodhouse (at the bottom of the Royal Mile) and my recommended B&B neighborhood. For an exhilarating hike, connect these two zones with a moderately strenuous 30-minute walk along the **Salisbury Crags**—reddish cliffs with sweeping views over the city. Or, for a more serious climb, make the ascent to the summit of **Arthur's Seat,** the 822-foot-tall remains of an extinct volcano. You can run up like they did in *Chariots of Fire,* or just stroll—at

the summit, you'll be rewarded with commanding views of the town and surroundings. On May Day, be on the summit at dawn and wash your face in the morning dew to commemorate the Celtic holiday of Beltane, the celebration of spring. (Morning dew is supposedly very good for your complexion.)

You can do this hike either from the bottom of the Royal Mile, or from the B&B neighborhood.

From the Royal Mile: Begin in the parking lot below the Palace of Holyroodhouse. Facing the cliff, you'll see two trailheads. For the easier hike along the base of the Salisbury Crags, take the trail to the right. At the far end, you can descend into the Dalkeith Road area or—if you're up for more hiking—continue steeply up the switchbacked trail to the Arthur's Seat summit. If you know you'll want to ascend Arthur's Seat from the start, take the wider path on the left from the Holyroodhouse parking lot (easier grade, through the abbey ruins and "Hunter's Bog").

From the B&B Neighborhood: If you're staying in this area, enjoy a pre-breakfast or late-evening hike starting from the other side (in June, the sun comes up early, and it stays light until nearly midnight). From the Commonwealth Pool, take Holyrood Park Road, bear left at the first roundabout, then turn right at the second roundabout (onto Queen's Drive). Soon you'll see the

On top of Arthur's Seat

Whisky shop

trailhead, and make your choice: Bear right up the steeper "Piper's Walk" to **Arthur's Seat** (about a 20-minute hike from here, up a steeply switchbacked trail). Or bear left for an easier ascent up the "Radial Road" to the **Salisbury Crags,** which you can follow—with great views over town—all the way to Holyrood-house Palace.

By Car: If you have a car, you can drive up most of the way to Arthur's Seat from behind (follow the one-way street from the palace, park safely and for free by the little lake, and hike up).

▲**CALTON HILL**

For an easy walk for fine views over all of Edinburgh, head up to Calton Hill—the monument-studded bluff that rises up from the eastern end of the New Town. From the Waverley Station area, simply head east on Princes Street (which becomes Waterloo Place).

About five minutes after passing North Bridge, watch on the right for the gated entrance to the **Old Calton Cemetery**—worth a quick walk-through for its stirring monuments to great Scots.

The views from the cemetery are good, but for even better ones, head back out to the main road and continue a few more minutes on Waterloo Place. Across the street, steps lead up into **Calton Hill.** Explore. Informational plaques identify the key landmarks. At the summit of the hill is the giant, unfinished replica of the Parthe-

non, honoring those lost in the Napoleonic Wars. Donations to finish it never materialized, leaving it with the nickname "Edinburgh's Disgrace." Nearby, the old observatory is filled with an avant-garde art gallery, and the back of the hillside boasts sweeping views over the Firth of Forth and Edinburgh's sprawl. Back toward the Old Town, the tallest tower celebrates Admiral Horatio Nelson—the same honoree of the giant pillar on London's Trafalgar Square. The best views are around the smaller, circular Dugald Stewart Monument, with postcard panoramas overlooking the spires of the Old Town and the New Town.

Whisky and Gin Tasting
Whisky Tasting
One of the most accessible places to learn about whisky is at the **Scotch Whisky Experience** on the Royal Mile, an expensive but informative overview to whisky, including a tasting (listed in "Sights," earlier).

To get more into sampling whisky, try one of the early-evening tastings at the **Cadenhead's Whisky Shop** on the Royal Mile. They're a hit with aficionados (£25, Mon-Fri at 17:45, best to book ahead in peak season; shop open Mon-Sat 10:30-17:30, closed Sun, 172 Canongate, tel. 0131/556-5864, www.wmcadenhead.com).

At **Whiski Rooms Shop,** just off the Royal Mile, you can order a flight in the bar (includes written info on the whiskies) or opt for a guided tasting, which you can book in advance (flights and tours start around £25, daily 10:00-18:00, bar until 24:00, both open later in Aug, 4 North Bank Street, tel. 0131/225-1532, www. whiskirooms.com).

Gin Distillery Tours

The residents of Edinburgh drink more gin per person than any other city in the United Kingdom, and the city is largely responsible for the recent renaissance of this drink, so it's only appropriate that you visit a gin distillery while in town. Two distilleries right in the heart of Edinburgh offer hourlong tours with colorful guides who discuss the history of gin, show you the stills involved in the production process, and ply you with libations. Both tours are popular and fill up; book ahead on their websites.

Pickering's is located in a former vet school and animal hospital at Summerhall, halfway between the Royal Mile and the B&B neighborhood—you'll still see cages lining the walls (£10, 3/day Thu-Sun, meet at the Royal Dick Bar in the central courtyard at 1 Summerhall, tel. 0131/290-2901, www.pickeringsgin.com).

Edinburgh Gin is in the New Town, next to the Waldorf Astoria Hotel. Besides the basic tour, there's a connoisseur tour with more tastings and a gin-making tour (basic tour £10, 3/day daily, 1A Rutland Place, tel. 0131/656-2810, www.edinburghgin.com). If you can't get on to one of their tours, visit their Heads & Tales bar to taste their gins (daily 17:00-24:00).

Edinburgh's Festivals

Every summer, Edinburgh's annual festivals turn the city into a carnival of the arts. The season begins in June with the international film festival (www.edfilmfest.org. uk); then the jazz and blues festival in July (www.edinburghjazzfestival.com).

In August a riot of overlapping festivals known collectively as the **Edinburgh Festival** rages simultaneously—international,

fringe, book, and art, as well as the Military Tattoo. There are enough music, dance, drama, and multicultural events to make even the most jaded traveler giddy with excitement. Every day is jammed with formal and spontaneous fun. Many city sights run on extended hours. It's a glorious time to be in Edinburgh...if you have (and can afford) a room.

If you'll be in town in August, book your room and tickets for major events (especially the Tattoo) as far ahead as you can lock in dates. Plan carefully to ensure you'll have time for festival activities as well as sightseeing. Check online to confirm dates; the best overall website is www. edinburghfestivals.co.uk. Several publications—including the festival's official schedule, the *Edinburgh Festivals Guide Daily, The List, Fringe Program,* and *Daily Diary*—list and evaluate festival events.

The official, more formal **Edinburgh International Festival** is the original. Major events sell out well in advance (ticket office at the Hub, in the former Tolbooth Church near the top of the Royal Mile, tel. 0131/473-2000, www. hubtickets.co.uk or www.eif.co.uk).

The less formal **Fringe Festival,** featuring edgy comedy and theater, is huge—with 2,000 shows—and has eclipsed the original festival in popularity (ticket/info office just below St. Giles' Cathedral on the Royal Mile, 180 High Street, bookings tel. 0131/226-0000, www.edfringe.com). Tickets may be available at the door, and half-price tickets for some events are sold on the day of the show at the Half-Price Hut, located at The Mound, near the Scottish National Gallery.

The **Military Tattoo** is a massing of bands, drums, and bagpipes, with groups from all over the former British Empire and beyond. Displaying military finesse with a stirring lone-piper finale, this grand spectacle fills the Castle Esplanade (nightly during most of Aug except Sun, performances Mon-Fri at 21:00, Sat at 19:30 and 22:30, £25-63, booking starts in Dec, Fri-Sat shows sell out first, all seats generally sold out by early summer, some scattered same-day tickets may be available; office open Mon-Fri 10:00-16:30, closed Sat-Sun, during Tattoo open until show time and closed Sun; 32 Market Street, behind Waverley Station, tel. 0131/225-1188, www.edintattoo.co.uk).

Shopping

Shops are usually open around 10:00-18:00 (later on Thu, shorter hours or closed on Sun). Tourist shops are open longer hours.

Rick's Tip: *If you want to be sure you're buying local merchandise,* **check if the labels read: "Made in Scotland."** *"Designed in Scotland" actually means "Made in China."*

Shopping Streets and Neighborhoods

Near the Royal Mile: The Royal Mile is intensely touristy, mostly lined with interchangeable shops selling made-in-China souvenirs. There are some gems, too, such as the delightful **Pinnies & Poppy Seeds** (selling handmade shortbread made fresh daily, at 26 St. Mary's Street) and **Cranachan & Crowdie** (stocked with Scottish edibles and crafts from many producers, at 263 Canongate). Both are within a block of each other near World's End.

In general, the area near **Grassmarket,** an easy stroll from the top of the Royal Mile, offers more originality. **Victoria Street,** which climbs steeply downhill from the Royal Mile (near the Hub/Tolbooth Church) to Grassmarket, has a fine concentration of local chain shops, including I.J. Mellis Cheesemonger and Walker Slater for designer tweed (both described later), plus Calzeat (scarves, throws, and other textiles), a Harry Potter store, and more clothing and accessory shops. **Candlemaker Row,** exiting Grassmarket opposite Victoria Street, is a little more artisan, with boutiques selling hats (everything from dapper men's caps to outrageous fascinators), jewelry, art, design items, and even fossils. The street winds a couple of blocks up toward the National Museum.

If it's **whisky** you want, try the shops I recommend for tasting (see page 75); they're on or near the Royal Mile.

In New Town: For mass-market shopping, you'll find plenty of big chain stores along **Princes Street.** In addition to Marks & Spencer, H&M, Zara, Primark, and a glitzy Apple Store, you'll also see the granddaddy of Scottish department stores, Jenners (generally daily 9:30-18:30, open later on Thu, shorter hours on Sun). Parallel to Princes Street, **George Street** has higher-end chain stores (including many from London, such as L.K. Bennett, Molton Brown, and

Victoria Street, lined with shops

Karen Millen). Just off St. Andrew Square is a branch of the high-end London department store Harvey Nichols.

For more local, artisan shopping, check out **Thistle Street,** lined with some fun eateries and a good collection of shops. You'll see some fun boutiques selling jewelry, shoes, and clothing. This is also the home of Howie Nicolsby's 21st Century Kilts, which attempts to bring traditional Scottish menswear into the present day.

Night Walks
▲▲LITERARY PUB TOUR
This two-hour walk is interesting even if you think Sir Walter Scott won an Oscar for playing General Patton. You'll follow the witty dialogue of two actors as they debate whether the great literature of Scotland was high art or the creative re-creation of fun-loving louts fueled by a passion for whisky. You'll wander from the Grassmarket over the Old Town and New Town, with stops in three pubs, as your guides share their takes on Scotland's literary greats. The tour meets at the Beehive Inn on Grassmarket (£14, book online and save £2, May-Sept nightly at 19:30, April and Oct Thu-Sun, Jan-March Fri and Sun, Nov-Dec Fri only, tel. 0800-169-7410, www.edinburghliterarypubtour. co.uk).

▲GHOST WALKS
A variety of companies lead spooky walks around town, providing an entertaining and affordable night out (offered nightly, most around 19:00 and 21:00, easy socializing for solo travelers). These two options are the most established.

The theatrical and creatively staged **The Cadies & Witchery Tours,** the most established outfit, offers two different 1.25-hour walks: "Ghosts and Gore" (April-Aug only, in daylight and following a flatter route) and "Murder and Mystery" (year-round, after dark, hillier, more surprises and scares). The cost for either tour is the same (£10, includes book of stories, leaves from top of Royal Mile, outside the Witchery Restaurant, near Castle Esplanade, reservations required, tel. 0131/225-6745, www.witcherytours.com).

Auld Reekie Tours offers a scary array of walks daily and nightly (£12-16, 60-90 minutes, leaves from front steps of the Tron Church building on Cockburn Street, tel. 0131/557-4700, www.auldreekietours.com). Auld Reekie focuses on the paranormal, witch covens, and pagan temples, taking groups into the "haunted vaults" under the old bridges (complete with screaming Gothic "jumpers").

Scottish Folk Evenings

A variety of £35-40 dinner shows, generally for tour groups intent on photographing old cultural clichés, are held in the huge halls of expensive hotels. (Prices are bloated to include 20 percent commissions.) Your "traditional" meal is followed by a full slate of swirling kilts, blaring bagpipes, and Scottish folk dancing with an old-time music hall emcee. If you like Lawrence Welk, you're in for a treat. But for most travelers, these are painfully cheesy. You can sometimes see the show without dinner for about two-thirds the price. The TI has fliers on all the latest venues.

Prestonfield House, a luxurious venue near the Dalkeith Road B&Bs, offers its kitschy "Taste of Scotland" folk evening with or without dinner Sunday to Friday. For £50, you get the show with two drinks and a wad of haggis; £65 buys you the same, plus a three-course meal and a half-bottle of wine (be there at 18:45, dinner at 19:00, show runs 20:00-22:00, April-Oct only). It's in the stables of "the handsomest house in Edinburgh," which is now home to the Rhubarb Restaurant (Priestfield Road, a 10-minute walk from Dalkeith Road B&Bs, tel. 0131/225-7800, www.scottishshow.co.uk).

For something more lowbrow—and arguably more authentic—in summer, you can watch the Princes Street Gardens Dancers perform a range of Scottish country dancing. The volunteer troupe will demonstrate each dance, then invite spectators to give it a try (£5, June-July Mon 19:30-21:30, at Ross Bandstand in Princes Street Gardens—in the glen just

below Edinburgh Castle, tel. 0131/228-8616, www.princesstreetgardensdancing.org.uk). The same group offers summer programs in other parts of town (see website for details).

Theater

Even outside festival time, Edinburgh is a fine place for lively and affordable theater. Pick up *The List* for a complete rundown of what's on (free at TI; also online at www.list.co.uk).

▲▲Live Music in Pubs

While traditional music venues have been eclipsed by beer-focused student bars, Edinburgh still has a few good pubs that can deliver a traditional folk-music (trad) fix. The monthly *Gig Guide* (free at TI, accommodations, and various pubs, www.gigguide.co.uk) lists several places each night that have live music, divided by genre (pop, rock, world, and folk).

South of the Royal Mile: Sandy Bell's is a tight little pub with live folk music nightly from 21:30 (near National Museum of Scotland at 25 Forrest Road, tel. 0131/225-2751). Food is very simple (toasted sandwiches and pies), drinks are cheap, tables are small, and the vibe is local. They also have a few sessions earlier in the day (Sat at 14:00, Sun at 16:00, Mon at 17:30).

Captain's Bar is a cozy, music-focused pub with live sessions of folk and traditional music nightly around 21:00—see

Grassmarket has pubs with live music.

website for lineup (4 South College Street, http://captainsedinburgh.webs.com).

The Royal Oak is another good—if small—place for a dose of folk and blues (just off South Bridge opposite Chambers Road at 1 Infirmary Street, tel. 0131/557-2976).

The **Grassmarket** neighborhood (below the castle) bustles with live music and rowdy people spilling out of the pubs. Thanks to the music and crowds, you'll know where to go...and where not to. Have a beer and follow your ear to places like **Biddy Mulligans** or **White Hart Inn** (both on Grassmarket). **Finnegans Wake,** on Victoria Street (which leads down to Grassmarket), also has live music in a variety of genres each night.

On the Royal Mile: Three characteristic pubs within a few steps of each other on High Street (opposite Radisson Hotel) offer a fun setting, classic pub architecture and ambience, and live music for the cost of a beer: **Whiski Bar** (mostly trad and folk; nightly at 22:00), **Royal Mile** (variety of genres; nightly at 22:00), and **Mitre Bar** (acoustic pop/rock with some trad; Fri-Sun at 21:30).

In the New Town: All the beer drinkers seem to head for the pedestrianized Rose Street, famous for having the most pubs per square inch anywhere in Scotland—and plenty of live music.

EATING

Reservations for restaurants are essential in August and on weekends, and a good idea anytime. Children aren't allowed in many of the pubs.

In case Edinburgh is your first stop in Scotland, be aware that haggis, a Scottish specialty, consists of chopped organ meat often encased sausage-like in sheep intestines. Some people love it.

The Old Town

Pricey places abound on the Royal Mile (listed later). While those are tempting, I prefer the two areas described first, each within a few minutes' walk of the Mile—just far enough to offer better value and a bit less touristy crush.

On Victoria Street, Near Grassmarket

$$$$ **Grainstore Restaurant,** a sedate and dressy world of wood, stone, and candles tucked away above busy Victoria Street, has served Scottish produce with a French twist for more than two decades. While they have inexpensive £14 two-course lunch specials, dinner is à la carte. Reservations are recommended (daily 12:00-14:30 & 18:00-21:30, 30 Victoria Street, tel. 0131/225-7635, www. grainstore-restaurant.co.uk).

$$$ **Maison Bleue** Restaurant is popular for their à la carte French/Scottish/North African menu and dinner special before 18:30 (18:00 on Fri-Sat; open daily 12:00-22:00, 36 Victoria Street, tel. 0131/226-1900).

$ **Oink** carves from a freshly roasted pig each afternoon for sandwiches that come in "oink" or "grunter" sizes. Watch the pig shrink in the front window throughout the day (daily 11:00-18:00 or whenever they run out of meat, cash only, 34 Victoria Street, tel. 01890/761-355). Another location is at the bottom end of the Royal Mile, near the parliament building (at 82 Canongate).

Near the National Museum

These restaurants are happily removed from the Royal Mile melee and skew to a youthful clientele with few tourists. After passing the Greyfriars Bobby statue and the National Museum, fork left onto Forrest Road.

$ **Union of Genius** is a creative soup kitchen that also serves good salads and fresh-baked breads. The "flight" comes with three small cups of soup and three types of bread. Line up at the counter, then either take your soup to go or sit in the cramped interior, with a couple of tables and counter seating (Mon-Fri

10:00-16:00, Sat from 12:00, closed Sun, 8 Forrest Road, tel. 0131/226-4436).

$$ Mums is a kitschy diner serving up comfort food just like mum used to make. The menu runs to huge portions of heavy, greasy Scottish/British standards—bangers (sausages), meat pies, burgers, and artery-clogging breakfasts (served until 12:00)—all done with a foodie spin, including vegetarian options (Mon-Sat 9:00-22:00, Sun from 10:00, 4A Forrest Road, tel. 0131/260-9806).

Along the Royal Mile

Though the eateries along this most-crowded stretch of the city are invariably touristy, the scene is fun. Sprinkled in this list are some places a block or two off the main drag offering better values and maybe fewer tourists.

SIT-DOWN RESTAURANTS

These are listed roughly in downhill order, starting at the castle. You'll have more success getting into any of these with a reservation, especially on weekends.

$$$$ The Witchery by the Castle is set in a lushly decorated 16th-century building just below the castle on the Royal Mile, with wood paneling, antique candle-sticks, tapestries, and opulent red leather upholstery. Frequented by celebrities, tourists, and locals out for a splurge, the restaurant's emphasis is on pricey Scottish meats and seafood. Their Secret Garden dining room, in a separate building farther back, is also a special setting—down some steps and in a fanciful room with French doors opening on to a terrace. Reserve ahead for either space, dress smartly, and bear in mind you're paying a premium for the ambience (two-course lunch specials—also available before 17:30 and after 22:30, three-course dinner menu, daily 12:00-23:30, tel. 0131/225-5613, www. thewitchery.com).

$$$ Angels with Bagpipes, conveniently located across from St. Giles' Cathedral, serves sophisticated Scottish staples in its dark, serious, plush interior (two- and three-course lunches, tasting menus at dinner, daily 12:00-21:30, 343 High Street, tel. 0131/220-1111, www. angelswithbagpipes.co.uk).

$$$ Devil's Advocate is a popular gastropub that hides down the narrow lane called Advocates Close, directly across the Royal Mile from St. Giles'. With an old cellar setting—exposed stone and heavy beams—done up in modern style, it feels like a mix of old and new Edinburgh. Creative whisky cocktails kick off a menu that dares to be adventurous, but with a respect for Scottish tradition (daily 12:00-22:00, later for drinks, 8 Advocates Close, tel. 0131/225-4465).

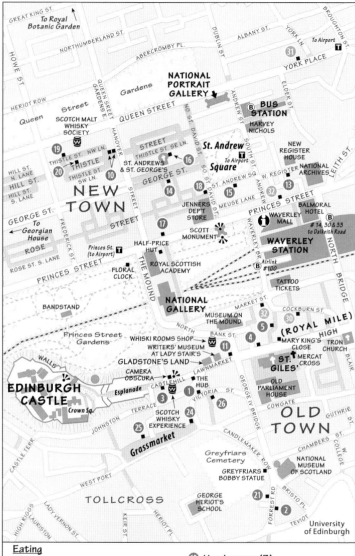

Eating

1. Grainstore, Maison Bleue & Oink
2. Union of Genius & Mums
3. The Witchery by the Castle
4. Angels with Bagpipes
5. Devil's Advocate
6. Wedgwood Restaurant
7. Edinburgh Larder
8. Mimi's Bakehouse Picnic Parlour
9. Clarinda's Tea Room
10. Hendersons (3)
11. Deacon Brodie's Tavern
12. The World's End Pub
13. Café Royal
14. The Dome Restaurant
15. Dishoom
16. St. Andrew's & St. George's Church Undercroft Café
17. Marks & Spencer Food Hall
18. Sainsbury's

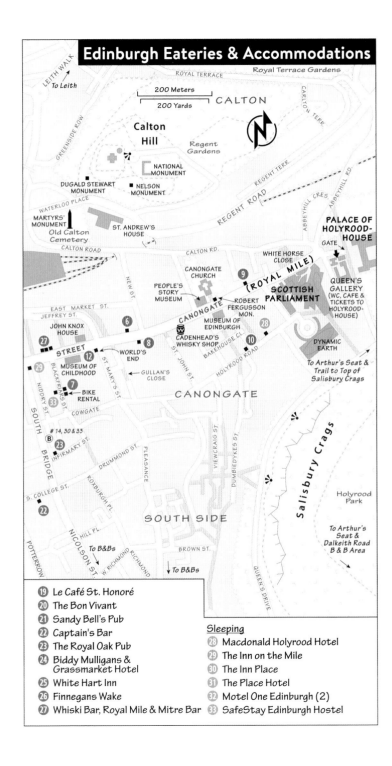

Edinburgh Eateries & Accommodations

ROYAL TERRACE

Royal Terrace Gardens

200 Meters
200 Yards

CALTON

LEITH WALK
To Leith

GREENSIDE ROW

Calton
Hill

Regent
Gardens

NATIONAL
MONUMENT

DUGALD STEWART
MONUMENT

NELSON
MONUMENT

CARLTON TERR.

REGENT TERR.

REGENT ROAD

WATERLOO PLACE

MARTYRS'
MONUMENT

Old Calton
Cemetery

ST. ANDREW'S
HOUSE

CALTON ROAD

ABBEYHILL CRES

ABBEYHILL RD.

PALACE OF
HOLYROOD-
HOUSE

GATE

CALTON RD.

WHITE HORSE
CLOSE

CANONGATE
CHURCH

❾

(ROYAL MILE)

SCOTTISH
PARLIAMENT

QUEEN'S
GALLERY
(WC, CAFE &
TICKETS TO
HOLYROOD-
HOUSE)

PEOPLE'S
STORY
MUSEUM

ROBERT
FERGUSSON
MON.

CANONGATE

MUSEUM OF
EDINBURGH

CADENHEAD'S
WHISKY SHOP

❷❽

❿

BAKEHOUSE CL.

HOLYROOD ROAD

DYNAMIC
EARTH

EAST MARKET ST.
JEFFREY ST.

JOHN KNOX
HOUSE

NEW ST.

❻

To Arthur's Seat &
Trail to Top of
Salisbury Crags

❷❼

STREET

❽

WORLD'S
END

❶❷

ST. MARY'S ST.

ST. JOHN ST.

GULLAN'S
CLOSE

CANONGATE

BLACKFRIARS ST.

❷❾

MUSEUM OF
CHILDHOOD

❼

BIKE
RENTAL

Salisbury Crags

NIDDRY ST.

COWGATE

SOUTH BRIDGE

14, 30 & 33

Ⓑ

❷❸

INFIRMARY ST.

DRUMMOND ST.

PLEASANCE

VIEWCRAIG ST.

DUMBIEDYKES ST.

Holyrood
Park

S. COLLEGE ST.

ROXBURGH PL.

❷❷

SOUTH SIDE

HILL PL.

NICOLSON ST.

W. RICHMOND

To B&Bs

RICHMOND

BROWN ST.

To Arthur's
Seat &
Dalkeith Road
B & B Area

POTTERROW

To B&Bs

QUEEN'S DRIVE

❶❾ Le Café St. Honoré
❷⓿ The Bon Vivant
❷❶ Sandy Bell's Pub
❷❷ Captain's Bar
❷❸ The Royal Oak Pub
❷❹ Biddy Mulligans &
     Grassmarket Hotel
❷❺ White Hart Inn
❷❻ Finnegans Wake
❷❼ Whiski Bar, Royal Mile & Mitre Bar

Sleeping
❷❽ Macdonald Holyrood Hotel
❷❾ The Inn on the Mile
❸⓿ The Inn Place
❸❶ The Place Hotel
❸❷ Motel One Edinburgh (2)
❸❸ SafeStay Edinburgh Hostel

$$$$ Wedgwood Restaurant is romantic, contemporary, chic, and as gourmet as possible with no pretense. Paul Wedgwood cooks while his wife Lisa serves with appetizing charm. The cuisine: creative, modern Scottish with an international twist and a whiff of Asia. The pigeon and haggis starter is scrumptious. Paul and Lisa believe in making the meal the event of the evening—don't come here to eat and run. I like the ground level with the Royal Mile view, but the busy kitchen ambience in the basement is also fine (fine wine by the glass, daily 12:00-15:00 & 18:00-22:00, reservations advised, 267 Canongate on Royal Mile, tel. 0131/558-8737, www.wedgwoodtherestaurant.co.uk).

QUICK, EASY, AND CHEAP LUNCH OPTIONS

$ Edinburgh Larder promises "a taste of the country" in the center of the city. They focus on high-quality, homestyle breakfast and lunches made from seasonal, local ingredients. The café, with table service, is a convivial space with rustic tables filled by local families. The takeaway shop next door has counter service and a few dine-in tables (Mon-Fri 8:00-16:00, Sat-Sun from 9:00, 15 Blackfriars Street, tel. 0131/556-6922).

$ Mimi's Bakehouse Picnic Parlour, a handy Royal Mile outpost of a prizewinning bakery, serves up baked goods—try the scones—and sandwiches in their cute and modern shop (daily 9:00-18:00, 250 Canongate, tel. 0131/556-6632).

$ Clarinda's Tea Room, near the bottom of the Royal Mile, is a charming and girlish time warp—a fine and tasty place to relax after touring the Mile or the Palace of Holyroodhouse. Stop in for a quiche, salad, or soup lunch. It's also great for sandwiches and tea and cake anytime (Mon-Sat 9:00-16:30, Sun from 10:00, 69 Canongate, tel. 0131/557-1888).

$$ Hendersons is a bright and casual local chain with good vegetarian dishes to go or eat in (daily 9:00-17:00, 67 Holyrood Road—three minutes off Royal Mile near

Scottish Parliament end, tel. 0131/557-1606; for more details, see the Hendersons listing later, under "The New Town").

HISTORIC PUBS ALONG THE MILE

To drink a pint or grab some forgettable pub grub in historic surroundings, consider one of the landmark pubs described on my self-guided walk: **$$ Deacon Brodie's Tavern,** at a dead-center location on the Royal Mile (a sloppy pub on the ground floor with a sloppy restaurant upstairs) or **$$ The World's End Pub,** farther down the Mile at Canongate (a colorful old place dishing up hearty meals from a creative menu in a fun, dark, and noisy space, live music Thu-Sat 21:00, 4 High Street). Both serve pub meals and are open long hours daily.

The New Town

In the Georgian part of town, you'll find a bustling world of office workers, students, and pensioners doing their thing. All of these eateries are within a few minutes' walk of the TI and Waverley Station.

Elegant Spaces near Princes Street

These places provide a staid glimpse at grand old Edinburgh. The ambience is generally better than the food.

Café Royal is a movie producer's dream pub—the perfect fin de siècle setting for a coffee, beer, or light meal. (In fact, parts of *Chariots of Fire* were filmed here.) Drop in, if only to admire the 1880 tiles featuring famous inventors (daily 12:00-14:30 & 17:00-21:30, bar food available all day, two blocks from Waverley Mall on 19 West Register Street, tel. 0131/556-1884, www.caferoyaledinburgh.co.uk). There are two eateries here: the noisy **$$ pub** and the dressier **$$$ restaurant**, specializing in oysters, fish, and game (reserve for dinner—it's quite small and understandably popular).

$$$$ The Dome Restaurant, in what was a fancy bank, serves modern international cuisine around a classy bar and under the elegant 19th-century skylight dome. With soft jazz and chic, white-tablecloth ambience, it feels a world apart. Come here not for the food, but for the opulent atmosphere (daily 12:00-23:00, food served until 21:30, reserve for dinner, open for a drink any time under the dome; the adjacent, more intimate Club Room serves food Mon-Thu 10:00-16:00, Fri-Sat until 21:30, closed Sun; 14 George Street, tel. 0131/624-8624, www.thedomeedinburgh.com).

Casual and Cheap near St. Andrew Square

$$ Dishoom, in the New Town, is the first non-London outpost of this popular Bombay café. You'll enjoy upscale Indian cuisine in a bustling, dark, 1920s dining room on the second floor overlooking St. Andrew Square. You can also order from the same menu in the basement bar at night (daily 9:00-23:00, 3A St. Andrew Square, tel. 0131/202-6406).

$ St. Andrew's and St. George's Church Undercroft Café, in the basement of a fine old church, is the cheapest place in town for lunch (Mon-Fri lunch only, closed Sat-Sun, at 13 George Street, just off St. Andrew Square, tel. 0131/225-3847).

Supermarkets: Marks & Spencer Food Hall is just a block from the Scott Monument and the picnic-perfect Princes Street Gardens (Mon-Sat 8:00-19:00, Thu until 20:00, Sun 11:00-18:00, 54 Princes Street—separate stairway next to main M&S entrance leads directly to food hall, tel. 0131/225-2301). **Sainsbury's** supermarket, a block off Princes Street, also offers grab-and-go items (daily 7:00-22:00, on corner of Rose Street on St. Andrew Square, across the street from Jenners).

Hip Eateries on and near Thistle Street

$$$ Le Café St. Honoré, tucked away like a secret bit of old Paris, is a charming place with friendly service and walls lined by wine bottles. It serves French-Scottish cuisine in tight, Old World, cut-glass elegance to a dressy crowd (three-course lunch and dinner specials, daily 12:00-14:00 & 17:30-22:00, reservations smart—ask to sit upstairs, down Thistle Street from Hanover Street, 34 Northwest Thistle Street Lane, tel. 0131/226-2211, www.cafesthonore.com).

$$$ The Bon Vivant is woody, youthful, and candlelit, with a rotating menu of French/Scottish dishes, a good cocktail list, and a companion wine shop next door. They have fun tapas plates and heartier dishes, served either in the bar up front or in the restaurant in back (daily 12:00-22:00, 55 Thistle Street, tel. 0131/225-3275, www.bonvivantedinburgh.co.uk).

$$ Hendersons has fed a generation of New Town vegetarians hearty cuisine and salads. Even carnivores love this place for its delectable salads, desserts, and smoothies. Henderson's has two separate eateries: Their main restaurant, facing Hanover Street, is self-service by day but has table service after 17:00. Each evening after 19:00, they have pleasant live music—generally guitar or jazz (Mon-Sat 9:00-22:00, Sun 10:30-16:00, between Queen and George streets at 94 Hanover Street, tel. 0131/225-2131). Just around the corner on Thistle Street, **Henderson's Vegan** has a strictly vegan menu and feels a bit more casual (daily 12:00-21:30, tel. 0131/225-2605).

In the B&B Neighborhood

Pub Grub

$$ The Salisbury Arms Pub, with a nice garden terrace and separate restaurant area, serves upscale, pleasing traditional classics with yuppie flair in a space that exudes more Martha Stewart and Pottery Barn than traditional public house (book ahead for restaurant, food served daily 12:00-22:00, across from the pool at 58 Dalkeith Road, tel. 0131/667-4518, www.thesalisburyarmsedinburgh.co.uk).

$$ The Old Bell Inn, with an old-time sports-bar ambience—fishing, golf, horses, televisions—serves pub meals. This is a classic "snug pub"—all dark woods and brass beer taps, littered with evocative knickknacks. It comes with sidewalk seating and a mixed-age crowd (bar tables can be reserved, food served daily until 21:15, 233 Causewayside, tel. 0131/668-1573, http://oldbelledinburgh.co.uk).

Other Eateries

$$$$ Aizle is a delicious night out. They serve a set £45 five-course tasting menu based on what's in season—ingredients are listed on the chalkboard (with notice, they can accommodate dietary restrictions). The restaurant is intimate but unpretentious, and they serve only 36 people a night to keep the experience special and unrushed (dinner only Wed-Sun, this is not a walk-in type of place—book ahead at least a week, 107 St. Leonard's Street—five minutes past the Royal Commonwealth Pool, tel. 0131/662-9349, www.aizle.co.uk).

$$ Southpour is a nice place for a local beer, craft cocktail, or a reliable meal from a menu of salads, sandwiches, meat dishes, and other comfort foods. The brick walls, wood beams, and giant windows give it a warm and open vibe (daily 10:00-22:00, 1 Newington Road, tel. 0131/650-1100).

$$ Ristorante Isola is a calm and casual place with 15 tables surrounding a bright yellow bar. They serve pizzas, pastas, and meat or seafood *secondi* with an emphasis on Sardinian specialties (Mon-Tue 17:00-22:30, Wed-Sun 12:00-22:30, 85 Newington Road, tel. 0131/662-9977).

$$ Voujon Restaurant serves a fusion menu of Bengali and Indian cuisines. Vegetarians appreciate the expansive yet inexpensive offerings (daily 17:00-23:00, 107 Newington Road, tel. 0131/667-5046).

Groceries: Several grocery stores are on the main streets near the restaurants, including Sainsbury's Local and Co-op on South Clerk Road, and Tesco Express and another Sainsbury's Local one block over on Causewayside (all open late—until at least 22:00).

SLEEPING

To stay in the city center, you'll likely have to stay in a larger hotel or more impersonal guesthouse. For the classic B&B experience, look to the area south of town, along Dalkeith Road. From the B&Bs, it's a long walk to the city center (about 25 minutes) or a quick bus or taxi/Uber ride.

While many of my B&B listings are not cheap (generally around £90-130), most come with friendly hosts and great cooked breakfasts. And they're generally cheaper than staying at a city-center hotel.

Note that during the Festival in August, prices skyrocket and most places do not accept bookings for one- or even two-night stays. If coming in August, book far in advance.

Conventions, rugby matches, school holidays, and weekends can make finding a room tough at other times of year, too. In winter, when demand is light, some B&Bs close, and prices at all accommodations get soft.

B&Bs South of the City Center

At these not-quite-interchangeable places, character is provided by the personality quirks of the hosts and sometimes the decor. In general, cash is preferred and can lead to discounted rates. Book direct—you will pay a much higher rate through a booking service.

Near the B&Bs, you'll find plenty of fine eateries (see "Eating in Edinburgh," earlier). A few places have their own private parking; others offer access to easy, free street parking (ask when booking—or better yet, don't rent a car for your time in Edinburgh). The nearest launderette is Ace Cleaning Centre (which picks up and drops off; see page 40).

Taxi or Uber fare between the city center and the B&Bs is about £7. If taking the bus from the B&Bs into the city, hop off at the South Bridge stop for the Royal Mile (£1.60 single ride, £4 day ticket, use exact change; see later for more bus specifics). Most of my B&Bs near Dalkeith Road are located south of the Royal Commonwealth Pool. This comfortable, safe neighborhood is a ten-minute bus ride from the Royal Mile.

To get here from the train station, catch the bus around the corner on North Bridge: Exit the station onto Princes Street, turn right, cross the street, and walk up the bridge to the bus stop in front of the Marks & Spencer department store (#14, #30, or #33). About 10 minutes into the ride, after following South Clerk Street for a while, the bus makes a left turn, then a right. Depending on where you're staying, you'll get off at the first or second stop after the turn (confirm specifics with your B&B).

$$ Gil Dun Guest House, with eight rooms—some contemporary, others more traditional—is on a quiet cul-de-sac just off Dalkeith Road. It's comfortable, pleasant, and managed with care by Gerry and Bill; Maggie helps out and keeps things immaculate (family rooms, two-night minimum in summer preferred, limited off-street parking, 9 Spence Street, tel. 0131/667-1368, www.gildun.co.uk, gildun. edin@btinternet.com).

$$ Gifford House, on busy Dalkeith Road, is a bright, flowery retreat with six peaceful rooms (some with ornate cornices and views of Arthur's Seat) and compact, modern bathrooms (RS%, family rooms, cash preferred, street parking, 103 Dalkeith Road, tel. 0131/667-4688, www.giffordhouseedinburgh.com, giffordhouse@btinternet.com, David and Margaret).

$$ AmarAgua Guest House is an inviting Victorian home away from home, with five welcoming rooms, a Japanese garden, and eager hosts (one double has private bath down the hall, 2-night minimum, no kids under 12, street parking, 10 Kilmaurs Terrace, tel. 0131/667-6775, www. amaragua.co.uk, reservations@amaragua. co.uk, Lucia and Kuan).

$$ Hotel Ceilidh-Donia (KAY-lee-DON-yah), with 17 rooms, is bigger and more hotel-like than other nearby B&Bs, with a bar and a small reception area, but managers Kevin and Susan and their staff provide a guesthouse warmth. The back deck is a pleasant place to sit on a warm day (family room, two-night minimum on peak-season weekends, 14 Marchhall Crescent, tel. 0131/667-2743, www. hotelceilidh-donia.co.uk, reservations@ hotelceilidh-donia.co.uk).

$$ Ard-Na-Said B&B, in an elegant 1875 Victorian house, has seven bright, spacious rooms with modern bathrooms, including one ground-floor room with a pleasant patio (two-night minimum preferred in summer, off-street parking, 5 Priestfield Road, tel. 0131/283-6524, mobile 07476-606-202, www.ardnasaid. co.uk, info@ardnasaid.co.uk, Audrey Ballantine and her son Steven).

$$ Dunedin Guest House (dun-EE-din) is bright and plush, with seven well-decorated rooms, an angelic atrium, and a spacious breakfast room/lounge with TV (family rooms, one room with private bath down the hall, includes continental breakfast, extra charge for cooked breakfast, limited off-street parking, 8 Priestfield Road, tel. 0131/468-3339, www.dunedinguesthouse. co.uk, reservations@dunedinguesthouse. co.uk, Mary and Tony).

$ Airdenair Guest House is a hands-off guesthouse, with no formal host greeting (you'll get an access code to let yourself in) and a self-serve breakfast buffet. But the price is nice and the five simple rooms are well-maintained (29 Kilmaurs Road, tel. 0131/468-0173, http://airdenair-edinburgh.co.uk, contact@airdenair-edinburgh.co.uk, Duncan).

Hotels in the City Center

While a B&B generally provides more warmth, character, and lower prices, a city-center hotel gives you more walkability and access to sights and Edinburgh's excellent restaurant and pub scene. Prices are very high in peak season and drop

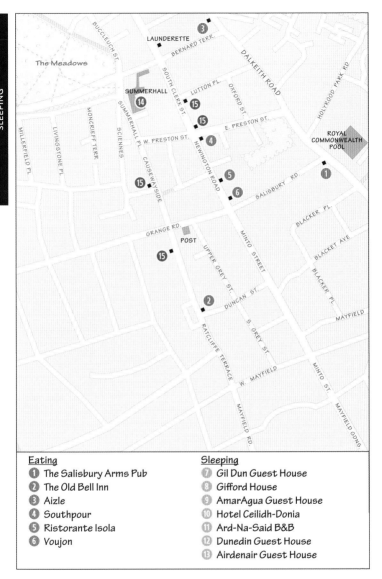

Eating
1. The Salisbury Arms Pub
2. The Old Bell Inn
3. Aizle
4. Southpour
5. Ristorante Isola
6. Voujon

Sleeping
7. Gil Dun Guest House
8. Gifford House
9. AmarAgua Guest House
10. Hotel Ceilidh-Donia
11. Ard-Na-Said B&B
12. Dunedin Guest House
13. Airdenair Guest House

substantially in off-season (a good time to shop around). In each case, I'd skip the institutional breakfast and eat out. You'll generally pay about £10 a day to park near these hotels.

$$$$ Macdonald Holyrood Hotel is a four-star splurge, with 157 rooms up the street from the parliament building and Palace of Holyroodhouse. With its classy marble-and-wood decor, fitness center, spa, and pool, it's hard to leave. On a gray winter day in Edinburgh, this could be worth it (pricey breakfast, elevator, pay valet parking, near bottom of Royal Mile, across from Dynamic Earth, 81 Holyrood Road, tel. 0131/528-8000,

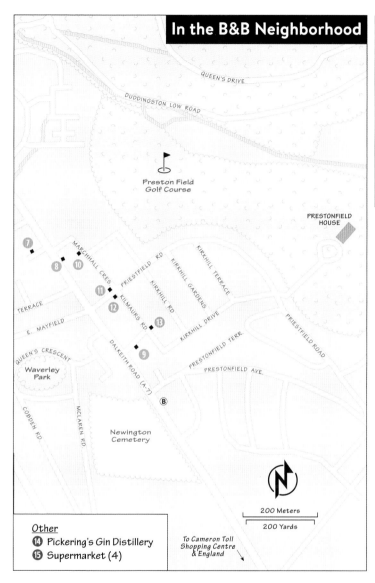

In the B&B Neighborhood

Preston Field
Golf Course

PRESTONFIELD
HOUSE

Waverley
Park

Newington
Cemetery

200 Meters

200 Yards

Other
⑭ Pickering's Gin Distillery
⑮ Supermarket (4)

To Cameron Toll
Shopping Centre
& England

www.macdonaldhotels.co.uk, newres@
macdonald-hotels.co.uk).

$$$$ The Inn on the Mile is your trendy, central option, filling a renovated old bank building right in the heart of the Royal Mile (at North Bridge/South Bridge). The nine bright and stylish rooms are an afterthought to the busy upmarket pub, which is where you'll check in. If you don't mind some noise (from the pub and the busy street) and climbing lots of stairs, it's a handy home base (breakfast extra, complimentary drink, 82 High Street, tel. 0131/556-9940, www.theinnonthemile.co.uk, info@theinnonthemile.co.uk).

$$$$ The Inn Place, part of a small

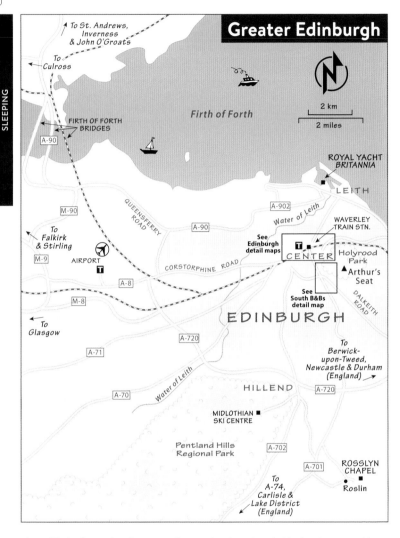

Greater Edinburgh

To St. Andrews,
Inverness
& John O'Groats

To Culross

FIRTH OF FORTH
BRIDGES

A-90

Firth of Forth

2 km

2 miles

ROYAL YACHT
BRITANNIA

LEITH

M-90

A-902

QUEENSFERRY ROAD

Water of Leith

WAVERLEY
TRAIN STN.

To
Falkirk
& Stirling

A-90

M-9

AIRPORT

See
Edinburgh
detail maps

CENTER

Holyrood
Park

CORSTORPHINE ROAD

Arthur's
Seat

A-8

See
South B&Bs
detail map

DALKEITH ROAD

M-8

To
Glasgow

EDINBURGH

A-720

To
Berwick-
upon-Tweed,
Newcastle & Durham
(England)

A-71

A-70

Water of Leith

HILLEND

A-720

MIDLOTHIAN
SKI CENTRE

Pentland Hills
Regional Park

A-702

A-701

ROSSLYN
CHAPEL

Roslin

To
A-74,
Carlisle &
Lake District
(England)

---

chain, fills the former headquarters of *The Scotsman* newspaper—a few steep steps below the Royal Mile—with 41 characterless, minimalist rooms ("bunk rooms" for 6-8 people, best deals on weekdays, breakfast extra, elevator, 20 Cockburn Street, tel. 0131/526-3780, www.theinnplaceedinburgh.co.uk, reception@theinnplaceedinburgh.co.uk).

$$$ Grassmarket Hotel's 42 rooms are quirky and fun, from *the Dandy* comic-book wallpaper to the giant wall map of Edin-

burgh equipped with planning-your-visit magnets. The hotel is in a great location right on Grassmarket overlooking the Covenanters Memorial and above Biddy Mulligans Bar (family rooms, two-night minimum on weekends, elevator only serves half the rooms, 94 Grassmarket, tel. 0131/220-2299, www.grassmarkethotel.co.uk).

$$$ The Place Hotel, sister of the Inn Place listed earlier, has a fine New Town location 10 minutes north of the train station. It occupies three grand Georgian townhouses, with no elevator and long flights of stairs leading up to the 47 contemporary, no-frills rooms. Their outdoor terrace with retractable roof and heaters is a popular place to unwind (save money with a smaller city double, 34 York Place, tel. 0131/556-7575, www.yorkplace-edinburgh.co.uk, frontdesk@yorkplace-edinburgh.co.uk).

$$ Motel One Edinburgh Royal, part of a stylish German budget hotel chain, is between the train station and the Royal Mile; it feels upscale and trendy for its price range (208 rooms, pay more for a park view or less for a windowless "budget" room with skylight, breakfast extra, elevator, 18 Market Street, tel. 0131/220-0730, www.motel-one.com, edinburgh-royal@motel-one.com; second location in the New Town/shopping zone at 10 Princes Street).

Chain Hotels in the Center: Besides my recommendations earlier, you'll find a number of cookie-cutter chain hotels close to the Royal Mile, including **Jurys Inn** (43 Jeffrey Street), **Ibis Hotel** (two convenient branches: near the Tron Church and another around the corner along the busy South Bridge), **Holiday Inn Express** (two locations: just off the Royal Mile at 300 Cowgate and one in the New Town), and **Travelodge Central** (just below the Royal Mile at 33 St. Mary's Street; additional locations in the New Town).

Hostel

¢ SafeStay Edinburgh, just off the Royal Mile, rents 272 bunks in pleasing purple-accented rooms. Dorm rooms have 4 to 12 beds, and there are also a few private singles and twin rooms (all rooms have private bathrooms). Bar 50 in the basement has an inviting lounge. Half of the rooms function as a university dorm during the school year, becoming available just in time for the tourists (breakfast extra, kitchen, laundry, free daily walking tour, 50 Blackfriars Street, tel. 0131/524-1989, www.safestay.com, reservations-edi@safestay.com).

TRANSPORTATION

Getting Around Edinburgh

Many of Edinburgh's sights are within walking distance of one another, but **buses** come in handy—especially if you're staying at a B&B south of the city center. Double-decker buses come with fine views upstairs. It's easy once you get the hang of it: Buses come by frequently (screens at bus stops show wait times) and have free, fast Wi-Fi on board. The only hassle is that you must pay with exact change (£1.60/ride, £4/all-day pass). As you board, tell your driver where you're going (or just say "single ticket") and drop your change into the box. Ping the bell as you near your stop. You can pick up a route map at the TI or at the transit office at Old Town end of Waverley Bridge (tel. 0131/555-6363, www.lothianbuses.com). Edinburgh's single **tram** line (also £1.60/ride) is designed more for locals than tourists; it's most useful for reaching the airport.

The 1,300 **taxis** cruising Edinburgh's streets are easy to flag down (ride between downtown and the B&B neighborhood costs about £7; rates go up after 18:00 and on weekends). They can turn on a dime, so hail them in either direction. **Uber** also works well here.

Arriving and Departing

By Plane

Edinburgh Airport is located eight miles northwest of the center (airport code: EDI, tel. 0844-481-8989, www.edinburghairport.com).

Taxis or **Uber rides** between the airport and city center are about £20-25 (25 minutes to downtown or Dalkeith Road).

The airport is also well connected to central Edinburgh by tram and bus. Just follow signs outside; the tram tracks are straight ahead, and the bus stop is to the right, along the main road in front of the terminal. **Trams** make several stops in town, including along Princes Street and at St. Andrew Square (£5.50, buy ticket from machine, runs every 10 minutes from early morning until 23:30, 35 minutes, www.edinburghtrams.com).

The Lothian **Airlink bus #100** drops you at Waverley Bridge (£4.50, £7.50 round-trip, runs every 10 minutes, 30 minutes, tel. 0131/555-6363, http://lothianbuses.co.uk).

Whether you take the tram or bus to the center, to continue on to my recommended B&Bs south of the city center, you can either take a taxi (about £7) or hop on a city bus (for directions, see "Sleeping in Edinburgh," earlier). To get from the B&Bs to the Airlink or tram stops downtown, you can take a taxi...or ride a city bus to North Bridge, turn left at the grand Balmoral Hotel, and walk a short distance down Princes Street. Turn right up St. Andrew Street to catch the tram at St. Andrew Square, or continue up to the next bridge, Waverley, for the Airlink bus.

By Train

Arriving by train at Waverley Station puts you in the city center and below the TI. Taxis line up outside, on Market Street or Waverley Bridge. For the TI or bus stop, follow signs for Princes Street and ride up several escalators. From here, the TI is to your left, and the city bus stop is two blocks to your right. Train info: Tel. 0345-748-4950, www.nationalrail.co.uk.

TRAIN CONNECTIONS

From Edinburgh by Train to: Glasgow (10/hour, 50 minutes), **St. Andrews** (train to Leuchars, 2/hour, 1 hour, then 10-minute bus into St. Andrews), **Stirling** (2/hour, 1 hour), **Pitlochry** (6/day direct, 2 hours), **Inverness** (6/day direct, 3.5 hours, more with transfer), **Oban** (5/day, 4.5 hours, change in Glasgow), **York** (3/hour, 2.5 hours), **London** (2/hour, 4.5 hours).

By Bus

Edinburgh's bus station (with luggage lockers) is in the New Town, just off St. Andrew Square, two blocks north of the train station. For long-distance bus info, stop by the station or check Scottish Citylink (tel. 0871-266-3333, www.citylink.co.uk), National Express (www.nationalexpress.com), or Megabus (www.megabus.com).

BUS CONNECTIONS

Direct buses go to **Glasgow** (Citylink bus #900, 4/hour, 1.5 hours), **Inverness** (express #G90, 2/day, 3.5 hours; slower #M90, 6/day, 4 hours), **Pitlochry** (Citylink #M90, 3/day, 2.5 hours), **Stirling** (every 2 hours on Citylink #909, 1 hour).

To reach most destinations in the **Highlands**—including **Oban, Fort William, Glencoe,** or **Portree** on the Isle of Skye—you'll have to transfer. It's usually fastest to take the train to Glasgow and change to a bus there. For details, see "Getting Around the Highlands" on page 171.

Rick's Tip: *If you plan to* **rent a car, pick it up on your way out** *of Edinburgh—you won't need it in town.*

By Car

Car Rental: These places have offices both in the town center and at the airport—**Avis** (24 East London Street, tel. 0844-544-6059, airport tel. 0844-544-6004), **Europcar** (Waverley Station, near platform 2, tel. 0871-384-3453, airport tel. 0871-384-3406), **Hertz** (10 Picardy Place, tel. 0843-309-3026, airport tel. 0843-309-3025), and **Budget** (24 East London Street, tel. 0844-544-9064, airport tel. 0844-544-4605).

BEST OF THE REST

The historic city of Stirling is the crossroads of Scotland: Equidistant from Edinburgh and Glasgow (less than an hour from both), and rising above a plain where the Lowlands meet the Highlands, it's no surprise that Stirling has hosted many of the biggest names (and biggest battles) of Scottish history. Everyone from Mary, Queen of Scots to Bonnie Prince Charlie has passed through the gates of its stately, strategic castle.

You'll likely pass near Stirling at least once as you travel through Scotland. It's easy to visit by car and is well-connected by trains and buses with major towns.

Just south of Stirling is the town of Falkirk, which has two interesting sights (easiest for drivers to reach): You can take a spin in a fascinating Ferris wheel for boats, and ogle the gigantic horse-head sculptures called *The Kelpies*.

STIRLING

Every Scot knows the city of Stirling (pop. 41,000) deep in their bones. This patriotic heart of Scotland is like Bunker Hill, Gettysburg, and the Alamo, all rolled into one. Stirling perches on a ridge overlooking Scotland's most history-drenched plain: a flat expanse—cut through by the twisting River Forth and the meandering stream called Bannockburn—that divides the Lowlands from the Highlands. And capping that ridge is Stirling's formidable castle, the seat of the final kings of Scotland.

From a traveler's perspective, Stirling is a pleasant mini-Edinburgh, with a steep spine leading up to that grand castle. It's busy with tourists by day, but sleepy at night. The town, and its castle, may lack personality—but both are striking and strategic.

Orientation

Stirling's old town is situated along a long, narrow hill. At its base are the train and bus stations and a thriving (but characterless) commercial district; at its apex is the castle. The old town feels like a steeper, shorter, less touristy, and far less characteristic version of Edinburgh's Royal Mile.

Day Plan: Visit the castle, the town's main sight (allow 2-3 hours). With extra time, consider a walking tour and see more of the sights. Drivers can add the two Falkirk sights, roughly 12 miles away (though these can also be visited on the way to or from Stirling).

Getting There: Stirling is linked by train with Edinburgh (2/hour, 1 hour), Glasgow (3/hour, 45 minutes), Pitlochry (5/day direct, 1 hour), and Inverness (6/day direct, 3 hours). It's also connected by Scottish Citylink **bus** with Glasgow (hourly on #M8, 45 minutes) and Edinburgh (every 2 hours on #909, 1 hour).

Arrival in Stirling: The castle sits at the very tip of a steep old town. Drivers should follow the *Stirling Castle* signs uphill through town to the esplanade and park at the £4 lot just outside the castle gate.

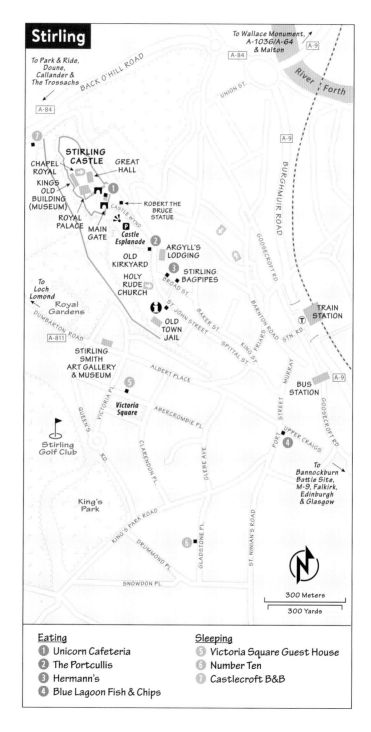

Stirling

To Wallace Monument,
A-1036/A-64
& Malton

To Park & Ride,
Doune,
Callander &
The Trossachs

BACK O'HILL ROAD

UNION ST.

River Forth

A-84

A-9

A-84

A-9

BURGHMUIR ROAD

STIRLING CASTLE

GREAT HALL

CHAPEL ROYAL

KINGS OLD BUILDING (MUSEUM)

ROYAL PALACE

MAIN GATE

CASTLE WYND

ROBERT THE BRUCE STATUE

Castle Esplanade

ARGYLL'S LODGING

OLD KIRKYARD

STIRLING BAGPIPES

HOLY RUDE CHURCH

BROAD ST.

GOOSECROFT RD.

To Loch Lomond

Royal Gardens

DUMBARTON ROAD

A-811

St. JOHN STREET

BAKER ST.

FRIARS

STN. RD.

TRAIN STATION

OLD TOWN JAIL

SPITTAL ST.

KING ST.

BARNTON ROAD

STIRLING SMITH ART GALLERY & MUSEUM

ALBERT PLACE

MURRAY

BUS STATION

A-9

GOOSECROFT RD.

Victoria Square

ABERCROMBIE PL.

QUEEN'S RD.

VICTORIA PL.

PORT STREET

UPPER CRAIGS

Stirling Golf Club

CLARENDON PL.

GLEBE AVE.

To Bannockburn Battle Site, M-9, Falkirk, Edinburgh & Glasgow

King's Park

KING'S PARK ROAD

DRUMMOND PL.

GLADSTONE PL.

ST. NINIAN'S ROAD

SNOWDON PL.

N

300 Meters

300 Yards

Eating
1 Unicorn Cafeteria
2 The Portcullis
3 Hermann's
4 Blue Lagoon Fish & Chips

Sleeping
5 Victoria Square Guest House
6 Number Ten
7 Castlecroft B&B

Without a car, you can hike the 20-minute uphill route from the train or bus station to the castle, or take a taxi (about £5).

Tourist Information: The TI is a five-minute walk below the castle, just inside the gates of the Old Town jail (daily 10:00-17:00, free Wi-Fi, St. Johns Street, tel. 01786/475-019).

Sights

▲▲STIRLING CASTLE

"He who holds Stirling, holds Scotland." These fateful words have been proven, more often than not, to be true. Stirling Castle's prized position—perched on a volcanic crag overlooking a bridge over the River Forth, the primary passage between the Lowlands and the Highlands—has long been the key to Scotland. This castle was the preferred home of Scottish kings and queens in the Middle Ages; today it's one of the most historic—and most popular—castles in Scotland. While its interiors are pretty empty and new-feeling, the castle still has plenty to offer: spectacular views over a gentle countryside, tales of the dynamic Stuart monarchs, and several exhibits that try to bring the place to life.

Cost and Hours: £15, daily April-Sept 9:30-18:00, Oct-March until 17:00, last entry 45 minutes before closing, Regimental Museum closes one hour before castle, good café, tel. 01786/450-000, www.stirlingcastle.gov.uk.

Tours: The included 40-minute **guided tour** helps you get your bearings—both to the castle, and to Scottish history (generally on the hour 10:00-16:00, often on the half-hour, too, departs from inside the main gate near the well). Docents posted throughout can tell you more, and you can rent a £3 **audioguide.**

Background: King David I built the first real castle here in the 12th century. But Stirling Castle's glory days were in the 16th century, when it became the primary residence of the Stuart (often spelled "Stewart") monarchs, who turned it into a showpiece of Scotland—and a symbol of one-upmanship against England.

The 16th century was a busy time for royal intrigues here: James IV married the sister of England's King Henry VIII, thereby knitting together the royal families of Scotland (the Stuarts) and England (the Tudors). Later, James V further expanded the castle. Mary (who became the Queen

Stirling Castle

of Scots) spent her early childhood at the castle before being raised in France. As queen and as a Catholic, she struggled against the rise of Protestantism in her realm. But when Mary's son, King James VI, was crowned King James I of England, he took his royal court with him away from Stirling to London—never to return.

During the Jacobite rebellions of the 18th century, the British military took over the castle—bulking it up and destroying its delicate beauty. Even after the Scottish threat had subsided, it remained a British garrison, home base of the Argyll and Sutherland regiments. (You'll notice the castle still flies the Union Jack of the United Kingdom.) Today, while Stirling Castle is fully restored and gleaming, it feels new and fairly empty—with almost no historic artifacts.

❍ SELF-GUIDED TOUR

Begin on the esplanade, just outside the castle entrance, with its grand views.

The Esplanade: The castle's esplanade, a military parade ground in the 19th century, is a tour-bus parking lot today. As you survey this site, remember that Stirling Castle bore witness to some of the most important moments in Scottish history.

To the right as you face the castle, **King Robert the Bruce** looks toward the plain called Bannockburn, where he defeated the English army in 1314. Squint off to the horizon on Robert's left to spot the pointy stone monument capping the hill called Abbey Craig. This is the **Wallace Monument,** marking the spot where the Scottish warrior William Wallace surveyed the battlefield before his victory in the Battle of Stirling Bridge (1297).

These great Scots helped usher in several centuries of home rule. In 1315, Robert the Bruce's daughter married into an on-the-rise noble clan called the Stuarts, who had distinguished themselves fighting at Bannockburn. When their son Robert became King Robert II of Scotland in 1371, he kicked off the Stuart dynasty. Over the next few generations, their headquarters—Stirling Castle—flourished. The fortified grand entry showed all who approached that James IV (r. 1488-1513) was a great ruler with a powerful castle.

• Head through the first gate into Guardroom Square, where you can buy your ticket, check tour times, and consider renting the audioguide. Then continue up through the inner gate.

James IV's yellow Great Hall

Gardens and Battlements: Once through the gate, follow the passage to the left into a delightful grassy courtyard called the **Queen Anne Garden.** This was the royal family's playground in the 1600s. Imagine doing a little lawn bowling with the queen here.

In the casemates lining the garden is the **Castle Exhibition.** Its "Come Face to Face with 1,000 Years of History" exhibit provides an entertaining and worthwhile introduction to the castle. You'll meet each of the people who left their mark here, from the first Stuart kings to William Wallace and Robert the Bruce.

Leave the garden the way you came and make a sharp U-turn up the ramp to the top of the **battlements.** From up here, this castle's strategic position is evident: Defenders had a 360-degree view of enemy armies approaching from miles away. These battlements were built in 1710, long after the castle's Stuart glory days, in response to the early Jacobite rebellions (from the Latin word for "James"). By this time, the successes of William Wallace and Robert the Bruce were a distant memory; and through the 1707 Act of Union, Scotland had become welded to England. Bonnie Prince Charlie—descendant of those original Stuart "King Jameses" who built this castle—later staged a series of uprisings to try to reclaim the throne of Great Britain for the Stuart line, frightening England enough for it to further fortify the castle. And sure enough, Bonnie Prince Charlie found himself—ironically—laying siege to the fortress that his own ancestors had built: Facing the main gate (with its two round towers below the UK flag), notice the pockmarks from Jacobite cannonballs in 1746.

• *Now head back down to the ramp and pass through that main gate, into the...*

Outer Close: As you enter this courtyard, straight ahead is James IV's yellow **Great Hall.** To the left is his son **James V's royal palace,** lined with finely carved Renaissance statues. In 1540, King James V, inspired by French Renaissance châteaux he'd seen, had the castle covered with about 200 statues and busts to "proclaim the peace, prosperity, and justice of his reign" and to validate his rule. Imagine the impression all these classical gods and goddesses made on visitors. The message: James' rule was a Golden Age for Scotland.

The **guided tours** of the castle depart from just to your right, near the well. Beyond that is the Grand Battery, with its cannons and rampart views and, underneath that, the Great Kitchens. We'll see both at the end of this tour.

• *Hike up the ramp between James V's palace and the Great Hall (under the crenellated sky bridge connecting them). You'll emerge into the...*

Inner Close: Standing at the center of Stirling Castle, you're surrounded by Scottish history. This courtyard was the core of the 12th-century castle. From here, additional buildings were added—each by a different monarch. Facing downhill, you'll see the Great Hall. To the left is the Chapel Royal—where Mary, Queen of Scots was crowned in 1543. Opposite that, to the right, is the royal palace (containing the Royal Apartments)—notice the "I5" monogram above the windows (for the king who built it: James, or Iacobus in Latin, V). Upstairs in this same palace is the Stirling Heads Gallery. And behind you is the Regimental Museum.

• *We'll visit each of these in turn. First, at the far-left end of the gallery with the coffee stand, step into...*

The Great Hall: This is the largest secular space in medieval Scotland. Dating from 1503, this was a grand setting for the great banquets of Scotland's Renaissance kings. One such party, to which all the crowned heads of Europe were invited, reportedly went on for three full days. This was also where kings and queens would hold court, earning it the nickname "the parliament." The impressive hammer-beam roof is a modern reconstruction,

The Great Hall

modeled on the early 16th-century roof at Edinburgh Castle. It's made of 400 local oak trees, joined by wooden pegs. If you flipped it over, it would float.

• *At the far end of the hall, climb a few stairs and walk across the sky bridge into James V's palace. Here you can explore...*

The Royal Apartments: Six ground-floor apartments are colorfully done up as they might have looked in the mid-16th century, when James V and his queen, Mary of Guise, lived here. Costumed performers play the role of palace attendants, happy to chat with you about medieval life. You'll begin in the King's Inner Hall, where he received guests. Notice the 60 carved and colorfully painted oak medallions on the ceiling. The medallions are carved with the faces of Scottish and European royalty. These are copies, painstakingly reconstructed after expert research. You'll soon see the originals up close (and upstairs) in the Stirling Heads Gallery.

Continue (left of the fireplace) into the other rooms (each with actors in costumes who love to interact): the King's Bedchamber, with a four-poster bed supporting a less-than-luxurious rope mattress; and then the Queen's Bedchamber,

the Inner Hall, and the Outer Hall, offering a more vivid example of what these rich spaces would have looked like.

• *From the queen's apartments, you'll exit into the top corner of the Inner Close. Directly to your left, up the stairs, is the...*

Stirling Heads Gallery: This is, for me, the castle's highlight—a chance to see the originals of the elaborately carved and painted portrait medallions that decorated the ceiling of the king's presence chamber. Each one is thoughtfully displayed and lovingly explained. Don't miss the video at the end of the hall.

• *If you were to leave this gallery through the intended exit, you'd wind up back down in the Queen Anne Garden. Instead, backtrack and exit the way you came in to return to the Inner Close, and visit the two remaining sights.*

The Chapel Royal: One of the first Protestant churches built in Scotland, the Chapel Royal was constructed in 1594 by James VI for the baptism of his first son, Prince Henry. The faint painted frieze high up survives from Charles I's coronation visit to Scotland in 1633. Clearly the holiness of the chapel ended in the 1800s when the army moved in.

Regimental Museum: At the top of the Inner Close, in the King's Old Building, is the excellent **Argyll and Sutherland Highlanders Museum.** Another highlight of the castle, it's barely mentioned in castle promotional material because it's run by a different organization. With lots of tartans, tassels, and swords, it shows how the fighting spirit of Scotland was absorbed by Britain. The two regiments, established in the 1790s to defend Britain in the Napoleonic age and combined in the 1880s, have served with distinction in British military campaigns for more than two centuries. Their pride shows here in the building that has served as their headquarters since 1881. The "In the Trenches" exhibit is a powerful look at World War I, with accounts from the battlefield. Up the spiral stairs, the exhibit continues through

The Royal Apartments

World War II and conflicts in the Middle East to the present day.

• When you're ready to move on, consider the following scenic route back to the castle exit.

Rampart Walk to the Kitchen: The skinny lane between church and museum leads to the secluded Douglas Garden at the rock's highest point. Belly up to the ramparts for a commanding view, including the Wallace Monument. From here you can walk the ramparts downhill to the Grand Battery, with its cannon rampart back at the Outer Close. The Outer Close was the service zone, with a well and the kitchen (below the cannon rampart). The great banquets of James VI didn't happen all by themselves, as you'll appreciate when you explore the fine medieval kitchen exhibit (where mannequin cooks oversee medieval recipes); to find it, head down the ramp and look for the *Great Kitchens* sign.

• Your castle visit ends here.

Rick's Tip: *For a **scenic route** down into town, consider a detour through the **old Kirkyard cemetery**. The rocky crag in the middle offers a fine viewpoint.*

Experiences
In Stirling

OLD KIRKYARD STROLL

Stirling has a particularly evocative old cemetery in the kirkyard (churchyard) just below the castle. For a soulful stroll, sneak down the stairs where the castle meets the esplanade parking lot (near the statue of the Scotsman fighting in the South African War). From here, you can wander through the tombstones—Celtic crosses, Victorian statues, and faded headstones—from centuries gone by. Work your way over to the Church of the Holy Rude (well worth a visit), where you can re-enter the town.

▲HISTORIC AND HAUNTED WALKS

David Kinnaird, a local actor/historian, gives history walks by day and haunted walks by night in Stirling. Each walk meets at the TI (inside the gates of the Old Town Jail), lasts 75 minutes, and costs £4 for readers of this book (tel. 01592/874-449, www.stirlingghostwalk.com). Just show up and pay him directly. David's historic walks (May-Sept Fri-Sun at 12:00, 14:00, and 16:00) tell the story of Stirling as you wander through town. His "Happy Hang-man" haunted walks through the old kirk-yard cemetery involve more storytelling (July-Aug Tue-Sat at 20:30, Sept-June Fri-Sat at 20:00).

OLD TOWN JAIL

Stirling's jail was built during the Victorian Age, when the purpose of imprisonment was shifting from punishment to rehabil-itation. While there's little to see today, theatrical 30-minute tours entertain fam-ilies with a light and funny walk through one section of the jail. You'll end at the top of the tower for a Q&A with a command-ing view of the surrounding countryside.

Cost and Hours: £6.50, July-Sept only, tours every 30 minutes daily 10:15-17:15, St. John Street, www.destinationstirling.com.

▲STIRLING BAGPIPES

This fun little shop, just a block below the castle on Broad Street, is worth a visit for those curious about bagpipes. Owner Alan refurbishes old bagpipes here, but also makes new ones from scratch, in a workshop on the premises. The pleasantly cluttered shop, which is a bit of a neigh-borhood hangout, is littered with bagpipe components—chanters, drones, bags, covers, and cords. If he's not too busy, Alan can answer your questions. He'll explain how the most expensive parts of the bag-pipe are the "sticks"—the chanter and drones, carved from blackwood—while the bag and cover are cheap. A serious set costs £700...beginners should instead consider a £40 starter kit that includes a practice chanter (like a recorder) with a book of sheet music and a CD.

Cost and Hours: Free, Mon-Sat 10:00-18:00, closed Sun, 8 Broad Street, tel. 01786/448-886, www.stirlingbagpipes.com.

Near Stirling

Two engaging landmarks sit just outside the town of Falkirk, 12 miles south of Stir-ling. Taken together, *the Kelpies* and the Falkirk Wheel offer a welcome change of pace from Scottish countryside kitsch.

▲THE KELPIES

Unveiled in 2014 and standing over a hundred feet tall, these two giant steel horse heads have quickly become a sym-bol of this town and region. They may seem whimsical, but they're rooted in a mix of mythology and real history: Kelpies are magical, waterborne, shape-shifting sprites of Scottish lore, who often took the form of a horse. And historically, horses—the ancestors of today's Budweiser Clydesdales—were used as beasts of bur-den to power Scotland's industrial output. These statues stand over old canals where hardworking horses towed heavily laden barges. A café nearby sells drinks and light meals, and a free visitors center shows how the heads were built. A 30-minute guided tour through the inside of one of the great beasts shows how they're sup-ported by a sleek steel skeleton.

Cost and Hours: Always open and free to view (£3 to park); visitors center open daily 9:30-17:00. Tours—£7.50, daily at the bottom of every hour 10:30-16:30, fewer tours Oct-March, tel. 01324/506-850, www.thehelix.co.uk.

Getting There: *The Kelpies* are in a park called the Helix, just off the M-9 motorway—you'll spot them looming high over the motorway as if inviting you to exit. For a closer look, exit the M-9 for the A-905 (Falkirk/Grangemouth), then follow *Falkirk/A-904* and brown *Helix Park & Kelpies* signs.

▲▲FALKIRK WHEEL

At the opposite end of Falkirk stands this remarkable modern incarnation of Scot-tish technical know-how.

The 115-foot-tall Falkirk Wheel, opened in 2002, is a modern take on a classic engi-neering challenge: linking the Forth and Clyde Canal below with the aqueduct of the Union Canal, 80 feet above. Rather than using rising and lowering water through several locks, the wheel simply picks boats up and—ever so slowly—takes them where they need to go, like a giant waterborne elevator. In the 1930s, it took

The Kelpies

half a day to ascend or descend through 11 locks; now it takes only five minutes.

Cost and Hours: Wheel is free to view, visitors center (with cafeteria) open daily 10:00-17:30, park open until 20:00, shorter hours Nov-mid-March; cruises run about hourly and cost £13, call or go online to check schedule and book your seat, tel. 0870-050-0208, www.thefalkirkwheel. co.uk.

Getting There: Exit the M-876 motorway for A-883/Falkirk/Denny, then follow brown *Falkirk Wheel* signs. Parking is free and a short walk from the wheel.

Visiting the Wheel: Twice an hour, the wheel springs (silently) to life: Gates rise up to seal off each of the water-filled gondolas, and then the entire structure slowly rotates a half-turn to swap the positions of the lower and upper boats—each of which stays comfortably upright.

Each hour, a barge takes 96 people (listening to a recorded narration explaining everything) into the Falkirk Wheel for the slow and graceful ride. Once at the top, the barge cruises a bit of the canal. The slow-motion experience lasts 50 minutes.

Eating and Sleeping

If eating near Stirling Castle, choose among the **$$ Unicorn Cafeteria,** tucked under the castle's casemates; **$$ The Portcullis** pub, just below the castle esplanade; and the classier **$$$$ Hermann's,** a block below the esplanade (top of Broad Street). At the bottom of town, a string of cheap chain pubs and ethnic eateries cluster near Dumbarton Road, including the **Blue Lagoon Fish & Chips** (Port Street).

If overnighting, consider these B&Bs (all with easy parking): the plush **$$$ Victoria Square Guest House** (10 rooms, faces park, no kids under 12, 20-minute walk to castle, 12 Victoria Square, www.victoriasquareguesthouse. com); the traditional, Scottish-feeling **$ Number Ten** (3 rooms, lovely back garden, no kids under 5, 10 Gladstone Place, www.cameron-10.co.uk); and, nearest the castle, the immaculate **$$ Castlecroft B&B** (5 rooms, shared deck, Ballengeich Road, www.castlecroft-uk.co.uk).

Glasgow

Glasgow (GLAS-goh)—astride the River Clyde—is a friendly, attractive city, with Victorian facades and distinctive Art Nouveau buildings, courtesy of its star architect, Charles Rennie Mackintosh.

In its heyday a century ago, Glasgow was Britain's second-largest city, after London. It had 1.2 million people, twice the size of today. An industrial powerhouse, Glasgow produced 25 percent of the world's oceangoing ships. But by the mid-20th century, it had become rough and run-down.

In the 1980s, city leaders embarked on rejuvenating Glasgow. Today this revitalized city, abuzz with restaurants and nightlife, offers visitors a warm welcome.

Glaswegians (rhymes with "Norwegians") are the chattiest people in Scotland—with the most entertaining (and impenetrable) accent.

Edinburgh may have a more royal aura, but Glasgow has down-to-earth appeal. In Glasgow, there's no upper-crust history, and no one puts on airs. One Glaswegian told me, "The people of Glasgow have a better time at a funeral than the people of Edinburgh have at a wedding." Locals are happy to introduce you to their fun-loving, laid-back way of life.

GLASGOW IN 2 DAYS

Day 1: Follow my "Get to Know Glasgow" self-guided walk of the city center, tying together the most important sights in the city's core (visit the interior of the Tenement House).

In the afternoon, take the two-hour hop-on, hop-off bus tour, which is convenient for getting the bigger picture and reaching three important sights away from the center: the Cathedral Precinct, the Riverside Museum, and the Kelvingrove Museum (though it's easy to visit the Kelvingrove tomorrow at the end of the West End Walk).

On any evening: Have dinner in the West End, settle in at a pub with live music, or watch a movie at the Grosvenor Cinema.

Day 2: Follow my West End Walk to explore Glasgow's appealing residential zone, which has some of the city's best restaurants as well as a number of worthwhile sights, including the Kelvingrove Museum (has a Mackintosh exhibit) and the Mackintosh House at the Hunterian Gallery.

through the heart of town (the third street of the Zed, Argyle Street, is busy with traffic and less appealing).

The **West End** is a posh suburb, with big homes, upscale apartment buildings, and lots of green space. The area has three pockets of interest: near the Hillhead subway stop, with a lively restaurant scene and the Botanic Gardens; the University of Glasgow campus, with its stately buildings and fine museums; and, just downhill through a sprawling park, the area around the Kelvingrove Museum, with a nearby strip of trendy bars and restaurants (Finnieston).

Tourist Information

The TI is inside the Gallery of Modern Art on Royal Exchange Square, downstairs. They hand out a good, free map and brochures on Glasgow and the rest of Scotland (daily 10:00-17:00, www. visitscotland.com).

Tours

HOP-ON, HOP-OFF BUS

CitySightseeing connects Glasgow's far-flung historic sights in a two-hour loop and lets you hop on and off as you like for two days. Buses are frequent (every 10-20 minutes, 9:30-18:20, service ends earlier in off-season) and alternate between live guides and recorded narration (both are equally good). The route covers the city very well, and the guide does a fine job of describing activities at each stop. While the first stop is on George Square, you can hop on and pay the driver anywhere along the route (£15, tel. 0141/204-0444, www. citysightseeingglasgow.co.uk).

WALKING TOURS

Walking Tours in Glasgow was started by Jenny and Liv, two recent University of Glasgow graduates who love their city. The city center tour starts in George Square and covers about 3.5 miles in 2.5 hours (daily 10:30 and 14:00; off-season tours by request). They also run a West

ORIENTATION

Although it's often thought of as a "second city," Glasgow is actually Scotland's biggest (pop. 600,000, swelling to 1.2 million within Greater Glasgow—that's one out of every five Scots).

The tourist's Glasgow has two parts: the businesslike downtown (train stations, commercial zone, and main shopping drag) and the residential West End (B&Bs, restaurants, and nightlife). Both areas have good sights, and both are covered in this chapter by self-guided walks.

Glasgow's **downtown** is a tight grid of boxy office buildings and shopping malls, making it feel more like a midsized American city. The walkable city center has two main drags, both lined with shops and crawling with shoppers: Sauchiehall Street (pronounced "Suckyhall," running west to east) and Buchanan Street (running north to south). These two pedestrian malls—part of a shopping zone nicknamed the Golden Zed—make a big zig and zag

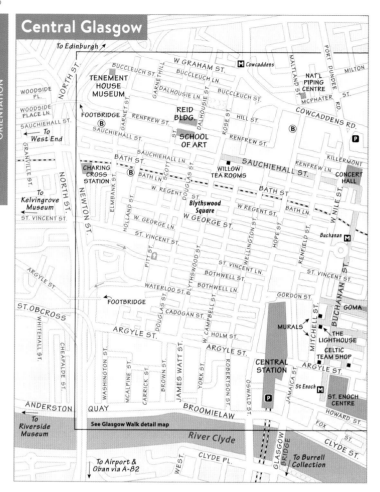

Central Glasgow

End tour at 14:30 that requires advance booking (£10, www.walkingtoursin.com, walkingtoursinglasgow@gmail.com).

Those with a specific interest in **Mackintosh** architecture should consider the 2.25-hour Mackintosh-themed city walking tours given by students of the Glasgow School of Art (£20, 4/week).

LOCAL GUIDES

Joan Dobbie, a native Glaswegian and registered Scottish Tourist Guide, will give you the insider's take on Glasgow's sights (£135/half-day, £200/day, tours on foot or by public transit—no tours by car,

tel. 01355/236-749, mobile 07773-555-151, joan.leo@lineone.net).

Ann Stewart is a former high-school geography teacher turned Blue Badge guide who is excited to show you around Glasgow or take you on an excursion outside the city (£150/4 hours, £220/8 hours, mobile 07716-358-997, www.comeseescotland.com, ann@comeseescotland.com).

HIGHLANDS DAY TRIPS

Most of the same companies that do Highlands side-trips from Edinburgh also operate trips from Glasgow. If you'd like to spend an efficient day away from the

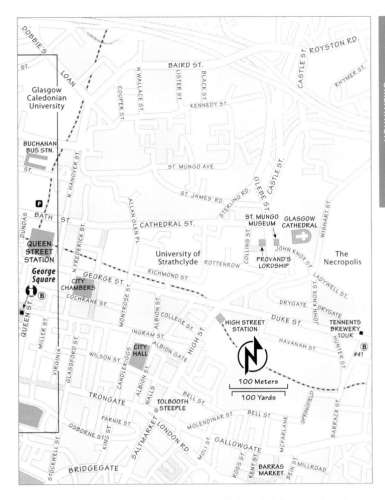

city, skim the descriptions and listings on page 40, and then check each company's website or browse the brochures at the TI for details.

Helpful Hints

Safety: The city center, which is packed with ambitious career types during the day, can feel deserted at night. While the area between Argyle Street and the River Clyde has been cleaned up in recent years, parts can still feel sketchy. As in any big city, use common sense and don't wander down dark, deserted alleys.

The Golden Zed shopping drag, the Merchant City area (east of the train stations), and the West End all bustle with crowded restaurants well into the evening and feel well populated in the wee hours.

Sightseeing: Almost every sight in Glasgow is free, but request £3-5 donations (www.glasgowmuseums.com). While these donations are not required, I like to consider what the experience was worth and decide if and how much to donate as I leave.

Laundry: Majestic Launderette will pick up and drop off at your B&B or hotel (call to arrange); they also have a

GLASGOW AT A GLANCE

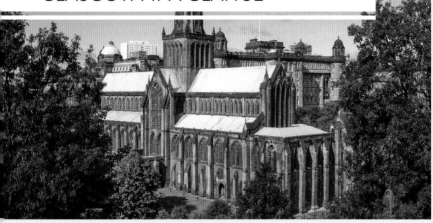

▲▲**Tenement House** Well-preserved 1930s-era middle-class residence offering nostalgic look at Scotland's past. **Hours:** April-Oct daily 13:00-17:00, July-Aug from 11:00, closed Nov-March. See page 121.

▲▲**Tennent's Brewery Tour** Scotland's biggest brewery showing how they brew and bottle the popular beer. **Hours:** Tours depart daily at 10:00, 12:00, 14:00, 16:00, & 18:00. See page 124.

▲▲**Kelvingrove Art Gallery and Museum** "Scottish Smithsonian" displaying separate collections of art (including a fine Mackintosh exhibit) and natural history. **Hours:** Mon-Thu and Sat 10:00-17:00, Fri and Sun from 11:00. See page 126.

▲▲**Riverside Museum** Showcasing many types of transportation—stagecoaches, cars, subways, and ships—plus toys and more, in a kid-friendly way. **Hours:** Mon-Thu and Sat 10:00-17:00, Fri and Sun from 11:00. See page 127.

▲**National Piping Centre** Sharing the proud history of the country's iconic bagpipes—Scotland's soundtrack. **Hours:** Mon-Thu 9:00-19:00, Fri until 17:00, Sat until 15:00, closed Sun. See page 121.

▲**Glasgow Cathedral** Rare example of a pre-Reformation Scottish cathedral. **Hours:** Mon-Sat 9:30-17:30, Sun 13:00-17:00; Oct-March until 16:00. See page 123.

▲**Necropolis** Evocative 19th-century graveyard behind the cathedral. See page 124.

▲**St. Mungo Museum of Religious Life and Art** Secular museum promoting religious understanding, summarizing the world's faiths and how each addresses life's rites of passage. **Hours:** Tue-Thu and Sat 10:00-17:00, Fri and Sun from 11:00, closed Mon. See page 124.

▲**Hunterian Gallery and Mackintosh House** Art gallery of Scottish artists, plus a walk though Mackintosh's reconstructed home. **Hours:** Tue-Sat 10:00-17:00, Sun 11:00-16:00, closed Mon. See page 125.

▲**Hunterian Museum** Eclectic collection of a medical researcher, with fossils, Roman artifacts, and examples of life's deformities. **Hours:** Tue-Sat 10:00-17:00, Sun 11:00-16:00, closed Mon. See page 126.

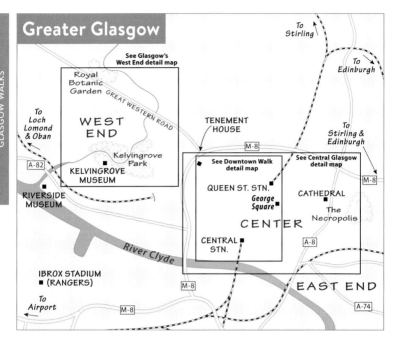

Greater Glasgow

To Stirling

To Edinburgh

See Glasgow's West End detail map

Royal Botanic Garden

GREAT WESTERN ROAD

TENEMENT HOUSE

To Stirling & Edinburgh

M-8

To Loch Lomond & Oban

WEST END

See Downtown Walk detail map

See Central Glasgow detail map

A-82

Kelvingrove Park

KELVINGROVE MUSEUM

QUEEN ST. STN.

CATHEDRAL

M-8

George Square

The Necropolis

RIVERSIDE MUSEUM

CENTER

CENTRAL STN.

A-8

River Clyde

IBROX STADIUM
■ (RANGERS)

M-8

EAST END

To Airport

M-8

A-74

---

launderette near the Kelvingrove Museum in the West End (self-serve or full-serve, Mon-Fri 8:00-18:00, Sat until 16:00, Sun 10:00-16:00, 1110 Argyle Street, tel. 0141/334-3433).

GLASGOW WALKS

These two self-guided walks introduce you to Glasgow's most interesting (and very different) neighborhoods: the downtown zone, and the residential and university sights of the West End.

◉ Get to Know Glasgow: The Downtown Core

Glasgow isn't romantic, but it has an earthy charm, its people are a joy to chat with, and architecture buffs love it. The more time you spend here, the more you'll appreciate the edgy, artsy vibe and the quirky, fun-loving spirit. Be sure to look up—above the chain restaurants and mall stores—and you'll discover a wealth of imaginative facades, complete with ornate friezes and

expressive sculptures. These buildings transport you to the heady days around the turn of the 20th century—when the rest of Britain was enthralled by Victorianism, but Glasgow set its own course, thanks largely to the artistic bravado of Charles Rennie Mackintosh and his Art Nouveau friends (the "Glasgow Four"). This walking tour takes about 1.5 hours (plus sightseeing stops along the way).

• *Start at the St. Enoch subway station, at the base of the pedestrian shopping boulevard, Buchanan Street. (This is a short walk from Central Station, or a longer walk or quick cab ride from Queen Street Station.) Stand at the intersection of Argyle and Buchanan, where the square hits the street (with your back to the glassy subway entry). Take a moment to get oriented.*

❶ Argyle Street and Nearby

The grand pedestrian boulevard, Buchanan Street, leads uphill to the Royal Concert Hall. This is the start of the "Golden Zed"—the nickname for a

Z-shaped pedestrian boulevard made of three streets: Buchanan, Sauchiehall, and Argyle. This district (with the top shops in town) is also called the "Style Mile."

Before heading up Buchanan Street, take a quick detour down Argyle to see a couple slices of Glasgow life. Step into the extremely green sports store (at #154).

The **Celtic Shop** is green. That's the color of Glasgow's dominant (for now) soccer team. It's hard for outsiders to fathom the intensity of the rivalry between Glasgow's Celtic and Rangers. Celtic, founded by an Irish Catholic priest to raise money for poor Irish immigrants in the East End, is—naturally—green and favored by Catholics. Rangers, with team colors of the Union Jack (red, white, and blue), are more likely to be supported by Unionist and Protestant families. Wander into the shop (minimizing or hiding any red or blue you might be wearing). Check out the energy in the photos and shots of the stadium filled with 60,000 fans. You're in a world where red and blue don't exist.

Now head around the corner from the Celtic Shop and walk a few steps down the alley (Mitchell Street). While it seems a bit seedy, it should be safe...but look out for giant magnifying glasses and taxis held aloft by balloons. City officials have cleverly co-opted street artists by sanctioning huge, fun, and edgy **graffiti murals** like these. The girl with the magnifying glass is painted by graffiti artist Smug (see the

girl's necklace). In the taxi painting, the driver is actually the artist and the license plate alludes to his tag name: Rogue-One. (By the way, there are no actual bricks on that wall.) Glasgow produces a free booklet called *City Centre Mural Trail* (also available at www.citycentremuraltrail.co.uk), which explains all this fun art around town.

• *Now return to the base of...*

❷ *Buchanan Street*

Buchanan Street has a friendly vibe with an abundance of street musicians. As you stroll uphill, keep an eye out for a few big landmarks: **Frasers** (#45, on the left) is a vast and venerable department store, considered the "Harrods of Glasgow." The **Argyll Arcade** (#30, opposite Frasers), dating from 1827 with a proud red-sandstone facade, is the oldest arcade in town. It's filled mostly with jewelry and comes with security guards dressed in Victorian-era garb. **Princes Square** (at #48, just past Argyll Arcade) is a classic old building dressed with a modern steel peacock and foliage. Step inside to see the delightfully modernized Art Nouveau atrium.

At #97 (50 yards up, on the left) is one of two Mackintosh-designed **Willow Tea Rooms** (the other location, described later in this walk, is the original). This central location is designed to capitalize on the trendiness of Mackintosh.

Celtic Shop

Graffiti mural

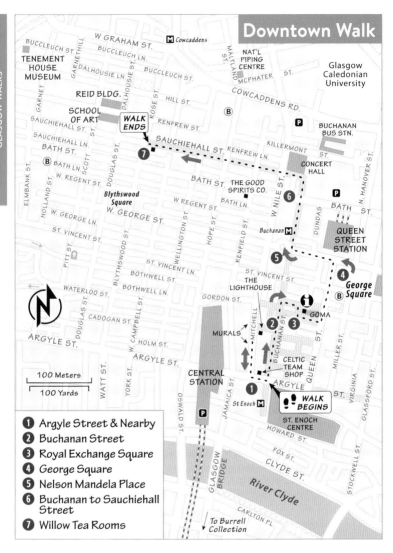

GLASGOW
GLASGOW WALKS

W GRAHAM ST. **M** Cowcaddens

BUCCLEUCH ST.
BUCCLEUCH HILL
GARNET HILL
BUCCLEUCH LN.

**TENEMENT
HOUSE
MUSEUM**
DALHOUSIE LN.
BUCCLEUCH ST.

NAT'L
PIPING
CENTRE
MAITLAND ST.
MCPHATER ST.

Glasgow
Caledonian
University

REID BLDG.
HILL ST.
ROSE ST.
DALHOUSIE ST.
COWCADDENS RD.
B

**SCHOOL
OF ART**
SAUCHIEHALL ST.
**WALK
ENDS**
RENFREW ST.
B
P
**BUCHANAN
BUS STN.**

SAUCHIEHALL LN.
BATH ST.
7
SAUCHIEHALL ST. RENFREW LN.
KILLERMONT ST.

B BATH LN.
GARNET
W. REGENT ST.
DOUGLAS ST.
SCOTT ST.
BATH ST. THE GOOD
SPIRITS CO.
W NILE ST.
6
CONCERT
HALL
N. HANOVER ST.

ELMBANK ST.
HOLLAND ST.
*Blythswood
Square*
W REGENT ST.
BATH LN.
DUNDAS
BATH ST.

W. GEORGE LN.
W. GEORGE ST.
HOPE ST.
RENFIELD ST.
Buchanan **M**
**QUEEN
STREET
STATION**

ST. VINCENT ST.
PITT ST.
BLYTHSWOOD ST.
ST. VINCENT LN.
5

WATERLOO ST.
BOTHWELL ST.
WELLINGTON ST.
ST. VINCENT ST.
4
*George
Square*
B

N
DOUGLAS ST.
BOTHWELL LN.
THE
LIGHTHOUSE
GORDON ST.
i
GoMA

CADOGAN ST.
W. CAMPBELL ST.
MITCHELL ST.
2 **3**
QUEEN ST.
MILLER ST.

ARGYLE ST.
W. HOLM ST.
MURALS
BUCHANAN ST.
CELTIC
TEAM
SHOP
VIRGINIA ST.

ARGYLE ST.
YORK ST.
WATT ST.
**CENTRAL
STATION**
JAMAICA ST.
1
ARGYLE ST.
**WALK
BEGINS**
GLASSFORD ST.

| 100 Meters |
| 100 Yards |

OSWALD ST.
P
St Enoch **M**
**ST. ENOCH
CENTRE**
HOWARD ST.

1 Argyle Street & Nearby
2 Buchanan Street
3 Royal Exchange Square
4 George Square
5 Nelson Mandela Place
6 Buchanan to Sauchiehall
Street
7 Willow Tea Rooms

GLASGOW
BRIDGE
FOX ST.
CLYDE ST.
STOCKWELL ST.

River Clyde

CARLTON PL.
↓ *To Burrell
Collection*

*• Just past the tearooms, turn down the alley
on the right, called Exchange Place. You'll
pass the recommended Rogano restaurant
on your right before emerging onto...*

❸ Royal Exchange Square

The centerpiece of this square—which
marks the entrance to the shopping zone
called Merchant City—is a stately, Neoclassical, bank-like building.

Today the mansion houses the **Glasgow
Gallery of Modern Art,** nicknamed
GoMA. Circle around the building to the
main entry (at the equestrian statue of the
Duke of Wellington, often creatively decorated as Glasgow's favorite conehead),
and step back to take in the Neoclassical facade. The temporary exhibits inside
GoMA are generally forgettable, but the
museum does have an unusual charter: It

Glasgow Gallery of Modern Art

George Square

displays only the work of living artists (free, £2 suggested donation, daily 10:00-17:00, TI inside and downstairs).

• *Facing the fanciful GoMA facade, turn right up Queen Street. Within a block, you'll reach...*

❹ George Square

This square, the centerpiece of Glasgow, is filled with statues and lined with notable buildings, such as the Queen Street train station and the Glasgow City Chambers. (It's the big Neoclassical building standing like a secular church to the east; pop in to see its grand ground floor.) In front of the City Chambers stands a monument to Glaswegians killed fighting in the World Wars. The square is decorated with a *Who's Who* of statues depicting great Glaswegians. Find James Watt (the only guy with a chair; he perfected the steam engine that helped power Europe into the Industrial Age), as well as Scotland's two top literary figures: Robert Burns and Sir Walter Scott (capping the tallest pillar in the center). The twin equestrian statues are of Prince Albert and a skinny Queen Victoria—a rare image of her in her more svelte youth.

• *Just past skinny Vic and Robert Peel, turn left onto West George Street, and cross Buchanan Street to the tall church in the middle of...*

❺ Nelson Mandela Place

This first public space named for Nelson Mandela honors the man who, while still in prison, helped bring down apartheid in South Africa. The square was renamed in the 1980s while apartheid was still in place—and when the South African consulate was on it. Subsequently, anyone sending the consulate a letter had to address it with the name of the man who embodied the anti-apartheid spirit: Mandela.

• *Head uphill on Buchanan Street.*

❻ Buchanan Street to Sauchiehall Street

A short distance uphill is the glass entry to Glasgow's subway. Soon after, on the right, you'll pass the Buchanan Galleries, an indoor mall that sprawls through several city blocks (filled with shopping temptations and offering a refuge in rainy weather).

Whisky Side-Trip: For a fun education in whisky, take a little detour. At Buchanan Galleries, head left down Bath Street 1.5 blocks to #23, where stairs lead down into **The Good Spirits Company.** This happy world of whisky is run by two young aficionados (Shane and Matthew) and their booze-geek staff. They welcome you to taste and learn (Mon-Sat 10:00-19:00, Sun 12:00-17:00, tel. 0141/258-8427).

• *Returning to Buchanan Street, continue uphill to the top.*

At the top of Buchanan Street stands the **Glasgow Royal Concert Hall**. Its steps are a favorite perch where local office workers munch lunch and enjoy the street scene.

• *From here, the Golden Zed zags left, Buchanan Street becomes Sauchiehall Street, and the shopping gets cheaper and less elegant. Walk a few blocks, passing "Pound Shops" (the equivalent of "dollar stores"), newspaper hawkers, beggars, buskers, souvenir shops, and a good bookstore. Enjoy the people-watching. Just before the end of the pedestrian zone, on the left side (at #217), are the...*

❼ Willow Tea Rooms

Tearooms were hugely popular during the industrial boom of the late 19th century. As Glasgow grew, more people moved to the suburbs, meaning that office workers couldn't easily return home for lunch. And during this age of Victorian morals, the temperance movement was trying to discourage the consumption of alcohol. Tearooms were designed to be an appealing alternative to eating in pubs.

These tearooms, opened in 1903, are an Art Nouveau masterpiece by Charles Rennie Mackintosh. He made his living from design commissions, including multiple tearooms for businesswoman Kate Cranston. Mackintosh designed everything here—down to the furniture, lighting, and cutlery. He took his theme for the café from the name of the street it's on— *saugh* is the Scots' word for willow.

In the design of these tearooms, there was a meeting of the (very modern) minds. In addition to giving office workers an alternative to pubs, Cranston also wanted a place where women could gather while unescorted—in a time when traveling solo could give a woman a less-than-desirable reputation. An ardent women's rights supporter, Cranston requested that the rooms be bathed in white, the suffragettes' signature color.

At the Willows, you can have tea or just browse the exhibits showcasing his designs along with Mackintosh-inspired jewelry. The almost-hidden Room de Luxe dining room (upstairs) appears just as it did in Mackintosh's day, though most features are reproductions, such as the chairs and the doors, which were too fragile to survive.

• *Our walk ends here. Within a few minutes' stroll are three more sights. One of those is the*

Nelson Mandela Place

Glasgow Royal Concert Hall

Charles Rennie Mackintosh (1868-1928)

Charles Rennie Mackintosh brought an exuberant Art Nouveau influence to the architecture of his hometown. His designs challenged the city planners of this otherwise practical, working-class port city to create beauty in the buildings they commissioned.

As a student traveling in Venice and Ravenna, Mackintosh fell under the spell of Byzantine design, and in Siena he saw a unified, medieval city design he would try to import—but with a Scottish flavor and palette—to Glasgow.

When Mackintosh was at the Glasgow School of Art, the Industrial Age dominated life. Factories belched black soot as they burned coal and forged steel. Mackintosh and his artist friends drew inspiration from nature and created some of the first Art Nouveau buildings, paintings, drawings, and furniture. His first commission came in 1893, to design an extension to the Glasgow Herald building. More work followed, including the Glasgow School of Art and the Willow Tea Rooms.

A radical thinker, Mackintosh shared credit with his artist wife, Margaret MacDonald (who specialized in glass and metalwork). He once famously said, "I have the talent...Margaret has the genius." The two teamed up with another husband-and-wife duo—Herbert MacNair and Margaret's sister, Frances MacDonald—to define a new strain of Scottish Art Nouveau, called the "Glasgow Style." These influential couples were known as "the Glasgow Four."

Mackintosh's works show a strong Japanese influence, particularly in his use of black-and-white contrast to highlight the idealized forms of nature. He also drew inspiration from the Arts and Crafts movement, with an eye to simplicity, clean lines, respect for tradition, and an emphasis on precise craftsmanship over mass production. Mackintosh inspired other artists, such as painter Gustav Klimt and Bauhaus founder Walter Gropius, but his vision was not appreciated in his own time as much as it is now; he died poor. Now, a century after Scotland's greatest architect set pencil to paper, his hometown is at last celebrating his unique vision.

In Glasgow, there are four main Mackintosh sights (listed in order of importance): The Mackintosh House (a reconstruction of his 1906 home filled with his actual furniture); the Kelvingrove Art Gallery (with a wonderful exhibit of his work); the Willow Tea Rooms (a functioning tea room entirely furnished in the Mackintosh style); and the Glasgow School of Art (gutted by fire and closed until 2019).

Glasgow School of Art, which was gutted by a 2014 fire. Before the fire, this building, designed by 28-year-old Charles Rennie Mackintosh, attracted architects from far and wide. Now it's closed for a few years for repairs.

Two additional sights (described later) lie within a five-minute stroll (in different directions). The remarkably preserved Tenement House offers a fascinating glimpse into Glasgow lifestyles in the early 1900s. And the National Piping Centre goes beyond the clichés and provides a better appreciation for the history and musicality of Scotland's favorite instrument.

◑ West End Walk

Glasgow's West End—just a quick subway, bus, or taxi ride from downtown—is the city's top residential neighborhood. (Since this walk is most worthwhile as a scenic way to connect several important museums, be sure to do this when they're open.) This area has great recommended restaurants, nightlife, and accommodations (all described later). This walk begins at the Hillhead subway stop, meanders through dining and residential zones, explores some grand old university buildings (and related museums), and ends with a wander through the park to the Kelvingrove Museum—Glasgow's top museum. (Walk route shown on page 118).

• *Start at the Hillhead subway station. Exiting the station, turn right and walk four short blocks up...*

Byres Road: This is a main thoroughfare through a trendy district. A block before the big intersection, notice the **Waitrose** supermarket on the left. In Britain, this upscale grocery is a sure sign of a posh neighborhood.

Approaching the corner with Great Western Road, you'll see a church spire on the right. Dating from 1862, this church was converted into a restaurant and music venue called **Òran Mòr** (Gaelic for "The Great Music"). Step into the entryway to see the colorful murals (by Alasdair Gray, a respected Glaswegian artist and novelist). Consider a drink or meal in their pub (try some whisky—they have more than 300 varieties). Also check what's on while you're in town, as this is a prime music and theater venue.

• *If the weather's good, cross Great Western Road and head into the...*

Glasgow Botanic Gardens: This inviting parkland is the Glaswegians' favorite place to enjoy a break from the bustling city. And, like so many things in Glasgow, it's free.

Head into the park. If the sun's out, it'll be jammed with people enjoying some rare rays. Young lads wait all winter for the day when they can cry, "Sun's oot, taps aff!" and pull off their shirts to make the most of it.

In addition to the finely landscaped gardens, the park has two inviting greenhouse pavilions—both free and open to

Glasgow Botanic Gardens

Greenhouse pavilion

the public. The big white one on the right (from 1873, open 10:00-18:00) is the more elegant, with classical statues scattered among the palm fronds (but beware the killer plants, to the left as you enter).

When you're done in the park, head back out the way you came in.

• *Cross back over Great Western Road and backtrack (past the Òran Mòr church/restaurant) one block down Byres Road. Turn left down Vinicombe Street (across from the Waitrose). Now we'll explore...*

Back-Streets West End: Peek inside the **Hillhead Bookclub**—a former cinema that's been converted into a hipster bar/restaurant serving affordable food (described later, under "Eating in Glasgow"). A half-block after that, turn right and walk (on Crawnworth Street) along the row of red-sandstone **tenements**. While that word has negative connotations stateside, here a "tenement" is simply an apartment building.

Across the street from this tenement row (at #12) is a **baths club**—a private swimming pool, like an exclusive health club back home.

After the baths, turn right down Cresswell Street. A half-block down on the right, turn left down **Cresswell Lane**—an inviting, traffic-free, brick-floored shopping and dining zone. While the Golden Zed downtown is packed with chain stores, this is where you'll find charming one-off boutiques.

Browse your way to the end of the lane, cross the street, and continue straight to the even more appealing **Ashton Lane,** strung with fairy lights. Scout this street and pick a place to return for dinner tonight. Fancy a film? Halfway down the street on the right, the Grosvenor Cinema shows both blockbusters and art-house fare.

• *When you reach the end of the lane, take a very sharp left up the stairs (with the beer garden for Brel on your left). At the top of the stairs, turn right along the road. You're now walking through the modern part of the...*

University of Glasgow Campus: Founded in 1451, this is Scotland's second-oldest university (after St. Andrews). Its 24,000 students sprawl through the West End. Unlike the fancy "old university" buildings, this area is gloomy and concrete.

• *Eventually you'll reach a wide cross street, University Avenue. Turn left up this street and walk two more blocks uphill. At the traffic light, the Hunterian Gallery and Mackintosh House are just up the hill on your left, and the Hunterian Museum is across the street on the right.*

Hunterian Gallery and Mackintosh House: First, stop in at the Hunterian Gallery to tour the Mackintosh House. In the morning, visits are by tour only; later you can free flow (admission is limited). Ask if there's a wait, and if so, spend your time either in the adjacent gallery, the wonderful university cafeteria (across the lane, cheap and cheery lunch), or the

Typical "tenements"

Ashton Lane

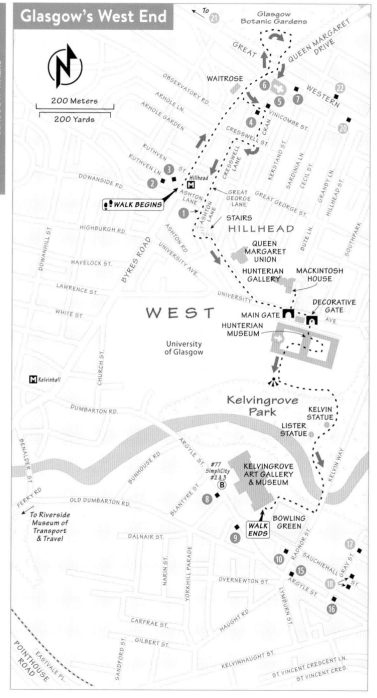

Glasgow's West End

200 Meters
200 Yards

To

Glasgow
Botanic Gardens

GREAT

QUEEN MARGARET DRIVE

WAITROSE

WESTERN

OBSERVATORY RD.

ARHOLE LN.

ARHOLE GARDEN

VINICOMBE ST.

CRAN...

CRESSWELL ST.

KERSTAND ST.

SARDINIA LN.

CECIL ST.

GRANBY LN.

HILLHEAD ST.

RUTHVEN ST.

RUTHVEN LN.

DOWANSIDE RD.

Hillhead

WALK BEGINS

ASHTON LANE

CRESSWELL LANE

ASHTON LANE

GREAT GEORGE LANE

GREAT GEORGE ST.

STAIRS

HILLHEAD

BUTE LN.

SOUTHPARK

HIGHBURGH RD.

ASHTON RD.

UNIVERSITY AVE.

QUEEN MARGARET UNION

DOWANHILL ST.

HAVELOCK ST.

BYRES ROAD

LAWRENCE ST.

UNIVERSITY

HUNTERIAN GALLERY

MACKINTOSH HOUSE

WHITE ST.

WEST

MAIN GATE

DECORATIVE GATE

AVE.

HUNTERIAN MUSEUM

University
of Glasgow

CHURCH ST.

Kelvinhall

Kelvingrove
Park

KELVIN STATUE

DUMBARTON RD.

LISTER STATUE

KELVIN WAY

BENALDER ST.

ARGYLE ST.

#77
SimpliCity
#2 & 3
B

KELVINGROVE
ART GALLERY
& MUSEUM

FERRY RD.

BUNHOUSE RD.

BLANTYRE ST.

OLD DUMBARTON RD.

To Riverside
Museum of
Transport
& Travel

DALNAIR ST.

NARIN ST.

YORKHILL PARADE

WALK
ENDS

BOWLING
GREEN

RADNOR ST.

SAUCHIEHALL

GRAY ST.

ST.

OVERNEWTON ST.

ARGYLE ST.

LYMBURN ST.

POINTHOUSE ROAD

EASTVALE PL.

SANDFORD ST.

GILBERT ST.

CARFRAE ST.

HAUGHT RD.

KELVINHAUGHT ST.

ST VINCENT CRESCENT LN.

ST VINCENT CRES.

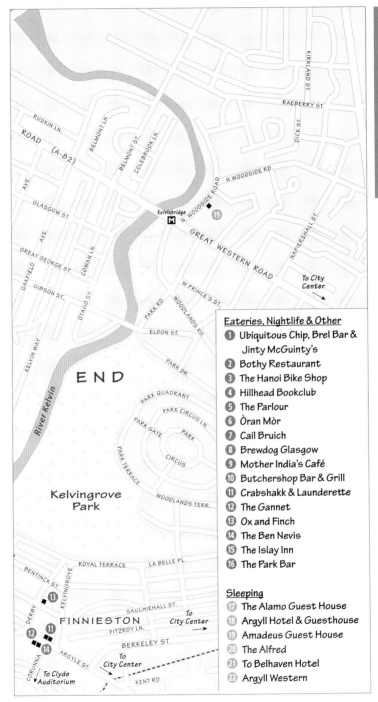

Eateries, Nightlife & Other

1. Ubiquitous Chip, Brel Bar & Jinty McGuinty's
2. Bothy Restaurant
3. The Hanoi Bike Shop
4. Hillhead Bookclub
5. The Parlour
6. Òran Mòr
7. Cail Bruich
8. Brewdog Glasgow
9. Mother India's Café
10. Butchershop Bar & Grill
11. Crabshakk & Launderette
12. The Gannet
13. Ox and Finch
14. The Ben Nevis
15. The Islay Inn
16. The Park Bar

Sleeping

17. The Alamo Guest House
18. Argyll Hotel & Guesthouse
19. Amadeus Guest House
20. The Alfred
21. To Belhaven Hotel
22. Argyll Western

Universtity of Glasgow cloister

Kelvingrove Park

Hunterian Museum across the street. All three sights (the Mackintosh House, Hunterian Gallery, and Hunterian Museum) are important if you have the time and energy (all are described later, in "Sights").

• *When you're done here, head for the Hunterian Museum in the university's big old main building across University Avenue. Instead of going through the main gate, go to the left end of the building facing the street to find a more interesting decorative gate.*

University of Glasgow Main Building: Take a good look at the gate, which is decorated with the names of illustrious alums. Pick out the great Scots: James Watt, King James II, Adam Smith, Lord Kelvin, William Hunter (the namesake of the university's museums), and Donald Dewar, a driving force behind devolution who became Scotland's first "First Minister" in 1999.

Go through the gate and face the main university building. Stretching to the left is Graduation Hall, where commencement takes place. Head straight into the building, ride the elevator to floor 4, and enjoy the **Hunterian Museum.**

After you visit the Hunterian Museum, find the grand staircase down (in the

room with the Antonine Wall exhibit). You'll emerge into one of the twin quads enclosed by the enormous ensemble of university buildings. Veer right to find your way into the atmospheric, Neo-Gothic **cloisters** that support the wing separating the two quads. These are modeled after the Gothic cloisters in the lower chapel of Glasgow Cathedral, across town. On the other side, you'll pop out into the adjoining quad. Head out the door at the bottom of the quad.

Leaving the university complex, head for the tall flagpole on a bluff overlooking a grand view. The turreted building just below is the Kelvingrove Museum, where this walk ends. (If you get turned around in the park, just head for those spires.)

• *From the flagpole, turn left and head to the end of the big building. Head down the stairs leading through the woods on your right (marked James Watt Building). When you reach the busy road, turn right along it for a short distance, then—as soon as you can—angle to the right back into the green space of...*

Kelvingrove Park: Another of Glasgow's favorite parks, this originated in the Victorian period, when there was a renewed focus on trying to get people out into green spaces. One of the first things you'll come to is a big statue of **Lord Kelvin** (1824-1907). Born William Thomson, he chose to take the name of the River Kelvin, which runs through Glasgow (and gives its name to many other things here, including the museum we're headed to). One of the most respected scientists of his time, Kelvin was a pioneer in the field of thermodynamics, and gave his name (or, actually, the river's) to a new, absolute unit of temperature measurement designed to replace Celsius and Fahrenheit.

Just past Kelvin, bear left at the statue of **Joseph Lister** (1827-1912, of "Listerine" fame—he pioneered the use of antiseptics to remove infection-causing germs from the surgical environment), and take the bridge across the River Kelvin. Once across the bridge, turn right toward the museum.

Now's the time to explore the Kelvingrove Museum, (described later).

• When you're finished at the museum, exit out the back end, toward the busy road. Several recommended restaurants are ahead and to the left, in the Finnieston neighborhood (see "Eating," later). Or, if you'd like to hop on the subway, just turn right along Argyle Street and walk five minutes to the Kelvinhall station.

SIGHTS

Downtown

▲▲TENEMENT HOUSE

Here's a chance to drop into a perfectly preserved 1930s-era middle-class residence. The National Trust for Scotland bought this otherwise ordinary row home, located in a residential neighborhood, because of the peculiar tendencies of Miss Agnes Toward (1886-1975). For five decades, she kept her home essentially unchanged. The kitchen calendar is still set for 1935, and canisters of licorice powder (a laxative) still sit on the bathroom

shelf. It's a time-warp experience, where Glaswegian old-timers enjoy coming to reminisce about how they grew up.

Cost and Hours: £6.50, April-Oct daily 13:00-17:00, July-Aug from 11:00, closed Nov-March, guidebook-£3, 145 Buccleuch Street (pronounced "ba-KLOO"), down from the top of Garnethill, tel. 0141/333-0183, www.nts.org.uk.

Visiting the House: Buy your ticket on the main floor, and poke around the little museum. Tenements like these were typical for every class except the richest. Then head upstairs to the apartment, which is staffed by caring volunteers. Ring the doorbell to be let in. Explore the four little rooms. Imagine a world without electricity (Miss Toward was a late adapter, making the leap to electricity only in 1960). Ask about the utility of the iron stove. Ponder the importance of that drawer full of coal and how that stove heated her entire world. Ask why the bed is in the kitchen. As you look through the rooms laced with Victorian trinkets—such as the ceramic dogs on the living room's fireplace mantle—consider how different they are from Mackintosh's stark, minimalist designs from the same period.

▲NATIONAL PIPING CENTRE

If you consider bagpipes a tacky Scottish cliché, think again. At this small but insightful museum, you'll get a scholarly lesson in the proud history of the bagpipe. For those with a healthy attention span for history or musical instruments—ideally both—it's fascinating. On Thursdays, Fridays, and Saturdays at 11:00 and 14:00 a piper is on hand to perform, answer questions, and show you around the collection. At other times, if it's quiet, ask the ticket-sellers to tell you more—some are bagpipe students at the music school across the street. The center also offers a shop, lessons, a restaurant, and accommodations.

Cost and Hours: £4.50, includes audioguide, Mon-Thu 9:00-19:00, Fri

National Piping Centre

until 17:00, Sat until 15:00, closed Sun, 30 McPhater Street, tel. 0141/353-5551, www.thepipingcentre.co.uk.

Visiting the Museum: The collection is basically one big room packed with well-described exhibits, including several historic bagpipes. The thoughtful, beautifully produced audioguide—which mixes a knowledgeable commentary with sound bites of bagpipes being played and brief interviews with performers—feels like a 40-minute audio-documentary on the BBC. The 15-minute film shown at the end of the room sums up the collection helpfully.

Rick's Tip: For fun, **try the set of bagpipes and chanters** *in the Piping Centre. The fingering is easy if you play the recorder, but keeping the bag inflated is exhausting.*

GLASGOW SCHOOL OF ART
When he was just 28 years old—and still a no-name junior draughtsman for a big architectural firm—Charles Rennie Mack-intosh won the contest to create a new home for the Glasgow School of Art. He threw himself into the project, designing every detail of the building, inside and out. Remember that this work was the Art Nouveau original, and that Frank Lloyd Wright, the Art Deco Chrysler Building, and everything that resembles it came well after Charles Rennie Mack's time.

Unfortunately, the building was badly damaged by a fire in May 2014. It likely won't open again until 2019 at the earliest.

For now, you can visit the small, free exhibition about Mackintosh, including an impressive model of the School of Art (shop, exhibition, and tour desk open daily during renovation 10:00-16:30).

Cathedral Precinct
Today's towering cathedral is mostly 13th century—the only great Scottish church to survive the Reformation intact. In front of the cathedral (near the street), you'll see an attention-grabbing statue of **David Livingstone** (1813-1873). Livingstone—the Scottish missionary/explorer/cartographer

who discovered a huge waterfall in Africa and named it in honor of his queen, Victoria—was born eight miles from here.

Nearby, the St. Mungo Museum of Religious Life and Art, built on the site of the old Bishop's Castle, is a unique exhibit covering the spectrum of religions. And the Necropolis, blanketing the hill behind the cathedral, provides an atmospheric walk through a world of stately Victorian tombstones. From there you can scan the city and look down on the brewery where Tennent's Lager (a longtime Glasgow favorite) has been made since 1885. And, if the spirit moves you, hike on down and tour the brewery (described later).

The following sights are within close range of each other. As you face the cathedral, the St. Mungo Museum is on your right (with handy public WCs). The brewery is a 10-minute walk away.

To reach these sights from Buchanan Street, turn east on Bath Street, which soon becomes Cathedral Street, and walk about 15 minutes (or hop a bus along the main drag—try bus #38, or #57, confirm with driver that the bus stops at the cathedral). To head to the Kelvingrove Museum after your visit, from the cathedral, walk two blocks up Castle Street and catch bus #19 (on the cathedral side).

▲GLASGOW CATHEDRAL

This blackened, Gothic cathedral is a rare example of an intact pre-Reformation Scottish cathedral. The zealous Reformation forces of John Knox ripped out the stained glass and ornate chapels of the Catholic age, but they left the church standing. The church is aching to tell its long and fascinating story and volunteers are standing by to do just that.

Cost and Hours: Free, £3 suggested donation; Mon-Sat 9:30-17:30, Sun 13:00-17:00; Oct-March until 16:00; request a free tour or join one in progress; near junction of Castle and Cathedral Streets, tel. 0141/552-8198, www.glasgowcathedral.org.uk.

Visiting the Cathedral: Inside, look up to see the wooden barrel-vaulted ceiling, and take in the beautifully decorated section over the choir ("quire"). The choir screen is the only pre-Reformation screen surviving in Scotland. It divided the common people from the priests and big shots of the day, who got to worship closer to the religious action. The cathedral's glass dates mostly from the 19th century.

Step into the choir and enjoy the east end with the four evangelists presiding high above in stained glass. Two seats (with high backs, right of altar) are reserved for Queen Elizabeth II and her husband Prince Philip, the Duke of Edinburgh.

Step into the lower church (down stairs on right as you face the choir), where the central altar sits upon St. Mungo's tomb. Mungo was the seventh-century Scottish monk and mythical founder of Glasgow who

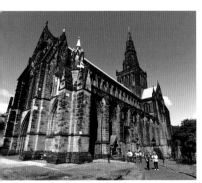

Glasgow Cathedral

Cathedral interior

Necropolis

established the first wooden church on this spot and gave Glasgow its name. Notice the ceiling bosses (decorative caps where the ribs come together) with their colorfully carved demons, dragons, and skulls.

Rick's Tip: *On Cathedral Square, you'll find the cute* **Empire Coffee Box,** *where Rocco is ready to* **caffeinate** *you from this old-style police call box.*

▲NECROPOLIS

From the cathedral, a lane leads over the "bridge of sighs" into the park filled with grand tombstones. Glasgow's huge burial hill has a wistful, ramshackle appeal. A stroll among the tombstones of the eminent Glaswegians of the 19th century gives you a glimpse of Victorian Glasgow and a feeling for the confidence and wealth of the second city of the British Empire in its glory days.

If the cemetery's main black gates are closed, see if you can get in and out through a gate off the street to the right.

▲ST. MUNGO MUSEUM OF RELIGIOUS LIFE AND ART

This secular, city-run museum, just in front of the cathedral, aims to promote religious understanding. Built in 1990 on the site of the old Bishop's Castle, it provides a handy summary of major and minor world religions, showing how each faith handles various rites of passage across the human life span: birth, puberty, marriage, death, and everything in between and after. Start with the 10-minute video overview on the first floor, and finish with a great view from the top floor of the cathedral and Necropolis. Ponder the Zen Buddhist garden out back as you leave.

Cost and Hours: Free, £3 suggested donation, Tue-Thu and Sat 10:00-17:00, Fri and Sun from 11:00, closed Mon, free WCs downstairs, cheap ground-floor café, 2 Castle Street, tel. 0141/276-1625, www.glasgowmuseums.com.

▲▲TENNENT'S BREWERY TOUR

Tennent's, founded in 1740, is now the biggest brewery in Scotland, spanning 18 acres. They give serious hour-long tours showing how they make "Scotland's favorite pint," and how they fill 700 kegs per hour and 1,000 bottles per minute (you'll see more action Mon-Fri). It's hot and sweaty inside, with 100 steps to climb on your tour. When you're done (surrounded by "the Lager Lovelies"—cans from 1965 to 1993 that were decorated with cover girls), you'll enjoy three samples followed by a pint of your choice (£10, tours depart daily at 10:00, 12:00, 14:00, 16:00, & 18:00; call or book online; 161 Duke Street, 0141/202-7145, www.tennentstours.com). To head back downtown, bus #41 stops in front of the brewery on Duke Street and goes to George Square.

The West End

These sights (except for the Riverside Museum) are linked by my West End Walk, covered earlier.

▲HUNTERIAN GALLERY AND MACKINTOSH HOUSE

Here's a sightseeing twofer: an art gallery offering a good look at some Scottish artists relatively unknown outside their homeland, and the chance to take a guided tour through the reconstructed home of Charles Rennie Mackintosh, decorated exactly the way he liked it. For Charles Rennie Mack fans—or anyone fascinated by the unique habitats of artists—it's well worth a visit.

Cost and Hours: Gallery—free, Tue-Sat 10:00-17:00, Sun 11:00-16:00, closed Mon, across University Avenue from the main university building, tel. 0141/330-4221, www.gla.ac.uk/hunterian. Mackintosh House—£5, same hours as gallery, last entry 45 minutes before closing. The Mackintosh House is open weekday mornings by 30-minute tour only (Tue-Fri 10:00-12:30, departs every 30 minutes). After 13:00, and all day Sat-Sun, the house is open without a tour, but only 12 people are allowed at a time, so there may be a short wait.

Visitor Information: First, check in at the reception desk to sign up for a tour of the Mackintosh House or see if there's a wait to get in. You'll also need to check

any bags (free lockers available). Spend your waiting time visiting the gallery, or, with a longer wait, head across the street to the Hunterian Museum (described later). If it's lunchtime, eat at **$ Food,** a cheap, healthy, fast, and modern student cafeteria across the lane from the museum that's open to the public.

Mackintosh House: In 1906, Mackintosh and his wife, Margaret MacDonald, moved into the end unit of a Victorian row house. Mackintosh gutted the place and redesigned it to his own liking—bathing the interior in his trademark style, a mix of curving, organic lines and rigid, proto-Art Deco functionalism. They moved out in 1914, and the house was demolished in the 1960s—but the university wisely documented the layout and carefully removed and preserved all of Mackintosh's original furnishings. In 1981, when respect for Mackintosh was on the rise, they built this replica house and reinstalled everything just as Mackintosh had designed it. You'll see the entryway, dining room, drawing room, and bedroom—each one offering glimpses into the minds of these great artists. You'll see original furniture and

Portrait by a "Glasgow Boy"

decorations by Mackintosh and MacDonald, providing insight into their creative process.

Hunterian Art Gallery: The adjacent gallery is manageable and worth exploring. Circling one floor, you'll enjoy three thoughtfully described sections. One highlight is the modern Scottish art (1850-1960), focusing on two groups: the "Glasgow Boys," who traveled to France to study during the waning days of Realism (1880s), and, a generation later, the Scottish Colourists, who found a completely different inspiration in circa-1910 France—bright, bold, with an almost Picasso-like exuberance. The gallery also has an extensive collection of portraits by American artist James Whistler—Whistler's wife was of Scottish descent, as was Whistler's mother. (Hey, that has a nice ring to it.) The painter always found great support in Scotland, and his heir donated his estate to the University of Glasgow.

▲HUNTERIAN MUSEUM

The oldest public museum in Scotland was founded by William Hunter (1718-1783), a medical researcher. Today his natural science collection is housed in a huge and gorgeous space inside the university's showcase building. Everything is well presented and well explained. Ancient Roman artifacts on display include leather shoes, plumbing, weapons, and carved reliefs. The eclectic collection also includes musical instruments, a display on the Glasgow-built *Lusitania,* and a fine collection of fossils, including the aquatic dinosaur called plesiosaur (possibly a distant ancestor of the Loch Ness monster). But to some, most fascinating are the many examples of deformities—two-headed animals, body parts in jars, and so on (main hall, left of Romans). Ever the curious medical researcher, Hunter collected these for study, and these intrigue, titillate, and nauseate visitors to this day.

Cost and Hours: Free, Tue-Sat 10:00-17:00, Sun 11:00-16:00, closed Mon, Gilbert Scott Building, University Avenue, tel. 0141/330-4221, www.gla.ac.uk/hunterian.

▲▲KELVINGROVE ART GALLERY AND MUSEUM

This "Scottish Smithsonian" displays everything from a stuffed elephant to paintings by the great masters and what, for me, is the city's best collection of work by Charles Rennie Mackintosh. The well-described contents are impressively displayed in a grand, 100-year-old, Spanish Baroque-style building. The Kelvingrove claims to be one of the most-visited museums in Britain—presumably because of all the field-trip groups you'll see here. Watching all the excited Scottish kids—their imaginations ablaze—is as much fun as the collection itself.

Cost and Hours: Free, £5 suggested donation, Mon-Thu and Sat 10:00-17:00, Fri and Sun from 11:00, free tours at 11:00 and 14:30, Argyle Street, tel. 0141/276-9599, www.glasgowmuseums.com.

Hunterian Museum

Kelvingrove Art Gallery and Museum

Getting There: My self-guided West End Walk leads you here from the Hillhead subway stop, or you can ride the **subway** to the Kelvinhall stop. When you exit, turn left and walk five minutes. **Buses** #2 and #3 run from Hope Street downtown to the museum. It's also on the **hop-on, hop-off bus** route. No matter how you arrive, just look for the huge, turreted red-brick building.

Rick's Tip: Enjoy an **organ concert.** *At the top of the Kelvingrove's main hall, the huge pipe organ booms with a daily 30-minute recital at 13:00 (15:00 on Sun).*

Visiting the Museum: Built in 1901 to house the city collection, the museum is divided into two sections: Art ("Expression") and Natural ("Life"), each with two floors. The symmetrical floor plan can be confusing. Pick up a map and plan your strategy.

The "Expression" section, in the East Court, is marked by a commotion of heads—each with a different expression—raining down from the ceiling. This half of the museum focuses on artwork, including Dutch, Flemish, French, and Scottish Romanticism from the late 19th century. The exhibits on "Scottish Identity in Art" let you tour the country's scenic wonders and its history on canvas. The Mackintosh section, a highlight for many, demonstrates the Art Nouveau work of the "Glasgow Four," including Charles Rennie Mackintosh. Unfortunately, the museum's star

painting, Salvador Dalí's *Christ of St. John of the Cross,* will be on the road until 2020.

The "Life" section, in the West Court, features a menagerie of stuffed animals (including a giraffe, kangaroo, ostrich, and moose) with a WWII-era Spitfire fighter plane hovering overhead. Branching off are halls with exhibits ranging from Ancient Egypt to "Scotland's First People" to weaponry ("Conflict and Consequence").

▲▲RIVERSIDE MUSEUM

Located along the River Clyde, this high-tech, extremely kid-friendly museum—nostalgic and modern at the same time—is dedicated to all things transportation-related. Named the European museum of the year in 2013, visiting is a must for anyone interested in transportation and how it has shaped society.

Cost and Hours: Free, £5 suggested donation, Mon-Thu and Sat 10:00-17:00, Fri and Sun from 11:00, ground-floor café with £6-9 meals, upstairs coffee shop with basic drinks and snacks, 100 Pointhouse Place, tel. 0141/287-2720, www.glasgowmuseums.com.

Getting There: It's on the riverfront promenade, two miles west of the city center. **Bus** #100 runs between the museum and George Square (2/hour, last departure from George Square at 15:02, operated by McColl's), or you can take a **taxi** (£6-8, 10-minute ride from downtown). The museum is also included on the **hop-on, hop-off sightseeing**

Riverside Museum

Riverside Museum interior

The tall ship Glenlee

bus route (described earlier, under "Orientation").

Visiting the Museum: Most of the collection is strewn across one huge, wide-open floor. Upon entering, visit the info desk (to the right as you enter, near the shop) to ask about the free tours and activities that day—or just listen for announcements. Also pick up a map from the info desk, as the museum's open floor plan can feel a bit like a traffic jam at rush hour.

Diving in, explore the vast collection: stagecoaches, locomotives, double-decker trolleys, an entire wall stacked with vintage automobiles, and another wall with motorcycles. Learn about the opening of Glasgow's old-timey subway (Europe's third oldest). Explore the collections of old toys and prams, and watch a film about 1930s cinema. Stroll the re-creation of a circa-1900 Main Street, with video clips bringing each shop to life (there's one about a little girl who discovers her daddy was selling things to the pawn shop to pay the rent).

Don't miss the much smaller upstairs section, with great views over the River Clyde (cross the footbridge over the trains), additional exhibits about ships built here in Glasgow, and what may be the world's oldest bicycle.

Nearby: Be sure to head to the River Clyde directly behind the museum (just step out the back door). The *Glenlee,* one of five remaining tall ships built in Glasgow in the 19th century (1896), invites visitors to come aboard (free, daily 10:00-17:00, Nov-Feb until 16:00, tel. 0141/357-3699, www.thetallship.com). Good exhibits illustrate what it was like to live and work aboard the ship. Explore the officers' living quarters, then head below deck to the café and more exhibits. Below that, the cargo hold has kids' activities and offers the chance to peek into the engine room. As you board, note the speedboat river tour that leaves from here each afternoon (£10, 20 minutes).

EXPERIENCES

Shopping

Downtown, the **Golden Zed**—a.k.a. "Style Mile"—has all the predictable chain stores, with a few Scottish souvenir stands mixed among them. For more on this, see the start of my self-guided "Get to Know Glasgow" walk. The Glasgow Modern Art Museum (GoMA) has a quirky gift shop that many find enticing.

The West End also has some appealing shops. Many are concentrated on **Cresswell Lane** (covered in my self-guided West End Walk). Browsing here, you'll find an eclectic assortment of gifty shops, art galleries, design shops, hair salons, record stores, home-decor shops, and lots of vintage bric-a-brac. Be sure to poke into De Courcy's Arcade, a two-part warren of tiny offbeat shops.

Pubs and Clubs

Downtown: Bath Street's bars and clubs are focused on young professionals as well as students; the recommended Pot Still is a perfect place to sample Scotch whisky (see "Eating in Glasgow," later). Nearby, running just below the Glasgow School of Art, **Sauchiehall Street** is younger, artsier, and more student-oriented. The recently revitalized **Merchant City** zone, stretching just east of the Buchanan Street shopping drag, has a slightly older crowd and a popular gay scene.

West End: You'll find fun bars and music venues in **Hillhead,** on Ashton Lane and surrounding streets. **Finnieston,** just below the Kelvingrove Museum, is packed with trendy bars and restaurants.

Live Music

Glasgow has a great music scene, on its streets (talented buskers) and in its bars and clubs (with trad sessions—Scottish traditional music—and more). Check what's up in *The Skinny,* an info-packed alternative weekly (www.theskinny.co.uk), The List (www.list.co.uk), or *Gig Guide* (www.gigguide.co.uk).

Finnieston

The following pubs line up along Argyle Street.

The Ben Nevis hosts lively, toe-tap-

ping sessions three times a week. It's a good scene—full of energy but crowded. Show up early to grab a seat in this tiny pub, or be ready to stand (Wed, Thu, and Sun at 21:00, no food service—just snacks, #1147).

The Islay Inn has bands twice weekly—some traditional, some doing contemporary covers (music Fri and Sat at 21:00, food available, #1256, at corner with Radnor).

At **The Park Bar,** you'll find live music several nights a week, including traditional Scottish bands and sessions on Thursdays (Thu-Sun around 21:00, food available, #1202).

Hillhead

The Òran Mòr (www.oran-mor.co.uk) and **Hillhead Bookclub** (www.hillhead bookclub.co.uk) are popular live music venues (both recommended later, under "Eating in Glasgow").

Jinty McGuinty's has acoustic music every night, ranging from chart hits to Irish classics to soul and blues (daily at 21:30, 29 Ashton Lane).

Downtown

Twice weekly at **Babbity Bowster,** musicians take over a corner of this cute pub (under a recommended B&B) for a trad session. The music, energy, and atmosphere are top-notch (Wed and Sat at 15:00, solid pub grub, 16 Blackfriars Street).

Sloans, hidden away through a muraled tunnel off Argyle Street, is a fun pub with outdoor tables filling an alley. They have live traditional music on Wednesdays (21:00) and *ceilidh* dancing instruction on Fridays (£10, starts at 20:30, book ahead, food available, 108 Argyle Street, www.sloansglasgow.com).

Waxy O'Connor's is a massive, multilevel Irish bar featuring a maze of dark, atmospheric rooms, a tree climbing up a wall, and lots of live music (usually acoustic—check their website for days/times) and trad sessions on Sundays at 15:00

(food available, 44 West George Street, www.waxyoconnors.co.uk).

Movies

The Grosvenor Cinema, right on Ashton Lane in the heart of the bustling West End restaurant scene, is an inviting movie theater, with cushy leather seats in two theaters showing films big and small (most movies £10) and lots of special events. Wine and beer are available at the theater, or you can order cocktails and warm food at the bar next door and have it delivered to your seat (21 Ashton Lane, tel. 0845-166-6002, www.grosvenorcinema.co.uk).

EATING

Downtown

$ Martha's is ideal for hungry, hurried sightseers in search of a healthy and satisfying lunch. They serve a seasonal menu of wraps, rice boxes, soups, and other great meals made with Scottish ingredients but with eclectic, exotic, international flavors. Just line up (it moves fast), order at the counter, and then find a table or take your food to go (Mon-Fri 7:30-18:00, closed Sat-Sun, 142A St. Vincent Street, tel. 0141/248-9771).

$$$ Mussel Inn offers light, good-value fish dinners and seafood plates in an airy, informal environment. Their "kilo pot" of Scottish mussels is popular with locals and big enough to share ("lunchtime quickie" deals, daily specials, daily 12:00-14:30 & 17:00-22:00, 157 Hope Street, tel. 0141/572-1405).

$$ The Willow Tea Rooms, designed by Charles Rennie Mackintosh, has a diner-type eatery and a classy Room de Luxe. The cheap and cheery menu covers both dining areas (afternoon tea, Mon-Sat 9:00-17:00, Sun from 10:30, reservations smart, 217 Sauchiehall Street, tel. 0141/332-0521, www.willowtearooms.co.uk).

Rogano is a time-warp Glasgow institution that retains much of the same classy Art Deco interior it had when it opened in 1935. The restaurant has three distinct sections: **$$ The Rogano Bar** in front is an Art Deco diner with dressy outdoor seating and serves soups, sandwiches, and simple dishes; **$$$$ The Rogano Restaurant,** a fancy dining room at the back of the main floor, focuses on seafood, classic Scottish dishes, and afternoon tea (their early menu—until 19:00—is a good deal); **$$$ The Rogano Café,** a more casual yet still dressy bistro in the cellar, is filled with 1930s-Hollywood posters and offers a similar menu to the fancy restaurant, but cheaper (daily 12:00-16:00 & 18:00-21:30, 11 Exchange Place—just before giant Merchant City archway just off Buchanan Street, reservations smart, tel. 0141/248-4055, www.roganoglasgow.com).

$$ Tabac is a dark, mod, and artsy cocktail bar with spacious seating on a narrow lane just off Buchanan Street. They serve pizza, burgers, and big salads (daily 12:00-24:00, food served until 21:00, across from "The Lighthouse" at 10 Mitchell Lane, tel. 0141/572-1448).

$$$ Two Fat Ladies is a hardworking and dressy little place with a focus on food rather than atmosphere and a passion for white fish (early-bird menu until 18:15 a great value, daily 12:00-14:30 & 17:00-22:00, 118 Blythswood Street, tel. 0141/847-0088).

$$ CCA Saramago Bar and Courtyard Vegetarian Café, located on the first floor of Glasgow's edgy contemporary art museum, charges art-student prices for its designer, animal-free food (food served daily 12:00-22:00, free Wi-Fi, 350 Sauchiehall Street, tel. 0141/332-7959).

For Your Whisky: The Pot Still is an award-winning malt whisky bar dating from 1835 that's also proud of its meat pies. You'll see locals of all ages sitting in its leathery interior, watching football (soccer), and discussing their drinks. Give the friendly bartenders a little background on your beverage tastes, and they'll narrow

Explore Ashton Lane for dinner options.

down a good choice for you from their long list (daily 11:00–24:00, 154 Hope Street, tel. 0141/333-0980, Frank has the long beard).

In the West End

This hip, lively residential neighborhood/university district is worth exploring, particularly in the evening. The restaurant scene focuses on two areas (at opposite ends of my West End Walk): near the Hillhead subway stop and, farther down, in the Finnieston neighborhood near the Kelvingrove Museum. It's smart to book ahead at any of these places for weekend evenings.

Near Hillhead

There's a fun concentration of restaurants on the streets that fan out from the Hillhead subway stop (£8 taxi ride from downtown). If it's a balmy evening, several have convivial gardens designed to catch the evening sun. Before choosing a place, take a stroll and scout the Ashton Lane scene, which has the greatest variety of places (including Ubiquitous Chip and Brel Bar, recommended next).

$$$$ Ubiquitous Chip, aka "The Chip," is a beloved local landmark with a cou-ple inviting pubs and two great restaurant options. On the ground floor is their fine restaurant with beautifully presented contemporary Scottish dishes in a garden atrium. Their early-bird menu (order by 18:30) is a great value. Upstairs (looking down on the scene) is the less-formal, less-expensive, but still very nice brasserie (daily 11:00–22:00, 12 Ashton Lane, tel. 0141/334-5007, www.ubiquitouschip.co.uk).

$$ Brel Bar is a fun-loving place with a happy garden and a menu with burgers, mussels, and quality bar food. On a nice evening, its backyard beer garden is hard to beat (daily 12:00–24:00, 37 Ashton Lane, tel. 0141/342-4966).

$$$ Bothy Restaurant is a romantic place offering tasty, traditional Scottish fare served by waiters in kilts. Sit outside in the inviting alleyway or in the rustic-contemporary dining room (daily 12:00–22:00, down the lane opposite the subway station to 11 Ruthven Lane, tel. 0141/334-4040).

$$ The Hanoi Bike Shop, a rare-in-Scotland Vietnamese "street food" restaurant, serves Asian tapas that are healthy and tasty, using local produce. With tight seating and friendly service, the place has a fun energy (daily 12:00-23:00, 8 Ruthven Lane, tel. 0141/334-7165).

$$ Hillhead Bookclub is a youthful and quirky art-school scene, with lots of beers on tap, creative cocktails, retro computer games, ping-pong, and theme evenings like "drag queen bingo" night. The menu: meat pies, fish-and-chips, burgers, and salads (daily 10:00-21:30, 17 Vinicombe Street, tel. 0141/576-1700).

$$ The Parlour, across from the Hillhead Bookclub, gets all the evening sun on its terrace seating. It's young, fun, and pub-like, with pizza, tacos, burgers, and creative cocktails (daily 11:00-21:30, 28 Vinicombe Street, mobile 07943-852-973).

$$ Òran Mòr fills a converted church from the 1860s with a classic pub. They offer basic pub grub either inside or on the front-porch beer garden (daily 10:00-21:00, later on weekends, across from the Botanic Gardens at 731 Great Western Road, tel. 0141/357-600).

$$$$ Cail Bruich serves award-winning classic Scottish dishes with an updated spin in an elegant and romantic setting. Reservations are smart (classy tasting menus for £35-45, lunch Wed-Sun 12:00-14:00, dinner Mon-Sat 18:00-21:00, 725 Great Western Road, tel. 0141/334-6265, www.cailbruich.co.uk).

Facing the Kelvingrove Museum

These three places are immediately across from the Kelvingrove Museum. They're more basic and less trendy than the Finnieston places (a few blocks away, listed next) that will leave you with better memories.

$$ Brewdog Glasgow is a beer-and-burgers joint. It's a great place to sample Scottish microbrews (daily 12:00-24:00, 1397 Argyle Street, tel. 0141/334-7175, www.brewdog.com).

$$ Mother India's Café is a good stop if you crave Scotland's national dish: "a good curry" (about two plates per person makes a meal, daily 12:00-22:30, 1355 Argyle Street, tel. 0141/339-9145).

$$$ Butchershop Bar & Grill is a casual, rustic, American-style steak house featuring Scottish products (lunch and early-bird deals, daily 12:00-22:00, 1055 Sauchiehall Street, tel. 0141/339-2999, www.butchershopglasgow.com).

Trendy Finnieston Eateries on and near Argyle Street

This trendy, up-and-coming neighborhood—with a hipster charm in this hipster city—stretches east from in front of the Kelvingrove Museum (a 10-minute walk from the Kelvinhall or Kelvinbridge subway stops). Each of these is likely to require a reservation.

$$ Crabshakk, specializing in fresh, beautifully presented seafood, is a foodie favorite, with a very tight bar-and-mezzanine seating area and tables spilling out onto the sidewalk (daily 12:00-22:00, 1114 Argyle Street, tel. 0141/334-6127, www.crabshakk.com).

$$$ The Gannet emphasizes Scottish ingredients with a modern spin. It's relaxed and stylish (lunch Thu-Sat 12:00-14:00, dinner Tue-Sat 17:00-21:30, Sun 13:00-19:30, closed Mon, 1155 Argyle Street, tel. 0141/204-2081, www.thegannetgla.com).

$$ Ox and Finch, with a romantic setting, open kitchen, and smart clientele, serves modern international cuisine (daily 12:00-22:00, 920 Sauchiehall Street, tel. 0141/339-8627, www.oxandfinch.com).

SLEEPING

For accommodations, choose between downtown (bustling by day, nearly deserted at night, close to main shopping zone and some major sights, very expensive parking and one-way streets that cause headaches for drivers) and the West End (neighborhoody, best variety of restaurants, easier parking, easy access to West End sights and parks but a bus or subway ride from the center and train station).

Downtown

These accommodations are scattered around the city center. Glasgow also has all the predictable chains—**Ibis, Premier Inn, Travelodge, Novotel, Mercure, Jurys Inn, EasyHotel**—check online for deals.

$$$ Pipers' Tryst has eight simple rooms enthusiastically done up in good tartan style above a restaurant in the National Piping Centre. The location is handy, if not romantic, and it's practically a pilgrimage for fans of bagpipes (30 McPhater Street, tel. 0141/353-5551, www.thepipingcentre.co.uk, hotel@thepipingcentre.co.uk).

$$$ Z Hotel, part of a small "compact luxury" chain, offers 104 sleek, stylish rooms (some are very small and don't have windows). It's welcoming and handy to Queen Street Station, just a few steps off George Square (breakfast extra, air-con, elevator, free wine-and-cheese buffet each afternoon, 36 North Frederick Street, tel. 0141/212-4550, www.thezhotels.com, glasgow@thezhotels.com).

$$ Grasshoppers is a cheerful, above-it-all retreat on the sixth floor of a building overlooking Central Station. The 29 rooms are tight, with small "efficiency" bathrooms, but the welcome is warm and there's 24-hour access to fresh cupcakes, shortbread, and ice cream (free breakfast to those booking direct, optional buffet dinner, elevator, 87 Union Street, tel. 0141/222-2666, www.grasshoppersglasgow.com, info@grasshoppersglasgow.com).

$$ Motel One, part of a stylish German budget hotel chain, has 374 rooms and is located conveniently, right next to Central Station (corner of Oswald and Argyle streets, www.motel-one.com).

$ Babbity Bowster, named for a traditional Scottish dance, is a pub and restaurant renting five simple, mod rooms up top. It's located in the trendy Merchant City area (no breakfast, lots of stairs and no elevator, 10-minute walk from either station, 16 Blackfriars Street, tel. 0141/552-5055, www.babbitybowster.com, info@babbitybowster.com). The ground-floor **$$ pub** serves good grub (daily 12:00-22:00) and has twice-weekly sessions.

¢ The huge **Euro Hostel** (over 400 beds) is a well-run and well-located option for those on a tight budget (private rooms, family rooms, all rooms have en-suite bathrooms, breakfast extra, kitchen, bar, very central on the River Clyde near Central Station, 318 Clyde Street, tel. 0845-539-9956, www.eurohostels.co.uk, glasgow@eurohostels.co.uk).

In the West End

For a more appealing neighborhood experience, bunk in the West End—the upper-middle-class neighborhood just a few subway stops (or a 15-minute, £8 taxi ride) from downtown. As this is also one of the city's best dining zones, you'll likely come here for dinner anyway—so why not sleep here? My favorites in this area are the Alamo and Amadeus, which have the most personality.

Finnieston

These places are in an inviting residential area near the Kelvingrove Museum (not as handy to the subway, but easy by bus). They're close to the lively Argyle Street scene, with good restaurants and fun Gaelic pubs.

$$ The Alamo Guest House, energetically run by Steve and Emma, has rich, lavishly decorated public spaces and 10 comfortable rooms, including two luxury suites with bathtubs (family room, some rooms with bathroom down the hall, 2- or 3-night minimum stay on weekends in peak season, 46 Gray Street, tel. 0141/339-2395, www.alamoguesthouse.com, info@alamoguesthouse.com).

At the **$$ Argyll Hotel and Guest-house** you won't forget you're in Scotland. Each room is accessorized with a different

Central Glasgow Restaurants & Hotels

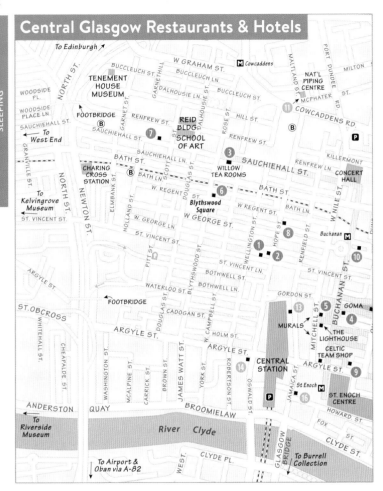

tartan and has info on the associated clan. The hotel has an elevator, breakfast room, and higher prices than the guesthouse (guesthouse customers must cross the street for breakfast and deal with stairs). Otherwise the rooms are just as nice and a bit larger in the guesthouse (family rooms, save money by skipping breakfast, 973 Sauchiehall Street, tel. 0141/337-3313, www.argyllhotelglasgow.co.uk, info@ argyllhotelglasgow.co.uk).

Near Kelvinbridge
$$ Amadeus Guest House, a classy ref-

uge just north of the large Kelvingrove Park, has nine modern rooms and artistic flourishes. It hides down a quiet street yet is conveniently located near the Kelvinbridge subway stop—just a 10-minute walk or one subway stop from the restaurant zone (includes continental breakfast, 411 North Woodside Road, tel. 0141/339-8257, www.amadeusguesthouse.co.uk, reservations@amadeusguesthouse.co.uk, Alexandra).

Hillhead
These places, overlooking the busy Great

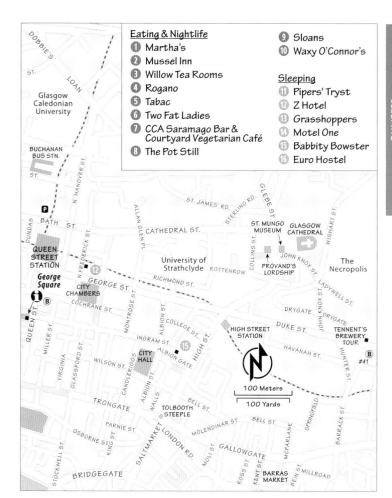

Eating & Nightlife
1. Martha's
2. Mussel Inn
3. Willow Tea Rooms
4. Rogano
5. Tabac
6. Two Fat Ladies
7. CCA Saramago Bar & Courtyard Vegetarian Café
8. The Pot Still
9. Sloans
10. Waxy O'Connor's

Sleeping
11. Pipers' Tryst
12. Z Hotel
13. Grasshoppers
14. Motel One
15. Babbity Bowster
16. Euro Hostel

Western Road, are close to the Botanic Gardens and Hillhead restaurant scene but farther from the center (10-minute walk to Hillhead subway stop or catch bus to center from Great Western Road).

$$ The Alfred, run by the landmark Òran Mòr restaurant/pub (located in the former church just up the street), brings a contemporary elegance to the neighborhood, with 14 new-feeling, stylish rooms (family room, includes continental breakfast, 1 Alfred Terrace, tel. 0141/357-3445, www.thealfredhotelglasgow.co.uk, alfred@thealfredhotelglasgow.co.uk).

$$ Belhaven Hotel, a little farther out (about 10 minutes past Byres Road), has 18 rooms in an elegant four-floor town-house with a pretty, tiled atrium (save money by skipping breakfast, bar in break-fast room serves drinks to guests, no ele-vator, 15 Belhaven Terrace, tel. 0141/339-3222, www.belhavenhotel.com, info@belhavenhotel.com).

$ Argyll Western, with 17 sleek and tartaned Scottish-themed rooms, feels modern, efficient, and a bit impersonal (breakfast extra, 6 Buckingham Terrace, tel. 0141/339-2339, www.argyllwestern.

co.uk, info@argyllwestern.co.uk, same family runs the Argyll Hotel, listed earlier).

TRANSPORTATION
Getting Around Glasgow
By City Bus
Most city-center routes are operated by First Bus Company (£2.20/ride, £4.50 for all-day ticket on First buses, buy tickets from driver, exact change required). Buses run every few minutes down Glasgow's main thoroughfares (such as Sauchiehall Street) to the downtown core (train stations). You can also get around the city via hop-on, hop-off bus (see "Tours in Glasgow," earlier).

By Taxi or Uber
Taxis are affordable, plentiful, and often come with nice, chatty cabbies (if your driver has an impenetrable Glaswegian accent, just smile and nod). Most taxi rides within the downtown area cost about £6; to the West End is about £8. Uber works particularly well in Glasgow and lets you make quick connections for about £5.

By Subway
Glasgow's cute little single-line subway system, nicknamed The Clockwork Orange, makes a six-mile circle that has 15 stops. While simple today, when it opened in 1896 it was a wonder (it's the world's third-oldest subway system, after those in London and Budapest). Though the subway is useless for connecting city-center sightseeing (Buchanan Street and St. Enoch are the only downtown stops), it's ideal for reaching sights farther out, including the Kelvingrove Museum (Kelvinhall stop) and West End restaurant/nightlife neighborhood (Hillhead stop). Ticket options are: £1.65 single trip, £4 for all-day ticket, or frequent riders can get a £3 Bramble card, which is reloadable (subway runs Mon-Sat 6:30-23:15, Sun 10:00-18:00, www.spt.co.uk/subway).

Arriving and Departing
If you're connecting with Edinburgh, note that the train is faster but the bus is cheaper.

Glasgow is considered the public-transit launchpad for the Highlands. For more info, see bus and train connections below, and "Getting Around the Highlands" on page 171.

Traveline Scotland has a journey planner that's linked to all of Scotland's train and bus schedule info. Go online (www.travelinescotland.com), call them at tel. 0871-200-2233, or use the individual websites listed later.

Rick's Tip: **On Sundays** and in the off-season, **bus and train schedules are dramatically reduced.** If you want to get to the Highlands by bus on a Sunday in winter, forget it.

By Train
Glasgow, a major Scottish transportation hub, has two main train stations, which are just a few blocks apart in the heart of town: **Central Station** (with a grand, genteel interior under a vast steel-and-glass Industrial Age roof) and **Queen Street Station** (more functional, with better connections to Edinburgh—take the exit marked Buchanan Street to reach the main shopping drag). Both stations have pay WCs and baggage storage. If going between the stations to change trains, you can walk five minutes or take the roundabout "RailLink" bus #398 (free with train ticket, otherwise £1.20, 5/hour; also goes to bus station). Train info: Tel. 0345-748-4950, www.nationalrail.co.uk.

TRAIN CONNECTIONS
From Glasgow's Queen Street Station to: Oban (5/day, 3 hours), **Fort William** (3/day, 4 hours), **Inverness** (5/day direct, 3 hours, more with change in Perth), **Edinburgh** (6/hour, 50 minutes), **Stirling** (3/hour, 45 minutes), **Pitlochry** (4/day direct,

1.5 hours, more with change in Perth).

From Glasgow's Central Station to:
York (hourly, 4 hours, more with change in Edinburgh), **London** (2/hour, 5 hours direct).

By Bus

Buchanan bus station is at Killermont Street, two blocks up the hill behind Queen Street Station (has luggage lockers; travel center open daily 9:00-17:00). It's a hub for reaching the Highlands. If you're coming from Edinburgh, you can take the bus to Glasgow and transfer here. Or, for a speedier connection, zip to Glasgow on the train, then walk a few short blocks to the bus station. (Ideally, try to arrive at Glasgow's Queen Street Station, which is closer to the bus station.) Bus info: Citylink—tel. 0871-266-3333, www.citylink.co.uk; National Express—tel. 0871-781-8181, www.nationalexpress.com.

BUS CONNECTIONS
From Glasgow to: Edinburgh (Citylink bus #900, 4/hour, 1.5 hours), **Oban** (Citylink buses #976 and #977; 5/day, 3 hours), **Fort William** (Citylink buses #914, #915, and #916; 8/day, 3 hours), **Glencoe** (Citylink buses #914, #915, and #916; 8/day, 2.5 hours), **Inverness** (5/day on Citylink express bus #G10, 3 hours; 1/day direct on National Express #588, 4 hours), **Portree** on the Isle of Skye (Citylink buses #915 and #916, 3/day, 7 hours), **Pitlochry** (1/day direct on National Express #588, 5/day on Megabus to Perth, then transfer to Citylink bus for Pitlochry, 2.5 hours—train is faster), **Stirling** (hourly on Citylink #M8, 45 minutes).

By Plane

Glasgow International Airport: Located eight miles west of the city, this airport has currency-exchange desks, a TI, luggage storage, and ATMs (code: GLA, tel. 0844-481-5555, www.glasgowairport.com). Taxis connect downtown to the airport for about £25. Your hotel can likely arrange a private

taxi service for £15, or you can take Uber.

Bus #500 zips to central Glasgow (every 10 minutes, 5:00-23:00, £7.50/one-way, £10/round-trip, 25 minutes to both train stations and the bus station, catch at bus stop #1). Slow bus #77 goes to the West End, stopping at the Kelvingrove Museum and rolling along Argyle Street (departs every 30 minutes, £5/one-way, 50 minutes).

Prestwick Airport: A hub for Ryanair, this airport is 30 miles southwest of the city center (code: PIK, tel. 0871-223-0700, ext. 1006, www.glasgowprestwick.com). The best connection is by train, which runs between the airport and Central Station (3/hour, 50 minutes, half-price with Ryanair ticket, trains also run to Edinburgh Waverley Station—about 2/hour, 2 hours). Stagecoach buses link the airport with Buchanan Bus Station (£10, 1-2/hour, 50 minutes, www.stagecoachbus.com).

By Car

Glasgow's downtown streets are steep, mostly one-way, congested with buses and pedestrians, and a horrible place to drive. Parking downtown is a hassle: Metered street parking is expensive (£3/hour) and limited to two hours during the day; garages are even more expensive (figure £25 for 24 hours).

Rick's Tip: *Ideally, do* **Glasgow without a car**—*for example, tour Glasgow by public transit, then* **pick up your rental car on your way out of town.**

If you are stuck with a car in Glasgow, try to sleep in the West End, where driving and parking are easier (and use public transportation or taxis as necessary).

The M-8 motorway, which slices through downtown Glasgow, is the easiest way in and out of the city. Ask your hotel for directions to and from the M-8, and connect with other highways from there.

If you'll be driving to Oban, see page 170 for a scenic route via Inveraray.

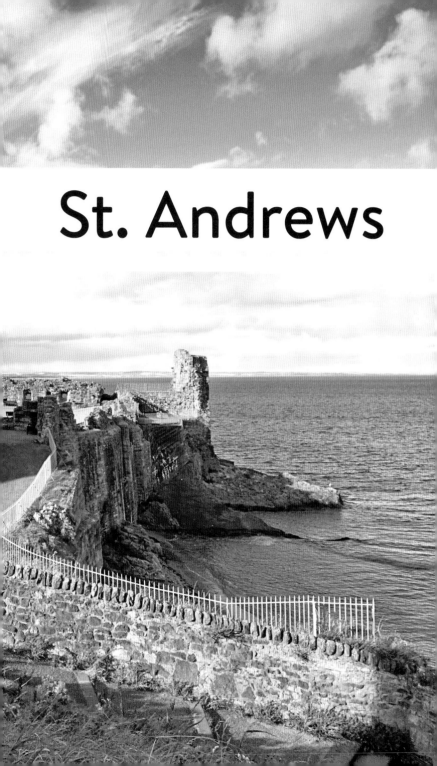

St. Andrews

S t. Andrews is synonymous with golf. But there's much more to this charming town than its famous links. Dramatically situated at the edge of a sandy bay, St. Andrews is the home of Scotland's most important university—think of it as the Scottish Cambridge. And centuries ago, the town was the religious capital of the country.

In its long history, St. Andrews has seen two boom periods. First, in the early Middle Ages, the relics of St. Andrew made the town cathedral one of the most important pilgrimage sites in Christendom. The faithful flocked here from all over Europe, leaving the town with a medieval all-roads-lead-to-the-cathedral street plan that survives today. But after the Scottish Reformation, the cathedral rotted away and the town became a forgotten backwater. A new wave of visitors arrived in the mid-19th century, when a visionary mayor (with the on-the-nose surname Playfair) began to promote the town's connection with the newly in-vogue game of golf. Most buildings in town date from this Victorian era.

St. Andrews remains a popular spot for students, golf devotees (from amateurs to professional golfers to celebrities), and occasionally Britain's favorite royal couple, Will and Kate (college sweethearts, U. of St. A. class of '05). With vast sandy beaches, golfing opportunities for pros and novices alike, playgrounds of castle and cathedral ruins, and a fun-loving student vibe, St. Andrews is an appealing place to take a vacation from your busy vacation.

Hugging the east coast of Scotland, the town is a bit off the main tourist track, but it's well connected by train to Edinburgh (via bus from nearby Leuchars), making it a worthwhile day trip from the capital. Better yet, spend a night (or more, if you're a golfer) to enjoy this university town after dark.

ST. ANDREWS IN 1 DAY

In the morning, follow my self-guided walk, which connects the golf course, the university quad, the castle, and the cathedral.

After lunch, dip into the British Golf Museum, watch the golfers on the Old Course, and play a round at "The Himalayas" putting green.

Before or after dinner, walk along the West Sands beach. Other evening options are a ghost tour, theater at the Byre, or pub-hopping in this pub-happy university town. Forgan's offers Scottish music and dancing on weekends.

If you're here to golf, reserve well in advance. But if you're not set on the

ST. ANDREWS AT A GLANCE

▲**The Old Course** The first golf course on the planet, attracting golfers from around the globe. See page 144.

▲**St. Andrews Cathedral** Ruined church once housing the relics of St. Andrew, with a cloister, cemetery, humble exhibit, and climbable tower. **Hours:** Daily April-Sept 9:30-17:30, Oct-March 10:00-16:00. See page 148.

▲**St. Andrews Preservation Trust Museum and Garden** A quaint 17th-century home, featuring replicas of an old-time grocery and pharmacy, plus a garden and old washhouse. **Hours:** June-Sept daily 14:00-17:00, closed off-season. See page 150.

▲**The Himalayas** Classy, fun minigolf course on challengingly hilly terrain. **Hours:** Mon-Fri 10:30-18:30, Sat until 18:00, Sun from 12:00, weekends only Oct and March. See page 152.

British Golf Museum Britain's best museum on the Scots' favorite sport. **Hours:** April-Oct Mon-Sat 9:30-17:00, Sun from 10:00; Nov-March daily 10:00-16:00. See page 145.

St. Andrews Castle Empty shell of a castle on the sea, offering striking views, underground tunnels, and a small museum. **Hours:** Daily April-Sept 9:30-17:30, Oct-March 10:00-16:00. See page 147.

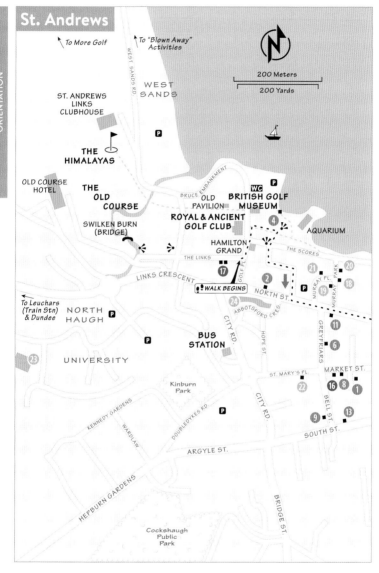

St. Andrews

To More Golf

To "Blown Away" Activities

WEST SANDS RD.

WEST SANDS

200 Meters
200 Yards

ST. ANDREWS LINKS CLUBHOUSE

THE HIMALAYAS

OLD COURSE HOTEL

THE OLD COURSE

BRUCE EMBANKMENT

OLD PAVILION

WC

BRITISH GOLF MUSEUM

ROYAL & ANCIENT GOLF CLUB

SWILKEN BURN (BRIDGE)

AQUARIUM

HAMILTON GRAND

THE SCORES

THE LINKS

LINKS CRESCENT

GOLF PL.

17

WALK BEGINS

21

MURRAY PL.

PARK

20

19

MURRAY

18

To Leuchars (Train Stn) & Dundee

NORTH HAUGH

2

NORTH ST.

24

ABBOTSFORD CRES.

P

11

CITY RD.

HOPE ST.

6

BUS STATION

GREYFRIARS

UNIVERSITY

23

Kinburn Park

ST. MARY'S PL.

MARKET ST.

22

16

8

1

KENNEDY GARDENS

WARDLAW

DOUBLEDYKES RD.

CITY RD.

9

BELL ST.

13

SOUTH ST.

ARGYLE ST.

HEPBURN GARDENS

BRIDGE ST.

Cockshaugh Public Park

famous Old Course, you'll have more flexibility getting a tee time on shorter notice. Read "Golfing" (later in chapter) for your options. Build your sightseeing around your course time and extend your visit by a half-day or more.

ORIENTATION

St. Andrews (pop. 16,000, plus several-thousand more students during term) is situated at the tip of a peninsula next to a broad bay. The town retains its old medieval street plan: Three main streets (North, Market, and South) converge at

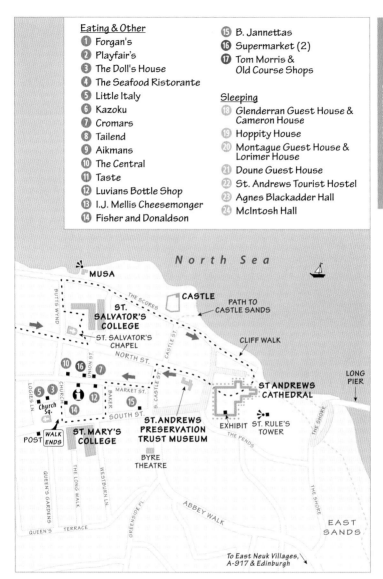

Eating & Other
1. Forgan's
2. Playfair's
3. The Doll's House
4. The Seafood Ristorante
5. Little Italy
6. Kazoku
7. Cromars
8. Tailend
9. Aikmans
10. The Central
11. Taste
12. Luvians Bottle Shop
13. I.J. Mellis Cheesemonger
14. Fisher and Donaldson
15. B. Jannettas
16. Supermarket (2)
17. Tom Morris & Old Course Shops

Sleeping
18. Glenderran Guest House & Cameron House
19. Hoppity House
20. Montague Guest House & Lorimer House
21. Doune Guest House
22. St. Andrews Tourist Hostel
23. Agnes Blackadder Hall
24. McIntosh Hall

the cathedral, which overlooks the sea at the tip of town. The middle street—Market Street—has the TI and many handy shops and eateries. North of North Street, the seafront street called The Scores connects the cathedral with the golf scene, which huddles along the West Sands beach at the base of the old town.

St. Andrews is compact: You can stroll across town—from the cathedral to the historic golf course—in about 15 minutes.

Tourist Information

St. Andrews' helpful TI is on Market Street, about two blocks in front of the cathedral (Mon-Sat 9:15-17:00, Sun from

10:00, closed Sun in winter; free Wi-Fi, 70 Market Street, tel. 01334/472-021, www. visitscotland.com).

Helpful Hints

School Term: The University of St. Andrews has two terms: spring semester ("Candlemas"), from mid-February through May; and fall semester ("Martinmas"), from mid-September until December. St. Andrews has a totally different vibe in the summer (June-mid-Sept), when most students leave and are replaced by upper-crust golfers and tourists.

Rick's Tip: *The best time to see* **students in traditional garb** *is during the* **Pier Walk on Sundays** *when school is in session. Around noon, students—with their red robes flapping in the North Sea wind—parade out to the end of the pier beyond the cathedral ruins.*

Sand Surfing and Adventure Activities: Nongolfers may enjoy some of the adventure activities offered by **Blown Away**—including "land yachting" (zipping across the beach in wind-powered go-carts), kayaking, and paddle boarding. Brothers Guy and Jamie McKenzie set up shop at the northern tip of the West Sands beach (sporadic hours—call first, mobile 07784-121-125, www.blownaway.co.uk, ahoy@blownaway.co.uk).

Ghost Tours: Richard Falconer, who has researched and written books on paranormal activity in the area, gives 1.5-hour tours mixing St. Andrews history with ghost stories (£12, tours at 16:00, 17:30, 19:30, and 21:00, must book ahead, text 0746-296-3163 or visit www.standrewsghosttours.com).

ST. ANDREWS WALK

This walk links all of St. Andrews' must-see sights and takes you down hidden medieval streets. Allow a couple of hours, or more if you detour for the sights along the way.

⊙ Self-Guided Walk

• *Start at the base of the seaside street called The Scores, overlooking the famous golf course.*

▲ The Old Course

You're looking at the mecca of golf. The 18th hole of the world's first golf course is a few yards away, on your left (for info on playing the course, see "Golfing," later).

The gray Neoclassical building to the right of the 18th hole is the clubhouse of the **Royal and Ancient Golf Club**—"R&A" for short. R&A is a private club with membership by invitation only; it was men-only until 2014, but now—finally!—women are also allowed to join. (In Scotland, men-only clubs lose tax benefits, which is quite costly, but they generally don't care about expenses because their membership is wealthy.) The shop (across the street from the 18th hole, next to Tom Morris—the oldest golf shop in the world) is a great spot to buy a souvenir for the golf lover back home. Even if you're not golfing, watch the action for a while. (Serious fans can walk around to the low-profile stone bridge across the creek called the Swilken Burn, with golf's single most iconic view: back over the 18th hole and the R&A Clubhouse.)

Rick's Tip: *Every five years, St. Andrews is swamped with about 100,000 visitors when it hosts the* **British Open** *(officially called "The Open Championship"; the next one will be the 150th in 2021). Unless you're a golf pilgrim, avoid the town at these times, as room rates skyrocket.*

Overlooking the course is the big red-sandstone **Hamilton Grand,** an old hotel that was turned into university dorms and then swanky apartments (rumor has it Samuel L. Jackson owns one). According to town legend, the Hamilton Grand was originally built to upstage the R&A Clubhouse by an American upset over being declined membership to the exclusive club.

The Old Course

• *Between Hamilton Grand and the beach is the low-profile British Golf Museum. I'd suggest saving it for later, but golfers may want to visit it now.*

British Golf Museum

This exhibit, which started as a small collection in the R&A Clubhouse across the street, is the best place in Britain to learn about the Scots' favorite sport. It's fascinating for golf lovers.

Cost and Hours: £8, April-Oct Mon-Sat 9:30-17:00, Sun from 10:00; Nov-March daily 10:00-16:00; café upstairs; Bruce Embankment, in the blocky modern building squatting behind the R&A Clubhouse by the Old Course, tel. 01334/460-046, www.britishgolfmuseum.co.uk.

Visiting the Museum: The compact, one-way exhibit reverently presents a meticulous survey of the game's history. Start with the film, then follow the counterclockwise route to learn about the evolution of golf—from the monarchs who loved and hated golf (including the king who outlawed it because it was distracting men from church and archery practice), to Tom Morris and Bobby

Jones, all the way up to the "Golden Bear" and a randy Tiger. Along the way, you'll see plenty of old clubs, balls, medals, and trophies, and learn about how the earliest "feathery" balls and wooden clubs were made. Touchscreens invite you to learn more, and you'll also see a "hall of fame" with items donated by today's biggest golfers. Finally, you'll have a chance to dress up in some old-school golfing duds and try out some of that antique equipment for yourself.

• *Turn your back to the golf course and walk through the park toward the obelisk (along the street called The Scores). Stop at the top of the bluff.*

Beach Viewpoint

The broad, two-mile-long sandy beach that stretches below the golf course is the **West Sands.** It's a wonderful place for a relaxing and/or invigorating walk. Or do a slo-mo jog, humming the theme to *Chariots of Fire*—this is the beach on which the characters run in the movie's famous opening scene.

From the bluff look at the **cliffs** on your right. The sea below was once called "Witches' Lake" because of all the women and men pushed off the cliff on suspicion of witchcraft.

The big obelisk is a **martyrs' monument,** commemorating all those who died for their Protestant beliefs during the Scottish Reformation.

The Victorian bandstand **gazebo** (between here and the Old Course) recalls the town's genteel heyday as a seaside resort, when the train line ran all the way to town.

• *Just opposite the obelisk, across The Scores and next to Alexander's Restaurant, walk down the tiny alley called...*

Gillespie Wynd

This winds through the back gardens of the city's stone houses. Notice how the medieval platting gave each landowner a little bit of street front and a long back garden. St. Andrews' street plan typifies that of a medieval pilgrimage town: All main roads lead to the cathedral; only tiny lanes, hidden alleys, and twisting "wynds" (rhymes with "minds") such as this one connect the main east-west streets.

• *The wynd pops you out onto North Street. Head left, past the cinema toward the church tower with the red clock face. It's on the corner of North Street and Butts Wynd. For some reason, this street sign often goes missing.*

St. Salvator's College

The tower with the red clock marks the entrance to St. Salvator's College. If you're a student, be careful not to stand on the **initials PH** in the reddish cobbles in front of the gate. These mark the spot where St. Andrews alum and professor Patrick Hamilton—the Scottish Reformation's most famous martyr—was burned at the stake. According to student legend, as he suffered in the flames, Hamilton threatened that any students who stood on this spot would fail their exams.

Now enter the grounds by walking through the arch under the tower. (If the entrance is closed, you can go halfway down Butts Wynd and enter, or at least look, through the gate to the green square.) This grassy square, known to students as **Sally's Quad,** is the heart of the university. As most of the university's classrooms, offices, and libraries are spread out across the medieval town, this quad is the one focal point for student

St. Salvator's College

gatherings. It's where graduation is held every July, and where almost the entire student body gathered on the wedding day of their famous alumni couple Prince William and Kate Middleton for a celebration complete with military flybys.

On the outside wall of St. Salvator's Chapel, under the arcade, are **display cases** holding notices and university information; if you're here in spring, you might see students nervously clustered here, looking to see if they've passed their exams.

Go through the simple wooden door and into the **chapel.** Dating from 1450, this is the town's most beautiful medieval church. It's a Gothic gem, with a wooden ceiling, 19th-century stained glass, a glorious organ, and what's supposedly the pulpit of reformer John Knox.

Stroll around Sally's Quad counterclockwise. On the east (far) side, stop to check out the crazy faces on the heads above the second-floor windows. Find the **university's shield** over the door marked *School 6*. The diamonds are from the coat of arms of the bishop who issued the first university charter in 1411; the crescent moon is a shout-out to Pope Benedict XIII, who gave the OK in 1413 to found the university (his given name was Peter de Luna); the lion is from the Scottish coat of arms; and the X-shaped cross is a stylized version of the Scottish flag (a.k.a. St. Andrew's Cross). On the next building to the left, facing the chapel, is St. Andrew himself (above door of building labeled *Lower & Upper College Halls*).

• *Exit the square and make your way back to Butts Wynd. Walk to the end; you're back at The Scores. Across the street and a few steps to the right is the…*

Museum of the University of St. Andrews (MUSA)

This free museum is worth a quick stop. The first room has some well-explained medieval artifacts. Find the copy of the earliest-known map of the town, made

in 1580—back when the town walls led directly to the countryside and the cathedral was intact. Notice that the street plan within the town walls has remained the same—but no golf course. The next room has some exhibits on student life, including the "silver arrow competition" (which determined the best archer on campus from year to year). The next room displays scientific equipment, great books tied to the school, and an exhibit on the Scottish Reformation. The final room has special exhibits. For a great view of the West Sands, climb to the rooftop terrace.

Cost and Hours: Free; Mon-Sat 10:00-17:00, Sun 12:00-16:00, shorter hours and closed Mon-Wed in winter; 7 The Scores, tel. 01334/461-660, www.st-andrews. ac.uk/musa.

• *Leaving the museum, walk left toward the castle. The turreted stone buildings along here (including one fine example next door to the museum) are built in the Neo-Gothic Scottish Baronial style, and most are academic departments. About 100 yards farther along, the grand building on the right is St. Salvator's Hall, the most prestigious of the university residences and former dorm of Prince William.*

Just past St. Salvator's Hall on the left are the remains of…

St. Andrews Castle

Overlooking the sea, the castle is an evocative empty shell—another casualty of the Scottish Reformation. With a small museum and good descriptions, it offers a quick king-of-the-castle experience in a striking setting.

Cost and Hours: £6, £9 combo-ticket includes cathedral exhibit, daily April-Sept 9:30-17:30, Oct-March 10:00-16:00, tel. 01334/477-196, www.historic-scotland. gov.uk.

Visiting the Castle: Your visit starts with a colorful, kid-friendly exhibit about the history of the castle. Built by a bishop to entertain visiting diplomats in the late 12th century, the castle was home to the

St. Andrews Castle

powerful bishops, archbishops, and cardinals of St. Andrews. In 1546, the cardinal burned a Protestant preacher at the stake in front of the castle. In retribution, Protestant reformers took the castle and killed the cardinal. In 1547, the French came to attack the castle on behalf of their Catholic ally, Mary, Queen of Scots. During the ensuing siege, a young Protestant refugee named John Knox was captured and sent to France to row on a galley ship. Eventually he traveled to Switzerland and met the Swiss Protestant ringleader, John Calvin. Knox brought Calvin's ideas back home and became Scotland's greatest reformer.

Next, head outside to explore. The most interesting parts are underground: the "bottle dungeon," where prisoners were sent, never to return (peer down into it in the Sea Tower); and the tight "mine" and even tighter "counter-mine" tunnels (follow the signs, crawling is required to reach it all; go in as far as your claustrophobia allows). This shows how the besieging pro-Catholic Scottish government of the day dug a mine to take (or "undermine") the castle—but were followed at every turn by the Protestant counter-miners.

Nearby: Just below the castle is a small beach called the **Castle Sands,** where university students take a traditional and chilly morning dip on May 1. Supposedly, doing this May Day swim is the only way to reverse the curse of having stepped on Patrick Hamilton's initials (explained earlier).

• *Leaving the castle, turn left and continue along the bluff on The Scores, which soon becomes a pedestrian lane leading directly to the gate to the cathedral graveyard. Enter it to stand amid the tombstone-strewn ruins of...*

▲St. Andrews Cathedral

Between the Great Schism and the Reformation (roughly the 14th-16th centuries), St. Andrews was the ecclesiastical capital of Scotland—and this was its showpiece church. Today the site features the remains of the cathedral and cloister (with walls and spires pecked away by centuries of scavengers), a graveyard, and a small exhibit and climbable tower.

Cost and Hours: Cathedral ruins-free, exhibit and tower-£5, £9 combo-ticket includes castle; daily April-Sept 9:30-17:30, Oct-March 10:00-16:00, tel.

The ruined St. Andrews Cathedral and its graveyard

01334/472-563, www.historic-scotland.gov.uk.

Background: It was the relics of the Apostle Andrew that first put this town on the map and gave it its name. There are numerous legends associated with the relics. According to one version, in the fourth century, St. Rule was directed in a dream to bring the relics northward from Constantinople. When the ship wrecked offshore from here, it was clear that this was a sacred place. Andrew's bones (an upper arm, a kneecap, some fingers, and a tooth) were kept on this site, and starting in 1160, the cathedral was built and pilgrims began to arrive. Since St. Andrew had a direct connection to Jesus, his relics were believed to possess special properties, making them worthy of pilgrimages on par with St. James' relics in Santiago de Compostela, Spain (of Camino de Santiago fame). St. Andrew became Scotland's patron saint; in fact, the white "X" on the blue Scottish flag evokes the diagonal cross on which St. Andrew was crucified (he chose this type of cross because he felt unworthy to die as Jesus had).

Visiting the Cathedral: You can stroll around the cathedral **ruins**—the best part of the complex—for free. First, walk between the two ruined but still towering ends of the church, which used to be the apse (at the sea end, where you entered) and the main entry (at the town end). Visually trace the gigantic footprint of the former church in the ground, including the bases of columns—like giant sawed-off tree trunks. Plaques identify where elements of the church once stood.

Looking at the one wall that's still standing, you can see the architectural changes that were made over the 150 years the cathedral was built—from the rounded, Romanesque windows at the front to the more highly decorated, pointed Gothic arches near the back. Try to imagine this church in its former majesty, when it played host to pilgrims from all over Europe.

The church wasn't destroyed all at once, like all those ruined abbeys in England (demolished in a huff by Henry VIII when he broke with the pope). Instead, because the Scottish Reformation was more gradual, this church was slowly picked apart over time. First just the decorations were removed from inside the cathedral. Then the roof was pulled down to make use of its lead. Without a roof, the cathedral fell further and further into disrepair, and was quarried by locals for its handy precut stones (which can still be found in the walls of many old St. Andrews homes). The elements—a big storm in the 1270s and a fire in 1378—also contributed to the cathedral's demise.

The surrounding **graveyard,** dating from the post-Reformation Protestant era, is much more recent than the cathedral. In this golf-obsessed town, the game even infiltrates the cemeteries: Many notable golfers from St. Andrews are buried here, including four-time British Open winner Young Tom "Tommy" Morris.

Go through the surviving wall into the former **cloister,** marked by a gigantic grassy square in the center. You can still see the cleats up on the wall, which once supported beams. Imagine the cloister back in its heyday, its passages filled with strolling monks.

At the end of the cloister is a small **exhibit** (entry fee required), with a relatively dull collection of old tombs and other carved-stone relics that have been unearthed on this site. Your ticket also includes entry to the surviving **tower of St. Rule's Church** (the rectangular tower beyond the cathedral ruins that was built to hold the precious relics of St. Andrew about a thousand years ago). If you feel like hiking up the 157 very claustrophobic steps for the view over St. Andrews' rooftops, it's worth the price.
• *Leave the cathedral grounds on the town side of the cathedral. Angling right, head down North Street. Just ahead, on the left, is the adorable...*

▲St. Andrews Preservation Trust Museum and Garden

Filling a 17th-century fishing family's house that was protected from developers, this museum is a time capsule of an earlier, simpler era. The house itself seems built for Smurfs, but it once housed 20 family members. The ground floor features replicas of a grocer's shop and a "chemist's" (pharmacy), using original fittings from actual stores. Upstairs are temporary exhibits. Out back is a tranquil garden (dedicated to the memory of a beloved professor) with "great-grandma's washhouse," featuring an exhibit about the history of soap and washing. Lovingly presented, this quaint, humble house provides a nice contrast to the big-money scene around the golf course at the other end of town.

Cost and Hours: Free but donation requested, generally open June-Sept daily 14:00-17:00, closed off-season, 12 North Street, tel. 01334/477-629, www.standrewspreservationtrust.org.
• *From the museum, hang a left around the next corner to South Castle Street. Soon you'll reach...*

Market Street

At the top of Market Street—one of the most atmospheric old streets in town—look for the tiny white house on your left, with the cute curved staircase. What's that chase scene on the roof?

Now turn right down Market Street (which leads directly to the town's center, but we'll take a curvier route). Notice how the streets and even the buildings are smaller at this oldest end of town, as if the whole city is shrinking as the streets close in on the cathedral. Homeowners along Market Street are particularly proud of their address, and recently pooled their money to spiff up the cobbles and sidewalks.

Passing an antique bookstore on your right, take a left onto Baker Lane, a.k.a. Baxter Wynd. You'll pass a tiny and inviting public garden on your right before landing on South Street.
• *Turn right and head down South Street. After 50 yards, cross the street and enter a gate marked by a cute gray facade and a university insignia.*

St. Mary's College

This is the home of the university's School of Divinity (theology). If the gate's open, find the peaceful quad, with its gnarled tree that was purportedly planted by Mary, Queen of Scots. To get a feel of student life from centuries past, try poking your nose into one of the old classrooms.

• *Back on South Street, continue to your left. Some of the plainest buildings on this stretch of the street have the most interesting history—several of them were built to fund the Crusades. Turn right on Church Street. You can end this walk at charming Church Square—perhaps while enjoying a decadent pastry from the recommended Fisher and Donaldson bakery. Or, if you continue a few more yards down Church Street, you'll spill onto Market Street and the heart of town.*

EXPERIENCES

Golfing

St. Andrews is the Cooperstown of golf. While St. Andrews lays claim to founding the sport (the first record of golf being played here was in 1553), nobody knows exactly where and when people first hit a ball with a stick for fun. In the Middle Ages, St. Andrews traded with the Dutch; some historians believe they picked up a golf-like Dutch game played on ice and translated it to the bonnie rolling hills of Scotland's east coast. Since the grassy beachfront strip just outside St. Andrews was too poor to support crops, it was used for playing the game—and, centuries later, it still is. For much more on the sport, visit the British Golf Museum (described earlier).

THE OLD COURSE

The Old Course hosts the British Open every five years (next in 2021). At other times it's open to the public for golfing. The famous Royal and Ancient Golf Club (R&A) doesn't actually own the course, which is public and managed by the St. Andrews Links Trust. Drop by the St. Andrews Links Clubhouse, overlooking the beach near the Old Course (open long hours daily). They have a well-stocked shop, a restaurant, and a rooftop garden with nice views over the Old Course.

Old Course Tours: One-hour guided tours visit the 1st, 17th, and 18th holes (£10, daily April-May at 11:00, June-Sept at 11:00 and 14:00, leaves from the St. Andrews Links Clubhouse, tel. 01334/466-666, www.standrews.com).

Teeing Off at the Old Course: Playing at golf's pinnacle course is pricey (£175/person, less off-season), but open to the public—subject to lottery drawings for tee times and reserved spots by club members. You can play the Old Course only if you have a handicap of 24 (men) or 36 (women and juniors) or better; bring along your certificate or card. If you don't know your handicap—or don't know what "handicap" means—then you're not good enough to play here (they want to keep the game moving). If you play, you'll do nine holes out, then nine more back in—however, all but four share the same greens.

Reserving a Tee Time: To ensure a specific tee time at the Old Course, reserve a year ahead during a brief window between late August and early September (fill out form at www.standrews.com). Otherwise, some tee times are determined each day by a lottery called the "daily ballot." Enter your name on their website, in person, or by calling 01334/466-666—by 14:00 two days before (2 players minimum, 4 players max). They post the results online at 16:00. Note that no advance reservations are taken on Saturdays or in September, and the courses are closed on Sundays—which is traditionally the day reserved for townspeople to stroll.

Rick's Tip: Golfers save money by *skipping the Old Course and* **playing at other courses** *nearby, which are less expensive and easier to reserve.*

Other Courses: Two of the seven St. Andrews Links courses are right next to the Old Course—the New Course and the Jubilee Course. And the modern clifftop Castle Course is just outside the city. These are cheaper, and it's much easier to get a tee time (£75 for New and Jubilee, £120 for Castle Course, much less for others). It's usually possible to get a tee time for the same day or next day (if you want a guaranteed reservation, make it at least 2 weeks in advance). The Castle Course has great views overlooking the town, but even more wind to blow your ball around.

Club Rental: You can rent decent-quality clubs around town for about £30. The **Auchterlonies** shop has a good reputation (on Golf Place—a few doors down from the R&A Clubhouse, tel. 01334/473-253, www.auchterlonies.com); you can also rent clubs from the St. Andrews Links Clubhouse for a few pounds more.

▲**THE HIMALAYAS**

The St. Andrews Ladies' Putting Club, better known as "The Himalayas" (for its dramatically hilly terrain), is basically a very classy (but still relaxed) game of minigolf. The course presents the perfect opportunity for nongolfers (female or male) to say they've played the links at St. Andrews—for less than the cost of a Coke. It's remarkable how this cute little patch of undulating grass can present even more challenging obstacles than the tunnels, gates, and distractions of a miniature golf course back home. Flat shoes are required (no high heels). You'll see it on the left as you walk toward the St. Andrews Links Clubhouse from the R&A Clubhouse.

Cost and Hours: £3 for 18 holes. The putting green is open to nonmembers (tourists like you) Mon-Fri 10:30-18:30, Sat until 18:00, Sun from 12:00, weekends only Oct and March, closed in winter, tel. 01334/475-196, www.standrewsputtingclub.com.

EATING

Restaurants

$$$ Forgan's is tempting and popular, tucked back in a huge space behind Market Street in what feels like a former warehouse. It's done up country-kitschy, with high ceilings, cool lanterns, and a fun energy. It serves up hearty food and offers a tempting steak selection (daily 12:00-22:00, reservations smart, 110 Market Street, tel. 01334/466-973, www.forgansstandrews.co.uk). On Friday and Saturday nights after 22:30, they have live *ceilidh* (traditional Scottish) music, and everyone joins in the dancing; consider reserving a booth for a late dinner, then stick around for the show. They also have live acoustic music on Thursday evenings.

$$$ Playfair's, a restaurant and steakhouse downstairs in the Ardgowan Hotel between the B&B neighborhood and the Old Course, has a cozy/classy interior and outdoor seating at rustic tables set just below the busy street. Their bar next door also serves food (daily 12:00-22:00, off-season weekdays open for dinner only, 2 Playfair Terrace on North Street, tel. 01334/472-970).

$$$ The Doll's House serves dressed-up Scottish cuisine in a stone-and-wood interior or at tables on the square in front, complete with fur throws on the chairs (daily 10:00-22:00, across from Holy Trinity Church at 3 Church Square, tel. 01334/477-422).

$$$$ The Seafood Ristorante, in a modern glassy building overlooking the beach near the Old Course, is like dining in an aquarium. They serve high-end Italian with a focus on seafood in a formal space with floor-to-ceiling windows providing unhindered views (minimum £20/person food order at dinner, daily 12:00-14:30 & 18:00-21:30, reservations a must on weekends and in summer, Bruce Embankment, tel. 01334/479-475, www.theseafoodristorante.com).

$$ Little Italy is a crowded Italian joint with all the clichés—red-and-white checkered tablecloths, replica Roman busts, a bit of freneticism, and even a moped in the wall. But the food is authentically good and the menu is massive. It's popular—make reservations (daily 12:30-22:30, 2 Logies Lane, tel. 01334/479-299).

$$ Kazoku is a casual and satisfying sushi bar that also serves some hot Japanese dishes (seared scallops on a bed of haggis, anyone?). It's a family business—the name means "family" in Japanese (daily 12:00-14:30 & 17:00-21:30, 6A Greyfriars Gardens, tel. 01334/477-750).

Fish-and-Chips: $ Cromars is a local favorite for takeaway fish-and-chips (and burgers). At the counter, you can order yours to go, or—in good weather—enjoy it at the sidewalk tables; farther in is a small **$$ sit-down restaurant** with more choices (both open daily 11:00-22:00, at the corner of Union and Market, tel. 01334/475-555). **Tailend** also has a **$ takeaway counter** up front (fish-and-chips) and a **$$ restaurant** with a bigger selection in the back (daily 11:30-22:00, 130 Market Street, tel. 01334/474-070).

Beer, Coffee, and Whisky

Pubs: There's no shortage in this college town. These aren't "gastropubs," but they all serve straightforward pub fare (all open long hours daily).

Aikmans, run by Barbara and Malcolm (two graduates from the university who couldn't bring themselves to leave), features a cozy wood-table ambience, a focus on ales, live music (usually Fri-Sat), and simple soups, sandwiches, and snacks (32 Bell Street, tel. 01334/477-425). **The Central,** right along Market Street, is a St. Andrews standby, with old lamps and lots of brass (77 Market Street, tel. 01334/478-296).

Coffee: $ Taste, a little café just across the street from the B&B neighborhood, has the best coffee in town and a laidback, borderline-funky ambience that feels like a big-city coffeehouse back home. It also serves cakes and light food (daily 7:00-18:00 in summer, open later when students are back, 148 North Street, tel. 01334/477-959).

Whisky: Luvians Bottle Shop—run by three brothers (Luigi, Vincenzo, and Antonio)—is a friendly place to talk, taste, and purchase whisky. Distilleries bottle unique single-cask vintages exclusively for this shop to celebrate the British Open every five years (ask about the 21-year-old Springbank they received in 2015 to commemorate the tournament). With nearly 50 bottles open for tastings, a map of Scotland's whisky regions, and helpful team members, this is a handy spot to learn about whisky. They also sell fine wines and a wide range of microbrews (Mon-Sat 10:00-22:00, Sun from 12:30, 66 Market Street, tel. 01334/477-752).

Rick's Tip: *For the* **town's best gelato,** *head to* **B. Jannettas,** *which has been around for more than a century. Choose from 50-plus flavors (daily 9:00-22:00, 31 South Street).*

Picnic Food and Sweets

Cheese: I.J. Mellis Cheesemonger, the excellent Edinburgh shop with a delectable array of Scottish, English, and international cheeses, has a branch here (Mon-Sat 9:00-19:00, Sun 10:00-17:00, 149 South Street, tel. 01334/471-410).

Pastries: Fisher and Donaldson is beloved for its rich, affordable pastries and chocolates. Listen as the straw-hatted bakers chat with customers, then try their Coffee Tower—like a giant cream puff filled with rich, lightly coffee-flavored cream—or their top seller, the fudge doughnut (Mon-Sat 6:00-17:00, closed Sun, just around the corner from the TI at 13 Church Street, tel. 01334/472-201).

Supermarkets: You can stock up for a picnic at **Tesco** or **Sainsbury's Local** on Market Street.

SLEEPING

Owing partly to the high-roller golf tourists flowing through the town, St. Andrews' accommodations are quite expensive. During graduation week in June, hotels often require a four-night stay and book up quickly. All of the guesthouses I've listed are on the streets called Murray Park and Murray Place, between North Street and The Scores in the Old Town. If you need to find a room on the fly, look around in this same neighborhood, which has far more options than the ones I've listed below.

$$$ Glenderran Guest House offers five plush rooms (including two true singles) and a few nice breakfast extras (no kids under 12, pay same-day laundry, 9 Murray Park, tel. 01334/477-951, www. glenderran.com, info@glenderran.com, Ray and Maggie).

$$ Hoppity House is a bright and contemporary place, with attention to detail and fun hosts Gordon and Heather, who are helpful and generous with travel tips. There's a lounge and kitchen for guest use and a storage closet for golf equipment. You may find a stuffed namesake bunny or two hiding out among its four impeccable rooms (cash or PayPal only, fridges in rooms, 4 Murray Park, tel. 01334/461-116, mobile 07701-099-100, www.hoppityhouse.co.uk, enquiries@hoppityhouse.co.uk).

$$ Cameron House has five clean and simple rooms around a beautiful stained-glass atrium (two-night minimum in summer, 11 Murray Park, tel. 01334/472-306, www.cameronhouse-sta.co.uk, info@cameronhouse-sta.co.uk, Donna).

$ Montague Guest House has richly furnished public spaces—with a cozy, leather-couches lounge/breakfast room—and eight nice rooms (21 Murray Park, tel. 01334/479-287, www.montaguehouse.com, info@montagueguesthouse.com, Raj and Judith).

$$ Lorimer House has six comfortable, tastefully decorated rooms, including one on the ground floor (two-night minimum preferred, no kids under 12, 19 Murray Park, tel. 01334/476-599, www.lorimerhouse.com, info@lorimerhouse.com, Mick and Chris).

$$ Doune Guest House's seven rooms provide a more impersonal but perfectly comfortable place to stay in St. Andrews (breakfast extra, two-night minimum preferred in summer, 5 Murray Place, tel. 01334/475-195, www.dounehouse.com, info@dounehouse.com).

¢ St. Andrews Tourist Hostel has 44 beds in colorful 5- to 8-bed rooms about a block from the base of Market Street. The high-ceilinged lounge is a comfy place for a break, and the friendly staff is happy to recommend their favorite pubs (kitchen, St. Mary's Place, tel. 01334/479-911, www.hostelsstandrews.com, info@hostelsstandrews.com).

University Accommodations

In the summer (early June-Aug), some of the University of St. Andrews' student-housing buildings are tidied up and rented out to tourists. I've listed the most convenient options below (website for both: www.discoverstandrews.com; pay when reserving). Both of these include breakfast and Wi-Fi. Because true single rooms are rare in St. Andrews' B&Bs, these dorms are a good option for solo travelers.

$ Agnes Blackadder Hall has double beds and private bathrooms; it's more comfortable, but also more expensive and less central (North Haugh, tel. 01334/467-000, agnes.blackadder@st-andrews.ac.uk).

$ McIntosh Hall is cheaper and more central, but it only has twin beds and shared bathrooms (Abbotsford Crescent, tel. 01334/467-035, mchall@st-andrews.ac.uk).

TRANSPORTATION

Arriving and Departing
By Train

The nearest train station is in the village of Leuchars, five miles away. From there, a

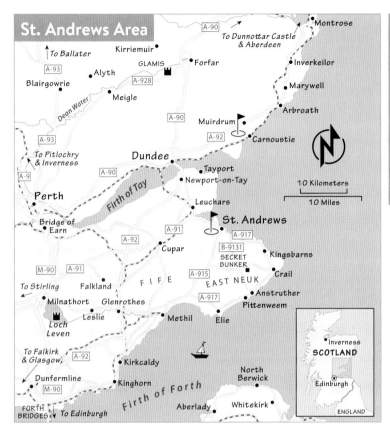

St. Andrews Area

10-minute bus ride takes you right into St. Andrews (2-4/hour, buy ticket from driver, buses meet most trains—see schedule at bus shelter for next bus to St. Andrews; while waiting, read the historical info under the nearby flagpole). St. Andrews' bus station is near the base of Market Street—a short walk from most B&Bs and the TI. A taxi from Leuchars into St. Andrews costs about £14.

Train Connections from Leuchars to: **Edinburgh** (1-2/hour, 1 hour), **Glasgow** (2/hour, 2 hours, transfer in Haymarket), **Inverness** (roughly hourly, 3.5 hours, 1-2 changes). Trains run less frequently on Sundays. Train info: Tel. 0345-748-4950, www.nationalrail.co.uk.

By Car

For a short stay, drivers can park anywhere along the street in the town center (pay-and-display, coins only, 2-hour limit, monitored Mon-Sat 9:00-17:00, Sun from 13:00). For longer stays, ask your hotelier for advice. You can park for free along certain streets near the center (such as the small lot near the B&B neighborhood around Murray Place, and along The Scores), or use one of the pay-and-display lots near the entrance to town.

Oban & the
Inner Hebrides

For a taste of Scotland's west coast, the port town of Oban is equal parts endearing and functional. This busy little ferry-and-train terminal has no important sights, but makes up the difference in character, in scenery (with its low-impact panorama of overlapping islets and bobbing boats), and with one of Scotland's best distillery tours. Oban is also convenient: It's midway between the Lowland cities (Glasgow and Edinburgh) and the Highland riches of the north (Glencoe, Isle of Skye). And it's the "gateway to the isles," with handy ferry service to the Hebrides Islands.

Oban is ideally situated for a busy and memorable full-day side-trip to three of the most worthwhile Inner Hebrides: big, rugged Mull; pristine little Iona, where buoyant clouds float over its historic abbey; and Staffa, a remote, grassy islet inhabited only by sea birds. (The best of the Inner Hebrides—the Isle of Skye—is covered in its own chapter.) Sit back, let someone else do the driving, and enjoy a tour of the Inner Hebrides.

OBAN & THE INNER HEBRIDES IN 2 DAYS

You'll need two nights to enjoy Oban's main attraction: the side-trip to Mull, Iona, and Staffa. There are few actual sights in Oban itself, beyond the excellent distillery tour, but—thanks to its manageable size, scenic waterfront setting, and great restaurants—the town is an enjoyable place to linger.

Drivers coming from Glasgow can follow a scenic route via Inveraray (see page 170), arrive in Oban by midday, get oriented to the town, and take the distillery tour (and visit more sights as time allows). Devote the next day to visiting the islands.

Evening options in Oban include dinner at a seafood restaurant, live traditional music at pubs, music and dancing at Skipinnish Ceilidh House, a movie at the Phoenix Cinema, or a waterfront stroll.

OBAN

Oban (pronounced OH-bin) is a low-key resort. Its winding promenade is lined by gravel beaches, ice-cream stands, fish-and-chips joints, a tourable distillery, and a good choice of restaurants. Everything in Oban is close together, and the town seems eager to please its many visitors: Wool and tweed are perpetually on sale, and posters announce a variety of day tours to Scotland's wild and wildlife-strewn western islands. When the rain clears, sun-starved Scots sit on benches along the Esplanade, leaning back to catch some rays. Wind, boats, gulls, layers of islands, and the promise of a wide-open Atlantic beyond give Oban a rugged charm.

OBAN & THE INNER HEBRIDES AT A GLANCE

▲▲**Oban** Handy, personable port for the Inner Hebrides, with a few sights of its own, including a distillery tour. See page 158.

▲▲▲**Day Trip to Inner Hebrides** Fascinating ferry-and-bus tour of three distinctly different islands: Mull, Iona, and Staffa. See page 172.

▲**Mull** A large, mountainous island with Ben More ("Big Mountain"), foggy scenery, laid-back people, and ferries to Iona and Staffa. See page 175.

▲▲**Iona** Small, historic island, considered the birthplace of Christianity in Scotland, with an abbey and town. See page 176.

▲**Staffa** Tiny, uninhabited island featuring puffins (cute migratory birds) and Fingal's Cave, with unusual basalt formations. See page 179.

The Scottish Highlands

Filled with natural and historical mystique, the Highlands are where Scottish dreams are set, amid legends of Bonnie Prince Charlie, crumbling castles, and tunes played by kilt-clad pipers.

The Highlands are covered with mountains, lochs, and glens, scarcely leaving a flat patch of land for building a big city. Inverness is the Highlands' de facto capital, and often claims to be the region's only city. The Highlands occupy more than half of Scotland's area, but are populated by less than five percent of its people.

Scotland's Hebrides Islands (among them Skye, Mull, Iona, and Staffa), while not strictly the Highlands, are often included simply because they share much of the same culture, clan history, and Celtic ties.

Orientation

Oban, with about 10,000 people, is where the train system of Scotland meets the ferry system serving the Hebrides Islands. As "gateway to the isles," its center is not a square or market, but its harbor. Oban's

business action, just a couple of streets deep, stretches along the harbor and its promenade.

Tourist Information: Oban's TI, located at the North Pier, sells bus and ferry tickets, is well stocked with

The Highlands are where you'll most likely see Gaelic—the old Celtic language that must legally accompany English on road signs.

As you travel through the countryside, keep an eye out for shaggy Highland cattle called "hairy coos." They're big and have impressive horns, but are best known for their adorable hair falling into their eyes.

Scotland is a hiker's paradise...as long as you have rain gear and bug spray. From late May through September, the Highlands swarm with midges (like "no-see-ums"). If visiting in summer, consider bringing or buying bug spray (locals recommend Avon's Skin So Soft).

Highlanders are an outdoorsy bunch. For a fun look at local athletics, check whether your trip coincides with one of the Highland Games that enliven towns in summer (www.shga.co.uk).

Most games take place between mid-June and late August (usually on Saturdays). They're typically a one-day affair. Expect feats of strength (shot put and log tossing), Highland dance competition, races (track and cross-country), and a fun, family-friendly scene.

brochures, and has free Wi-Fi (generally daily July-Aug 9:00-19:00; April-June 9:00-17:30; Sept-March 10:00-17:00; 3 North Pier, tel. 01631/563-122, www.oban.org.uk).

Helpful Hints

Laundry: You'll find **Oban Quality Laundry** tucked a block behind the main drag just off Stevenson Street (same-day drop-off service, no self-service, Mon-Fri 9:00-17:00, Sat until 13:00, closed Sun, tel.

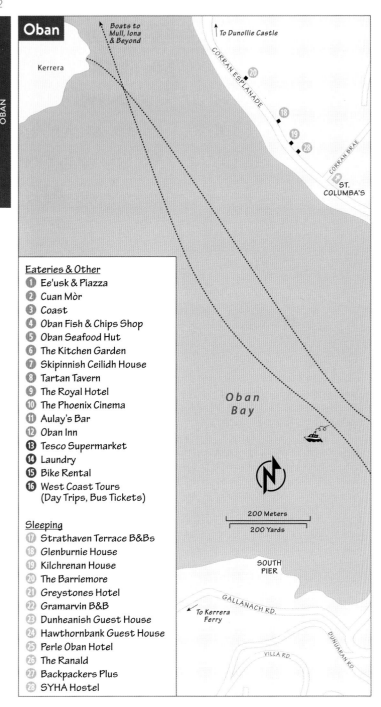

Oban

Boats to Mull, Iona & Beyond

To Dunollie Castle

Kerrera

CORRAN ESPLANADE

20

18

19 28

CORRAN BRAE

ST. COLUMBA'S

Oban Bay

200 Meters
200 Yards

SOUTH PIER

GALLANACH RD.

To Kerrera Ferry

DUNUARAN RD.

VILLA RD.

Eateries & Other

1 Ee'usk & Piazza
2 Cuan Mòr
3 Coast
4 Oban Fish & Chips Shop
5 Oban Seafood Hut
6 The Kitchen Garden
7 Skipinnish Ceilidh House
8 Tartan Tavern
9 The Royal Hotel
10 The Phoenix Cinema
11 Aulay's Bar
12 Oban Inn
13 Tesco Supermarket
14 Laundry
15 Bike Rental
16 West Coast Tours
   (Day Trips, Bus Tickets)

Sleeping

17 Strathaven Terrace B&Bs
18 Glenburnie House
19 Kilchrenan House
20 The Barriemore
21 Greystones Hotel
22 Gramarvin B&B
23 Dunheanish Guest House
24 Hawthornbank Guest House
25 Perle Oban Hotel
26 The Ranald
27 Backpackers Plus
28 SYHA Hostel

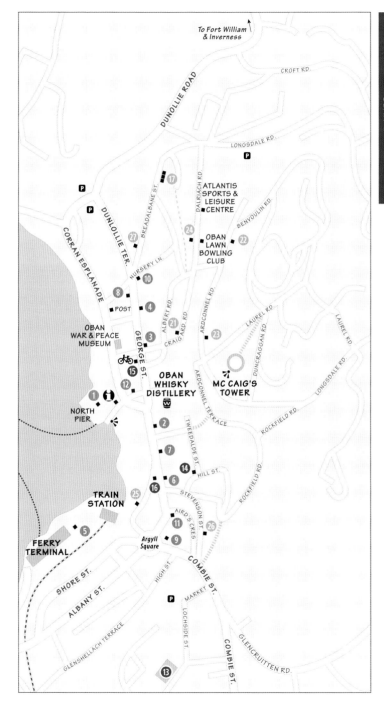

The port town of Oban

01631/563-554). The recommended **Back-packers Plus** hostel (page 170) will also do laundry for nonguests.

Supermarket: The giant **Tesco** is a five-minute walk from the train station (Mon-Sat until 24:00, Sun until 20:00, walk through Argyll Square and look for entrance to large parking lot on right, Lochside Street).

Bike Rental: Oban Cycles is on the main drag (£25/day, Tue-Sat 10:00-17:00, closed Sun-Mon, 87 George Street, tel. 01631/566-033).

Rick's Tip: *If leaving Oban by bus in peak season, it's wise to* book bus tickets the day before—*either at the TI, or at the West Coast Tours office.*

Bus and Island Tour Tickets: West Coast Tours, a block from the train station in the bright-red building along the harbor, sells bus and island tour tickets (Tue-Sat 6:30-17:30, Sun-Mon 8:30-17:30, 17 George Street, tel. 01631/566-809, www.westcoasttours.co.uk).

Highland Games: Oban hosts its touristy Highland Games every August (www.obangames.com), and the more local-oriented Lorne Highland Games each June (www.lorne-highland-games.org.uk).

Tours

For the best day trip from Oban, tour the islands of Mull, Iona, and/or Staffa (offered daily Easter-Oct, described later). With more time or other interests, consider one of many other options you'll see advertised.

WILDLIFE TOURS

If you just want to go for a boat ride, the easiest option is the one-hour seal-watching tour (£10, various companies—look for signs at the harbor). But to really get a good look at Scottish coastal wildlife, several groups—including **Coastal Connection** (based in Oban) and **Sealife Adventures** and **SeaFari** (based in nearby coastal towns)—run whale-watching tours that seek out rare minke whales, basking sharks, bottlenose dolphins, and porpoises. For an even more ambitious itinerary, the holy grail is Treshnish Island (out past Staffa), which brims with puffins, seals, and other sea critters. Options abound—check at the TI for information.

OPEN-TOP BUS TOURS

If the weather is good and you don't have a car, you can go by bus for a spin out of Oban for views of nearby castles and islands, plus a stop near McCaig's Tower with narration by the driver (£7, departs train station 4/day June-Sept only, 1.5 hours, www.citysightseeingoban.com).

Sights

▲THE BURNED-OUT SIGHTSEER'S VISUAL TOUR FROM THE PIER

If weather permits, get oriented to the town while taking a break: Head out to the North Pier, just past the TI, and find the benches that face back toward town (in front of the recommended Piazza restaurant). Take a seat and get to know Oban.

Scan the harborfront from left to right, surveying the mix of grand Victorian sandstone buildings and humbler modern storefronts. At the far-right end of town is the **ferry terminal** and—very likely—a huge ferry loading or unloading. The townscape seems dominated by Caledonian MacBrayne, Scotland's biggest ferry company. CalMac's 30 ships serve 24 destinations and transport more than 4 million passengers a year. The town's port has long been a lifeline to the islands.

Hiding near the ferry terminal is the **train station.** With the arrival of the train in 1880, Oban became the unofficial capital of Scotland's west coast and a destination for tourists.

Tourism aside, herring was the first big industry. A dozen boats still fish commercially—you'll see them tucked around the ferry terminal.

After fishing, big industries here historically included tobacco (imported from the American colonies), then whisky. At the left end of the embankment, find the building marked *Oban Whisky Distillery*. With the success of its whisky, the town enjoyed an invigorating confidence, optimism, and, in 1811, a royal charter. Touring Oban's distillery is the best activity in Oban.

Above the distillery, you can't miss the odd mini-Colosseum. This is **McCaig's Tower,** an employ-the-workers-and-build-me-a-fine-memorial project undertaken by an Oban tycoon in 1900. McCaig died before completing the structure, so his complete vision for it remains a mystery. This is an example of a "folly"—that uniquely British notion of an idiosyncratic structure erected by a colorful aristocrat.

While the building itself is nothing to see up close, a 10-minute hike through a Victorian residential neighborhood leads you to a peaceful garden and a commanding view (nice at sunset).

Now turn and look out to sea, and imagine this: At the height of the Cold War, Oban played a critical role when the world's first two-way transatlantic telephone cable was laid from Gallanach Bay to Newfoundland in 1956—a milestone in global communication. This technology later provided the White House and the Kremlin with the "hotline" that was created after the Cuban Missile Crisis to avoid a nuclear conflagration.

▲▲OBAN WHISKY DISTILLERY TOURS

Founded in 1794, Oban Whisky Distillery produces more than 25,000 liters a week, and exports much of that to the US. Their exhibition (upstairs, free to all) gives a quick, whisky-centric history of Oban and Scotland.

The distillery offers serious and fragrant one-hour tours explaining the process from start to finish, with two smooth samples of their signature product: Oban whisky is moderately smoky ("peaty") and characterized by notes of sea salt, citrus, and honey. You'll also receive a whisky glass and a discount coupon for the shop. This is the handiest whisky tour you'll encounter—just a block off the harbor—and one of the best. Arrive 10 minutes before your tour starts to check out the exhibition upstairs. Then your guide will walk you through each step of the process: malting, mashing, fermentation, distillation, and maturation. Photos are not allowed inside.

Cost and Hours: Tours cost £10, are limited to 16 people and depart every 20 to 30 minutes. Tours fill up, so book in advance by phone, online, or in person to get a firm spot. Unless it's really a busy day, you should be able to drop in and pay for a tour leaving in the next hour or so, then easily pass time in the town center. Generally open July-Sept Mon-Fri 9:30-19:30,

Sat-Sun until 17:00; March-June and Oct-Nov daily 9:30-17:30; Dec-Feb daily 12:30-16:00; last tour 1.25 hours before closing, Stafford Street, tel. 01631/572-004, www.discovering-distilleries.com.

Serious Tasting: Connoisseurs can ask about their "exclusive tour," which adds a visit to the warehouse and four premium tastings in the manager's office (£40, 2 hours, likely July-Sept, Mon, Wed, and Fri at 16:00 only, reservation required).

OBAN WAR & PEACE MUSEUM

Opened in 1995 on the 50th anniversary of Victory in Europe Day, this charming little museum focuses on Oban's experience during World War II. But it covers more than just war and peace. Photos show Oban through the years, and a 15-minute looped video gives a simple tour around the town and region. Volunteer staffers love to chat about the exhibit—or anything else on your mind (free; May-Oct Mon-Sat 10:00-18:00, Sun until 16:00; off-season daily until 16:00; next to Regent Hotel on the promenade, tel. 01631/570-007, www.obanmuseum.org.uk).

DUNOLLIE CASTLE AND MUSEUM

In a park just a mile up the coast, a ruined castle and an old house hold an intimate collection of clan family treasures. This spartan, stocky castle with 10-foot walls offers a commanding, windy view of the harbor—a strategic spot back in the days when transport was mainly by water. For more than a thousand years, clan chiefs ruled this region from this ancestral home of Clan MacDougall, but the castle was abandoned in 1746. The adjacent house, which dates from 1745, shows off the MacDougall clan's heritage with a handful of rooms filled with a humble yet fascinating trove of treasures. While the exhibit won't dazzle you, the family and clan pride in the display, their "willow garden," and the walk from Oban make the visit fun.

To get there, head out of town along the harborfront promenade. At the war memorial (with inviting seaview benches), cross the street. A gate leads to a little lane, lined with historic and nature boards along the way to the castle.

Cost and Hours: £5.50, April-Oct Mon-Sat 10:00-16:00, Sun from 13:00, closed Nov-March, free tours given most days at 11:00 and 14:00, tel. 01631/570-550, www.dunollie.org.

Experiences
Sports

ATLANTIS LEISURE CENTRE

This industrial-type sports center is a good place to get some exercise on a rainy day or let the kids run wild for a few hours. It has a rock-climbing wall, tennis courts, indoor "soft play centre" (for kids under 5), and an indoor swimming pool with a big water slide. The outdoor playground is free and open all the time. (Pool only-£4.20, no rental towels or suits, fees for other activities; open Mon-Fri 6:30-21:30, Sat-Sun 9:00-18:00; on the north end of Dalriach Road, tel. 01631/566-800, www.atlantisleisure.co.uk.)

OBAN LAWN BOWLING CLUB

The club has welcomed visitors since 1869. This elegant green is the scene of a wonderfully British spectacle of old men tiptoeing wishfully after their balls. It's fun to watch, and—if there's no match scheduled and the weather's dry—anyone can rent shoes and balls and actually play (£5/person; informal hours, but generally daily 10:00-12:00 & 14:00-16:00 or "however long the weather lasts"; just south of sports center on Dalriach Road, tel. 01631/570-808, www.obanbowlingclub.com).

Quick Island Excursion

ISLE OF KERRERA

Functioning like a giant breakwater, the Isle of Kerrera (KEH-reh-rah) makes Oban possible. Just offshore from Oban, this stark but very green island offers a quick, easy opportunity to get that romantic island experience. In contrast, the isles of Mull, Iona, and Staffa are farther out and require a full day to visit (described later in this chapter). For a quicker glimpse at the Inner Hebrides, consider Kerrera.

While it has no proper roads, it offers nice hikes, a ruined castle, and a few sheep farms. It's also a fine place to bike (ask for advice at bike rental shop). You may see the Kerrera ferry filled with sheep heading for Oban's livestock market.

Getting There: You have two options for reaching the island. A boat operated by the Oban Marina goes from Oban's North Pier to the Kerrera Marina in the northern part of the island (£5 round-trip, every two hours, book ahead at tel. 01631/565-333, www.obanmarina.com).

A ferry departs from Gallanach (two miles south of Oban) and goes to the middle of the island. This is the best option if you want to hike to Kerrera's castle (passengers only, £4.50 round-trip, bikes free, runs 10:30-18:00 with a break 12:30-14:00, none in off-season, 5-minute ride, tel. 01475/650-397, www.calmac.co.uk. To reach Gallanach, drive south, following the coast road past the ferry terminal (parking available).

Eating on Kerrera: $$ Waypoint Bar & Grill has a laid-back patio with a simple menu of steak, burgers, and seafood. On a nice day the open-air waterside setting is unbeatable (late May-Sept Tue-Sun 18:00-21:00, bar opens at 17:00, closed Mon and in winter, reservations highly recommended, tel. 01631/565-333, www.obanmarina.com).

Nightlife

Little Oban has a few options for entertaining its many visitors; check www.obanwhatson.co.uk. Fun low-key activities may include open-mic, disco, or quiz theme nights in pubs; occasional Scottish folk shows; coffee meetings; and—if you're lucky—duck races. On Wednesday nights, the Oban Pipe Band plays in the square by the train station.

Music and Group Dancing: On many summer nights, you can climb the stairs to the **Skipinnish Ceilidh House,** a sprawling venue on the main drag for music and dancing (the owners are professional musicians Angus and Andrew). There's *ceilidh* (KAY-lee) dancing a couple of times per week, where you can learn some group dances to music performed by a folk band (including, usually, a piper). These group dances are a lot of fun—wallflowers and bad dancers are warmly welcomed, and the staff is happy to give you pointers (£8, May-Sept Mon & Thu at 21:00). They also host concerts by folk and traditional bands (check website for schedule, 34 George Street, tel. 01631/569-599, www.skipinnishceilidhhouse.com).

Traditional Music: Various pubs and hotels in town have live traditional music in the summer; ask your B&B host or the TI for the latest. Try the **Tartan Tavern,** a block off the waterfront at 3 Albany Terrace or **The Royal Hotel,** just above the train station on Argyll Square.

Cinema: The Phoenix Cinema is volunteer-run and booming (140 George Street, tel. 01631/562-905, www.obanphoenix.com).

Characteristic Pubs: Aulay's Bar, with decor that shows off Oban's maritime heritage, has two sides, each with a different personality (I like the right-hand side). Having a drink here invariably comes with a good "blether" (conversation), and the gang is local (daily 11:00-24:00, 8 Airds Crescent, just around the corner from the train station and ferry terminal). The **Oban Inn,** right on the harborfront, is also a fun and memorable place for a pint and possibly live music.

Eating

Oban brags that it is the "seafood capital of Scotland," and indeed its sit-down restaurants (listed first) are surprisingly high quality for such a small town. For something more casual, consider a fish-and-chips joint.

Sit-Down Restaurants

These fill up in summer, especially on weekends. To ensure getting a table, you'll want to book ahead. The first four are generally open daily from 12:00-15:00 and 17:30-21:00.

$$$ **Ee'usk** (Scottish Gaelic for "fish") is a popular, stylish, place on the waterfront. It has a casual-chic, yacht-clubby atmosphere, with a bright and glassy interior and sweeping views on three sides—fun for watching the ferries come and go. They sometimes offer an early-bird special until 18:45, and their seafood platters are a hit. Reservations are recommended (no kids under age 12 at dinner, North Pier, tel. 01631/565-666, www.eeusk.com, MacLeod family).

$$$ **Cuan Mòr** is a popular, casual restaurant that combines traditional Scottish food with modern flair—both in its crowd-pleasing cuisine and in its furnishings, made of wood, stone, and metal scavenged from the beaches of Scotland's west coast (brewery in back, 60 George Street, tel. 01631/565-078). Its harborside tables on the sidewalk are popular when it's warm.

$$$$ **Coast** proudly serves fresh local fish, meat, and veggies in a mod pine-and-candlelight atmosphere. As everything is cooked to order and presented with care—this is no place to dine and dash (two- and three-course specials, closed Sun for lunch, 104 George Street, tel. 01631/569-900, www.coastoban.co.uk).

$$ **Piazza,** next door to Ee'usk, is a casual, family-friendly place serving basic Italian dishes with a great harborfront location. They have some outdoor seats and big windows facing the sea (smart to reserve ahead July-Aug, tel. 01631/563-628, www.piazzaoban.com).

$$ **Oban Fish and Chips Shop** serves praiseworthy haddock and mussels among other tasty options in a cheery cabana-like dining room. Consider venturing away from basic fish-and-chips into a world of more creative seafood dishes—

like their tiny squat lobster. You can bring your own wine for no charge (daily, sit-down restaurant closes at 21:00, takeaway available later, 116 George Street, tel. 01631/567-000).

Lunch

$ **Oban Seafood Hut,** in a green shack facing the ferry dock, is a finger-licking festival of cheap and fresh seafood. John and Marion sell smaller bites (such as cold sandwiches), as well as some bigger cold platters and a few hot dishes (picnic tables nearby, daily from 10:00 until the boat unloads from Mull around 18:00).

$ **The Kitchen Garden** is fine for soup, salad, or sandwiches. It's a deli and gourmet-foods store with a charming café upstairs (daily 9:00-17:30, 14 George Street, tel. 01631/566-332).

Sleeping

Rick's Tip: *Especially in Oban,* **B&Bs** *offer a much* **better value** *than its hotels.*

On Strathaven Terrace

The following B&Bs line up on a quiet, flowery street that's nicely located two blocks off the harbor, three blocks from the center, and a 10-minute walk from the train station. Rooms here are more compact than those on the Esplanade and don't have views, but the location can't be beat.

By car, as you enter town from the north, turn left immediately after King's Knoll Hotel, and take your first right onto Breadalbane Street. ("Strathaven Terrace" is actually just the name for this row of houses on Breadalbane Street.) The alley behind the buildings has tight, free parking for all of these places.

$$ **Rose Villa Guest House** has six crisp and cheery rooms (at #5, tel. 01631/566-874, stuartcameronsmith@yahoo.co.uk, Stuart and Jacqueline).

$ Raniven Guest House has five simple, tastefully decorated rooms and gracious, fun-loving hosts Moyra and Stuart (cash only, 2-night minimum in summer, continental breakfast, at #1, tel. 01631/562-713, www.ranivenoban.com, bookings@ranivenoban.com).

$ Sandvilla B&B rents five pleasant, polished rooms (2-night minimum in summer, at #4, tel. 01631/564-483, www.holidayoban.co.uk, sandvilla@ holidayoban.co.uk, Josephine and Robert).

Along the Esplanade

These are along the Corran Esplanade, which stretches north of town above a cobble beach; they are a 10-minute walk from the center. For the most part, they offer much more spacious rooms than places in town (and many rooms have beautiful bay views).

$$ Glenburnie House, a stately Victorian home, has an elegant breakfast room overlooking the bay. Its 12 spacious, comfortable, classy rooms feel like plush living rooms (closed mid-Nov-March, tel. 01631/562-089, www.glenburnie.co.uk, stay@glenburnie.co.uk, Graeme).

$$ Kilchrenan House, the turreted former retreat of a textile magnate, has 16 large rooms, most with bay views. The stunning rooms #5, #9, and #15 are worth the few extra pounds, while the "standard" rooms in the newer annex are a good value (2-night minimum in summer, welcome drink of whisky or sherry, family rooms, closed Nov-Feb, tel. 01631/562-663, www.kilchrenanhouse.co.uk, info@ kilchrenanhouse.co.uk, Colin and Frances).

$$ The Barriemore, at the very end of Oban's grand waterfront Esplanade, is a welcome refuge after a day of exploration. Its 14 well-appointed rooms come with robes, sherry, etc. It has a nice front patio, spacious breakfast room, and glassed-in sunporch with a view of the water (family suite, tel. 01631/566-356, www.barriemore.co.uk, info@barriemore.co.uk, Jan and Mark).

Above the Town Center

These places perch on the hill above the main waterfront zone—a short (but uphill) walk from all of the action. Many rooms come with views, and are priced accordingly.

$$$ Greystones is an enticing splurge. It fills a big, stately, turreted mansion at the top of town with five spacious rooms that mix Victorian charm and sleek gray-and-white minimalism. The lounge and breakfast room offer stunning views over Oban and the offshore isles (closed Nov-mid-Feb, 13 Dalriach Road, tel. 01631/358-653, www.greystonesoban.co.uk, stay@ greystonesoban.co.uk).

$$ Gramarvin B&B feels a little more homey, with just two rooms. Window seats in each room provide a lovely view over Oban, but be warned—the climb up from town and then up their stairs is steep (skip breakfast to save a few pounds, cash only, 2-night minimum in summer preferred, on-street parking, Benvoulin Road, tel. 01631/564-622, Mary and Joe).

$$ Dunheanish Guest House offers six pleasant rooms (two on the ground floor) and wide-open views from its perch above town, which you can enjoy from the front stone patio, breakfast room, and several guest rooms (parking, Ardconnel Road, tel. 01631/566-556, www.dunheanish. com, info@dunheanish.com, William and Linda).

$ Hawthornbank Guest House fills a big Victorian sandstone house with seven traditional-feeling rooms. Half of the rooms face bay views, and the other half overlook the town's lawn bowling green (2-night minimum in summer, Dalriach Road, tel. 01631/562-041, www.hawthornbank.co.uk, info@ hawthornbank.co.uk).

Hotels in the Town Center

A number of hotels are in the center of town along or near the main drag—but you'll pay heavily for the convenience.

$$$$ Perle Oban Hotel is your luxury boutique splurge. Right across from the harbor, it has 59 super-sleek rooms with calming sea-color walls, decorative bath tile floors, and rain showers (suites, fancy restaurant, bar with light bites, pay parking, Station Square, tel. 01631/700-301, www. perleoban.com, stay@perleoban.com).

$$$ The Ranald is a modern change of pace from the B&B scene in Oban. This narrow, 17-room, three-floor hotel has a budget-boutique atmosphere (family rooms, bar, no elevator, street or off-site parking, a block behind the Royal Hotel at 41 Stevenson Street, tel. 01631/562-887, www.theranaldhotel.com, info@ theranaldhotel.com).

Hostels

¢ Backpackers Plus is central, laid-back, and fun. It fills part of a renovated old church with a sprawling public living room, 47 beds, and a staff generous with travel tips (includes breakfast, great shared kitchen, pay laundry service, 10-minute walk from station, on Breadalbane Street, tel. 01631/567-189, www.backpackersplus. com, info@backpackersplus.com). They have two other locations nearby with private rooms.

¢ The official SYHA hostel, on the scenic waterfront Esplanade, is in a grand building with 87 beds and smashing views of the harbor and islands from the lounges and dining rooms. While institutional, this place is quite nice (all rooms en suite, private rooms available, also has family rooms and 8-bed apartment with kitchen, breakfast extra, pay laundry, kitchen, tel. 01631/562-025, www. syha.org.uk, oban@syha.org.uk).

TRANSPORTATION

Arriving and Departing
By Train

Oban's small train station has a ticket window and lockers (both open Mon-Sat 5:00-20:30, Sun 10:45-18:00. Train info: Tel. 0845-748-4950, www.nationalrail. co.uk).

Train Connections to: Glasgow (6/day, fewer on Sun, 3 hours), Edinburgh (5/day with transfer in Glasgow, 4.5 hours).

By Bus

Buses arrive and depart from a roundabout, marked by a stubby clock tower, just before the entrance to the train station. You can buy bus tickets at the West Coast shop near the bus stop, or at the TI across the harbor. Book in advance during peak times (tel. 0871-266-3333, www. citylink.co.uk).

If departing Oban to explore more of the Highlands, catch a bus to Fort William (a transit hub), then another bus to the Isle of Skye or to Inverness. For an overview of bus connections (to and from Oban, and more), see the "Getting Around the Highlands" sidebar.

By Car

For tips on driving, see the "Getting Around the Highlands" sidebar and "Driving" in Practicalities.

To help you make the most of the drive from Glasgow to Oban, then on to Glencoe and Fort Williams (and more of the Highlands), here are route tips:

FROM GLASGOW TO OBAN VIA INVERARAY—THE SCENIC ROUTE

Leaving Glasgow on the A-82, you'll soon be driving along the west bank of Loch Lomond (the first picnic turnout has the best views of this famous lake). Halfway up the loch at the town of Tarbet, the road forks. The signs for Oban keep you on the direct route along the A-82.

But, for the scenic option that takes you past Loch Fyne to Inveraray (about 30 minutes longer to drive), keep left for the A-83 (toward Campbeltown). You'll pass the village of Arrochar, drive along Loch Long, and head through mountains. At the summit, stop at the large parking lot on your left (signed for *Argyll Forest Park*); stretch your legs here, at the aptly named Rest-and-Be-Thankful Pass. Heading

Getting Around the Highlands

By Car

The Highlands are made for joyriding. There are a lot of miles, but they're scenic, the roads are good, and the traffic is light. Drivers enjoy plenty of tempting stops. Be careful, but don't be timid about passing. Don't wait too long to gas up—village gas stations are few and far between, and can close unexpectedly. Get used to single-lane roads: Slow down on blind corners—you never know when an oncoming car (or a road-blocking sheep) is right around the bend. If you encounter an oncoming vehicle, rules of the road dictate that the driver closest to a pullout will use it—even if they have to back up.

By Public Transportation

Glasgow is the gateway to this region (so you'll most likely have to transfer there if coming from Edinburgh). The **train** zips from Glasgow to Fort William, Oban, and Kyle of Lochalsh in the west; and up to Stirling, Pitlochry, and Inverness in the east. For more remote destinations (such as Glencoe), the bus is better.

Most of the **buses** are operated by Scottish Citylink. You can pay the driver in cash when you board. But in peak season—when these buses fill up—it's smart to buy tickets at least a day in advance: Book at www.citylink.co.uk, call 0871-216-3333, or stop by a bus station or TI.

Glasgow's Buchanan Station is the main Lowlands hub for reaching Highlands destinations. From Edinburgh, it's best to transfer in Glasgow (fastest by train, also possible by bus)—though there are direct buses from Edinburgh to Inverness, where you can connect to Highlands buses. Once in the Highlands, Inverness and Fort William serve as the main bus hubs.

Note that bus frequency can be substantially reduced on Sundays and in the off-season (Oct-mid-May). Unless otherwise noted, I've listed bus information for summer weekdays. Always confirm schedules locally and online.

These handy bus routes connect most Highland destinations covered in this book:

Glasgow and Oban: Buses #976 and #977 (5/day, 3 hours).

Glasgow and Inverness: Bus #G10 (express: 5/day, 3 hours) and National Express #588 (1/day, 4 hours; www.nationalexpress.com).

Glasgow and Fort William (and Portree): Buses #914, #915, and #916 (8/day, stop at Glencoe en route, 2.5 hours to Glencoe, 3 hours total to Fort William). Several of the #915 and #916 buses continue to **Portree** on the Isle of Skye (3/day, 7 hours for the full run).

Oban and Fort William: Bus #918 (2/day, stop en route at Ballachulish, a half-mile from Glencoe; 1 hour to Ballachulish, 1.5 hours total to Fort William). From Fort William, transfer to bus #915 or #916 for **Portree** (3/day, 4 hours; see previous listing).

Fort William and Inverness: Buses #19 and #919 (7/day, 2 hours).

Inverness and Portree (Isle of Skye): Bus #917 (3/day, 3 hours).

Inverness and Edinburgh: Buses #M90 and #G90 (express #G90, 2/day, 3.5 hours; slower #M90, some stop in Pitlochry, 6/day, 4 hours).

down from the pass, you'll drive through Glen Kinglas and soon reach Loch Fyne (well-known for its elegant **$$$$ Loch Fyne Seafood Restaurant and Deli;** open daily from noon, no reservations, www. lochfyne.com).

Looping around Loch Fyne, you'll approach Inveraray. Keep an eye on the right (when crossing the bridge, have your camera ready) for the dramatic, turreted Inveraray Castle, the residence of the Duke of Argyll. It's worth a stop for its lavishly decorated interior, well-described room by room, with docents happy to answer questions about the family and castle. Highlights include the Armory Hall decorated with weaponry; the upstairs with a room dedicated to Downton Abbey and another to the duke's photos; and the finely manicured gardens (£11, April-Oct daily 10:00-17:45, closed Nov-March, last entry 45 minutes before closing, nice café in basement, buy tickets at car park booth, tel. 01499/302-203, www. inveraray-castle.com).

After visiting the castle, explore the lovely town of Inveraray on Loch Fyne. Browse the main street—lined with touristy shops and cafés all the way to the church at its top. There's free parking on the main street and plenty of pay-and-display parking near the pier (TI open daily, on Front Street, tel. 01499/302-063; public WCs at end of nearby pier).

To continue directly to Oban from Inveraray (about an hour), leave town through the gate at the woolen mill and get on the A-819, which takes you through Glen Aray and along Loch Awe. A left turn on the A-85 takes you into Oban.

FROM OBAN TO GLENCOE AND FORT WILLIAM

It's an easy one-hour drive from Oban to Glencoe. From Oban, follow the coastal A-828 toward Fort William. After about 20 miles—as you leave the village of Appin—you'll see the photogenic Castle Stalker marooned on a lonely island (you can pull over at the Castle Stalker View

Café for a good photo from just below its parking lot). At North Ballachulish, you'll reach a bridge spanning Loch Leven; rather than crossing the bridge, turn off and follow the A-82 into the Glencoe Valley for about 15 minutes. After exploring the dramatic valley, make a U-turn and return through Glencoe village. To continue on to Fort William, backtrack to the bridge at North Ballachulish (great view from bridge) and cross it, following the A-82 north.

THE INNER HEBRIDES

For the best day trip to see the dramatic and historic Inner Hebrides (HEB-rid-eez) islands, take a tour from Oban to Mull, Iona, and Staffa. Though this trip is spectacular and worth ▲▲▲ when it's sunny, it's worthwhile in any weather (but if rain or rough seas are expected, I'd skip the Staffa option). For an even more in-depth look at the Inner Hebrides, head north to Skye (covered in another chapter).

Getting Around the Islands
Visiting Mull and Iona

To visit Mull and ultimately Iona, you'll take a huge ferry run by Caledonian MacBrayne (CalMac) from Oban to the town of Craignure on Mull (45 minutes). From there, you'll ride a bus or drive across Mull to its westernmost ferry terminal, called Fionnphort (1.25 hours), where you can catch the ferry to Iona (10 minutes). It's a long journey, but it's all incredibly scenic; you also get about two hours of free time on Iona. There are several ways to do this.

By Tour (Easiest): If you book a tour with **West Coast Tours,** all of the transportation is taken care of. The CalMac ferry leaves from the Oban pier daily at 9:50 (as schedule can change from year to year, confirm times locally; board at least

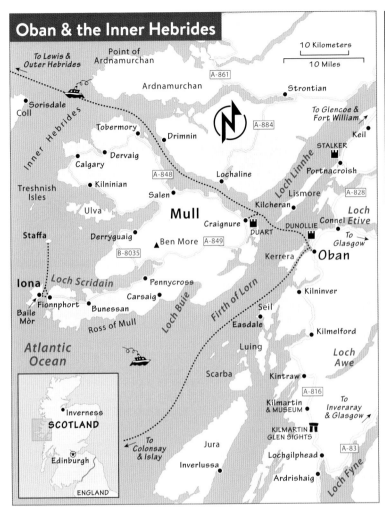

Oban & the Inner Hebrides

To Lewis &
Outer Hebrides
Point of
Ardnamurchan

Ardnamurchan
A-861

Strontian

10 Kilometers
10 Miles

Sorisdale
Coll

To Glencoe &
Fort William

Keil

Inner Hebrides

Tobermory
Drimnin

STALKER

Dervaig
Calgary

Loch Linnhe

Portnacroish

Kilninian
A-848
Lochaline

Lismore
A-828

Treshnish
Isles

Salen
Kilcheran

Ulva

Mull

Loch
Connel Etive

Staffa

Derryguaig

Craignure
DUART

DUNOLLIE

To
Glasgow

Ben More
A-849

Kerrera

Oban

B-8035

Iona
Loch Scridain

Pennycross

Kilninver

Fionnphort
Bunessan

Carsaig

Seil

Baile
Mòr

Ross of Mull

Loch Buie

Firth of Lorn

Easdale

Kilmelford

Atlantic
Ocean

Luing

Loch
Awe

Scarba

Kintraw

A-816

Inverness

SCOTLAND

Kilmartin
& MUSEUM

To
Inveraray
& Glasgow

Edinburgh

To
Colonsay
& Islay

Jura

Inverlussa

KILMARTIN
GLEN SIGHTS

Lochgilphead

A-83

ENGLAND

Ardrishaig

Loch Fyne

20 minutes before departure). You can buy tickets online at www.westcoasttours.co.uk, from the West Coast Tours office, or from the Tour Shop Oban at the ferry building (tel. 01631/562-244, tourshop@calmac.co.uk). Book as far in advance as possible for July and August (tickets can sell out). When you book their tour, you'll receive a strip of tickets—one for each leg; if you book online, you must go to the West Coast Tours office and collect tickets in person (£35; April-Oct only, no tours Nov-March).

Rick's Tip: The **best interior seats on the Oban-Mull ferry**—with the biggest windows—are in the sofa lounge on the "observation deck" (level 4) at the back end of the boat. (Follow signs for the toilets, and look for the big staircase to the top floor).

The ferry has a fine cafeteria with hot meals and packaged sandwiches, a small snack bar on the top floor (hot drinks and basic sandwiches), and a bookshop. If it's a clear day, ask a local or a crew

Day-tripping by ferry to the islands

member to point out Ben Nevis, the tallest mountain in Britain. Five minutes before landing on Mull, you'll see the striking 13th-century Duart Castle on the left.

Walk-on passengers disembark from deck 3, across from the bookshop (port side). Upon arrival in Mull, find your **bus** for the entertaining and informative ride across the Isle of Mull. The right (driver's) side offers better sea views during the second half of the journey to Fionnphort, while the left side has fine views of Mull's rolling wilderness. The driver spends the entire ride chattering away about life on Mull, slowing to point out wildlife, and sharing adages like, "If there's no flowers on the gorse, snogging's gone out of fashion." These hardworking locals make historical trivia fascinating—or at least fun. At Fionnphort, you'll board a small, rocking **ferry to Iona.** You'll have about two hours to roam freely around the island before returning to Oban (arrives around 18:00).

By Public Transit: If you want an early start (and want to avoid some crowds), have more time on Iona, or don't get a space on the tour described earlier, you can take the early ferry and public bus across Mull, paying individually per leg (Tue-Sat

only; approximate round-trip prices: £7 for Oban-Mull ferry, £15 for public bus across Mull, £3.50 for Mull-Iona ferry).

Take the first boat of the day (departs about 7:30, buy ticket at Oban ferry terminal), then connect at Mull to bus #496 to Fionnphort (departs 8:25, 80 minutes, buy ticket from driver, no tour narration, no guarantee you'll get to sit), then hop on the Iona ferry (every 30 minutes, buy ticket from small trailer ferry office; if closed, purchase ticket from ferry worker at the dock; cash or credit/debit cards accepted; leaving Iona, do the same, as there's no ferry office). You'll have about four hours on Iona and will need to return to Fionnphort in time for the bus back (15:15). It's important to confirm all of these times locally (just pop in to the West Coast Tours office or the ferry terminal Tour Shop).

By Car: You can do this trip on your own by driving your car onto the ferry to Mull, but space is limited so book way in advance. Because of tight ferry timings, you'll wind up basically following the tour buses anyway, you'll miss all of the commentary, and no visitor cars are allowed on Iona (£26 round-trip for the car, plus passengers, www.calmac.co.uk).

The coast of Mull

Visiting Staffa

With two extra hours, you can add a side-trip to Staffa along with your Mull/Iona visit. Like the route listed earlier, you'll ferry from Oban to Mull, take a bus across Mull to Fionnphort, and then board a **Staffa Tours** boat (35-minute trip, about an hour of free time on Staffa). From Staffa you'll head to Iona for about two hours before returning to Mull for the bus then ferry back to Oban. You can either depart on the 9:50 ferry, returning around 20:05 (£60) or do the "early bird" tour (£55, Tue-Sat only, depart at 7:30, return 18:00; book through West Coast Tours or Staffa Tours—mobile 07831-885-985, www.staffatours.com).

For a more relaxed schedule, **Staffa Trips** offers a guided tour with the same route as the one listed earlier, but with more time on Staffa and Iona (£60, Tue-Sat only, depart at 7:30, return 19:10, tel. 01681/700-358, www.staffatrips.co.uk).

Turus Mara offers nature/wildlife tours to just Staffa or Staffa and the small island of Ulva, departing from Oban (book at Tour Shop at Oban ferry terminal or contact Turus Mara—tel. 01688/400-242, www.turusmara.com).

Mull

The Isle of Mull, the second largest of the Inner Hebrides (after Skye), has nearly 300 scenic miles of coastline and castles and a 3,169-foot-high mountain. Called Ben More ("Big Mountain" in Gaelic), it was once much bigger. At 10,000 feet tall, it made up the entire island of Mull—until a volcano erupted. Things are calmer now, and, similarly, Mull has a noticeably laid-back population. My bus driver reported that there are no deaths from stress, and only a few from boredom.

With steep, fog-covered hillsides topped by cairns (piles of stones, sometimes indicating graves) and ancient stone circles, Mull has a gloomy, otherworldly charm. Bring plenty of rain protection and wear layers in case the sun peeks through the clouds.

On the far side of Mull, the caravan of tour buses unloads at Fionnphort, a tiny ferry town. The ferry to the island of Iona takes about 200 walk-on passengers. Confirm the return time with your bus driver, then hustle to the dock to make the first trip over (otherwise, it's a 30-minute wait; on very busy days, those who dillydally may not fit on the first ferry). At the dock, there's a small ferry-passenger building with a meager snack bar and a pay WC; a more enticing seafood bar is across the street. After the 10-minute ride, you wash ashore on sleepy Iona (free WC on this side), and the ferry mobs that crowded you on the boat seem to disappear up the main road and into Iona's back lanes.

The **About Mull Tours and Taxi** service can get you around Mull (tel. 01681/700-507 or mobile 0788-777-4550, www.aboutmull.co.uk). They also do day tours of Mull, focusing on local history and wildlife (half-day tours also available, or ask about shorter Mull tour combined with drop-off and pick-up at Fionnphort ferry dock for quick Iona trip, minimum 2 people, must book ahead).

Iona

The tiny island of Iona, just 3 miles by 1.5 miles, is famous as the birthplace of Christianity in Scotland. If you're on a day trip, you'll have about two hours here on your own before you retrace your steps (your bus driver will tell you which return ferry to take back to Mull).

A pristine quality of light and a thoughtful peace pervades the stark, (nearly) car-free island and its tiny community. With buoyant clouds bouncing playfully off distant bluffs, sparkling-white crescents of sand, and lone tourists camped thoughtfully atop huge rocks just looking out to sea, Iona is a place that's perfect for meditation. To experience Iona, it's important to get out and take a little hike; you can follow some or all of my self-guided walk outlined later. And you can easily climb a peak—nothing's higher than 300 feet above the sea.

Orientation

The ferry arrives at the island's only real village, Baile Mòr, with shops, a restaurant/pub, accommodations, a Spar grocery (up the road from dock, has free island maps), and no bank (get cash back with a purchase at the grocery store). The only taxi on Iona is **Iona Taxi** (mobile 07810-325-990, www.ionataxi.co.uk). Iona's official website has good information (www.isle-of-iona.net).

◉ Iona Walk

Here's a basic self-guided route for exploring Iona on foot (since no private cars are

The little isle of Iona, with its big abbey

History of Iona

St. Columba (521-597), an Irish scholar, soldier, priest, and founder of monasteries, stopped on Iona in 563 and established an abbey. Columba's monastic community flourished, and Iona became the center of Celtic Christianity. Missionaries from Iona spread the gospel throughout Scotland and northern England, while scholarly monks established Iona as a center of art and learning. The *Book of Kells*—perhaps the finest piece of art from "Dark Ages" Europe—was probably made on Iona in the eighth century.

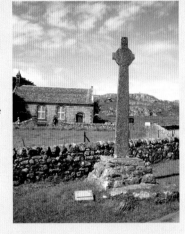

Slowly, the importance of Iona ebbed. Vikings massacred 68 monks in 806. Fearing more raids, the monks evacuated most of Iona's treasures to Ireland (including the *Book of Kells,* now in Dublin). Much later, with the Reformation, the abbey was abandoned, and most of its finely carved crosses were destroyed.

Iona's population peaked at about 500 in the 1830s; today it's only around 200. But in our generation, a new religious community has given the abbey fresh life. The Iona Community is an ecumenical gathering of men and women who seek new ways of living the gospel in today's world, with a focus on worship, peace and justice issues, and reconciliation (http://iona.org.uk).

permitted unless you're a resident or have a permit). With the standard two hours on Iona that a day trip allows, you will have time for a visit to the abbey (with a guided tour and/or audioguide) and then a light stroll; or do the entire walk described later, but skip the abbey (unless you have time for a quick visit on your way back).

Nunnery Ruins: From the ferry dock, head directly up the single paved road that passes through the village and up a small hill to visit one of Britain's best-preserved medieval nunneries (free).

Immediately after the nunnery, turn right on North Road. You'll curve up through the fields—passing the parish church.

Heritage Center: This little museum, tucked behind the church (watch for signs), is small but well done, with displays on local and natural history and a tiny tearoom (free but donation requested, closed Sun and in off-season, tel. 01681/700-576, www.ionaheritage.co.uk).

St. Oran's Chapel and Iona Abbey: Continue on North Road. After the road swings right, you'll soon see **St. Oran's Chapel,** in the graveyard of the Iona Abbey. This chapel is the oldest church building on the island. Inside you'll find a few grave slabs carved in the distinctive Iona School style, which was developed by local stone-carvers in the 14th century. On these tall, skinny headstones, look for the depictions of medieval warrior aristocrats with huge swords. Many more of these carvings have been moved to the abbey, where you can see them in its cloister and museum.

It's free to see the graveyard and chapel; the ▲**Iona Abbey** itself has an admission fee, but it's worth the cost just to sit in the stillness of its lovely, peaceful interior courtyard (£7.50, tel. 01681/700-512, www.historicenvironment.scot—search for "Iona Abbey").

The abbey marks the site of Christianity's arrival in Scotland. You'll see Celtic crosses, the original shrine of St. Columba, a big church slathered with medieval carvings, a tranquil cloister, and an excellent museum with surviving fragments of this site's fascinating layers of history. While the present abbey, nunnery, and graveyard go back to the 13th century, much of what you'll see was rebuilt in the 20th century.

At the entrance building, pick up your included audioguide, and ask about the good 30-minute guided tours (4/day and well worthwhile). Then head toward the church. You'll pass two faded **Celtic crosses** (and the base of a third); the originals are in the museum at the end of your visit.

Facing the entrance to the church, you'll see the original **shrine to St. Columba** on your left—a magnet for pilgrims.

Head inside the **church.** It feels like an active church—with hymnals neatly stacked in the pews—because it is, thanks to the Iona Community. While much

of this space has been rebuilt, take a moment to look around. Plenty of original medieval stone carving (especially the capitals of many columns) still survives. Some of the newer features of the church—including the base of the baptismal font near the entrance, and the main altar—are carved from locally quarried Iona marble: white with green streaks.

When you're ready to continue, find the poorly marked door into the **cloister.** (As you face the altar, it's about halfway down the nave on the left, before the transept.) This space is filled with harmonious light, additional finely carved capitals (these are modern re-creations), and—displayed along the walls—several more of the tall, narrow tombstones like the ones displayed in St. Oran's Chapel. On these, look for a couple of favorite motifs: the long, intimidating sword (indicating a warrior of the Highland clans) and the ship with billowing sails (a powerful symbol of this seafaring culture).

Around the far side of the cloister is the shop. But before leaving, don't overlook the easy-to-miss **museum.** (To find it, head outside and walk around the left side of the abbey complex, toward the sea.) This modern, well-presented space exhibits a remarkable collection of original stonework from the abbey—including what's left of the three Celtic crosses out front—all eloquently described.

Iona Abbey

Iona cloister

Iona Community's Welcome Centre: Just beyond and across the road from the abbey is the Iona Community's Welcome Centre (free WCs), which runs the abbey with Historic Scotland and hosts modern-day pilgrims who come here to experience the birthplace of Scottish Christianity. (If you're staying longer, you could attend a worship service at the abbey—check the schedule; tel. 01681/700-404, www.iona.org.uk.) Its gift shop is packed with books on the island's important role in Christian history.

Views: A 10-minute walk on North Road past the welcome center brings you to the footpath for **Dùn Ì,** a steep but short climb with good views of the abbey looking back toward Mull.

North Beach: Returning to the main road, walk another 20-25 minutes to the end of the paved road, where you'll arrive at a gate leading through a sheep- and cow-strewn pasture to Iona's pristine white-sand beach. Dip your toes in the Atlantic and ponder what this Caribbean-like alcove is doing in Scotland. Be sure to allow at least 40 minutes to return to the ferry dock.

Staffa

Those more interested in nature than in church history will enjoy the trip to the wildly scenic Isle of Staffa. Completely uninhabited (except for seabirds), Staffa is a knob of rock draped with a vibrant green carpet of turf. Remote and quiet, it feels like a Hebrides nature preserve.

Most day trips give you an hour on Staffa—barely enough time to see its two claims to fame: The basalt columns of Fingal's Cave, and (in summer) a colony of puffins. To squeeze in both, be ready to hop off the boat and climb the staircase. Partway up to the left, you can walk around to the cave (about 7 minutes). Or continue up to the top, then turn right and walk across the spine of the grassy island (about 10-15 minutes) to the cove where the puffins gather. (Your captain should point out both options and let you know how active the puffins have been.)

▲▲FINGAL'S CAVE

Staffa's shore is covered with bizarre, mostly hexagonal basalt columns that stick up at various heights. It's as if the earth were offering God his choice of thousands of six-sided cigarettes. (The island's name likely came from the Old Norse word for "stave"—the building timbers these columns resemble.) This is the other end of Northern Ireland's popular Giant's Causeway. You'll walk along the uneven surface of these columns, curling around the far side of the island, until you can actually step inside the gaping mouth of a cave—where floor-to-ceiling columns and crashing waves combine to create a powerful experience. Listening

Isle of Staffa, bordered by basalt columns

Fingal's Cave

Puffin, resident of Staffa

to the water and air flowing through this otherworldly space inspired Felix Mendelssohn to compose his overture, *The Hebrides*.

While you're ogling the cave, consider this: These unique formations were created by volcanic eruptions more than 60 million years ago. As the surface of the lava flow quickly cooled, it contracted and crystallized into columns (resembling the caked mud at the bottom of a dried-up lakebed, but with deeper cracks). As the rock later settled and eroded, the columns broke off into the many stair-like steps that now honeycomb Staffa.

▲▲PUFFINS

A large colony of Atlantic puffins settles on Staffa each spring and summer during mating season (generally early May through early August). The puffins tend to scatter when the boat arrives. But after the boat pulls out and its passengers hike across the island, the very tame puffins' curiosity gets the better of them. First you'll see them flutter up from the offshore rocks, with their distinctive, bobbing flight. They'll zip and whirl around, and finally they'll start to land on the lip of the cove. Sit quietly, move slowly, and be patient, and soon they'll get close. (If any seagulls are nearby, shoo them away—puffins are undaunted by humans, who do them no harm, but they're terrified of predator seagulls.)

In the waters around Staffa—on your way to and from the other islands—also keep an eye out for a variety of **marine life,** including seals, dolphins, porpoises, and the occasional minke whale, fin whale, or basking shark (a gigantic fish that hinges open its enormous jaw to drift-net plankton).

BEST OF THE REST

Some of Scotland's most spectacular—and most accessible—natural wonders are in the valley called Glencoe, just an hour north of Oban. Beyond Glencoe, Fort William—a touristy transportation hub—can be a handy lunch stop.

GLENCOE

This valley is the essence of the wild, powerful, and stark beauty of the Highlands. Along with its scenery, Glencoe offers a good dose of bloody clan history: In 1692, government Redcoats (led by a local Campbell commander) came to the valley, and they were sheltered and fed for 12 days by the MacDonalds—whose leader had been late in swearing an oath to the British monarch. Then, on the morning of February 13, the soldiers were ordered to rise up early and kill their sleeping hosts, violating the rules of Highland hospitality and earning the valley the nickname "The Weeping Glen." Thirty-eight men were killed outright; hundreds more fled through a blizzard, and some 40 addi-

tional villagers (mostly women and children) died from exposure. It's fitting that such an epic, dramatic incident should be set in this equally epic, dramatic valley, where the cliffsides seem to weep (with running streams) when it rains.

Orientation

The most appealing town here is the sleepy one-street village of Glencoe, worth a stop for its folk museum and its status as the gateway to the valley. (The slightly larger and more modern town of Ballachulish, a half-mile away, has more services, including a grocery store.)

Day Plan: On a quick visit, this area warrants a few hours. Wander through Glencoe village, tour its modest museum, then drive up Glencoe valley for views. But if you have a day or two to linger in the Highlands, Glencoe is an ideal place to do it. Settle in for a night (or more) to make time for a more leisurely drive and to squeeze in a hike or two.

Getting There: For **drivers,** the valley of Glencoe is an easy side-trip just off the

Glencoe Valley

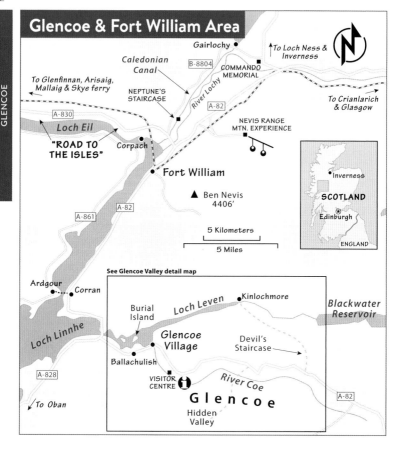

See Glencoe Valley detail map

main A-828/A-82 road between Oban and points north (such as Fort William and Inverness). If you're coming from the north, the signage can be tricky—at the roundabout south of Fort William, follow signs to *Crianlarich* and *A-82*.

Citylink buses #914, #915, or #916 stop at Glencoe Crossroads (a short walk to village center) and nearby Ballachulish, heading north to **Fort William** (8/day, 30 minutes) or south to **Glasgow** (2.5 hours). Stagecoach bus #44 runs from either Glencoe Crossroads or Ballachulish to **Fort William** (hourly, fewer on Sun). From Ballachulish, you can take Citylink bus #918 to **Oban** (2/day, 1 hour).

Tourist Information: Your best source of information—especially for walks and hikes—is the **Glencoe Visitor Centre** (described under "Sights"). The nearest **TI** is in the next town, Ballachulish (buried inside a huge gift shop, open daily, tel. 01855/811-866, www.glencoetourism. co.uk). For more information on the area, see www.discoverglencoe.com.

Sights

GLENCOE VILLAGE

Glencoe village is just a line of houses sitting beneath the brooding mountains. The town's hub of activity is its grocery store (with an ATM, open daily). The only real sight in town is the folk museum (described next). But walking the main street gives a good glimpse of village Scotland. From the free parking lot at the entrance to town, go for a stroll. You'll pass lots of little B&Bs renting two or three rooms, the stony Episcopal church, the folk museum, the town's grocery store, and the village hall.

Rick's Tip: *For a* **hike right from Glencoe village,** *cross the bridge in town and continue straight up to Glencoe Lochan (follow signs)—it's a 20-minute uphill walk. Once there, a helpful orientation panel suggests three one-mile walking loops—mostly around the beautiful lake.*

GLENCOE AND NORTH LORN FOLK MUSEUM

This gathering of thatched-roof, early 18th-century croft houses is a volunteer-run community effort. It's jammed with local history, creating a huggable museum filled with humble exhibits gleaned from the town's closets and attics. Be sure to look for the museum's little door that leads out back, where additional, smaller buildings are filled with everyday items (furniture, farm tools, and so on) and more exhibits (£3, Easter-Sept Mon-Sat 10:00-16:30, closed Sun and off-season, tel. 01855/811-664, www.glencoemuseum.com).

GLENCOE VISITOR CENTRE

This modern facility, a mile past Glencoe village up the A-82 into the dramatic valley, is designed to resemble a *clachan,*

Glencoe and North Lorn Folk Museum

or traditional Highland settlement. The information desk inside the shop at the ranger desk is your single best resource for advice (and maps or guidebooks) about local walks and hikes. At the back of the complex you'll find a viewpoint with a handy 3-D model of the hills for orientation. There's also a pricey exhibition about the surrounding landscape, the region's history, wildlife, mountaineering, and conservation. It's worth the time to watch the more-interesting-than-it-sounds two-minute video on geology and the 14-minute film on the Glencoe Massacre, which thoughtfully traces the events leading up to the tragedy rather than simply recycling romanticized legends (free, exhibition-£6.50; April-Oct daily 9:30-17:30; Nov-March Thu-Sun 10:00-16:00, closed Mon-Wed; free Wi-Fi, café, tel. 01855/811-307, www.glencoe-nts.org.uk).

Glencoe Valley Driving (and Hiking) Tour

If you have a car, spend an hour or so following the A-82 through the valley, past the Glencoe Visitor Centre, up into the desolate moor beyond, and back again. You'll enjoy grand views, dramatic craggy hills, and, if you're lucky, a chance to hear a bagpiper in the wind. Roadside Highland buskers often set up here on good-weather summer weekends.

If you're up for a hike, I've pointed out trailheads along the way. Many routes are not particularly well marked, so it's essential to get very specific instructions (from the rangers at the Glencoe Visitor Centre) and equip yourself with a good map (the Ordnance Survey Explorer Map #384, sold at the center).

● **Self-Guided Driving Tour:** Leaving Glencoe village on the A-82, it's just a mile to the **Glencoe Visitor Centre** (on the right). Soon after, the road pulls out of the forested hills and gives you unobstructed views of the U-shaped valley.

About a mile after the visitors center, on the left, is a parking lot for **Signal Rock and**

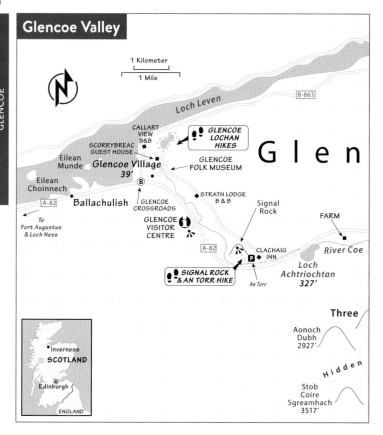

Glencoe Valley

1 Kilometer

1 Mile

Loch Leven

B-863

G l e n

CALLART VIEW B&B

GLENCOE LOCHAN HIKES

SCORRYBREAC GUEST HOUSE

GLENCOE FOLK MUSEUM

Eilean Munde

Glencoe Village 39'

Eilean Choinnech

A-82   Ballachulish

B

GLENCOE CROSSROADS

STRATH LODGE B & B

Signal Rock

FARM

To Fort Augustus & Loch Ness

GLENCOE VISITOR CENTRE

A-82

P   CLACHAIG INN

River Coe

SIGNAL ROCK & AN TORR HIKE

An Torr

Loch Achtriochan 327'

Three

Aonoch Dubh 2927'

SCOTLAND
• Inverness

Hidden

Edinburgh

ENGLAND

Stob Coire Sgreamhach 3517'

An Torr, a popular place for easy-to-moderate forested hikes (a panel at the trailhead describes your options). Just beyond, also on the left, is a single-track road leading to the recommended **Clachaig Inn,** a classic hikers' pub.

Continuing along the A-82, you'll hit a straight stretch, passing a lake (Loch Achtriochan), and then a small farm, both on the right. After the farm, the valley narrows a bit as you cut through Glencoe Pass. On the right, you'll pass two small parking lots. Pull into the second one for perhaps the best viewpoint of the entire valley, with point-blank views (directly ahead) of the steep ridge-like mountains known as the **Three Sisters.** Hike about 100 feet away from the pullout to your own private bluff to enjoy the view

alone. This is also the starting point for the **Hidden Valley** hike.

As you continue your drive, you'll pass a raging waterfall in a canyon—the Tears of the MacDonalds—on the right. After another mile or so—through more glorious waterfall scenery—watch on the left for the **Coffin Cairn,** which looks like a stone igloo (parking is just across the road if you want a photo op). Just after the cairn, look on the left for pullout parking for the easy-to-moderate **hike to The Study,** a viewpoint overlooking the road you just drove down (about 45-60 minutes round-trip).

After this pullout, you'll hit a straightaway for about a mile, followed by an S-curve. At the end of the curve, look for the pullout parking on the left, just

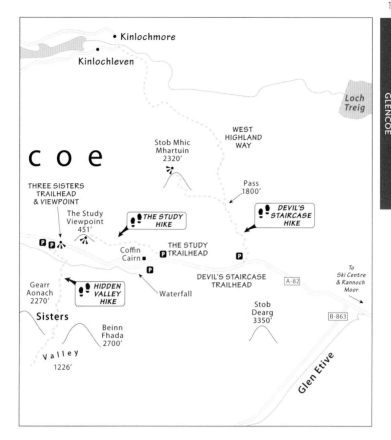

before the stand of pine trees. This is the trailhead for the **Devil's Staircase** hike, high into the hills (a strenuous 800-foot gain to the pass at the top, about 1.5 hours round-trip).

Continuing past here, you're nearing the end of the valley. The intimidating peak called the Great Shepherd of Etive (on the right) looms like a dour watchman, guarding the far end of the valley. Soon you'll pass the turnoff (on the right) for **Glen Etive,** an even more remote-feeling valley. Continuing past that, the last sign of civilization (on the right) is the Glencoe Ski Centre. And from here, the terrain flattens out as you enter the vast **Rannoch Moor**—50 bleak square miles of heather, boulders, and barely enough decent land to graze a sheep. Robert Louis Stevenson called it the "Highland Desert."

You could keep driving as far as you like—but the moor looks pretty much the same from here on out. Turn around and head back through Glencoe...it's scenery you'll hardly mind seeing twice.

Eating

In the village, **$$$ The Glencoe Gathering** specializes in seafood with a Scottish twist (daily, at junction of A-82 and Glencoe village), and the **$ Glencoe Café** has soups, sandwiches, and homemade baked goods (daily). Set in a stunning valley a few miles from the village, **$$ Clachaig Inn** serves solid pub grub all day long.

Sleeping

These B&Bs are along or just off the main road through the middle of the village: **$$ Beechwood Cottage B&B,** a shoes-off, slippers-on kind of place (www.beechwoodcottage.scot); the welcoming **$$ Heatherlea B&B** (www.heatherleaglencoe.com); and the cozy and homey **$ Ghlasdruim B&B** (http://ghlasdruim.co.uk).

Options just outside town, with good proximity to both the village and valley, include the comfortable **$$ Strath Lodge** (www.strathlodgeglencoe.com) and the hiker-friendly **$$ Clachaig Inn** (with recommended pub, frontdesk@clachaig.com).

FORT WILLIAM

Fort William—after Inverness, the second biggest town in the Highlands (pop. 10,000)—is Glencoe's opposite. While Glencoe is a humble one-street village, appealing to hikers and nature lovers, Fort William feels like one big Scottish shopping mall. But given its strategic position—between Glencoe and Oban in the south, Inverness in the east, and the Isle of Skye in the west—you're likely to pass through Fort William at some point during your Highlands explorations.

Orientation

While "just passing through" is the perfect plan here, Fort William can provide a good opportunity to stock up on whatever you need (last supermarket before Inverness), grab lunch, and get any questions answered at the TI.

Arrival in Fort William: Parking lots flank the main pedestrian zone, High Street. The train and bus stations sit side by side just north of the old town center, where you'll find a handy pay parking lot.

Tourist Information: The TI is on the car-free main drag (daily, free Wi-Fi, 15 High Street, tel. 01397/701-801). Free public WCs are up the street, next to the parking lot.

Sights

▲WEST HIGHLAND MUSEUM

Fort William's only real sight is its humble but well-presented museum. Its exhibits are genuinely insightful about local history and Highland life.

Cost and Hours: Free, £3 suggested donation, Mon-Sat 10:00-17:00, and maybe Sun in high season; Nov-Dec

On top of Ben Nevis, Britain's highest peak

and March until 16:00, closed Sun; closed Jan-Feb; midway down the main street on Cameron Square, www.westhighlandmuseum.org.uk).

BEN NEVIS

From Fort William, take a peek at Britain's highest peak, Ben Nevis (4,406 feet). Thousands walk to its summit each year. On a clear day, you can admire it from a distance. Scotland's only mountain cable cars—at the **Nevis Range Mountain Experience**—can take you to a not-very-lofty 2,150-foot perch on the slopes of Aonach Mòr for a closer look (£14, 15-minute ride, generally open daily but closed in high winds and winter—call ahead, signposted on the A-82 north of Fort William, tel. 01397/705-825, www.nevisrange.co.uk).

Eating and Sleeping

For lunch and picnics, try **$ Deli Craft** (61 High Street) or **$ Hot Roast Company** (127 High Street). For lunch or dinner, **$$ The Grog & Gruel** serves real ales, good pub grub, and Tex-Mex/Cajun dishes (66 High Street).

If spending the night, the Hobbit-cute **$ Gowan Brae B&B** ("Hill of the Big Daisy") has loch or garden views (Union Road, www.gowanbrae.co.uk).

Transportation
Getting Around

Fort William is a major transit hub for the Highlands.

BY BUS

From Fort William to: Glencoe or **Ballachulish** (all Glasgow-bound buses—#914, #915, and #916; 8/day, 30 minutes; also Stagecoach bus #44, hourly, fewer on Sun), **Oban** (bus #918, 2/day, 1.5 hours), **Portree** on the Isle of Skye (buses #914, #915, and #916, 3/day, 3 hours), **Inverness** (buses #19 and #919, 7/day, 2 hours), **Glasgow** (buses #914, #915, and #916; 8/day, 3 hours). To reach **Edinburgh,** take the bus to Glasgow, then transfer to a train or bus (figure 5 hours total).

BY TRAIN

From Fort William to: Glasgow (3/day, 4 hours), **Mallaig**/ferry to Isle of Skye (4/day, 1.5 hours; take 30-minute ferry to Armadale, where Stagecoach bus #52 connects to destinations on Skye).

BY CAR

From Fort William to Loch Ness and Inverness: Head north out of Fort William on the A-82. After about eight miles, in the village of Spean Bridge, take the left fork (staying on the A-82). The A-82 sweeps north and follows the Caledonian Canal, passing through **Fort Augustus** (a good lunch stop, with its worthwhile Caledonian Canal Visitor Centre), and then follows the north side of Loch Ness on its way to Inverness.

From Oban to Fort William via Glencoe: See page 172 in the Oban chapter.

From Fort William to the Isle of Skye: You have two options: Head north on the A-82 to Invergarry, and turn left (west) on the A-87, which you'll follow to Kyle of Lochalsh and the **Skye Bridge** to the island.

Or, head west on the A-830 through Glenfinnan, then catch the **ferry** from Mallaig to Armadale on the Isle of Skye. The scenic drive between Fort William and Mallaig is called the "Road to the Isles." Be sure you allow enough time to make it to Mallaig at least 20 minutes before the Skye ferry departs (figure at least 90 minutes of driving time from Fort William to the ferry, not including stops). In summer it's smart to reserve a spot on the ferry the day before, either online or by phone. For specifics, see "Arriving and Departing" at the end of the Isle of Skye chapter.

Isle of Skye

The rugged, remote-feeling Isle of Skye has a reputation for unpredictable weather, but it also offers some of Scotland's best scenery. Narrow, twisty roads wind around Skye in the shadows of craggy, black, bald mountains, and the coastline is ruffled with peninsulas and sea lochs (inlets).

Skye is the Inner Hebrides' largest island (over 600 square miles), but it's still manageable: You're never more than five miles from the sea. The island has only about 13,000 residents; roughly a quarter live in the main village, Portree. The mountain-like Cuillin Hills separate the northern part of the island (Portree, Trotternish, Dunvegan) from the south (Skye Bridge, Kyleakin, Sleat Peninsula).

Set up camp in Portree, Skye's charming, low-key tourism hub. Then dive into Skye's attractions. Drive around the appealing Trotternish Peninsula, enjoying scenic beauty: rolling fields, stony homes, and stark vistas of jagged rock formations. Go for a hike in the dramatic Cuillin Hills, sample a peaty dram of whisky, and walk across a desolate bluff to a lighthouse at the end of the world. Visit your choice of clan castles. Or just settle in, slow down, and enjoy island life.

ISLE OF SKYE IN 2 DAYS

Day 1: Starting from your home base at Portree, drive around the Trotternish Peninsula (could hike to the Old Man of Storr, visit the Skye Museum of Island Life, stop by Duntulm Castle ruins, and more). Hikers may want to get advice from Portree's TI on longer hikes.

Day 2: Tour Dunvegan Castle, take the distillery tour, and hike to the Fairy Pools.

Skye is best explored by car (rentable in Portree), though minibus tours do cover the island's major sights (as do public buses, but slowly and less efficiently).

Whether you like to hike or just don't want to rush a good thing, the island is easily worth two days. But if you have only **one day**, visit the three big sights—Dunvegan Castle, Talisker Distillery, and the Trotternish Peninsula, with its memorable Skye Museum of Island Life.

If you'll be taking the Skye Bridge to or from the island, be sure to get the picture-postcard view of Eilean Donan Castle on the mainland.

For details on arriving on Skye by ferry (from Mallaig on the mainland) and departing by bridge, see the end of this chapter.

ISLE OF SKYE AT A GLANCE

▲▲▲**Trotternish Peninsula Loop Drive** Exploring the northern peninsula (best in good weather), featuring striking natural beauty, hikes, ruined castles, and a fine museum. See page 201.

▲▲**Portree Harbor** Colorful, scenic harborfront of the island's top town. See page 196.

▲▲**The Quiraing** Jagged, mountainous ridge with distinctive formations. See page 203.

▲▲**Skye Museum of Island Life** Cluster of huts showing lifestyles of islanders 150 years ago. See page 204.

▲▲**Dunvegan Castle** Interesting, tourable residence of MacLeod clan, with lush gardens. See page 205.

▲▲**Talisker Distillery** Good whisky tours (by reservation) at distillery operating since 1830. See page 207.

▲▲**Cuillin Hills** Southern craggy ridge of island, offering views and hikes (including Fairy Pools Hike). See page 208.

▲**Kilt Rock** Sea cliff with volcanic formations resembling pleats of Scotland's national dress. See page 202.

▲**The Fairy Glen** Hilly, pond-strewn valley where locals claim fairies live. See page 205.

▲**Dun Beag Fort** Island's best-preserved Iron Age fort. See page 207.

▲**Eilean Donan Castle** Photogenic castle (with cozy but less notable interior), just 100 years old, on mainland. See page 210.

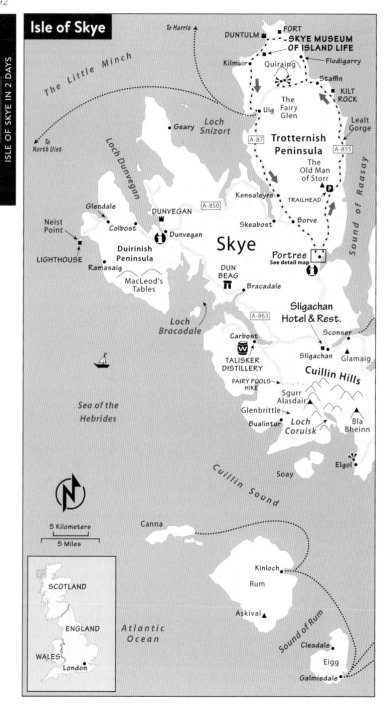

Isle of Skye

To Harris

DUNTULM · FORT

SKYE MUSEUM OF ISLAND LIFE

Kilmuir · Quiraing

Flodigarry

Staffin

KILT ROCK

The Fairy Glen

Uig

Lealt Gorge

The Little Minch

Geary

Loch Snizort

A-87 · **Trotternish Peninsula**

To North Uist

The Old Man of Storr

A-855

Loch Dunvegan

Glendale

DUNVEGAN

A-850

Kensaleyre

TRAILHEAD

P

Sound of Raasay

Neist Point

Colbost

Dunvegan

Skeabost

Borve

LIGHTHOUSE

Duirinish Peninsula

Ramasaig

MacLeod's Tables

Skye

Portree
See detail map

DUN BEAG

Bracadale

Loch Bracadale

A-863

Sligachan Hotel & Rest.

Sconser

Carbost

W

TALISKER DISTILLERY

Sligachan

Glamaig

Cuillin Hills

Sea of the Hebrides

FAIRY POOLS HIKE

Sgurr Alasdair

Glenbrittle

Bualintur

Loch Coruisk

Bla Bheinn

Elgol

Cuillin Sound

Soay

N

5 Kilometers

5 Miles

Canna

Kinloch

Rum

Askival

Atlantic Ocean

Sound of Rum

Cleadale

Eigg

Galmisdale

SCOTLAND

ENGLAND

WALES

London

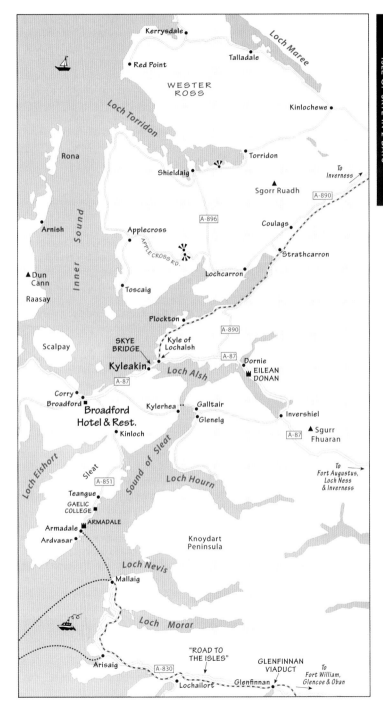

PORTREE

Skye's main attraction is its natural beauty, not its villages. But of those villages, the best home base is Portree (pore-TREE), Skye's largest settlement, transportation hub, and tourism center—ideally located for exploring Skye's quintessential sights on the Trotternish Peninsula loop drive.

Portree is nestled deep in its protective, pastel harbor; overlapping peninsulas just offshore guard it from battering west coast storms. Most of today's Portree dates from its early-19th-century boom time as a kelp-gathering and herring-fishing center.

As the most popular town on Scotland's most popular island, Portree is jammed with visitors in the summer. There are lots of hotels and B&Bs (which book up well in advance) and an abundance of good restaurants (the best of which merit reservations).

Orientation

Although Portree doesn't have any real sights, it does boast a gorgeous harbor area and—in the streets above—all of the necessary tourist services: a good TI, fine B&Bs, great restaurants, a grocery store, a launderette, and so on. The main business zone of this functional town of about 3,000 residents is in the tight grid of lanes on the bluff just above the harbor, anchored by Portree's tidy main square, Somerled Square. From here, buses fan out across the island and to the mainland.

Portree

B&Bs line the roads leading out of town.

Tourist Information: Portree's helpful TI is a block off the main square (June-Aug Mon-Sat 9:00-18:30, Sun until 17:00; off-season Mon-Sat 9:30-16:30, closed Sun; free Wi-Fi, just below Bridge Road, tel. 01478/612-137, www.visitscotland.com).

This is the island's most useful TI, though shops in smaller towns (including Dunvegan) host basic "information points."

Helpful Hints

WCs: Public WCs are across the street and down a block from the TI, across from the hostel.

Laundry: A **self-service launderette** is below the Independent Hostel, just off the main square (usually 11:00-21:00, last load starts at 20:00, The Green, tel. 01478/613-737).

Bike Rental: Island Cycles rents bikes in the middle of town, just off the main square (£10/half-day, £20/24 hours, best to reserve in advance in high season, Mon-Sat 9:00-17:00, closed Sun, shorter hours in winter, The Green, tel. 01478/613-121, www.islandcycles-skye.co.uk).

Car Rental: To make the most of your time on Skye, rent a car. Several options line up along the road to Dunvegan and charge around £40-60/day (most are closed Sun; smart to call several days ahead in peak season, but worth trying last-minute). The most user-friendly option is **M2 Motors,** which can pick you up at your B&B or the bus station (tel. 01478/613-344, www.m2-motors.co.uk). If they're booked up, try **Jansvans** (tel. 01478/612-087, www.jans.co.uk), **Highland Motors/HM Hire** (based nearby in Borve but can pick up in Portree, tel. 01470/532-264, www.hm-hire.co.uk), or **Morrison** (tel. 01478/612-688, www.morrisoncarrental.com).

Parking: As you enter town, you'll see signs on the right directing you to a free parking lot below, at water level—after

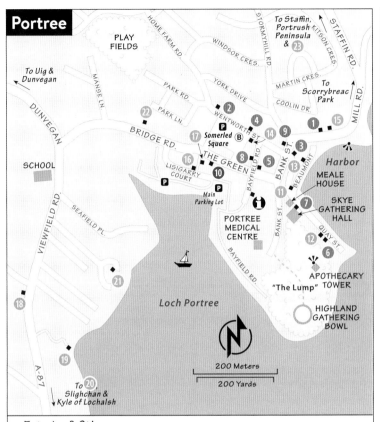

Portree

PLAY FIELDS

To Uig & Dunvegan

To Staffin, Portrush Peninsula & 23

SCHOOL

Somerled Square

Harbor

MEALE HOUSE

SKYE GATHERING HALL

Main Parking Lot

PORTREE MEDICAL CENTRE

APOTHECARY TOWER

"The Lump"

Loch Portree

HIGHLAND GATHERING BOWL

200 Meters
200 Yards

To Slighchan & Kyle of Lochalsh

Eateries & Other

1. Scorrybreac
2. The Isles Inn
3. Café Arriba & The Chippy
4. The Café
5. L'Incontro Pizza
6. Sea Breezes
7. The Harbour Fish & Chips Shop
8. Fat Panda
9. Co-op Grocery & Relish
10. Bike Rental

Sleeping

11. Rosedale Hotel
12. Pink Guest House
13. Marine House
14. The Portree Hotel
15. Ben Tianavaig
16. Portree Youth Hostel
17. Portree Independent Hostel & Launderette
18. Duirinish Guest House
19. Fishers Rock
20. To Greenacres Guest House
21. Seaforth Cottage
22. Easdale B&B
23. To Ballintoy Bed and Breakfast

parking, just head up the stairs to the TI. You can also pay-and-display to park in the main town square (2-hour max, free after 18:00).

Town Walk: Michelle Rhodes leads guided one-hour town walks through Portree by request. While there's not a lot to say about the town, it's fun to have a local to explain things, and Michelle is a fine storyteller (£10 per person, call or email to set a time; mobile 07833-073-951, tel. 01478/611-915, www.skyehistoryandheritagetours.co.uk, michellelorrainerhodes@gmail.com). She also offers all-day guided driving tours around the island, tailored to your interests. Her specialty: clan battles, fairies, myths, and legends (£150 for two, £75/extra person).

Sights

There's not a turnstile in town, but Portree itself is fun to explore. Below I've described the village's three areas: the main square and "downtown," the harborfront, and the hill above the harbor.

SOMERLED SQUARE AND THE TOWN CENTER

Get oriented to Portree on the broad main square, with its mercat cross, bus stops, parking lot, and highest concentration of public benches.

Much of present-day Portree was the vision of Sir James MacDonald, who pushed to develop the town in the late 18th century. City leaders imported the impressive engineer Thomas Telford (famous for his many great canals, locks, and bridges) to help design the village's harbor and the roads connecting it to the rest of the island.

Wentworth Street, running from this square to the harbor, is the main shopping drag. Window-shop your way two blocks along Wentworth Street. Turn right on Bank Street. The **Royal Hotel,** built on the site of MacNab's Inn, was where Bonnie Prince Charlie bid farewell to Flora MacDonald following his crushing defeat at Culloden, then set sail, never again to return to Scotland.

Quay Street leads down the hill to...

▲▲PORTREE HARBOR

Portree's most pleasant space (unless you've got food the seagulls want) is its harbor, where colorful homes look out over bobbing boats and the surrounding peninsulas. As one of the most protected natural harbors on the west coast, it's the reason that Portree emerged as Skye's leading town. Find a scenic perch at the corner of the harbor and take it all in.

Notice the stone building with the sealed-off door at the base of the stairs leading up into town. This was the former **ice house,** which was in operation until the 1970s. The winch at the peak of the building was used to haul big blocks of ice into an enormous subterranean cellar, to preserve Atlantic salmon throughout the summer.

Survey the harbor, enjoying the **pastel homes**—which come with lots of local gossip. Rumor has it that these used to be more uniform, until a proud gay couple decided to paint their house pink (it's now a recommended B&B). What used to be a blue-and-white house next door (now an all-blue hotel) belonged to a fan of the West Ham United soccer team. Soon the other homeowners followed suit, each choosing their own color.

You may notice the busy fish-and-chips joint, with its customers standing guardedly against the nearby walls and vicious seagulls perched on rooftops ready to swoop down at the first sight of battered cod.

Go for a stroll along the Telford-built pier. Along here, a couple of different companies offer 1.5-hour excursions out to the sea-eagle nests and around the bay (ask the captains at the port, or inquire at the TI).

Experiences

ASCENDING "THE LUMP" (HILL ABOVE THE HARBOR)

For a different perspective on Portree—and one that gets you away from the tourists—hike up the bluff at the south end of the harbor. From the Royal Hotel, head up Bank Street.

After a few steps, you'll spot the white

Apothecary tower

Portree harbor

Meall House on your left—supposedly Portree's oldest surviving home (c. 1800) and once the sheriff's office and jail. Today it's a center for the Gaelic cultural organization Fèisean nan Gàidheal, which celebrates the Celtic tongue that survives about as well here on Portree as anywhere in Scotland. Hiding behind the Meall House, along the harborview path, is the stepped-gable **Skye Gathering Hall** (from 1879). This is where Portree's upper crust throws big, fancy, invitation-only balls on the days before and after Skye's Highland Games. The rest of the year, it hosts cultural events and—on most days—a fun little market with a mix of crafts and flea-market-type items.

Back on Bank Street, continue uphill. Soon you'll approach the **Portree Medical Centre**—one of just two hospitals on the entire Isle of Skye. (Is it just me, or do those parking spots each come with a graveyard cross?)

Just before the hospital's parking lot, watch on the left for the uphill lane through the trees. Use this to hike on up to the top of the hill that locals call "The Lump" (or, for those with more local pride, "Fancy Hill"). Emerging into the clearing, you'll reach a huge, flat **bowl** that was blasted out of solid rock to hold 5,000 people during Skye's annual Highland Gathering. In addition to the typical Highland dancing, footraces, and feats of strength, Skye's

games have a unique event: From this spot, runners climb downhill, swim across Loch Portree, ascend the hill on the adjacent peninsula, then swim back again.

Walk left, toward the harbor, then head left again onto a path leading away from the bowl; you'll run into a crenellated **apothecary tower.** It was built in 1834, not as a castle fortification but to alert approaching sailors that a pharmacist was open for business in Portree. It's usually open if you'd like to climb to the top for views over the harbor and the region—on a clear day, you can see all the way to the Old Man of Storr.

WALKS AND HIKES NEAR PORTREE

The Portree TI can offer advice about hikes in the area; if either of the below options interests you, get details there before you head out.

One popular choice, which doesn't require a car, is called the **Scorrybreac Path.** To get to the trailhead—three-quarters of a mile from Somerled Square—walk north out of Portree on Mill Road, veer right onto Scorrybreac Road when you're just leaving town (following the sign for *Budhmor*), then follow the coastline to the start of the hiking trail, marked by signs. From here, you'll walk along the base of a bluff with fine views back on Portree's colorful harborfront.

Drivers can tackle the more ambitious hike up to the **Old Man of Storr:** You'll drive about 15 minutes north of town (following the start of my Trotternish Peninsula Driving Tour) and park at the Old Man of Storr trailhead. Green trail signs lead you through a gate and up along a well-trod gravel path through a felled woodland. Once you've reached the top of the first bluff, take the right fork, and continue all the way up to the pinnacle. Plan on about two hours round-trip.

Eating

Note that Portree's eateries tend to close early (21:00 or 22:00), and the popular places can merit reservations any evening in the high season.

Up in Town

$$$$ Scorrybreac is Portree's best splurge, offering a delightful array of well-presented international dishes that draw from local ingredients and traditions. The cozy, modern, unpretentious dining room with eight tables fills up quickly, so reservations are a must (set multicourse menus only, Tue-Sun 17:30-22:30, closed Mon, 7 Bosville Terrace, tel. 01478/612-069, www.scorrybreac.com).

$$ The Isles Inn is a happening place, popular with hikers, with two halves serving the same menu—a brighter high-energy dining area and the darker pub—or you can sit at the bar. Offering a fun energy and warm service, they dish up simple, honest food one notch above pub grub. They have popular burgers, and their big slabs of salmon or haddock are served with fresh vegetables (daily 12:00-15:00 & 17:00-21:30, no reservations possible after 19:00, tel. 01478/612-129, facing the main square, Somerled Square). In summer, the Isles Inn hosts live music several nights a week from 21:30.

$$ Café Arriba is a fun and welcoming space offering refreshingly eclectic flavors in this small Scottish town. With a menu that includes local specialties, burgers, and Italian, this youthful, colorful, easygoing eatery's hit-or-miss cuisine is worth trying

(lots of vegetarian options, daily 7:00-18:00, Quay Brae, tel. 01478/611-830).

$$ The Café, a few steps off the main square, is a busy, popular home-town diner serving good crank-'em-out food to an appreciative local crowd. It's family-friendly, with a good selection of burgers and fish-and-chips (daily 9:00-15:30 & 17:30-21:00, Wentworth Street, tel. 01478/612-553). Their homemade ice cream from the stand in front is a nice way to finish your meal.

$$ L'Incontro Pizza is Portree's favorite place for pizza. A sprawling, family-friendly place, it can merit reservations, too (open 17:00-21:00, closed Mon, The Green, tel. 01478/612-535).

Dining on the Waterfront

Portree's little harbor has a scattering of good eateries but none have actual waterfront seating. My hunch: It's because of the mean seagulls that hang out here.

$$$ Sea Breezes is a popular choice, with plain decor and a seafood-focused menu. At this basic, salty, no-nonsense eatery, you'll likely need reservations for dinner (daily 12:30-14:00 & 17:30-21:30 in summer, shorter hours off-season, closed Nov-Easter, tel. 01478/612-016, www.seabreezes-skye.co.uk).

Eating Cheaper

Fish-and-Chips: Portree has two chippies: **$ The Harbour Fish & Chips Shop** is delightfully located on the charming harbor with good fish that's cheap and in big portions (daily 11:00-21:00, later in summer). The down side: Aggressive sea gulls drive diners up against the wall. It's funny to watch. For a more relaxing meal, **$ The Chippy** sells very basic fish-and-chips and burgers, just up the harbor lane (on Bank Street) with peaceful-if-grungy tables and no seagulls.

Takeaway in Town: The **Fat Panda** Asian restaurant on Bayfield Road is satisfying, the **Co-op** grocery (daily 8:00-23:00) has a small selection of sandwiches and other prepared foods, and **Relish** is a deli serving good fresh sandwiches (eat in or to go, end of Wentworth Street).

Eating Between Portree and Kyleakin

In Sligachan: The **Sligachan Hotel** (pronounced SLIG-a-hin) is a grand and rustic old hotel in an extremely scenic setting, nestled in the Cuillin Hills. Its Harta Restaurant offers "casual dining with fine food" and a big bar. Popular with campers and hikers, it's also family-friendly, with a playground. The Seumas Bar has a Scotsman-pleasing range of whiskies. Choose between the lovely **$$$ dining room** (nightly 18:30-21:00) and the big, open-feeling **$$ pub** serving microbrews and mountaineer-pleasing grub (long hours daily, food served until 21:30, pub closed Oct-Feb; on the A-87 between Kyleakin and Portree in Sligachan, tel. 01478/650-204).

Sleeping

Portree is crowded with hikers and tourists in July and August: Book your room well in advance. You may need to check with several places. If you're late to the game, you might have better luck with a hotel, Airbnb, or one of the B&Bs lacking websites. Spring and fall (March-June and Sept-Oct) are also busy, but a bit more manageable (and cheaper).

If looking last-minute, try the Facebook group "Skye Rooms," where hotels, B&Bs, and short-term apartments list their availability for the next day. Travelers looking for accommodations can also post their desired dates.

On the Harbor

$$$ Rosedale Hotel fills three former fishermen's houses with mazelike hallways and 23 rooms (some modern, some more traditional). With-it Neil runs the hotel with the help of his family including his mom, who cooks (family room and a few small, no-view, cheaper doubles available;

no elevator, restaurant, bar for guests only, parking lot down the road; Beaumont Crescent, tel. 01478/613-131, www.rosedalehotelskye.co.uk, reservations@rosedalehotelskye.co.uk).

$$ At **Pink Guest House,** energetic Robbie and Fiona rent 11 bright, spacious rooms (8 with sea views) on the harbor. The rates include a full Scottish breakfast and the hosts' youthful enthusiasm (large family rooms, Quay Street, tel. 01478/612-263, www.pinkguesthouse.co.uk, info@pinkguesthouse.co.uk).

$ Marine House, a cozy, welcoming, delightful time warp run by sweet Skye native Fiona Stephenson, has three simple, homey rooms (two with a private bathroom down the hall) and fabulous views of the harbor (cash only, reserved parking right on harbor, 2 Beaumont Crescent, tel. 01478/611-557, stephensonfiona@yahoo.com).

Up in Town

$$$$ The Portree Hotel is your basic, impersonal town-center accommodation (right on the main square) with 24 modernized rooms on three floors and no elevator (family rooms, bar/restaurant, no parking—must use public lots, tel. 01478/612-511, www.theportreehotel.com, contact@theportreehotel.com).

$$ Ben Tianavaig, on the busy road through town overlooking the harbor, offers four fresh and airy rooms (all with views). Charlotte and Bill are generous with travel tips, offer a breakfast special of the day, and foster a shoes-off tidiness (2-night minimum required, cash only, street parking out front; 5 Bosville Terrace, tel. 01478/612-152, www.ben-tianavaig.co.uk, info@ben-tianavaig.co.uk).

¢ Portree Youth Hostel, run by Hostelling Scotland (SYHA), is a modern-feeling, institutional, cinderblock-and-metal building with 54 beds in 16 rooms (private and family rooms available, continental breakfast extra, kitchen, laundry, tel. 01478/612-231, www.syha.org.uk, portree@syha.org.uk).

¢ **Portree Independent Hostel,** in the unmissable yellow building just off the main square, has 60 beds and equally bold colors inside (one double room and several 4-person rooms, no breakfast, kitchen, laundry, tel. 01478/613-737, www.hostelskye.co.uk, skyehostel@yahoo.co.uk).

South of Portree, off Viewfield Road

Viewfield Road, stretching south from Portree toward the Aros Centre, is B&B central. All offer convenient parking and are within walking distance of town (figure 10-15 minutes). All are well marked from the main road.

$$ **Duirinish Guest House** feels homey, modern, and tidy. With four rooms, it sits across the main road from the water (only a few obstructed sea views) but comes with a spacious guest lounge and a warm welcome (2-night minimum, closed Nov-March, tel. 01478/613-728, www.duirinish-bandb-skye.com, ruth.n.prior@hotmail.co.uk, Ruth and Allan).

$$ **Fishers Rock,** a serene waterfront retreat with a glassy, contemporary, light-filled view breakfast room, has a soothing energy and three rooms (2-night minimum, closed in winter, tel. 01478/612-122, www.fishersrock.com, fishersrock@btinternet.com, Heather).

$$ **Greenacres Guest House** feels estate-like and a bit more formal, with fine china on the table, manicured hedges in the garden, and a sunroom with views. The five rooms have different color schemes and styles (cash only, closed Oct-Easter, one of the farthest houses from town on Viewfield Road, about a 20-minute walk, tel. 01478/612-605, www.greenacres-skye.co.uk, greenacreskye@aol.com, Marie and Ewen).

$ **Seaforth Cottage** feels like a retired sea captain's home. Overlooking tidal flats, its garden is artfully littered with nautical flotsam and jetsam. The three simple rooms come with sea views and are a bit older, but priced accordingly (cash only, tel. 01478/612-040, ianskye48@hotmail.co.uk, gentle Ian).

$ **Easdale B&B** is another old-school place with three rooms, a bright breakfast room, and a large, traditional lounge set just above the busy main road (cash only, no kids, Bridge Road, tel. 01478/613-244—call to reserve; spunky, plainspoken, and happily computer-free Chrissie).

North of Portree, off Staffin Road

$$ **Ballintoy Bed and Breakfast,** set back from the road and surrounded by a large field, has three immaculate ground-floor rooms accessorized with fun pops of color and artwork (family room, 2-night minimum preferred, includes continental breakfast, 15-minute walk from town on Staffin Road, tel. 01478/611-719, www.ballintoy-skye.co.uk, ballintoyskye@gmail.com, Gillian and Gavin).

Sleeping Between Portree and Kyleakin

$$$ **Sligachan Hotel,** perched at a crossroads in the scenic middle of nowhere (yet handy for road-tripping sightseers) is a local institution and a haven for hikers. The hotel's 21 rooms are comfortable, if a bit dated and simple for the price, while the nearby campground and bunkhouse offer a budget alternative (closed Nov-Feb, on the A-87 between Kyleakin and Portree in Sligachan, hotel and campground tel. 01478/650-204, bunkhouse tel. 01478/650-458, www.sligachan.co.uk, reservations@sligachan.co.uk).

SIGHTS ON THE ISLE OF SKYE

It's most fun to tour Skye by car, stopping wherever you want. (Portree's car-rental agencies are listed in "Helpful Hints," earlier.)

Without a car, travelers can choose among day-long minibus tours, which are more time-efficient than relying on public buses. (For more on both, see "Getting Around the Isle of Skye," at the end of this chapter.)

I've organized the sights geographically, roughly from north (near Portree) to south.

This well-trodden tourist path around Skye is clearly the most memorable way for drivers to spend the day. The three big sights are Dunvegan Castle, Talisker Distillery, and Trotternish Peninsula, with its memorable Skye Museum of Island Life. It's possible—but rushed—to see all three in one day. (The challenge: The Skye Museum of Island Life closes at 17:00.)

To see all three, start with the first distillery tour at 9:30, tour the castle, and get to the museum by about 16:30. This will rush the wonderful natural sights along the peninsula, but it might be worth it if time is short and you want to experience it all.

While you could drive directly from the castle to the museum and then tour the peninsula in a clockwise direction, it's far more scenic to drive it in a counterclockwise route as proposed here. Summer days are long, and the light can be wonderful in the early evening for the scenic west coast of the Trotternish Peninsula. Another option is to skip the distillery, do the castle first, and then have a leisurely tour of the peninsula as laid out in this chapter. Of course, if you have two days, do it all at your own pace.

Trotternish Peninsula Loop Drive

This inviting peninsula north of Portree is packed with windswept castaway views, unique geological formations, and some of Scotland's most dramatic scenery. The following loop tour starts and ends in Portree, circling the peninsula counterclockwise. In good weather, a spin around Trotternish is the best activity Skye offers and is worth ▲▲▲.

With minimal stops, the drive will take about two hours—but it deserves the better part of a day. Note that during several stretches, you'll be driving on a paved single-track road; use the occasional "passing places" to pull over and allow faster cars to go by.

☛ Self-Guided Drive

• *Head north of Portree on the A-855, following signs for Staffin. About three miles out of town, you'll begin to enjoy some impressive views of the Trotternish Ridge. You'll be passing peat bogs and may notice stretches where peat has been cut from the fields by the roadside. As you pass the small loch on your right, straight ahead is the distinctive rock tower called the...*

Old Man of Storr

This 160-foot-tall tapered slab of basalt stands proudly apart from the rest of the Storr (as the mountain is called). The unusual landscape of the Trotternish Peninsula is due to massive landslides. This block slid down the cliff about 6,500 years ago and landed on its end, where it has slowly been whittled by weather into a pinnacle.

If you'd like to tackle the two-hour hike to the Old Man, start at the parking lot directly below the formation (for details on the hike, see page 197).

• *After passing the Old Man, enjoy the scenery on your right, overlooking nearby islands and the mainland.*

As you drive, you'll notice that Skye seems to have more sheep than people. During the Highland Clearances of the early 19th century, many human residents were forced to move off the island to make room for more livestock. The people who remain are some of the most ardently Gaelic Scots in Scotland. While only about one percent of all Scottish people speak Gaelic (pronounced "gallic"), one-third of Skye residents are fluent. A generation ago, it was illegal to teach Gaelic in schools; today, Skye offers its residents

Old Man of Storr

Lealt Gorge

the opportunity to enroll in Gaelic-only education, from primary school to college (Sabhal Mòr Ostaig, on Skye's Sleat Peninsula, is the world's only college with courses taught entirely in Scottish Gaelic.

• *About four miles after the Old Man parking lot, you'll pass a sign for the River Lealt. Immediately after, the turnoff on the right is an optional stop at the...*

Lealt Gorge

Where the River Lealt tumbles toward the sea, it carves out a long and scenic gorge. To stretch your legs, you can walk about five minutes along the lip of the gorge to reach a viewpoint overlooking a protected, pebbly cove and some striking rock formations. The formations on the left, which look like stacked rocks, are the opposite: They've been weathered by centuries of battering storms, which have peeled back any vegetation and ground the stones to their smooth state.

• *Continue along the road. Just after the village of Valtos (about 2 miles after the Lealt Gorge viewpoint), you'll reach a loch (left), next to a parking lot (right). Park at the well-marked Kilt Rock viewpoint to check out...*

▲Kilt Rock

So named because of its resemblance to a Scotsman's tartan, this 200-foot-tall sea cliff has a layer of volcanic rock with vertical lava columns that look like pleats (known as columnar jointing), sitting atop a layer of horizontal sedimentary rock. The formations in the opposite direction are just as amazing.

• *Continuing north, as you approach the village of* **Staffin,** *you'll begin to see interesting rock formations—basalt rock pillars—high on the hill to your left.*

If you need a public WC, partway through town, watch on the left for the Staffin Community Hall (marked *Talla Stafainn,* sharing a building with a grocer). Or for a coffee or lunch break, you could visit (on the right) the Columba 1400 Centre, a Christian-run retreat for struggling teens from big cities. They run a nice cafeteria and shop to support their work (Mon-Sat 10:00-20:00, closed Sun, tel. 01478/611-400).

• *Just after you leave Staffin, watch for signs on the left to turn off and head up to the quintessential Isle of Skye viewpoint—a rock formation called...*

The Quiraing

▲▲ *The Quiraing*

You'll get fine views of this jagged northern end of the Trotternish Ridge as you drive up. Landslides caused the dramatic scenery in this area, and each rock formation has a name, such as "The Needle" or "The Prison."

At the summit of this road, you'll reach a parking area.

Rick's Tip: *From the parking lot at the Quiraing,* **even a short walk** *to a nearby bluff—to get away from the cars and alone with the wind and the island wonder—***is rewarding.**

There are several exciting hikes from here for a closer look at the formations. If you've got the time, energy, and weather for an unforgettable hike, here's your chance. You can follow the trail toward the bluff and at the fork decide to stay level (to the base of the formations) or veer off to the left and switch back up (to the top of the plateau). Both paths are faintly visible from the parking area—if it's busy, you'll see hikers on each. Once up top, your reward is a view of the secluded green pla-

teau called "The Table," another landslide block, which isn't visible from the road.

• *You could continue on this road all the way to Uig, at the other end of the peninsula. But it's more interesting to backtrack, then turn left onto the main road (A-855, now single-track), to see the...*

Tip of Trotternish

A few miles north, after the village of Flodigarry, you'll pass the Flodigarry Hotel. Soon after, at the top of a ridge ahead, you'll see the remains of an old **fort** from World War II, when the Atlantic was monitored for U-boats from this position.

Farther down the road, at the tip of the peninsula, you'll pass (on the right) the crumbling remains of another fort, this one much older: **Duntulm Castle** (free, roadside parking, 5-minute walk from road), which was the first stronghold on Skye of the influential MacDonald clan. It was from here that the MacDonalds fought many fierce battles against Clan MacLeod. The castle was abandoned around 1730 for Armadale Castle on the southern end of Skye. While the castle ruins are fenced off, travelers venture in at their own risk. In the distance beyond, you can see the **Outer Hebrides**—the most rugged, remote, and Gaelic part of Scotland.

• *A mile after the castle, watch for the turnoff on the left to the excellent...*

▲▲Skye Museum of Island Life

This fine little stand of seven thatched stone huts, organized into a family-run museum, explains how a typical Skye family lived a century and a half ago.

Cost and Hours: £2.50, Easter-Sept Mon-Sat 9:30-17:00, closed Sun and Oct-Easter, tel. 01470/552-206, www.skyemuseum.co.uk, run by Margaret, Hector, and Dinah. Though there are ample posted explanations, the £1 guidebook is worth buying.

Visiting the Museum: The three huts closest to the sea are original (more than 200 years old). Most interesting is The Old Croft House, which was the residence of the Graham family until 1957. Inside you'll find three rooms: kitchen (with peat-burning fire), parents' "master bedroom," and a bedroom for the 10 kids. Nearby, The Old Barn displays farm implements, and the Ceilidh House (a gathering place for the entire community) contains dense but very informative displays about crofting (the traditional tenant-farmer lifestyle on Skye), the Gaelic language, and a fascinating wall of classic Skye postcards.

The four other huts, reconstructed here, house exhibits about weaving, the village smithy, and more.

• *After touring the museum, head out to the very end of the small road that leads past the parking lot, to a lonesome cemetery. Let yourself in through the gate to reach the tallest Celtic cross at the far end, which is the...*

Monument to Flora MacDonald

This fine old cemetery, with mossy and evocative old tombs to ponder, features a tall cross dedicated to the local heroine who rescued the beloved Jacobite hero Bonnie Prince Charlie at his darkest hour. (After the original was chipped away by 19th-century souvenir seekers, this more modern replacement was placed here.) After his loss at Culloden, and with a hefty price on his head, Charlie retreated to the Outer Hebrides. But the Hanover dynasty, which controlled the islands, was closing in. Flora MacDonald rescued the prince, disguised him as her Irish maid, Betty Burke, and sailed him to safety on Skye. (Charlie pulled off the ruse thanks to his soft, feminine features—hence the nickname "Bonnie," which means "beautiful" or "handsome.")

• *Return to the main road and proceed about six miles around the peninsula. Soon after what was once a loch (now a giant depression), you'll drop down over the town of Uig ("OO-eeg"), the departure point for ferries to the Outer Hebrides and a handy spot for*

Skye Museum of Island Life

Monument to Flora MacDonald

services (cafés, a gas station, pottery shop, brewery, and WC).

Continue past Uig, climbing the hill across the bay. To take a brief detour to enjoy some hidden scenery, consider a visit to the Fairy Glen. To find it, just after passing the big Uig Hotel, take a very hard left, marked for Sheadar and Balnaknock. Follow this single-track road about a mile through the countryside. You'll emerge into an otherworldly little valley. Wind through the valley to just past the tiny lake and park below the towering Fairy Castle rock.

▲The Fairy Glen

Whether or not you believe in fairies, it's easy to imagine why locals claim that they live here. With evocatively undulating terrain—ruffled, conical hills called "fairy towers" reflected in glassy ponds, rising up from an otherwise flat and dull countryside—it's a magical place. There's little to see on a quick drive-by, but hikers enjoy exploring these hills, discovering little caves, weathered stone fences, and delightful views. Hardy hikers enjoy clambering 10 minutes up to the top of the tallest rock tower, the "Fairy Castle." (By the way, the sheep are actually fairies until a human enters the valley.)

Rick's Tip: *As you explore the Fairy Glen, keep an eye out for "Skye landmines" (sheep droppings).*

• *Head back the way you came and continue uphill on the main road (A-87), with views down over Uig's port. Looking back at Uig, you can see a good example of Skye's traditional farming system—crofting.*

Traditionally, arable land on the island was divided into plots. If you look across to the hills above Uig, you can see strips of demarcated land running up from the water—these are crofts. Crofts were generally owned by landlords (mostly English aristocrats or Scottish clan chiefs, and later the Scottish government) and rented to tenant farmers. The crofters lived and worked under very difficult conditions and were lucky if they could produce enough potatoes and livestock to feed their families. Historically, rights to farm the croft were passed down from father to eldest son over generations, but always under the auspices of a wealthy landlord.

• *This tour is finished. From here, you can continue along the main road south toward Portree (and possibly continue from there to the Cuillin Hills). Or you can take the shortcut road just after Kensaleyre (B-8036) and head west on the A-850 to Dunvegan and its castle. All of your Skye options are described in the following pages.*

Northwest Skye
▲▲DUNVEGAN CASTLE

Perched on a rock overlooking a sea loch, Dunvegan Castle is the residence of the MacLeod (pronounced "McCloud") clan. One of Skye's preeminent clans, the MacLeods often clashed with their rivals, the MacDonalds. The current clan chief, Hugh Magnus MacLeod, is a film producer who divides his time between London and the castle, where his noble efforts are aimed at preserving Dunvegan for future generations. Worth ▲▲▲ to people named MacLeod, the castle offers an interesting look at Scotland's antiquated clan system, provides insight into rural Scottish aristocratic lifestyles, and has fine gardens that are a delight to explore. Dunvegan feels rustic and a bit worse-for-wear compared to some of the more famous Scottish castles closer to civilization.

Cost and Hours: £13, daily 10:00-17:30, closed mid-Oct-March, café in parking lot, tel. 01470/521-206, www.dunvegancastle.com.

Getting There: It's near the small town of Dunvegan in the northwestern part of the island, well signposted from the A-850 (free parking). From Portree, bus #56 takes you right to the castle's parking lot.

Visiting the Castle: Follow the one-way route through the castle, borrowing laminated descriptions in each room—and don't hesitate to ask the helpful docents if you have any questions. You'll start upstairs and then make your way to the ground floor with its unforgettable exhibit on the people of St. Kilda.

Up the main staircase and looping left, you reach the **bedroom.** On the elegant canopy bed, look for the clan's seal and motto, carved into the headboard. The words "Hold Fast," which you'll see displayed throughout the castle, recall an incident where a MacLeod chieftain saved a man from being gored by a bull by literally taking the bull by the horns and wrestling it to the ground.

Beyond the bedroom, you'll ogle several more rooms, including the dining room (with portraits of clan chieftains and the MacLeod family) and the library, crammed with rich, leather-bound books.

Then you're routed back across the top of the stairs to the right wing, with the most interesting rooms. The 14th-century **drawing room** is the oldest part of the

castle—it served as the great hall of the medieval fortress. In the 18th century, a clan chief's new bride requested that it be modernized, so they added a drop ceiling and painted plaster walls.

Leaving the drawing room, notice the entrance to the **dungeon**—a hold-over from that stout medieval fortress. Squeeze inside the dungeon and peer down into the deep pit. (Hey, is that a MacDonald rotting down there?)

At the end of this wing is the **north room,** a mini museum of the clan's most prestigious artifacts. In the display case in the corner, find Rory Mor's Horn—made from a horn of the subdued bull that gave the clan its motto. Other artifacts include bagpipes and several relics related to Bonnie Prince Charlie (including his vest). In the center glass case, next to a lock of Charlie's hair, is a portrait of Flora Mac-Donald and some items that belonged to her.

From here a staircase leads to the ground floor where you'll find some important exhibits in more utilitarian rooms. A glass case holds the Claymore

Dunvegan Castle

Sword—one of two surviving swords made of extremely heavy Scottish iron rather than steel. Dating from the late 15th or early 16th century, this unique weapon is the bazooka of swords—designed not for dexterous fencing, but for one big kill-'em-all swing.

The MacLeods owned the rugged and remote St. Kilda islands (40 miles into the Atlantic, the most distant bit of the British Isles). They collected rent from the hard-scrabble St. Kilda community of 100 or so (who were finally evacuated in 1930). The artifacts and dramatic photos of this community is a highlight of the castle visit. And, finally, you can watch a 12-minute video about the castle and the MacLeods, solemnly narrated by the 29th chief of the clan.

Between the castle and the parking lot are five acres of plush **gardens** to stroll through. Circling down to the sea loch, you'll enjoy grand views back up to the castle (and see a dock selling 30-minute boat rides on Loch Dunvegan to visit a seal colony on a nearby island—£6, tel. 01470/521-500).

Rick's Tip: Nature lovers head higher up in Dunvegan's gardens *to see its finer, hidden parts: the walled garden, the woodland walk up to the water garden (with a thundering waterfall and a gurgling stream), and the wide-open round garden.*

▲DUN BEAG FORT

If driving between the distillery and Dunvegan on A-863, you'll pass Skye's best-preserved Iron Age fort or "broch." This 2,000-year-old round stone tower caps a hill a 10-minute walk above its parking lot (just north of the village of Struan). The walk rewards you with an unforgettable chance to be alone in an ancient stone structure with a commanding view.

Western Skye
▲▲TALISKER DISTILLERY

Talisker, a Skye institution, has been distilling here since 1830 and takes the tours it offers seriously. This venerable whisky distillery is situated at the base of a hill

Lush Dunvegan Gardens

with 14 springs, and at the edge of a sea loch—making it easier to ship ingredients in and whisky out. On summer days, the distillery swarms with visitors: You'll sniff both peated and unpeated grains; see the big mash tuns, washbacks, and stills; and sample a wee dram at the end. Island whisky tends to be smokier than mainland whisky due to the amount of peat smoke used during malting. Talisker workers describe theirs as "medium smoky," with peppery, floral, and vanilla notes.

Cost and Hours: £10 for one-hour tour with tasting and a £5 voucher toward a bottle; Mon-Fri 9:30-17:00, open Sat-Sun April-Oct only, Sun from 11:00, last tour one hour before closing; 30 tours/day in summer, 4/day in off-season; on the loch in Carbost village, tel. 01478/614-308, www.malts.com. Be sure to call for a reservation (and plan on a 40-minute drive from Portree). Designated drivers who need to skip the tasting can ask for a dram to go.

Nearby: Note that the **Fairy Pools Hike**—an easy walk that includes some

Talisker Distillery

of the best Cuillin views on the island—starts from near Talisker Distillery (see next section).

Central Skye
▲▲CUILLIN HILLS

These rocky "hills" (which look more like mountains to me) stretch along the southern coast of the island, dominating Skye's landscape. Unusually craggy and alpine for Scotland, the Cuillin ("cool-in") seem to rise directly from the deep. You'll see them from just about anywhere on the southern two-thirds of the island, but no roads actually take you through the heart of the Cuillin—that's reserved for hikers and climbers, who love this area. To get the best views with a car, consider these options.

Sligachan: The road from the Skye Bridge to Portree is the easiest way to appreciate the Cuillin (you'll almost certainly drive along here at some point during your visit). These mountains are all that's left of a long-vanished volcano. As you approach, you'll see that there are three separate ranges (from right to left): red, gray, and black. The steep and challenging Black Cuillin is the most popular for serious climbers.

The crossroads of Sligachan has an old triple-arched Telford bridge—one of Skye's iconic views—and the landmark Sligachan Hotel (listed in "Eating" and "Sleeping," earlier). The village is nestled at the foothills of the Cuillin, and is a popular launch pad for mountain fun. The 2,500-foot-tall cone-shaped hill looming over Sligachan, named Glamaig ("Greedy Lady"), is the site of an annual 4.5-mile hill race in July: Speed hikers begin at the door of the Sligachan Hotel, race to the summit, run around a bagpiper, and scramble back down to the hotel. The record: 44 minutes (30 minutes up, 13 minutes down, 1 minute dancing a jig up top). A Gurkha from Nepal did it in near record time... barefoot.

Rick's Tip: *You're welcome to* **browse around the Sligachan Hotel**—*a virtual mountaineering museum with great old photos and artifacts throughout its ground floor (especially behind the reception desk).*

Fairy Pools Hike: Perhaps the best easy way to get some Cuillin views—and a sturdy but manageable hike—is to follow the popular trail to the Fairy Pools. This is relatively near Talisker Distillery (described earlier).

To reach the hike from the A-863 between Sligachan and Dunvegan, follow signs to *Carbost.* Just before reaching the village of Carbost, watch for signs and a turn-off on the left to *Glenbrittle.* Follow this one-track road through the rolling hills, getting closer and closer to the Cuillin peaks. The well-marked *Fairy Pools* turn-off will be on your right. Parking here, you can easily follow the well-tended trail down across the field and toward the rounded peaks. (While signs suggest a 9.5-mile, 4- to 5-hour loop, most people simply hike 30 minutes to the pools and back; it's mostly level.)

Very soon you'll reach a gurgling river, which you'll follow toward its source in the mountains. Because the path is entirely through open fields, you enjoy scenery the entire time (and you can't get lost). Soon the river begins to pool at the base of each waterfall, creating a series of picturesque pools. Although footing can be treacherous, many hikers climb down across the rocks to swim and sunbathe. This is a fun place to linger (bring a picnic, if not a swimsuit). As I overheard one visitor say, "Despite the fact that it's so cold, it's so invitin'!"

South Skye
KYLEAKIN
Kyleakin (kih-LAH-kin), the last town in Skye before the Skye Bridge, used to be a big tourist hub...until the bridge connecting it to the mainland enabled easier travel to Portree and other areas deeper

Fairy Pools

in the island. Today this unassuming little village, with a ruined castle (Castle Moil), a cluster of lonesome fishing boats, and a forgotten ferry slip is worth a quick look but little more.

Eating in Broadford: Up the road in Broadford is the Broadford Hotel, part of an upscale Skye hotel chain (Torrin Road at junction with Elgol, tel. 01471/822-204, www.broadfordhotel.co.uk). Its **$$$$ restaurant** is attempting to bring classy cuisine to this small town in a nice contemporary setting with harbor views (set multicourse menu only, daily from 18:00). The hotel's **$$ Gabbro Bar** is a relaxed pub grub bistro.

Skye's Sleat Peninsula
CLAN DONALD CENTRE AND ARMADALE CASTLE
Facing the sea just outside Armadale is the ruined castle of Clan Donald, also known as the MacDonalds (Mac/Mc = "son of"). Today it is the "spiritual home of clan Donald," a sprawling site with woodland walks, a ruined castle, and a clan history museum.

Armadale Castle—more of a mansion than a fortress—was built in 1790, during

Kyleakin

the relatively peaceful, post-Jacobite age. Today the ruins (which you can view, but not enter) anchor a visitors center that celebrates the MacDonald way of life. You'll explore its manicured gardens, ogle the castle ruins, and visit the Museum of the Isles. This modern, well-presented museum tells the history of Scotland and Skye through the lens of its most influential clan (only a few artifacts but good descriptions, includes 1.5-hour audioguide). While fascinating for people named MacDonald, it's pricey and not worth a long detour for anyone else. But because it's right along the main road near the Armadale-Mallaig ferry, it can be an enjoyable place to kill some time while waiting for your ferry. At the parking lot is a big shop and café with free WCs.

Cost and Hours: £8.50, Easter-Oct daily 9:30-17:30, closed off-season, 2 minutes north of the Armadale ferry landing, tel. 01471/844-305, www.clandonald.com.

Nearby: Heading north on the A-851 from the Clan Donald Centre, keep an eye out for **Sabhal Mòr Ostaig** (a big complex of white buildings on the point). Skye is proud to host this college, with coursework taught entirely in Scottish Gaelic. Its mission is to further the Gaelic language (spoken today by about 60,000 people).

On the Mainland, Near the Isle of Skye

▲EILEAN DONAN CASTLE

This postcard castle, watching over a sea loch from its island perch, is scenically (and conveniently) situated on the road between the Isle of Skye and Loch Ness. While the photo op is worth ▲▲, the interior—with cozy rooms—is worth only a peek and closer to ▲.

Strategically situated at the confluence of three sea lochs, this was the stronghold of the Mackenzies—a powerful clan that was, like the MacLeods at Dunvegan, a serious rival to the mighty MacDonalds. Though it looks ancient, the current castle is actually less than a century old. The original castle on this site (dating from 800 years ago) was destroyed in battle in 1719, then rebuilt between 1912 and 1932 by the Macrae family as their residence.

Cost and Hours: £7.50, good £6 guidebook; March-Oct daily 10:00-18:00, July-Aug from 9:00, may open a few days a week Nov-Feb—call ahead, last entry one

Eilean Donan Castle

hour before closing; café, tel. 01599/555-202, www.eileandonancastle.com.

Getting There: It's not actually on the Isle of Skye, but it's quite close, in the mainland town of Dornie. Follow the A-87 about 15 minutes east of Skye Bridge, through Kyle of Lochalsh and toward Loch Ness and Inverness. The castle is on the right side of the road, just after a long bridge. Buses that run between Portree and Inverness (including #915, #916, and #917) stop at Dornie, a short walk from the castle (6/day, 1 hour from Portree).

Visiting the Castle: Buy tickets at the visitors center, then walk across the bridge and into the castle complex, and make your way into the big, blocky keep. You'll begin with some audiovisual introductory exhibits (left of main castle entry), then work through the historic rooms. Docents posted throughout can tell you more. First you'll see the claustrophobic, vaulted Billeting Room (where soldiers had their barracks), then head upstairs to the inviting Banqueting Room, with grand portraits of the honorable John Macrae-Gilstrap and his wife (who spearheaded the modern rebuilding of the castle). This room comes to life when you get a docent to explain

the paintings and artifacts here. After the renovation, this was a sort of living room. Another flight of stairs takes you to the circa-1930 bedrooms, which feel more cozy and accessible than those in many other castles—and do a great job of evoking the lifestyles of the aristocrats who built the current version of Eilean Donan as their personal castle playset.

TRANSPORTATION

Getting Around the Isle of Skye
By Car

Once on Skye, you'll need a car to thoroughly enjoy the island. (Even if you're doing the rest of your trip by public transportation, a car rental is worthwhile here to make maximum use of your time; Portree-based car-rental options are listed in "Helpful Hints," near the beginning of this chapter.) The roads are simple and well signposted. But if you'll be exploring, a good map can be helpful. Sample driving times: Kyleakin and Skye Bridge to Portree—45 minutes; Portree to Dunvegan—30 minutes; Portree to the tip of Trotternish

Peninsula and back again—2 hours (more with sightseeing stops); Portree to Armadale/ferry to Mallaig—1 hour; Portree to Talisker Distillery—40 minutes.

By Public Bus

Skye can be frustrating by bus (slow and limited). Portree is the hub for bus traffic. Most buses within Skye are operated by Stagecoach (www.stagecoachbus.com; buy individual tickets or consider the £8.85 all-day Dayrider ticket; buy tickets onboard). From Portree, you can loop around the **Trotternish Peninsula** on bus #57A (counterclockwise route) or bus #57C (clockwise route; Mon-Sat 4/day in each direction, limited on Sun). Bus #56 connects Portree and **Dunvegan Castle** (3/day, does not run on Sun, 40 minutes). From Portree to **Kyleakin,** take the Inverness-bound Citylink #917 (3/day, 1 hour) or local bus #50 (2/day, 1 hour, none on Sat-Sun); to reach **Eilean Donan Castle,** take any Citylink bus heading toward Fort William or Inverness (#915, #916, and #917; get off at Dornie and walk, 6/day, 1 hour).

By Tour

Several operations on the island take visitors to hard-to-reach spots. Figure £40-45 per person to join an all-day island tour (about 8 hours). Compare the offerings at the following companies, which use smaller 8- or 16-seat minibuses: **Skye Scenic Tours** (tel. 01478/617-006, www.skyescenictours.com), **Tour Skye** (tel. 01478/613-514, www.tourskye.com), and **SkyeBus** (tel. 01470/532-428, www.realscottishjourneys.com).

Portree-based **Michelle Rhodes** also does tours around the island (see Portree's "Helpful Hints," earlier).

By Taxi or Shuttle

GoSkye offers a shuttle service to the Fairy Pools, Talisker Distillery, the Old Man of Storr, and the Quiraing (single trips or return, £8-12 one-way, tel. 01470/532-264, www.go-skye.co.uk). **Don's Taxis** is available for private rides (tel. 01478/613-100, www.donstaxis.vpweb.co.uk).

You can't go wrong.

Arriving and Departing

Situated between Oban/Glencoe and Loch Ness/Inverness, Skye fits neatly into a Highlands itinerary.

By Car

Your easiest bet is the slick **Skye Bridge** that crosses from Kyle of Lochalsh on the mainland to Kyleakin on Skye.

Rick's Tip: *To* **avoid seeing the same scenery twice,** *drivers can arrive at the Isle of Skye by ferry (from Mallaig), then take the Skye Bridge out, or vice versa.*

The island can also be reached by **car ferry.** The major ferry line connects the mainland town of Mallaig to Armadale on Skye (£15/car with 2 people, reservations required, April-late Oct 8/day each way, off-season very limited Sat-Sun connections, must check in at least 20 minutes before sailing or your place will be sold and you will not get on, can be canceled in rough weather, 30-minute trip, operated by Caledonian MacBrayne, toll-free tel. 0800-066-5000 or tel. 01475/650-397, can reserve online, www.calmac.co.uk).

For maximum scenery, use both the ferry and the bridge: Drivers coming from Fort William can take the "Road to the Isles" to Mallaig, then catch the ferry to Skye; then later, leave Skye via the Skye Bridge for Inverness, stopping at Eilean Donan Castle en route. (Reverse the route—bridge first, then ferry—if coming from Inverness.)

By Bus

Skye is connected to the outside world by Scottish Citylink buses (www.citylink.co.uk), which use Portree as their Skye hub. From Portree, buses connect to **Inverness** (bus #917, 3/day, 3.5 hours) and **Glasgow** (buses #915 and #916, 3/day, 7 hours, also stops at **Fort William** and **Glencoe**). For **Edinburgh,** you'll transfer in either Inverness or Glasgow (4/day, 8 hours total).

Inverness &
Loch Ness

I nverness, the Highlands' de facto capital, is an almost unavoidable stop on the Scottish tourist circuit. It's a pleasant town and an ideal springboard for some of the country's most famous sights. Hear the music of the Highlands in Inverness and the echo of muskets at Culloden, where government troops drove Bonnie Prince Charlie into exile and conquered his Jacobite supporters. Just to the southwest of Inverness, explore the locks and lochs of the Caledonian Canal while playing hide-and-seek with the Loch Ness monster.

INVERNESS & LOCH NESS IN 1 DAY

Though it has little in the way of sights, Inverness is a handy spot to spend a night or two between other Highland destinations. With two nights, you can easily find a full day's worth of sightseeing nearby: Choose among Loch Ness sights, the Culloden Battlefield, or a Highlands bus tour.

For evening fun, take your pick of live music, pub grub, whisky tastings, fine dining, and a riverside stroll.

Rick's Tip: **Drivers** *heading between Oban and Inverness can* **see the Loch Ness sights en route,** *rather than as a side-trip from Inverness.*

INVERNESS

Inverness is situated on the River Ness at the base of a castle (now used as a courthouse, but with a public viewpoint). Inverness' charm is its normalcy—it's a nice, midsize Scottish city that gives you a palatable taste of the "urban" Highlands and a contrast to cutesy tourist towns. It has a disheveled, ruddy-cheeked

grittiness and is well located for enjoying the surrounding countryside sights. Check out the bustling, pedestrianized downtown, or meander the picnic-friendly riverside paths and islands—best at sunset, when the light hits the castle and couples hold hands while strolling along the water and over its footbridges.

Orientation

Inverness, with about 70,000 people, has been one of the fastest-growing areas of Scotland in recent years. Marked by its castle, Inverness clusters along the River Ness. The TI is on High Street, an appealing pedestrian shopping zone a few blocks away from the river; nearby are the train and bus stations. Most of

Inverness

INVERNESS & LOCH NESS AT A GLANCE

Inverness Centrally located Highlands town, ideal as a home base for making day-trips. See page 216

▲▲▲**Culloden Battlefield** Site (with excellent museum) of the Highlanders' last stand and major defeat in 1746. **Hours:** Daily April-Oct 9:00-17:30, June-Aug until 18:00, Nov-Dec and Feb-March 10:00-16:00, closed Jan, See page 225.

Loch Ness Long, famous lake, hosting picturesque Urquhart Castle and monster exhibitions. See page 234.

▲**Loch Ness Centre & Exhibition** A thoughtful museum on the elusive, reclusive monster. **Hours:** Daily Easter-Oct 9:30-17:45, July-Aug until 18:45, Nov-Easter 10:00-16:15. See page 234.

▲**Urquhart Castle** A shell of a castle, beautifully perched on Loch Ness. **Hours:** Daily April-Sept 9:30-18:00, Oct until 17:00, Nov-March until 16:30. See page 235.

▲**Fort Augustus** A charming town on Loch Ness, with lake views and the Caledonian Canal Visitor Centre. See page 237.

Inverness Castle

my recommended B&Bs huddle atop a gentle hill behind the castle (a 10-minute uphill walk from the city center).

Tourist Information: At the TI, you can pick up the self-guided *City Centre Trail* walking-tour leaflet and the *What's On* weekly events sheet (June-Sept Mon-Sat 8:45-18:30, shorter hours on Sun and off-season, free Wi-Fi, 36 High Street, tel. 01463/252-401, www.inverness-scotland.com).

Helpful Hints

Festivals: The summer is busy with events. Book far ahead during these times, including the Etape Loch Ness bike race (early June), Highland Games (late June), Belladrum Tartan Heart Festival (music, late July), Black Isle farm show (early Aug), and Loch Ness Marathon (late Sept).

Bookstore: Leakey's Bookshop, in a converted church built in 1649, is the place to browse through teetering towers of musty old books and vintage maps. Climb the spiral staircase to the loft for views over the stacks (Mon-Sat 10:00-17:30, closed Sun, Church Street, tel. 01463/239-947, Charles Leakey).

Baggage Storage: The train station has lockers (Mon-Sat 6:40-20:30, Sun from 10:40), or you can leave your bag at the bus station's ticket desk (small fee, daily until 17:30).

Laundry: New City Launderette is near the west end of the Ness Bridge (self-service or same-day full-service, Mon-Sat 8:00-18:00, until 20:00 Mon-Fri in summer, Sun 10:00-16:00 year-round, 17 Young Street, tel. 01463/242-507). **Thirty Degrees Laundry** on Church Street is another option (full-service only, drop off before 10:00 for same-day service, Mon-Sat 8:30-17:30, closed Sun, a few blocks beyond Victorian Market at 84 Church Street, tel. 01463/710-380).

Tours

INVERNESS BIKE TOURS

Hard-working Alison leads small groups on two-hour bike tours. Her six-mile route is nearly all on traffic-free paths along canals and lochs outside of the city and comes with light guiding along the way. You'll pedal through Ness Island, stop at the Botanical Gardens, ride along the Caledonian Canal with its system of locks (you may even catch a boat passing through the locks), and cycle through a nature preserve (£21, no kids under 14, 10-person max; daily in season at 10:00, 13:00, and 16:00; best to book spot in advance online, goes even in light rain, meet near west end of Ness Bridge at Prime Restaurant at 5 Ness Walk, call or text mobile 07443-866-619, www.invernessbiketours.co.uk, info@invernessbiketours.co.uk). Arrive a bit early to size up your bike and helmet.

Excursions from Inverness

While thin on sights of its own, Inverness is a great home base for day trips. A variety of tour companies offer day trips—details and tickets are available at the TI. While the big sellers among Inverness day-trips are the many Loch Ness tours (because the monster is on every bucket list), I far prefer an Isle of Skye all-day joyride—which gives you a good look at Loch Ness and its famous castle along the way. Study the various websites for comparative details. For Isle of Skye tours in summer, it's a good idea to book about a week in advance.

LOCH NESS

The famous lake is just a 20-minute drive from Inverness. Tours will often include a short boat ride, a visit to Urquhart Castle, and a stop at the Loch Ness monster exhibits. The lake is not particularly scenic. The castle, while scenic, is just a shell. And the monster is mostly a promotional gimmick. Still, if you have no car, this can be the most efficient way to check this off your list. **Jacobite Tours** focuses on trips that include Loch Ness, from a one-hour basic boat ride to a 6.5-hour extravaganza. Their four-hour "Sensation" tour includes a guided bus tour with live narration, a half-hour Loch Ness cruise, and visits to Urquhart Castle and the Loch Ness exhibits (£35, www.jacobite.co.uk, tel. 01463/233-999).

ISLE OF SKYE

Several companies do good day tours to the Isle of Skye. They travel 110 miles (a

2.5-hour drive) to the heart of Skye (Portree). With about six hours of driving, and one hour for lunch in Portree, that leaves two or three hours for a handful of quick and scenic photo stops. All travel along Loch Ness so you can see Urquhart Castle and try for a monster sighting. And all stop for a view of Eilean Donan Castle. The longer rides loop around the Trotternish Peninsula.

Wow Scotland's ambitious 12-hour itinerary goes in a big bus. They depart at 8:30 from the Inverness bus station and include short but smart and adequate stops all along the way (£77, 5/week June-Aug, fewer departures in April-May and Sept, none Oct-March, tel. 01808/511-773, www.wowscotlandtours.com). I'd pay the extra for the £99 front row.

Highland Experience Tours runs another, shorter Isle of Skye itinerary in 24-seat buses (daily April-Oct, less off-season, 10 hours) but doesn't make it as far north as the Trotternish Peninsula (£55, tel. 01463/719-222, www.highlandexperience.com). They offer a variety of other daylong tours, including to the far north with John O'Groats, or a trip to Royal Deeside and the Speyside Whisky Trail.

Happy Tours Scotland organizes daily minibus tours on a 10-hour joy ride (getting all the way to Quiraing) with top-notch guides (£70, 8 people per minibus, daily at 8:30, leaves from 7 Ness Walk at Columba Hotel, mobile 07828-154-683, book at www.happy-tours.biz, run by Cameron). They also do other tours including itineraries focusing on Loch Ness, the *Outlander* books and TV series, a Speyside whisky tour, and private minibus tours.

Rabbie's Small Group Tours does 12-hour trips to Skye in its 16-seater buses for £52 nearly daily from Inverness. Their website explains their busy program (www.rabbies.com).

Iona Highland Tours takes eight people on several different Isle of Skye itineraries,

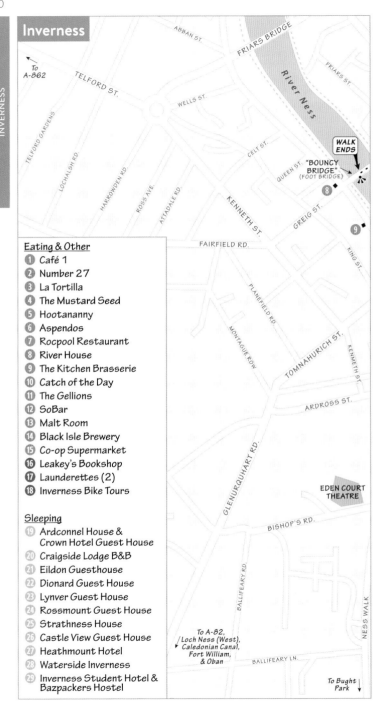

Inverness

To A-862

ABBAN ST.

FRIARS BRIDGE

FRIARS ST.

River Ness

TELFORD ST.

WELLS ST.

TELFORD GARDENS

LOCHALSH RD.

HARROWDEN RD.

ROSS AVE.

ATTADALE RD.

CELT ST.

WALK ENDS

QUEEN ST. "BOUNCY BRIDGE" (FOOT BRIDGE)

8

KENNETH ST.

GREIG ST.

KING ST.

9

FAIRFIELD RD.

PLANEFIELD RD.

MONTAGUE ROW

TOMNAHURICH ST.

KENNETH ST.

ARDROSS ST.

GLENURQUHART RD.

EDEN COURT THEATRE

BISHOP'S RD.

BALLIFEARY RD.

NESS WALK

To A-82, Loch Ness (West), Caledonian Canal, Fort William, & Oban

BALLIFEARY LN.

To Bught Park

Eating & Other

1 Café 1
2 Number 27
3 La Tortilla
4 The Mustard Seed
5 Hootananny
6 Aspendos
7 Rocpool Restaurant
8 River House
9 The Kitchen Brasserie
10 Catch of the Day
11 The Gellions
12 SoBar
13 Malt Room
14 Black Isle Brewery
15 Co-op Supermarket
16 Leakey's Bookshop
17 Launderettes (2)
18 Inverness Bike Tours

Sleeping

19 Ardconnel House & Crown Hotel Guest House
20 Craigside Lodge B&B
21 Eildon Guesthouse
22 Dionard Guest House
23 Lynver Guest House
24 Rossmount Guest House
25 Strathness House
26 Castle View Guest House
27 Heathmount Hotel
28 Waterside Inverness
29 Inverness Student Hotel & Bazpackers Hostel

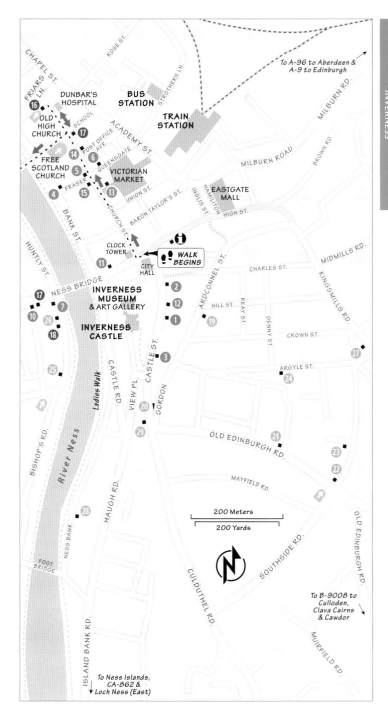

"Woe unto him that giveth his neighbour drink . . ."

including one that allows hiking time at the Fairy Pools (£70, 9 hours, tel. 01463/250-457, www.ionahighlandtours.com).

By Train Then Tour: To avoid a long bus ride or skip the sights along the way to Skye, take the train from Inverness to Kyle of Lochalsh, where a Skye-based tour company will pick you up and take you around. Try **Skye Tours** (tel. 01471/822-716, www.skye-tours.co.uk) or **Tour Skye** (tel. 01478/613-514, www.tourskye.com). The train leaves Inverness before 9:00 and arrives around 11:30; the return train is around 17:15 (covered by BritRail Pass).

THE ORKNEY ISLANDS

For a very ambitious itinerary, John O'Groats Ferries offers an all-day tour that departs Inverness at 7:15, drives you up to John O'Groats to catch the 40-minute passenger ferry, then a second bus takes you on a whistle-stop tour of Orkney's main attractions (with an hour in the town of Kirkwall) before returning you to Inverness by 21:00. While it's a long day, it's an efficient use of your time if you're determined to see Orkney (£74, daily June-Aug only, tel. 01955/611-353, www.jogferry.co.uk).

Inverness Walk

Humble Inverness has meager conventional sights, but its fun history and quirky charm become clear as you take this short self-guided walk.

• *Start at the clock tower.*

Clock Tower: The tower looming 130 feet above you is all that remains of a toll-booth building erected in 1791. This is the highest spire in town. Here, four streets—Church, Castle, Bridge, and High—come together, integrating God, defense, and trade—everything necessary for a fine city.

About 800 years ago, a castle was built on the bluff overhead and the town of Inverness coalesced right about here. For centuries, this backwater town's economy was based on cottage industries. Artisans who made things also sold them. In 1854, the train arrived, injecting energy and money from Edinburgh and Glasgow, and the Victorian boom hit. With the Industrial Age came wholesalers, distributors, mass production, and affluence. Much of the city was built during this era, in Neo-Gothic style—over-the-top and fanciful, like the City Hall (from 1882, kitty-corner to the clock tower). With the Victorian Age also came tourism.

Look for the **Bible quotes** chiseled into the wall across the street from the City Hall. A civic leader, tired of his council members being drunkards, edited these Bible verses for maximum impact, especially the bottom two.

Hiding just up the hill (behind the eyesore concrete home of the Inverness Museum and Art Gallery) is **Inverness Castle.** While the "castle" is now a courthouse, there is a small exhibition and a chance to climb to the top of the tower (£5).

Rick's Tip: It's worth **hiking up to the castle** *at some point during your visit* **to enjoy some of the best views** *of Inverness and its river.*

• *Walk a few steps away from the river (toward McDonald's)...*

Mercat Cross and Old Town Center: Standing in front of the City Hall is a well-worn mercat cross, which designated the market in centuries past. This is where the townspeople gathered to hear important proclamations, share news, watch hangings, gossip, and so on.

The yellow **Caledonian** building faces McDonald's at the base of High Street. (Caledonia was the ancient Roman name for Scotland.) It was built in 1847, complete with Corinthian columns and a Greek-style pediment, as the leading bank in town. Notice how nicely pedestrianized High Street welcomes people and seagulls...but not cars.

• *Next we'll head up Church Street, which begins between the clock tower and The Caledonian.*

Church Street: The street art you'll trip over at the start of Church Street is called **Earthquake**—a reminder of the quake that hit Inverness in 1816. As the slabs explain, the town's motto is "Open Heartedness, Insight, and Perseverance."

Stroll down Church Street. Look up above the modern storefronts to see Old World facades. **Union Street** (the second corner on the right)—stately, symmetrical, and Neoclassical—was the fanciest street in the Highlands when it was built in the 19th century. Its buildings had indoor toilets. That was big news.

Midway down the next block of Church Street (on the right), an alley marked by an ugly white canopy leads to the **Victorian Market.** Venturing down the alley, you'll pass **The Malt Room** (a recommended small, friendly whisky bar eager to teach you to appreciate Scotland's national tipple) and **The Old Market Bar** (a dive bar worth a peek). Stepping into the Victorian Market, you'll find a gallery of shops under an iron-and-glass domed roof dating from 1876. The first section seems abandoned, but delve deeper to find more active areas, where local shops mix with tacky "tartan tat" souvenir stands. If you're seriously into bagpipes, look for **Cabar Fèidh,** where American expat Brian sells CDs and sheet music,

High Street

Victorian Market

and repairs and maintains the precious instruments of local musicians.

Go back out of the market the way you came in, and continue down Church Street. At the next corner you come to **Hootananny,** famous locally for its live music (pop in to see what's on tonight). Just past that is **Abertarff House,** the oldest house in Inverness. It was the talk of the town in 1593 for its "turnpike" (spiral staircase) connecting the floors.

Continue about a block farther along Church Street. The lane on the left leads to the **"Bouncy Bridge"** (where we'll finish this walk). Opposite that lane (on the right) is **Dunbar's Hospital,** with four-foot-thick walls. In 1668, Alexander Dunbar was a wealthy landowner who built this as a poor folks' home.

A few steps farther up Church Street, walk through the iron gate on the left and into the churchyard (we're focusing on the shorter church on the right—ignore the bigger one on the left). Looking at the WWI and WWII memorials on the church's wall, it's clear which war hit Scotland harder. While no one famous is buried here, many tombstones go back to the 1700s. Being careful not to step on a rabbit, head for the bluff overlooking the river and turn around to see...

Old High Church: There are a lot of churches in Inverness (46 Protestant, 2 Catholic, 2 Gaelic-language, and one offering a Mass in Polish), but these days, most are used for other purposes. This one, dating from the 11th century, is the most historic (but is generally closed).

In the sixth century, the Irish evangelist monk St. Columba brought Christianity to northern England, the Scottish islands (at Iona), and the Scottish Highlands (in Inverness). He stood here amongst the pagans and preached to King Brude and the Picts.

Study the bell tower from the 1600s. The small door to nowhere (one floor up) indicates that back before the castle offered protection, this tower was the place of last refuge for townsfolk under attack. They'd gather inside and pull up the ladder. The church became a prison for Jacobites after the Battle of Culloden, and executions were carried out in the churchyard.

Every night at 20:00, the bell in the tower rings 100 times. It has rung like this since 1730 to remind townsfolk that it's dangerous to be out after dinner.

• *From here, you can circle back to the lane leading to the "Bouncy Bridge" and then hike out onto the bridge. Or you can just survey the countryside from this bluff.*

The River Ness: Emptying out of Loch Ness and flowing seven miles to the sea (a mile from here), this is one of the shortest rivers in the country. While it's shallow (you can almost walk across it), there are plenty of fish in it. In the 19th century, Inverness was smaller, and across the river

"Bouncy Bridge"

Old High Church

stretched nothing but open fields. Then, with the Victorian boom, the suspension footbridge (a.k.a. "Bouncy Bridge") was built in 1881 to connect new construction across the river with the town.

• *Your tour is over.*

Sights
In Inverness
INVERNESS MUSEUM AND ART GALLERY

This free, likable town museum is worth poking around on a rainy day to get a taste of Inverness and the Highlands. The ground-floor exhibits on geology and archaeology peel back the layers of Highland history: Bronze and Iron ages, Picts (including carved stones), Scots, Vikings, and Normans. Upstairs you'll find the "social history" exhibit (everything from Scottish nationalism to hunting and fishing) and temporary art exhibits.

Cost and Hours: Free, April-Oct Tue-Sat 10:00-17:00, shorter hours off-season, closed Sun-Mon year-round, cheap café, in ugly modern building on the way up to the castle, tel. 01463/237-114, www.highlifehighland.com.

INVERNESS CASTLE

Aside from nice views from the front lawn, a small exhibit on the ground floor, and a tower climb (£5 for a commanding city view), Inverness' biggest nonsight is not open to the public.

In 1715, the 15th-century castle that stood here was named Fort George by the English to demonstrate its control over the area. In 1745, it was destroyed by Bonnie Prince Charlie's Jacobite army and remained a ruin until the 1830s, when the present castle was built. The statue outside (from 1899) depicts Flora MacDonald, who helped Bonnie Prince Charlie escape from the English.

Near Inverness

Culloden can be reached by car or bus, but the other sights (Clava Cairns, Caw-

dor Castle, and the Leault sheepdog demonstration) are only doable by car.

▲▲▲CULLODEN BATTLEFIELD

Jacobite troops under Bonnie Prince Charlie were defeated at Culloden (kuh-LAW-dehn) by supporters of the Hanover dynasty (King George II's family) in 1746. This last major land battle fought on British soil spelled the end of Jacobite resistance and the beginning of the clan chiefs' fall from power. Wandering the desolate, solemn battlefield, you sense that something terrible occurred here. Locals still bring white roses and speak of "The '45" (as Bonnie Prince Charlie's entire campaign is called) as if it just happened. Be sure to visit the high-tech visitor center. Allow two hours here.

Cost and Hours: £11, £5 guidebook, daily April-Oct 9:00-17:30, June-Aug until 18:00, Nov-Dec and Feb-March 10:00-16:00, closed Jan, café, tel. 01463/796-090, http://www.nts.org.uk/culloden.

Tours: The included **audioguide** leads you through both the exhibition and the battlefield. There are several free tours daily along with costumed events (see schedule posted at entry).

Culloden Battlefield

Getting There: It's a 15-minute **drive** east of Inverness. Follow signs to *Aberdeen,* then *Culloden Moor*—the B-9006 takes you right there (well-signed on the right-hand side). Parking is £2. Public **buses** leave from Inverness' Queensgate Street and drop you off in front of the entrance (£5 round-trip ticket, bus #5, roughly hourly, 40 minutes, ask at TI for route/schedule updates). A **taxi** costs around £15 one-way.

Background: Charles Edward Stuart (1720-1788) was raised with a single purpose—to restore his family to the British throne. His grandfather, King James II (VII of Scotland), was deposed in 1688 by the English Parliament for his tyranny and pro-Catholic bias. The Stuarts remained exiled in France until 1745, when young Charlie crossed the Channel to Scotland to rally support for the Jacobite cause and retake the throne.

The charismatic "Bonnie" (handsome) Charlie led an army of 2,000 tartan-wearing Highlanders across Scotland, seizing Edinburgh. They picked up other supporters from the Lowlands and from England. Now 6,000 strong, they marched south toward London—advancing as far as Derby, just 125 miles

from the capital. But anticipated support for the Jacobites failed to materialize in the numbers they were hoping for (both in England and from France). The odds turned against them. Charles retreated to the Scottish Highlands, where many of his men knew the terrain and might gain an advantage when outnumbered. The English government troops followed closely on his heels.

Against the advice of his best military strategist, Charles' army faced the Hanoverian forces at Culloden Moor on flat, barren terrain that was unsuited to the Highlanders' guerrilla tactics. The Jacobites—many of them brandishing only broadswords, targes (wooden shields covered in leather and studs), and dirks (long daggers)—were mowed down by King George's cannons and horsemen. In less than an hour, the government forces routed the Jacobite army.

Charles fled with a price on his head. He escaped to the Isle of Skye, hidden by a woman named Flora MacDonald. Flora dressed Charles in women's clothes and passed him off as her maid.

Though usually depicted as a battle of the Scottish versus the English, in truth Culloden was a civil war between two

An Incident in the Rebellion of 1745 *by David Morier*

opposing dynasties: Stuart (Charlie) and Hanover (George).

The Battle of Culloden was the end of 60 years of Jacobite rebellions and the final stand of the Highlanders. From then on, clan chiefs were deposed; kilts, tartans, and bagpipes were outlawed; and farmers were cleared off their ancestral land, replaced by more-profitable sheep. Scottish culture would never fully recover from the events of the campaign called "The '45."

◐ **Self-Guided Tour:** Your tour takes you through two sections: the exhibit and the battlefield.

The Exhibit: As you pass the ticket desk, note the **family tree:** Bonnie Prince Charlie ("Charles Edward Stuart") and George II were distant cousins. Then the exhibit's shadowy-figure **touchscreens** connect you with historical figures who give you details from both the Hanoverian and Jacobite perspectives. A **map** shows the other power struggles happening in and around Europe, putting this fight for political control of Britain in a wider context. This battle was a key part of a larger struggle between Britain and its neighbors, primarily France, for control over trade and colonial power.

From here, your path through this building is cleverly designed to echo the course of the Jacobite army. Your short march (with lots of historic artifacts) gets under way as Charlie sails from France to Scotland, then finagles the support of Highland clan chiefs. As he heads south with his army to take London, you, too, are walking south. Along the way, maps show the movement of troops, and wall panels cover the buildup to the attack. Note the clever division of information: To the left and in red is the story of the "government" (a.k.a. Hanoverians/Whigs/English, led by the Duke of Cumberland); to the right, in blue, is the Jacobites' perspective (Prince Charlie and his Highlander/French supporters).

But you, like Charlie, don't make it to London—in the dark room at the end, you can hear Jacobite commanders arguing over whether to retreat back to Scotland. Pessimistic about their chances of receiving more French support, they decide to U-turn, and so do you.

By the time you reach the end of the hall, it's the night before the battle. Round another bend into a dark passage, and listen to the voices of the anxious troops. While the English slept soundly in their tents (recovering from celebrating the Duke's 25th birthday), the scrappy and exhausted Jacobite Highlanders struggled through the night to reach the battlefield.

At last the two sides meet. As you wait outside the theater for the next showing, study the chart depicting how the forces were arranged on the battlefield. Once inside the theater, you'll soon be surrounded by the views and sounds of a windswept moor. An impressive four-minute **360° movie** projects the re-enacted battle with you right in the center of the action. The movie drives home just how outmatched the Jacobites were.

The last room has **period weapons,** including ammunition and artifacts found on the battlefield, as well as **historical depictions** of the battle. Be sure to tour the

Culloden's visitor center

aftermath corridor and examine the **huge map,** giving you a bird's-eye view of the field through which you're about to roam.

The Battlefield: Leaving the visitors center, survey the battlefield (which you'll tour with the help of your audioguide). In the foreground is a cottage used as a makeshift hospital during the conflict. Red flags show the front line of the government army (8,000 troops). This is where most of the hand-to-hand fighting took place. The blue flags in the distance are where the Jacobite army (5,500 troops) lined up.

As you explore the battlefield, notice how uneven and boggy the ground is in parts, and imagine trying to run across this hummocky terrain with all your gear, toward almost-certain death.

The old stone memorial cairn, erected in 1881, commemorates the roughly 1,500 Jacobites buried in in this field. It's known as the Graves of the Clans. As you wander the battlefield, following the audioguide, you'll pass by other **mass graves,** marked by small headstones, and ponder how entire clans fought, died, and were buried here.

▲CLAVA CAIRNS

These well-preserved Neolithic burial chambers are nestled in the countryside just beyond the Culloden Battlefield. Dating from 3,000 to 4,000 years ago, they appear to be just some giant piles of rocks in a sparsely forested clearing, but the info plaque near the entry explains the site. There are three structures: a "ring cairn" with a central (and inaccessible) open space, flanked by two "passage cairns." The entrance shaft in each passage cairn lines up with the setting sun at the winter solstice. Each cairn is surrounded by a stone circle, and it's all framed by evocative trees.

Cost and Hours: Free, always open; just after passing Culloden Battlefield on the B-9006 coming from Inverness, signs point to Clava Cairns; follow twisty road a couple miles, over "weak bridge" to site.

▲CAWDOR CASTLE

This is the beautiful, homey residence of the Dowager Countess of Cawdor, an aristocratic branch of the Campbell family. You'll follow a one-way circuit around the castle with each room well-described with posted explanations (written by the countess'

Clava Cairns

late husband, the sixth Earl of Cawdor). Docents are happy to answer questions. The gardens are worth strolling. The small, nine-hole golf course on the grounds provides a quick, affordable way to have a Scottish golfing experience (£18/person with clubs; £4 for putting green only).

Cost and Hours: £11, good £5 guidebook; just off the A-96, 15 miles east of Inverness, and 6 miles beyond Culloden and Clava Cairns, May-Sept daily 10:00-17:30, closed Oct-April, www.cawdorcastle.com.

▲▲LEAULT WORKING SHEEPDOGS
Every afternoon (except Sat), Neil Ross presents a 45-minute, fascinating demonstration of his well-trained sheepdogs. You'll hunker down in a natural little amphitheater in the turf while Neil describes his work. Then the dogs get to work: With shouts and whistles, each dog follows commands, showing an impressive mastery over the sheep. Afterward, you'll meet (and pet) the border collie stars of the show, and may have the chance to feed lambs or try shearing sheep.

Cost and Hours: £5; open only for one demonstration per day: May-Oct Sun-Fri

at 16:00, closed Sat and Nov-April; exit A-9 at Kincraig, follow brown signs across A-9 to farm, tel. 01540/651-402, www. leaultworkingsheepdogs.co.uk.

Experiences

RIVER WALK
Consider an early-morning stroll in Inverness along the Ness Bank to capture the castle at sunrise, or a postdinner jaunt to Bught Park for a local shinty match. The path is lit at night. The forested islands in the middle of the River Ness—about a 10-minute walk south of the center— are a popular escape from the otherwise busy city.

Rick's Tip: *For a Highland treat,* **catch a shinty match,** *a combination of field hockey, hurling, and American football—but without pads. Ask the TI if any matches are on at Bught Park, or search online for Inverness Shinty Club.*

Past the islands, it's not as idyllic or as pedestrian-friendly, but in this zone

Cawdor Castle

Leault sheepdog demonstration

you'll find minigolf, the free Botanic Gardens (daily 10:00-17:00, until 16:00 Nov-March), and the huge Active Inverness leisure center, loaded with amusements including a swimming pool with adventure slides, a climbing wall, a sauna and steam area, and a gymnasium (www.invernessleisure.co.uk).

SCOTTISH FOLK MUSIC

While you can find traditional folk music sessions in pubs and hotel bars anywhere in town, two places are well-established as *the* music pubs. Neither charges a cover for the music, unless a bigger-name band is playing.

The Gellions has live folk and Scottish music nightly from 21:30. It has local ales on tap and brags it's the oldest bar in town (14 Bridge Street, tel. 01463/233-648, www.gellions.co.uk).

Hootananny is an energetic place with several floors of live rock, blues, or folk music, and drinking fun nightly. It's rock (upstairs) and reel (ground floor). Music in the main bar (ground floor) usually begins about 21:30 (traditional music sessions Sun-Wed, trad bands on weekends; also a daytime session on Sat afternoon at 14:30). On Friday and Saturday nights only, upstairs is the Mad Hatter's nightclub, complete with a cocktail bar (67 Church Street, tel. 01463/233-651, www.hootananny.co.uk).

BILLIARDS AND DARTS

SoBar is a sprawling pub with dartboards (free but £5 deposit), pool tables (£7.50 per hour), a museum worth of sports memorabilia, and the biggest TV screens in town (popular on big game nights). It's a fine place to hang out and meet locals if you'd rather not have live music (just across from the castle at 55 Castle Street, tel. 01463/229-780).

WHISKY TASTINGS AND BREW PUBS

For a whisky education, or just a fine cocktail, drop in to the intimate **Malt Room,** with whiskies ranging from £4 to £75. The whisky-plus-chocolate flight makes for a fun nightcap (just off Church Street in the alley leading to the Victorian Market, 34 Church Street, tel. 01463/221-888, Lee and Matt).

At the **Black Isle Brewery,** you can sample their local organic beers and ciders. Choose from 26 beers on tap (including some non-Black Isle brews), all listed on the TV screen over the bar (wood-fired pizzas, 68 Church Street, tel. 01463/229-920).

Eating

By the Castle

$$$ **Café 1** serves up high-quality modern Scottish and international cuisine with trendy, chic bistro flair. Fresh meat from their own farm adds to an appealing menu (lunch and early-bird dinner specials until 18:45, open Mon-Fri 12:00-14:30 & 17:00-21:30, Sat from 13:00 & 18:00, closed Sun, reservations smart, 75 Castle Street, tel. 01463/226-200, www.cafe1.net).

$$ **Number 27** has a straightforward, crowd-pleasing menu that offers something for everyone—burgers, pastas, and more. The food is surprisingly elegant for this price range (daily 12:00-15:00 & 17:00-21:00, generous portions, local ales on tap, 27 Castle Street, tel. 01463/241-999).

$$ **La Tortilla** has Spanish tapas, including spicy king prawns (the house specialty). It's a colorfully tiled and vivacious dining option that feels like Spain. With the tapas format, three family-style dishes make about one meal (daily 12:00-22:00, 99 Castle Street, tel. 01463/709-809).

Rick's Tip: *To* **eat upscale on a budget,** *take advantage of early-bird specials at the finer restaurants.*

In the Town Center

$$$$ **The Mustard Seed** serves Scottish food with a modern twist in an old church

with a river view. It's a lively place with nice outdoor tables over the river when sunny (early specials before 19:00, daily 12:00-15:00 & 17:30-22:00, reservations smart, on the corner of Bank and Fraser Streets, 16 Fraser Street, tel. 01463/220-220, www.mustardseedrestaurant.co.uk, Matthew).

$$ Hootananny is a spacious pub with a hardwood-and-candlelight vibe and a fun menu featuring dishes one step above pub grub (food served Mon-Sat 12:00-15:00 & 17:00-20:30, dinner only on Sun). The kitchen closes early to make way for the live music scene that takes over each night after 21:30.

$$ Aspendos serves up freshly pre-pared, delicious Turkish dishes in a spacious, dressy, and exuberantly deco-rated dining room (daily 12:00-21:30, 26 Queensgate, tel. 01463/711-950).

Picnic: There's a **Co-op** market with plenty of cheap picnic grub at 59 Church Street (daily until 22:00).

Across the River

$$$$ Rocpool Restaurant is a hit with locals, good for a splurge, and perhaps the best place in town. Owner/chef Steven Devlin serves creative modern Euro-pean food to a smart clientele in a sleek, contemporary dining room (early-bird weekday special until 18:45, open Mon-Sat 12:00-14:30 & 17:45-22:00, closed Sun, reservations essential; across Ness Bridge at 1 Ness Walk, tel. 01463/717-274, www.rocpoolrestaurant.com).

$$$$ River House, a classy, sophisti-cated, but unstuffy riverside place, is the brainchild of Cornishman Alfie—who prides himself on melding the seafood know-how of both Cornwall and Scotland, with a bit of Mediterranean flair (Mon-Sat 15:00-21:30, closed Mon off-season and Sun year-round, reservations smart, 1 Greig Street, tel. 01463/222-033, www.riverhouseinverness.co.uk).

$$$ The Kitchen Brasserie is a mod-ern building overlooking the river, popular for their homemade comfort food—pizza, pasta, and burgers (early-bird special until 19:00, daily 12:00-15:00 & 17:00-22:00, 15 Huntly Street, tel. 01463/259-119, www.kitchenrestaurant.co.uk, Christine).

Fish-and-Chips: Consider the **$ Catch of the Day** chippy for a nicely presented sit-down meal or to go (daily 12:00-14:00 & 16:30-22:00, closed Sun at lunch, a block over Ness Bridge on Young Street, mobile 07909-966-525).

Sleeping
B&Bs near the Town Center

These B&Bs are popular; book ahead for June through August (and during the peak times listed in "Helpful Hints," earlier), and be aware that some require a two-night minimum during busy times. The places I list are a 10- to 15-minute walk from the train station and town center. To get to the B&Bs, either catch a taxi (£5) or walk: From the train and bus stations, go left on Acad-emy Street. At the first stoplight (the sec-ond if you're coming from the bus station), veer right onto Inglis Street in the pedes-trian zone. Go up the Market Brae steps. At the top, turn right onto Ardconnel Street.

ON OR NEAR ARDCONNEL STREET

$$ Ardconnel House is a classic, tradi-tional place offering a nice, large guest lounge, along with six spacious and com-fortable rooms (family room, 2-night minimum preferred in summer, no children under 10, 21 Ardconnel Street, tel. 01463/240-455, www.ardconnel-inverness.co.uk, ardconnel@gmail.com, John and Elizabeth).

$ Craigside Lodge B&B has five large rooms with tasteful modern flair, nice tartan touches, and fun stuffed-animal doorstoppers. The breakfast room is a nice place to soak up city views (family room, no kids under 8, just above Castle Street at 4 Gordon Terrace, tel. 01463/231-576, www.craigsideguesthouse.co.uk, enquiries@craigsideguesthouse.co.uk, hospitable Paul and Mandy).

$ Crown Hotel Guest House has seven pleasant rooms (two with private bath down the hall) and is a bargain if you're willing to put up with a few quirks—some dated elements and owners who are still learning the ins and outs of running a guesthouse (family room, 19 Ardconnel Street, tel. 01463/231-135, www.crownhotel-inverness.co.uk, crownhotelguesthouse@gmail.com, Munawar and Asia).

AROUND OLD EDINBURGH ROAD AND SOUTHSIDE ROAD

$$ Eildon Guesthouse, set on a quiet corner, offers five tranquil rooms with spacious baths. The cute-as-a-button 1890s countryside brick home exudes warmth and serenity from the moment you open the gate (family rooms, 2-night minimum in summer, no kids under 10, in-room fridges, parking, 29 Old Edinburgh Road, tel. 01463/231-969, www.eildonguesthouse.co.uk, eildonguesthouse@yahoo.co.uk, Jacqueline).

$$ Dionard Guest House, wrapped in a fine hedged-in garden, has cheerful common spaces, six lovely rooms, and lively hosts Gail and Anne—best friends turned business partners (family suite, in-room fridges, they'll do guest laundry for free, 39 Old Edinburgh Road, tel. 01463/233-557, www.dionardguesthouse.co.uk, enquiries@dionardguesthouse.co.uk).

$$ Lynver Guest House will make you feel spoiled, with three large, boutiquey rooms (all with sitting areas), a backyard stone patio that catches the sun, and veggie and fish options at breakfast (2-night minimum preferred in summer, no kids under 10, in-room fridges, 30 Southside Road, tel. 01463/242-906, www.lynver.co.uk, info@lynver.co.uk, Michelle and Brian).

$$ Rossmount Guest House feels like home, with its curl-up-on-the-couch lounge space, unfussy rooms (five in all), and friendly hosts (two rooms share a bath and are cheaper, 2-night minimum in summer, Argyle Street, tel. 01463/229-749, www.rossmount.co.uk, mail@rossmount.co.uk, Ruth and Robert).

B&BS ACROSS THE RIVER

$$$ Strathness House has a prime spot on the river a block from Ness Bridge. Formerly a hotel, it's a bigger place, with 12 rooms and a large ground-floor lounge, but comes with the same intimate touches of a guesthouse. They cater to all diets at breakfast (family room for 3, no kids under 5, street or off-site parking, 4 Ardross Terrace, tel. 01463/232-765, www.strathnesshouse.co.uk, info@strathnesshouse.com, Joan and Javed).

$$ Castle View Guest House sits right along the River Ness at the Ness Bridge—and, true to its name, it owns smashing views of the castle. Its five big and comfy rooms (some with views) are colorfully furnished, and the delightful place is lovingly run by Eleanor (2A Ness Walk, tel. 01463/241-443, www.castleviewguesthouseinverness.com, enquiries@castleviewguesthouseinverness.com).

Hotels

Inverness has a number of big chain hotels. These tend to charge a lot but may be worth a look if the B&Bs are full or if it's outside the main tourist season. Options include the Inverness Palace Hotel & Spa (a Best Western fancy splurge right on the river with a pool and gym), Premier Inn (River Ness location), and Mercure. The following hotels are smaller and more local.

$$$ Heathmount Hotel's understated facade hides a chic retreat for comfort-seeking travelers. Its eight elegant rooms come with unique decoration, parking, and fancy extras (family room, no elevator, restaurant, Kingsmill Road, tel. 01463/235-877, www.heathmounthotel.com, info@heathounthotel.com,).

$$$ Waterside Inverness, in a nice, peaceful location along the River Ness, has 35 crisp rooms and a riverview restaurant (parking, 19 Ness

Bank, tel. 01463/233-065, www.thewatersideinverness.co.uk, info@thewatersideinverness.co.uk).

Hostels

¢ **Bazpackers Hostel,** a stone's throw from the castle, has a quiet, private feel for a hostel. There are 34 beds in basic dorms (private rooms with shared bath available, reception open 7:30-23:00, no curfew, pay laundry service, 4 Culduthel Road, tel. 01463/717-663, www.bazpackershostel.co.uk, info@bazpackershostel.co.uk). They also rent a small apartment nearby (sleeps up to 4).

¢ **Inverness Student Hotel** has 57 thin-mattressed beds in nine brightly colored rooms and a laid-back lounge overlooking the River Ness. The knowledgeable, friendly staff welcomes any traveler over 18 (breakfast extra, free tea and coffee, pay laundry service, kitchen, 8 Culduthel Road, tel. 01463/236-556, www.invernessstudenthotel.com, info@invernessstudenthotel.com).

Transportation
Getting Around the Highlands

With a car, the day trips around Inverness are easy. Without a car, side-trip to Loch Ness, Culloden, and other nearby sights by public bus or with a bus tour.

Arriving and Departing

Trains are generally best for connecting Inverness with Edinburgh, Stirling, Glasgow, and Pitlochry. Buses work well for connections with the Isle of Skye, Oban, and Glencoe.

BY TRAIN

The train station, two blocks from the bus station, is centrally located on Academy Street, several blocks east of the River Ness.

From Inverness by Train to: Pitlochry (hourly, 1.5 hours), **Stirling** (every 1-2 hours, 3 hours, some transfer in Perth), **Kyle of Lochalsh** near Isle of Skye (4/day, 2.5 hours), **Edinburgh** (hourly, 4 hours,

some with change in Perth), **Glasgow** (11/day, 3 hours, 4 direct, others change in Perth). The Caledonian Sleeper provides overnight service to **London** (www.sleeper.scot). Train info: tel. 0345-748-4950, www.nationalrail.co.uk.

BY BUS

The bus station is on Margaret Street, near the train station. Tickets are sold in advance online, by phone (tel. 0871-266-3333), or in person at the station (daily 7:45-18:15, baggage storage, tel. 01463/233-371).

Inverness has a handy direct bus to **Portree** on the Isle of Skye (bus #917, 3/day, 3 hours), but for other destinations in western Scotland, you'll first head for **Fort William** (bus #19 or #919, 8/day, 2 hours), then transfer to bus #918 for **Oban** (figure 4 hours total from Inverness) or **Glencoe** (bus stops at nearby Ballachulish; figure 3 hours total).

Inverness is also connected by direct bus to **Edinburgh** (express bus #G90, 2/day, 3.5 hours; slower bus #M90, 6/day, 4 hours) and **Glasgow** (5/day on Citylink express bus #G10, 3 hours; 1/day direct on National Express #588, 4 hours). Scottish Citylink: www.citylink.co.uk.

For bus travel to England, check National Express (www.nationalexpress.com) or Megabus (http://uk.megabus.com).

BY CAR

Inverness to Edinburgh (160 miles, 3.25 hours minimum): Leaving Inverness, follow signs to the A-9 (south, toward Perth). If you haven't seen the Culloden Battlefield yet, it's an easy detour: Just as you leave Inverness, head four miles east off the A-9 on the B-9006. Back on the A-9, it's a wonderfully speedy, scenic highway (A-9, M-90, A-90) all the way to Edinburgh. If you have time, consider stopping en route in Pitlochry (just off the A-9).

Inverness to Portree, Isle of Skye (110 miles, 2.5 hours): The drive from Inverness to Skye is pretty, but much less so than the valley of Glencoe or the Isle of Skye itself. You'll drive along boring Loch Ness and then follow signs to Portree and Skye on A-87 along Loch Cluanie.

Inverness to Fort William (65 miles, 1.5 hours): This city, southwest of Inverness via the A-82, is a good gateway to Oban and Glencoe.

LOCH NESS

I'll admit it: I had my zoom lens out and my eyes on the water. The local tourist industry thrives on the legend of the Loch Ness monster. It's a thrilling thought, and there have been several seemingly reliable "sightings" (by monks, police officers, and sonar imaging). But even if you ignore the monster stories, the loch is impressive: 23 miles long, less than a mile wide, 754 feet deep, and containing more water than all of the freshwater bodies of England and Wales combined. It's essentially the vast chasm of a fault line, filled with water.

Getting There: The Loch Ness sights are a 20-minute drive southwest of Inverness. To drive the full length of Loch Ness takes about 45 minutes. Fort William-bound buses #19 and #919 make stops at Urquhart Castle and Drumnadrochit (8/day, 40 minutes).

Sights

In July 1933, a couple swore they saw a giant sea monster shimmy across the road in front of their car by Loch Ness. Within days, ancient legends about giant monsters in the lake (dating as far back as the sixth century) were revived—and suddenly everyone was spotting "Nessie" poke its head above the waters of Loch Ness. Further sightings and photographic "evidence" have bolstered the claim that there's something mysterious living in this unthinkably deep and murky lake. (Most sightings take place in the deepest part of the loch, near Urquhart Castle.) Most witnesses describe a waterbound dinosaur (resembling the

real, but extinct, plesiosaur). Others cling to the slightly more plausible theory of a gigantic eel. And skeptics figure the sightings can be explained by a combination of reflections, boat wakes, and mass hysteria. The most famous photo of the beast (dubbed the "Surgeon's Photo") was later discredited—the "monster's" head was actually attached to a toy submarine. But that hasn't stopped various cryptozoologists from seeking photographic, sonar, and other proof.

And that suits the thriving local tourist industry just fine. The Nessie commercialization is so tacky that there are two different monster exhibits within 100 yards of each other, both in the town of Drumnadrochit. Of the two competing sites, Nessieland is pretty cheesy while the Loch Ness Centre and Exhibition (described later) is surprisingly thoughtful. Each has a tour-bus parking lot and more square footage devoted to their kitschy shops than to the exhibits. While Nessieland is a tourist trap, the Loch Ness Centre may appease that small part of you that knows the *real* reason you wanted to see Loch Ness.

▲LOCH NESS CENTRE & EXHIBITION

This exhibit has two parts: First you make six stops in a series of video rooms, and then you enter the exhibition explaining the history of the Great Glen and Loch Ness. It's spearheaded by Adrian Shine, a naturalist who has spent many years researching lake ecology and scientific phenomena. With video presentations

Loch Ness Centre

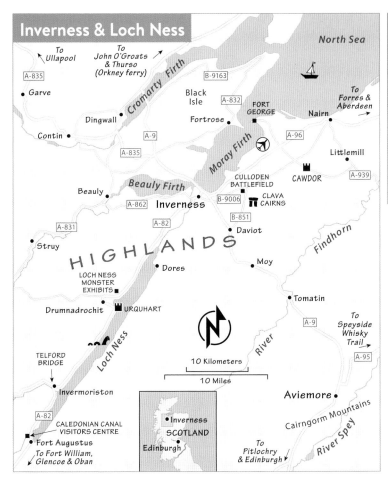

Inverness & Loch Ness

North Sea

To Ullapool
To John O'Groats & Thurso (Orkney ferry)

A-835

B-9163

Garve

Black Isle

A-832

FORT GEORGE

To Forres & Aberdeen

Dingwall

Fortrose

Nairn

Contin

A-9

Moray Firth

A-96

Littlemill

A-835

CULLODEN BATTLEFIELD

CAWDOR

A-939

Beauly Firth

Beauly

Inverness

B-9006

CLAVA CAIRNS

A-862

A-82

B-851

A-831

Daviot

H I G H L A N D S

Findhorn

Struy

Dores

Moy

LOCH NESS MONSTER EXHIBITS

Drumnadrochit

URQUHART

Tomatin

To Speyside Whisky Trail

A-9

River

10 Kilometers

A-95

TELFORD BRIDGE

Loch Ness

10 Miles

Invermoriston

Aviemore

A-82

SCOTLAND

Inverness

Cairngorm Mountains

CALEDONIAN CANAL VISITORS CENTRE

Fort Augustus
To Fort William, Glencoe & Oban

Edinburgh

To Pitlochry & Edinburgh

River Spey

and special effects, this exhibit explains the geological and historical environment that bred the monster story, as well as the various searches that have been conducted. Refreshingly, it retains an air of healthy skepticism instead of breathless monster-chasing. It also has some artifacts related to the search, such as a hippo-foot ashtray used to fake monster footprints and the *Viperfish*—a harpoon-equipped submarine used in a 1969 Nessie search.

Cost and Hours: £8, ask about RS%, daily Easter-Oct 9:30-17:45, July-Aug until 18:45, Nov-Easter 10:00-16:15, last entry 45 minutes before closing, in the big stone mansion

right on the main road to Inverness, tel. 01456/450-573, www.lochness.com.

▲URQUHART CASTLE

The ruins at Urquhart (UR-kurt), just up the loch from the Nessie exhibits, are gloriously situated with a view of virtually the entire lake and create a traffic jam of tourism on busy days.

The visitors center has a tiny exhibit with interesting castle artifacts and an eight-minute film taking you on a sweep through a thousand years of tumultuous history—from St. Columba's visit to the castle's final destruction in 1689. The castle itself, while dramatically situated

The Caledonian Canal

Two hundred million years ago, two tectonic plates collided, creating the land-mass we know as Scotland and leaving a crevice of thin lakes slashing diagonally across the country. This Great Glen Fault, from Inverness to Oban, is easily visible on any map.

British engineer Thomas Telford connected the lakes 200 years ago with a series of canals so ships could avoid the long trip around the north of the country. The Caledonian Canal runs 62 miles from Scotland's east to west coasts; 22 miles of it is manmade. Telford's great feat of engineering took 19 years to complete, opening in 1822 at a cost of one million pounds. But bad timing made the canal a disaster commercially. Napoleon's defeat in 1815 meant that ships could sail the open seas more freely. And by the time the canal opened, commercial ships were too big for its 15-foot depths. Just a couple of decades after the Caledonian Canal opened, trains made the canal almost useless...except for Romantic Age tourism. From the time of Queen Victoria (who cruised the canal in 1873), the canal has been a popular tourist attraction. To this day the canal is a hit with vacationers, recreational boaters, and lock-keepers who compete for the best-kept lock.

The scenic drive from Inverness along the canal is entertaining, with Drum-nadrochit (Nessie centers), Urquhart Castle, Fort Augustus (five locks), and Fort William (under Ben Nevis, with the eight-lock "Neptune's Staircase"). As you cross Scotland, you'll follow Telford's work—22 miles of canals and locks between three lochs, raising ships from sea level to 51 feet (Ness), 93 feet (Lochy), and 106 feet (Oich).

While Neptune's Staircase, a series of eight locks near Fort William, has been cleverly named to sound intriguing, the best lock stop is midway, at Fort Augustus, where the canal hits the south end of Loch Ness. In Fort Augustus, the **Caledonian Canal Visitor Centre,** overlooking the canal just off the main road, gives a good rundown on Telford's work.

Urquhart Castle on Loch Ness

and fun to climb through, is an empty shell. After its owners (who supported the crown) blew it up to keep the Jacobites from taking it, the largest medieval castle in Scotland (and the most important in the Highlands) wasn't considered worth rebuilding or defending, and was abandoned. Well-placed, descriptive signs help you piece together this once-mighty fortress. As you walk toward the ruins, take a close look at the trebuchet (a working replica of one of the most destructive weapons of English King Edward I), and ponder how this giant catapult helped Edward grab almost every castle in the country away from the native Scots.

Cost and Hours: £9, guidebook-£5, daily April-Sept 9:30-18:00, Oct until 17:00, Nov-March until 16:30, last entry 45 minutes before closing, café, tel. 01456/450-551, www.historic-scotland.gov.uk).

Rick's Tip: **Cruises on Loch Ness are as popular as they are pointless.** *The lake is scenic, but far from Scotland's prettiest— and the time-consuming boat trips show you little more than what you'll see from the road. I'd rather spend my time and money at Fort Augustus or Urquhart Castle.*

▲FORT AUGUSTUS

Perhaps the most idyllic stop along the Caledonian Canal is the little lochside town of Fort Augustus. It makes a delightful stop if you're driving through the area. Parking is easy. There are plenty of B&Bs, charming eateries, and an inviting park along the town's five locks. You can still see the capstans, surviving from the days when the locks were cranked open by hand.

The fine little **Caledonian Canal Visitor Centre** tells the story of the canal's construction (free, daily Easter-Oct, tel. 01320/366-493). Also, consider the pleasant little canalside stroll out to the head of the loch.

Eating in Fort Augustus: You can eat reasonably at a string of eateries all lining the same side of the canal. Consider **The Little Neuk,** a good café serving filled rolls and homemade soups; **The Lock Inn,** cozy and pub-like with great canalside tables, ideal if it's sunny; **The Bothy,** another pub with decent food; and the **Canalside Chip Shop** offering fish-and-chips to go (no seating, but plenty of nice spots on the canal). A small grocery store is at the gas station, next to the TI, which is a few steps from the canal just after crossing the River Oich (also housing the post office, a WC, and an ATM).

The town of Pitlochry, on the edge of Cairngorms National Park, has a green-hills-and-sandstone charm, a warm welcome, and a pair of great distilleries linked by a nice hike. Nearby you'll find a fascinating trip back to prehistory, at the Scottish Crannog Centre on Loch Tay.

At the east end of the Cairngorms, requiring more of a detour, is Balmoral Castle, Queen Elizabeth's country retreat.

PITLOCHRY

This likable tourist town, famous for its whisky and its hillwalking (both beloved by Scots), makes an enjoyable stop. Just outside the craggy Highlands, Pitlochry is set amid pastoral rolling hills that offer plenty of forest hikes. It seems that tourism is the town's only industry—with perhaps Scotland's highest concentration of woolens shops and outdoor outfitters.

Orientation

Plucky little Pitlochry (pop. 2,500) lines up along its tidy, tourist-minded main street, Atholl Road, which runs parallel to the River Tummel. Its two distilleries are a walk—or short drive—out of town (see my self-guided whisky walk). Navigate by following the black directional signs to Pitlochry's handful of sights.

Getting There: Pitlochry is linked by **train** with Inverness (almost hourly, 2 hours), Edinburgh (8/day direct, 2 hours), and Glasgow (9/day, 2 hours). For **drivers,** it's right off the A-9 highway connecting Inverness, Stirling, and Edinburgh.

Arrival in Pitlochry: The **train** station is on Station Road, off the main street. **Drivers** can park in the large pay-and-display lot next to the TI, in the center of town.

Tourist Information: The helpful TI, at one end of town, sells maps for local hill walks and scenic drives. Their good

Pitlochry

Pitlochry Path Network brochure is handy (Mon-Sat 9:30-17:30, Sun 10:00-16:00, longer hours in summer, shorter hours and closed Sun Nov-March; 22 Atholl Road, tel. 01796/472-215).

Rick's Tip: **Pitlochry's Highland Games** *are in early September (www. pitlochryhighlandgames.co.uk).*

Sights
Distilleries
Pitlochry's two distilleries can be linked by a relaxing two-hour hike (described below).

▲▲EDRADOUR DISTILLERY
This cute distillery (pronounced ED-rah-dower)—the smallest historic distillery in Scotland (est. 1825)—takes pride in making its whisky with a minimum of machinery, and maintains a proud emphasis on tradition. Small white-and-red buildings are nestled in a delightfully green Scottish hillside. ("Edradour"—also the name of the stream that gurgles through the complex—means "land between two rivers.") With its idyllic setting and gregarious spirit, it's one of the most enjoyable distillery tours in Scotland. If you like the whisky, buy some here and support the Pitlochry economy—this is one of the few independently owned distilleries left in Scotland.

Cost and Hours: £7.50 for a one-hour tour, departs 3/hour, April-Oct Mon-Sat 10:00-17:00, closed Sun and off-season, last tour departs one hour before closing, tel. 01796/472-095, www.edradour.com.

Getting There: If coming to the distillery by car, follow signs from the main road, 2.5 miles into the countryside.

BELL'S BLAIR ATHOL DISTILLERY
This big, ivy-covered facility is conveniently located (about a half-mile from the town center) and more corporate-feeling, offering hour-long tours with a wee taste at the end. I'd tour this only if you're a whisky completist, or if you lack the wheels or hiking stamina to reach Edradour.

Cost and Hours: £7.50, Easter-Oct tours depart 2/hour daily 10:00-17:00, July-Aug until 17:30, last tour departs one hour before closing; shorter hours, fewer tours, and closed Sat-Sun off-season; tel. 01796/482-003, www.discovering-distilleries.com/blairathol.

PITLOCHRY WHISKY WALK
A fun way to visit the distilleries is to hillwalk from downtown Pitlochry. The entire loop trip takes 2-3 hours, depending on how long you linger in the distilleries (at least an hour of walking each way). You'll see lush fern forests and a pretty decent waterfall. The walk is largely uphill on the way to the Edradour Distillery; wear good shoes, bring a rain jacket just in case, and be happy that you'll stroll easily downhill *after* you've had your whisky samples.

At the TI, pick up the *Pitlochry Path Network* brochure and follow along with its map. You'll be taking the **Edradour Walk** (marked on directional signs with yellow hiker icons; on the map it's a series of yellow dots). Leave the TI and head left along the busy A-924. The walk can be done in either direction, but I'll describe it counterclockwise.

Within 10 minutes, you'll walk under the railroad tracks and then come to **Bell's Blair Athol Distillery** on your left. If you're a whisky buff, stop in here. Otherwise, hold out for the much more atmospheric Edradour. You'll pass a few B&Bs and suburban homes, then a sign marked *Black Spout* on a lamppost. Just after this, you'll cross a bridge, then take the next left, walking under another stone rail overpass and away from the road. Following this path, you'll come to a clearing, and as the road gets steeper, you'll see signs directing you 50 yards off the main path to see the "Black Spout"—a wonderful waterfall well worth the few extra steps on your right.

At the top of the hill, you'll arrive in another clearing, where a narrow path hugs a huge field on your left. Low rolling

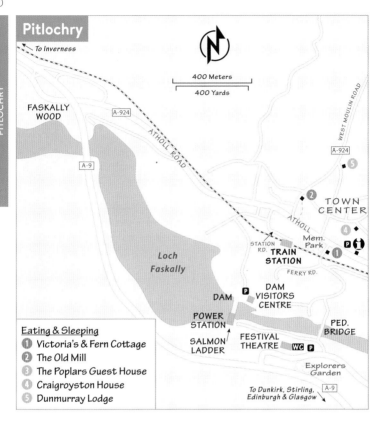

Pitlochry

To Inverness

400 Meters
400 Yards

FASKALLY WOOD

A-924

A-9

ATHOLL ROAD

WEST MOULIN ROAD

A-924

⑤

② TOWN CENTER

ATHOLL

④

STATION RD. **TRAIN STATION**

Mem. Park

P **ℹ**

①

Loch Faskally

FERRY RD.

DAM VISITORS CENTRE

DAM

P

POWER STATION

SALMON LADDER

FESTIVAL THEATRE

WC **P**

PED. BRIDGE

Explorers Garden

Eating & Sleeping
① Victoria's & Fern Cottage
② The Old Mill
③ The Poplars Guest House
④ Craigroyston House
⑤ Dunmurray Lodge

To Dunkirk, Stirling, Edinburgh & Glasgow

A-9

hills surround you in all directions. From here it's an easy 20 minutes to the **Edradour Distillery.**

Leaving the distillery, to complete the loop, head right, following the paved road (Old North Road). In about 50 yards, a sign points left into the field. Take the small footpath that runs along the left side of the road. (If you see the driveway with stone lions on both sides, you've gone a few steps too far.) You'll walk parallel to the route you took getting to the distillery, hugging the far side of the same huge field. The trail then swoops back downhill through the forest, until you cross the footbridge and make a left. You'll soon reach Knockfarrie Road—take this downhill; you'll pass a B&B and hear traffic noises as you emerge from the forest. The trail leads back to the highway, with the TI a few blocks ahead on the right.

Near Pitlochry
▲▲SCOTTISH CRANNOG CENTRE

Across Scotland, archaeologists know that little round islands on the lochs are evidence of crannogs—circular houses on stilts, dating to 500 years before Christ. Iron-Age Scots built on the water because in an age before roads, people traveled by boat, and because waterways were easily defended against rampaging animals (or people). Scientists have found evidence of 18 such crannogs on Loch Tay alone. One has been rebuilt, using mostly traditional methods, and now welcomes visitors. Guided by a passionate and well-versed expert, you'll spend about an

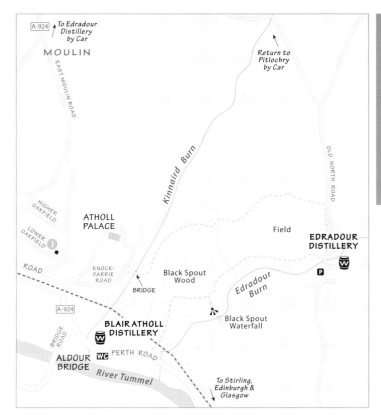

MOULIN

Return to
Pitlochry
by Car

EAST MOULIN ROAD

Kinnaird Burn

OLD NORTH ROAD

HIGHER OAKFIELD

ATHOLL
PALACE

LOWER OAKFIELD

Field

EDRADOUR
DISTILLERY

ROAD

KNOCK-
FARRIE
ROAD

Black Spout
Wood

Edradour Burn

BRIDGE

A-924

BLAIR ATHOLL
DISTILLERY

Black Spout
Waterfall

BRIDGE ROAD

ALDOUR
BRIDGE

WC PERTH ROAD

River Tummel

To Stirling,
Edinburgh &
Glasgow

hour visiting the crannog and learning about how its residents lived.

Cost and Hours: £10, family tickets available, daily 10:00-17:30, closed Nov-March, about 40 minutes outside Pitlochry, well-marked just outside the town of Kenmore on the south bank of Loch Tay, tel. 01887/830-583, www.crannog.co.uk.

Rebuilt hut at Scottish Crannog Centre

Eating and Sleeping

$$ Victoria's restaurant and coffee shop is a local favorite (daily, 45 Atholl Road). **$$$ The Old Mill,** tucked a block behind the main drag, has good Scottish food (daily). **$$$ Fern Cottage,** just behind Victoria's, has a dressier ambience (daily, Ferry Road).

Overnighters can choose from **$$ The Poplars Guest House,** perched regally on a meticulously landscaped hill high above the main road (at the end of Lower Oakfield at #27, www.poplars-pitlochry.com); **$$ Craigroyston House,** my sentimental favorite in Pitlochry (2 Lower Oakfield, www.craigroyston.co.uk); or **$$ Dunmurray Lodge,** a calming place to call home (72 Bonnethill Road, www.dunmurray.co.uk).

Pitlochry & Balmoral Castle Area

To John o'Groats

Helmsdale

Lairg • Brora

Golspie

40 Kilometers

40 Miles

Dornoch

North Sea

Inverness

SCOTLAND

Edinburgh

ENGLAND

Alness • Moray Firth

A-9

Elgin

Fraserburgh

Nairn

A-96

A-98

A-98

A-90

Dingwall

CAWDOR

Keith

Peterhead •

Inverness

CULLODEN
BATTLEFIELD
& CLAVA
CAIRNS

Craigellachie
Aberlour

GLENFIDDICH

Speyside

Huntly

A-82

URQUHART

GLENLIVET

Dufftown

Ellon

A-9

A-95

Note: Many whisky
distilleries found
in this area

A-96

Aberdeen

Loch Ness

LEAULT
WORKING
SHEEPDOGS

Aviemore

A-939

Ballater

River Dee

A-957

Laggan

Newtonmore

BALMORAL

Stonehaven

HIGHLAND
FOLK MUSEUM

Dalwhinnie

The Cairngorms

A-90

DUNNOTTAR

BLAIR

A-9

Brechin

Montrose

Pitlochry

GLAMIS

Forfar

Aberfeldy

Dunkeld

A-90

Kenmore

Loch
Tay

CRANNOG
CENTRE

Falls of
Dochart

Arbroath

Dundee

Killin

The Trossachs

Perth

North
Sea

A-84

Crief

St. Andrews

To Stirling

M-90

Crail

BALMORAL CASTLE

The Scottish home of the British royal family is wrapped in some of the most gorgeous scenery of Cairngorms National Park, in the forested valley of the River Dee. The Queen stays at her 50,000-acre private estate from August through early October. But in the months leading up to Her Majesty's arrival, the grounds and the castle's ballroom are open to visitors.

Queen Victoria and Prince Albert purchased Balmoral in 1848. Ever since, each British monarch has enjoyed retreating to this sprawling property, designed for hunting (red deer) and fishing (salmon). Today Balmoral has a huge staff, 80 miles of roads, a herd of Highland cattle, and a flock of Highland ponies, stout miniature horses useful for hauling deer carcasses over the hills.

Orientation

Day Plan: You'll need about 1.5 hours to tour the grounds and gardens. You can have lunch on the grounds or in the

Balmoral Castle

nearby village of Ballater.

Getting There: Balmoral is located on the east side of Cairngorms National Park, just off the A93 near Ballater.

Cost and Hours: £11.50, includes audioguide, April-July daily 10:00-17:00, closed Aug-March, arrive at least an hour before closing.

Information: Tel. 013397/42534, www. balmoralcastle.com.

Rick's Tip: *If you're caught up in the beauty of Balmoral,* **consider booking a ranger-led Land Rover safari** *through the grounds (£60, 3 hours, 2/day during the open season).*

◉ Visiting the Castle

From the parking lot (with a TI/gift shop, WCs, and the royal church across the street), walk across the River Dee to reach the ticket booth. From here, you can either hike 10 minutes to the palace, or hop on the free trolley.

Once at the stables, pick up your included audioguide and peruse a few exhibits, including an 8-minute orientation film. Peek into the Queen's garage to see her custom Bentley.

Then follow your audioguide on a short loop through the grounds and gardens before arriving at the palace. (To cut to the chase, or if the weather is bad, you can shortcut from the exhibit directly to the palace and the one room open to the public.) As you walk through the produce and flower gardens, ponder the unenviable challenge of trying to time all of the flowers to bloom and the produce to ripen at the same time, coinciding with the royal family's arrival in the first week of August (especially difficult given Scotland's notoriously uncooperative climate).

Finally you'll reach the single room in the palace open to the public: the palace ballroom. Display cases show off memorabilia (children's games played by royal tots, and a fully operational mini-Citroën that future kings and queens have enjoyed driving around). Near the exit, a touchscreen offers you a virtual glimpse at the tartaned private quarters that are off-limits to us commoners.

Nearby: For a free peek at another royal landmark, stop at **Crathie Kirk,** the small, stony, charming parish church where the royal family worships when they are at Balmoral, and where Queen Victoria's beloved servant John Brown is buried. The church is just across the highway from the Balmoral parking lot.

Scotland: Past & Present

Scotland is split geographically into two halves, each with a distinctly different character: the flatter, more Anglo-Saxon, London-like Lowlands in the south and the craggy, Celtic Highlands in the north. Since ancient times, the feisty people of Scotland—Highlanders and Lowlanders alike—have fought to preserve their region's identity. Their rabble-rousing national motto is *Nemo me impune lacessit*—"No one provokes me with impunity."

Prehistoric Origins, Roman Rebellion, and Highland Clans

Scotland's first inhabitants were hunter-gatherers who came north as the Ice Age receded (7000 BC). In Neolithic times (4500-2000 BC), a wave of farmer-herders arrived from the south.

Around 500 BC, the Celts moved in from Europe, bringing Iron-Age technology and the language that would develop into the Gaelic tongue. The Celts built hilltop forts with large stone towers.

In AD 80, Roman legions—having conquered England—marched north and established a camp near Edinburgh. They called today's Scotland "Caledonia" (a term you'll still see everywhere) and battled the fierce Celts, whom they dubbed "Picts" ("painted"; for their war paint). But

An ancient standing stone

the Picts would not surrender. Eventually, the Romans decided they had expanded far enough—and Scotland just wasn't worth the effort. It was mountainous, wild, and dangerous—not just with Picts, but with predatory beasts such as bears, wolves, and lynx. The Romans sealed off Caledonia with Hadrian's Wall, running more or less along the modern-day border between Scotland and England. From then on, while England was forever stamped with a Roman/European perspective, Scotland was set on a course that was isolated and Celtic.

Medieval Scotland was a stew of peoples: Picts in the northern Highlands, Anglo-Saxons (Germanic invaders) in the south, and the "Scoti" (Celtic cousins from Ireland) on the west coast. They established Gaelic as the chief language, and Christianity—brought from Ireland by St. Columba in the sixth century—as the dominant religion. Even at this early date, Scotland's geographical/ethnic boundary was already set: Gaelic/Celtic culture in the Highland north, English-friendly Anglo-Saxons in the Lowland south.

Iona Cross

Much of the Scottish realm united under a Gaelic warlord named Kenneth MacAlpin. In 843, in his capital at Scone, MacAlpin was crowned atop the Stone of Scone—making him the first king of Scots.

In the remote reaches of the Highlands and the Hebrides, communities were based on the clan system: tribes of people sharing a stretch of land managed by a chieftain, who served as a kind of caretaker for the people and future generations. Some clans were allies, either through intermarriage or through shared interests. Others were sworn enemies. One of the most famous rivalries was a three-way struggle between Clan Donald (or MacDonald), Clan Mackenzie, and Clan MacLeod, who clashed in several epic battles.

William Wallace, Robert the Bruce, and Medieval Independence

When King Malcolm III married the English Princess Margaret in 1070, it united the culture of the Highland Scots with that of the Lowland Anglo-Saxons. Increasingly, Scotland became ruled from the southern Lowlands and influenced by its southern neighbor, England. As English settlers moved north, they built castles and abbeys. They also brought with them a new social order—a hierarchical government that went beyond the small social unit of the Highland clan. But in the far reaches of Scotland, the clan system still flourished.

In 1286, the king of Scotland died without an heir. To settle the battle over succession, the Scots invited King Edward I of England to arbitrate. Edward seized the moment to assert his power over Scotland. He invaded, defeated the chosen successor, and stole the revered coronation stone—the Stone of Scone—taking it back to London (where it remained, almost untouched, until 1996).

Enraged, the Scots rallied around nobleman William Wallace. He defeated the English at Stirling Bridge (1297) and was named the "guardian of Scotland." Wallace marched his army into England, plundered its north, then returned to Scotland—where he was defeated at the Battle of Falkirk in 1298. Disgraced, Wallace retreated to the Highlands and waged guerrilla warfare against the English until he was finally betrayed, arrested, and executed in 1305.

The torch was passed to the earl of Carrick, Robert the Bruce, who united Scotland's many clans and defeated the English at the tide-turning Battle of Bannockburn (1314). Bruce was crowned King Robert, and his heirs would rule Scotland for the next four centuries under the Stuart family name (a.k.a. Stewart). Scotland had secured its independence. Over the next two centuries, Scotland's kings ruled from their castle in Stirling.

Mary, Queen of Scots; John Knox; and the Protestant Reformation

Everything changed when Henry VIII became king of England, sparking a bor-

der war with Scotland. In the Battle of Flodden (1513), Scotland was utterly defeated. Soon Scotland faced an even greater enemy. As the Reformation crept into Scotland (c. 1540-1560), it split the country in two. The Highlands remained Catholic, rural, pro-monarchy, and pro-French. The Lowlands grew increasingly Protestant, urban, anti-monarchy, and pro-English.

When the Scottish King James V died in 1542, his six-day-old daughter Mary was named Queen of Scots (r. 1542-1567). Mary grew up staunchly Catholic and was educated in France, where she married the French crown prince in 1558. By the time the newly widowed Mary arrived back home (in 1561) to rule her native Scotland, the teenage queen found a hostile country in the throes of a Protestant Reformation (known as the Scottish Reformation in Scotland).

One of the leaders of the Scottish Reformation was John Knox (1514-1572), who studied under the great Swiss reformer

Robert the Bruce

John Knox and Mary, Queen of Scots

John Calvin. Returning to Scotland, Knox hopped from pulpit to pulpit, and his feverish sermons incited riots of "born-again" iconoclasts who dismantled or destroyed Catholic churches and abbeys (including St. Andrews Cathedral). Knox's newly minted Church of Scotland gradually spread from the Lowlands to the Highlands. Catholicism was banned.

King James VI/I, King Charles I, and Civil War

Following an uprising in 1567, Mary was forced to abdicate in favor of her infant son, who became King James VI of Scotland. Raised a Protestant, James assumed official duties at age 17 (1584) and brought a tentative peace to religiously divided Scotland.

In the 1592 Golden Act, Presbyterianism triumphed, and was made the rule of law. Scotland went forward as a predominantly Protestant nation.

In 1603, Queen Elizabeth I—England's "virgin queen"—died without an heir. Her distant cousin, Scotland's King James VI, was next in line for the English throne. Upon leaving Edinburgh and being crowned England's King James I in London, he united Scotland and England. The two nations have been tied together, however fitfully, ever since.

James' son Charles I (1600-1649) was born and crowned in Scotland, but otherwise spent most of his life in England. Charles I traveled to St. Giles' Cathedral in Edinburgh; appointed a bishop who, in turn, anointed him; and eventually introduced his own prayer book. This was a bridge too far for the Scots, who rioted and signed the National Covenant. These "Covenanters" effectively declared their independence from the Church of England, and insisted that the Church of Scotland was under Scottish control. A revolution was brewing.

The Covenanters went on military raids into northern England. King Charles attempted to quell the uprising with promises of reform, but became distracted by problems closer to home: Civil war broke out in England, pitting Charles (and the monarchy and Anglicanism) against Oliver Cromwell (with his supporters in parliament and the Puritans). Scotland was also divided. The Covenanters backed Cromwell, while many Highlanders backed the king.

A Scottish army of 25,000 Covenanters invaded England, captured Charles I, and turned him over to Cromwell. On January 30, 1649, the English beheaded the king of Scotland.

England's Ascendancy and the Act of Union

Left without a king, Scotland's landed gentry crowned Charles' son at Scone on January 1, 1651 (the last coronation at Scone). But Cromwell marched north and put a decisive end to any ideas of Scottish independence. It was clear that Scotland could never again be independent without the approval of England.

James VI

Charles II (1630-1685) escaped to France, where he spent the next nine years in exile. In 1660 he was invited back to London, and in 1661, the English parliament invited him to take the English throne. The monarchy was restored, with Charles II (a Stuart) ruling both England and Scotland.

But the two countries remained bitterly divided over religion. After Charles II died, his Catholic successor—James II (James VII of Scotland)—was ousted by England's parliament in a coup d'état (called the Glorious Revolution), and replaced by a Protestant noble from the Dutch House of Orange-Nassau (King William III).

In Scotland, the newly ascendant Lowland Protestants set about forcing Highland Catholics to swear allegiance to the Protestant king. This culminated in the infamous Glencoe Massacre of 1692, where pro-William Protestants of the Campbell clan used the occasion as a pretext to slaughter their centuries-old enemy, the MacDonalds.

At the same time as Scotland's king was being forced into exile, the world was changing in other ways. England was on the rise as a naval and colonial superpower, and began encroaching on Scotland. Many Scots, particularly in the southern Lowlands, welcomed the English presence. These were people of Anglo-Saxon heritage, Calvinists and parliamentarians, and traders and industrialists who wanted to trade with wealthy England.

Due to a failed trading post venture in Panama (the Darien Scheme), Scotland went bankrupt. Members of the Scottish parliament (some of whom were bribed) agreed to accept a bailout from England, which came with one major string attached: the Act of Union. So in 1707, the Scottish nation was officially joined with England, becoming part of "Great Britain." The independence of the Scottish nation—led by the Stuart family since the days of Robert the Bruce—was over.

Jacobite Risings and Mass Emigrations

Or was it? Many Scots, especially in the Highlands, clung loyally to their ousted King James II (VII of Scotland) and his successors. They were called Jacobites—after the Latin "Jacobus" for James—and saw the Stuarts as their best hope to regain Scotland's independence.

In the first of two Jacobite "risings," a coalition of traditionalists, Highland clans, and Catholics rallied around James II's son in 1715. But English troops easily routed them, the grand hopes of "The '15" rebellion sputtered, and James Junior was sent scurrying back to his home-in-exile in France.

In 1745, a second rebellion was led by James II's grandson, known as "Bonnie Prince Charlie." That summer, the exiled Prince Charles sailed across the sea from France and landed in Scotland, where he raised an army of Highlanders and set out to re-establish the Stuart monarchy.

Bonnie Prince Charles

Within a few months, inspired by their charismatic leader, the Highlander forces had taken most of Scotland and even much of northern England. In their march toward London, they penetrated as far south as Derby—just 125 miles from the Tower of London. But the gains were ephemeral. Prince Charles' army was small (6,000 men) and disorganized; promised French support failed to materialize; and he had almost no popular support in the Lowlands, much less in England.

As better-equipped British troops advanced, Prince Charles pulled back to the Highlands. The two armies finally met in 1746 for one final, bloody conflict at Culloden Moor, just outside of Inverness, where Bonnie Prince Charlie's ragtag, kilted, bagpipe-bolstered army was routed and massacred. Charles himself escaped the chaos, dressed as a female servant to sail "over the sea to Skye," and ultimately died in exile in Rome. To this day, patriotic Scots lament the crippling blow dealt to the rebellion they call "The '45."

After Charlie's defeat, the authorities (aristocratic landowners with government assistance) came down brutally on those who had supported the Jacobites, targeting the Highland clans. Kilt-wearing was forbidden, the feudal clan system was dismantled, homes were burned, and valuables were plundered.

Landowners decided to make more efficient use of their land, bringing about the so-called "Highland Clearances" (which escalated following The '45, and peaked in the early 19th century). They evicted their farming populations and transformed the agricultural model (subsistence farming of locally used crops) to mass production (more profitable sheep). Many displaced farmers moved to cities for factory work (as this coincided with the burgeoning Industrial Revolution). Many others sought a better life in the New World. From the mid- to late-19th century, an estimated two million Scots emigrated, mostly to North America, Australia, and New Zealand. Meanwhile, back home, Highland culture all but died out. It was a bleak time for traditional life in Scotland.

Scotland Rebounds: Scottish Enlightenment, Industrial Revolution, and Highland Revival

Despite the difficult times in the Highlands, Lowlands Edinburgh thrived. In the last half of the 1700s, the city had become one of Europe's (and the world's) most intellectual cities. Edinburgh benefited from a rich university tradition, a strong Protestant work ethic, an educated middle class, and connections with a powerful England. Edinburgh was a city of secular, rational thinkers who embraced the scientific method and empirical observation. It's fitting that the Encyclopedia Britannica—the pre-Wikipedia authority on all things—was first published in Edinburgh in 1768.

As the Industrial Revolution dawned, Scotland became a powerhouse: Textiles were woven in large factories, powered by Watt's steam engine, which were fueled by Lanarkshire coal, then exported on iron ships built in the Clyde shipyards. Scotland was a global leader in pig iron exports and shipbuilding. Glasgow—an industrial center—overtook genteel Edinburgh as Scotland's biggest city.

In the early 19th century, the Scottish civil engineer Thomas Telford (1757-1834)—nicknamed "The Colossus of Roads"—designed roadways, bridges, canals, and locks to tie together the remotest corners of Scotland, effectively shrinking the country for the modern era. His masterpiece, the Caledonian Canal, is easy to see between Fort William and Inverness.

Meanwhile, Highland culture began to enjoy a renaissance. In the Romantic Age of the 19th century, tartans, kilts, bagpipes, and other aspects of Highland culture made a big comeback. In 1852,

Queen Victoria and Prince Albert purchased Balmoral Castle (in the shadow of the Highlands' Cairngorm Mountains) and proceeded to renovate it in a fanciful interpretation of the Scottish Baronial style. This signaled not just an acceptance, but a nostalgic embrace, of traditional Highland culture, just a century after it had been dismantled by the same monarchy.

This Scottish Baronial style, popularized by Sir Walter Scott, was a Romantic, Neo-Gothic celebration of medieval Highland castles. It features a stout sandstone structure with pointy turrets, fanciful finials, round towers, crenellated battlements, and narrow windows—based on Scotland's 16th-century tower houses. In many ways, this is Scotland's signature architectural style: You'll see it everywhere, from the urban streets of Glasgow to castles on the remotest fringes of Scotland.

Scotland Today: Devolution and Scottish Pride

By the last decades of the 20th century, change was percolating in Scotland. Since the 1980s, the main topic of Scottish political debate has become "devolution": the push to "devolve" authority over Scottish affairs from London to Scotland proper.

For centuries the notion of Scottish independence was rarely taken seriously. That began to change in the mid- to late-20th century. The independence-minded Scottish National Party (SNP), which had been founded as a fringe movement in 1934, won its first seat in the UK parliament in 1967. The discovery of North Sea oil in the late 1960s gave this often-overlooked corner of the United Kingdom some serious economic clout, and with it, more political pull.

The SNP gained seats in the UK parliament. When Prime Minister Tony Blair took office in May 1997, his Labour government (mindful of Scotland's strong working-class roots and long-standing support for the Labour Party) was open to the idea of devolution. After an overwhelming majority of Scots voted in favor of more autonomy, the UK parliament passed the Scotland Act 1998, creating a Scottish parliament that convened to much fanfare in Edinburgh on May 12, 1999. For the first time since the Act

Balmoral Castle

Scotland wants to be part of the United Kingdom . . . and the European Union.

of Union in 1707, Scotland had its own parliament.

With devolution, Edinburgh once again has become the actual self-governing capital of Scotland. Today the SNP is the most powerful party in Scotland (controlling 63 out of 129 seats in the Scottish parliament), and the third-largest party in the UK.

Today's supporters of Scottish independence take up ballots, not broadswords. On September 18, 2014, the Scottish people went to the polls to vote on a simple question: "Should Scotland be an independent country?" The results were clear: 55.3 percent of Scottish residents voted "no." Scotland will remain part of the United Kingdom—for now. The vote may be over, but the nationalists aren't done fighting yet.

In 2016, Britain voted to "Brexit" or leave the European Union. Most Scots voted to remain with the EU. Adding a new twist to the complicated political situation, it's likely that pro-EU Scotland would have voted for independence in 2014 had they known that the UK would vote to take them out of the EU two years later. Now, as the UK sorts out its messy situation with the EU, England's restless Celtic partners are wondering where their best future lies. And, at this point, nobody knows.

Practicalities

TOURIST INFORMATION

Before your trip, start with the Visit Scotland website, which contains a wealth of knowledge on destinations, activities, accommodations, and transport in Scotland (www.visitscotland.com).

   In Scotland, a good first stop is generally the tourist information office (abbreviated **TI** in this book). Officially called Visit Scotland Information Centres, these are all operated by the national tourist board (look for the purple signs). Some TIs have information on the entire country or at least the region, so try to pick up maps and printed information for destinations you'll be visiting later in your trip.

   Other Helpful Websites for Scotland:
To learn more about places around Scotland, see www.undiscoveredscotland.co.uk. For hiking advice, see www.walkhighlands. co.uk.

TRAVEL TIPS

Time Zones: Britain, which is one hour earlier than most of continental Europe, is five/eight hours ahead of the East/ West Coasts of the US. The exceptions are the beginning and end of Daylight Saving Time: Britain and Europe "spring forward" the last Sunday in March (two weeks after most of North America), and "fall back" the last Sunday in October (one week before North America). For a handy online time converter, see www. timeanddate.com/worldclock.

Business Hours: Most stores are open Monday through Saturday (roughly 9:00 or 10:00 to 17:00 or 18:00). In cities, some stores stay open later on Wednesday or Thursday (until 19:00 or 20:00).

Watt's Up? Britain's electrical system is 220 volts, instead of North America's 110 volts. Most newer electronics convert automatically, so you won't need a converter, but you will need an adapter plug with three square prongs, sold inexpensively at travel stores in the US.

Discounts: Discounts (called "concessions" or "concs" in Britain) for sights are generally not listed in this book. However, seniors (age 60 and over), youths under 18, and students and teachers with proper identification cards (www.isic.org) can get discounts at many sights—always ask. Some discounts are available only for British citizens.

HELP!

Emergency and Medical Help

Dial 999 or 112 for police help or a medical emergency. If you get sick, do as the locals do and go to a pharmacy and see a "chemist" (pharmacist) for advice. Or ask at your hotel for help—they'll know of the nearest medical and emergency services.

Theft or Loss

To replace a passport, you'll need to go in person to a US embassy (see later). If your credit and debit cards disappear, cancel and replace them. If your things are lost or stolen, file a police report, either on the spot or within a day or two; you'll need it to submit an insurance claim for rail passes or travel gear, and it can help with replacing your passport or credit and debit cards. For more information, see www.ricksteves.com/help.

Damage Control for Lost Cards

If you lose your credit or debit card, report the loss immediately to the respective

Avoiding Theft

Pickpockets are common in crowded, touristy places, but fortunately, violent crime is rare. Thieves don't want to hurt you; they just want your money and gadgets.

My recommendations: Stay alert and wear a money belt (tucked under your clothes) to keep your cash, debit card, credit card, and passport secure; carry only the money you need for the day in your front pocket.

Treat any disturbance (e.g., a stranger bumping into you, spilling something on you, or trying to get your attention for an odd reason) as a smoke screen for theft. Be on guard waiting in line at sights, at train stations, and while boarding and leaving crowded buses and subways. Thieves target tourists overloaded with bags or distracted by phones.

When paying for something, be aware of how much cash you're handing over (state the denomination of the bill when paying a cabbie) and count your change. There's no need to stress; just be smart and prepared.

global customer-assistance centers. Call these 24-hour US numbers collect: Visa (tel. 303/967-1096), MasterCard (tel. 636/722-7111), and American Express (tel. 336/393-1111). In Britain, to make a collect call to the US, dial 0-800-89-0011. Press zero or stay on the line for an operator. European toll-free numbers (listed by country) can be found at the websites for Visa and MasterCard. If you report your loss within two days, you typically won't be responsible for unauthorized transactions on your account, although many banks charge a liability fee of $50.

Embassies and Consulates

US Consulate in Edinburgh: 3 Regent Terrace, Mon-Fri 8:30-17:00, closed Sat-Sun, tel. 0131/556-8315; after-hours tel. 020/7499-9000, https://uk.usembassy.gov/embassy-consulates/edinburgh

Canadian Consulate in Edinburgh: Mobile 0770-235-9916 (business hours); after hours call the High Commission of Canada in London at tel. 020/7004-6000, www.unitedkingdom.gc.ca

MONEY

Here's my basic strategy for using money in Europe:

- Upon arrival, head for a cash machine (ATM) at the airport and withdraw some local currency, using a debit card with low international transaction fees.
- Pay for most purchases with a credit card with low (or no) international fees.
- Use cash for small purchases, tips, and transit fares.
- Keep your cards and cash safe in a money belt.

What to Bring

I pack the following and keep it all safe in my money belt.

Debit Card: Use at ATMs to withdraw local cash.

Credit Card: Use to pay for most items (at hotels, larger shops and restaurants, travel agencies, car-rental agencies, and so on).

Backup Card: Some travelers carry a third card (debit or credit; ideally from a different bank), in case one gets lost, demagnetized, eaten by a temperamental machine, or simply doesn't work.

US Dollars: I carry $100-200 US dollars as a backup. While you won't use it for day-to-day purchases, American cash in your money belt comes in handy for emergencies, such as if your ATM card stops working.

What NOT to Bring: Resist the urge to buy pounds before your trip or you'll pay

Exchange Rate

1 British pound (£1) = about $1.40

Britain uses the pound sterling. The British pound (£), also called a "quid," is broken into 100 pence (p). Pence means "cents." You'll find coins ranging from 1p to £2 and bills from £5 to £50.

While the pound sterling is used throughout the UK, Scotland prints its own bills, which are decorated with Scottish landmarks and VIPs. These are interchangeable with British pound notes, which are widely circulated here. The coins are the same throughout the UK.

To convert prices from pounds to dollars, add about 40 percent: £20=about $28, £50=about $70. (Check www.oanda.com for the latest exchange rates.)

the price in bad stateside exchange rates. Wait until you arrive to withdraw money.

Before You Go

Report your travel dates. Let your bank know that you'll be using your debit and credit cards in Europe, and when and where you're headed.

Know your PIN. Make sure you know the numeric, four-digit PIN for each of your cards, both debit and credit. Request it if you don't have one and allow time to receive the information by mail.

Adjust your ATM withdrawal limit. Find out how much you can take out daily and ask for a higher daily withdrawal limit if you want to get more cash at once. Note that European ATMs will withdraw funds only from checking accounts; you're unlikely to have access to your savings account.

Ask about fees. For any purchase or withdrawal made with a card, you may be charged a currency conversion fee (1-3 percent) and a Visa or MasterCard international transaction fee (1 percent).

In Europe

Using Cash Machines: European cash machines work just like they do at home—except they spit out local currency instead of dollars, calculated at the day's standard bank-to-bank rate. In most places, ATMs are easy to locate—in Britain ask for a "cashpoint." When possible, withdraw cash from a bank-run ATM located just outside that bank.

If your debit card doesn't work, try a lower amount—your request may have exceeded your withdrawal limit or the ATM's limit. If you still have a problem, try a different ATM or come back later—your bank's network may be temporarily down.

Avoid "independent" ATMs, such as Travelex, Euronet, Moneybox, Cardpoint, and Cashzone. These have high fees, can be less secure than a bank ATM, and may try to trick users with "dynamic currency conversion" (see later).

Exchanging Cash: Avoid exchanging money in Europe; it's a big rip-off. In a pinch you can always find exchange desks at major train stations or airports—convenient but with crummy rates.

Using Credit Cards: US cards no longer require a signature for verification, but don't be surprised if a European card reader generates a receipt for you to sign. Some card readers will accept your card as is; others may prompt you to enter your PIN (so it's important to know the code for each of your cards). If a cashier is present, you should have no problems.

At self-service payment machines (transit-ticket kiosks, parking, etc.), results are mixed, as US cards may not work in unattended transactions. If your card is rejected, look for a cashier who can process your card manually—or pay in cash.

Drivers Beware: Be aware of potential problems using a credit card to fill up at an unattended gas station, enter a parking garage, or exit a toll road. Carry cash and be prepared to move on to the next gas station if necessary. When approaching a toll plaza, use the "cash" lane.

Dynamic Currency Conversion: Some European merchants and hoteliers cheerfully charge you for converting your purchase price into dollars. If it's offered, refuse this "service." You'll pay extra for the expensive convenience of seeing your charge in dollars.

Tipping

Tipping in Britain isn't as automatic and generous as it is in the US. For special service, tips are appreciated, but not expected. As in the US, the proper amount depends on your resources, tipping philosophy, and the circumstances.

Restaurants: If a service charge is included in the bill, it's not necessary to tip. Otherwise, it's appropriate to tip about 10-12 percent for good service.

Taxis: For a typical ride, round up your fare a bit, but not more than 10 percent (for instance, if the fare is £7.40, pay £8).

Services: In general, if someone in the tourism or service industry does a super job for you, a small tip of a pound or two is appropriate...but not required. If you're not sure whether (or how much) to tip, ask a local for advice.

Getting a VAT Refund

Wrapped into the purchase price of your British souvenirs is a Value-Added Tax (VAT) of about 20 percent. You're entitled to get most of that tax back if you purchase more than £30 worth of goods at a store that participates in the VAT-refund scheme (although individual stores can require that you spend more). Typically, you must ring up the minimum at a single retailer—you can't add up your purchases from various shops to reach the required amount. (If the store ships the goods to your US home, VAT is not assessed on your purchase.)

Getting your refund is straightforward... and worthwhile if you spend a significant amount on souvenirs.

Get the paperwork. Have the merchant completely fill out the necessary refund document (either an official VAT customs form, or the shop or refund company's version of it). You'll have to present your passport at the store. Get the paperwork done before you leave the shop to ensure you'll have everything you need (including your original sales receipt).

Get your stamp at the border or airport. Process your VAT document at your last stop in the European Union (such as at the airport) with the customs agent who deals with VAT refunds. Arrive an additional hour early before you need to check in to allow time to find the customs office—and to stand in line.

Collect your refund. Many merchants work with a service that has offices at major airports, ports, or border crossings. These services, which extract their own fee (usually around 4 percent), can refund your money immediately in cash or credit your card.

Customs for American Shoppers

You can take home $800 worth of items per person duty-free, once every 31 days. As for alcohol, you can bring in one liter duty-free (it can be packed securely in your checked luggage).

To bring alcohol (or liquid-packed foods) in your carry-on bag on your flight home, buy it at a duty-free shop at the airport. You'll increase your odds of getting it onto a connecting flight if it's packaged in a "STEB"—a secure, tamper-evident bag. But stay away from liquids in opaque, ceramic, or metallic containers, which usually cannot be successfully screened (STEB or no STEB).

For details on allowable goods, customs rules, and duty rates, visit http://help.cbp.gov.

SIGHTSEEING

Sightseeing can be hard work. Use these tips to make your visits to Scotland's finest sights meaningful, fun, efficient, and painless.

Plan Ahead

Set up an itinerary that allows you to fit in all your must-see sights. For a one-stop look at opening hours, see the "At a Glance" sidebars for major destinations in this book. Most sights keep stable hours, but you can easily confirm the latest by checking with the TI or visiting museum websites.

Many museums are closed or have reduced hours at least a few days a year, especially on holidays such as Christmas, New Year's, and Bank Holiday Mondays in May and August. A list of holidays is on page 283. Check online for possible museum closures during your trip. Off-season, many museums have shorter hours.

At Sights

Here's what you can typically expect:

Entering: Be warned that you may not be allowed to enter if you arrive less than 30 to 60 minutes before closing time. Many sights have a security check, where you must open your bag or send it through a metal detector. Some sights require you to check daypacks and coats. (If you'd rather not check your daypack, try carrying it tucked under your arm like a purse as you enter.)

Photography: If the museum's photo policy isn't clearly posted, ask a guard. Generally, taking photos without a flash or tripod is allowed. Some sights ban selfie sticks; others ban photos altogether.

Expect Changes: Artwork can be on tour, on loan, out sick, or shifted at the whim of the curator. Pick up a floor plan as you enter, and ask museum staff if you can't find a particular item.

Audioguides and Apps: Many sights rent audioguides, which generally offer excellent recorded descriptions. If you bring your own earbuds, you can enjoy better sound. Museums and sights often offer free apps that you can download to your mobile device (check their websites).

Sightseeing Passes

Many sights in Scotland are managed by either Historic Scotland or the National

Trust for Scotland. Each organization has a combo-deal that can save some money for busy sightseers.

Historic Scotland's Explorer Pass covers its 77 properties, including Edinburgh Castle and Stirling Castle (£31/3 days out of any 5, £42/7 days out of any 14, www.historic-scotland.gov.uk/explorer). This pass allows you to skip the ticket-buying lines at Edinburgh and Stirling castles.

Membership in the **National Trust for Scotland** covers more than 350 historic houses, manors, and gardens throughout Great Britain, including 100 properties in Scotland. From the US, it's easy to join online through the Royal Oak Foundation, the National Trust's American affiliate (one-year membership: $65 for one person, $95 for two, family and student memberships, www.royal-oak.org). For more on National Trust for Scotland properties, see www.nts.org.uk.

PRACTICALITIES
EATING

Restaurant Code

Eateries in this book are categorized according to the average cost of a typical main course. Drinks, desserts, and splurge items (steak and seafood) can raise the price considerably.

$$$$ Splurge: Most courses over £20
$$$ Pricier: £15-20
$$ Moderate: £10-15
$ Budget: Under £10

In Great Britain, carryout fish-and-chips and other takeout food is **$**; a basic pub or sit-down eatery is **$$**; a gastropub or casual but more upscale restaurant is **$$$**; and a swanky splurge is **$$$$**.

EATING

These days, the stereotype of "bad food in Britain" is woefully dated. Britain has caught up with the foodie revolution, and I find it's easy to eat very well here.

Tipping: At pubs and places where you order at the counter, you don't have to tip. At restaurants and fancy pubs with waitstaff, it's standard to tip about 10-12 percent; you can add a bit more for finer dining or extra good service. Occasionally a service charge is added to your bill, in which case no additional tip is necessary—but this is rare in Scotland.

Restaurant Pricing

I've categorized my recommended eateries based on price, indicated with a dollar-sign rating (see sidebar). The price ranges suggest the average price of a typical main course—but not necessarily a complete meal.

The dollar-sign categories also indicate the overall personality and "feel" of a place.

Breakfast (Fry-Up)

The traditional fry-up or full Scottish breakfast—generally included in the cost of your room—is famous as a hearty way to start the day. Also known as a "heart attack on a plate," your standard fry-up comes with your choice of eggs, Canadian-style bacon and/or sausage, a grilled tomato, sautéed mushrooms, baked beans, and often haggis, black pudding, or a dense potato scone. Toast comes in a rack (to cool quickly and crisply) with butter and marmalade. Other options include porridge and sometimes pancakes or waffles. The meal is typically topped off with tea or coffee. Many B&B owners offer alternative, creative variations on the traditional breakfast.

Much as the full breakfast fry-up is a traditional way to start the morning, these days most places serve a healthier continental breakfast as well—with a buffet of yogurt, cereal, fruit, and pastries.

Haggis and Other Traditional Scottish Dishes

Scotland's most unique dish, **haggis,** began as a peasant food. Waste-conscious cooks wrapped the heart, liver, and lungs of a sheep in its stomach lining, packed in some oats and spices, and then boiled the lot. Traditionally served with "neeps and tatties" (turnips and potatoes), haggis was forever immortalized thanks to Robbie Burns' *Address to a Haggis*. To appreciate this iconic Scottish dish, think of how it tastes—not what it's made of.

Haggis—an acquired taste

The king of Scottish **black puddings** (blood sausage) is made in the Hebrides Islands. Called Stornoway, it's so famous that the European Union has granted it protected status. A mix of beef suet, oatmeal, onion, and blood, the sausage is usually served as part of a full Scottish breakfast.

Be on the lookout for other traditional Scottish taste treats. **Cullen skink** is Scotland's answer to chowder: a hearty, creamy fish soup, often made with smoked haddock. A **bridie** (or Forfar bridie) is a savory meat pastry similar to a Cornish pasty. A **Scotch pie**—small, double-crusted, and filled with minced meat, is a good picnic food. **Crowdie** is a dairy spread that falls somewhere between cream cheese and cottage cheese.

And for dessert, **cranachan** is similar to a trifle, made with whipped cream, honey, fruit (usually raspberries), and whisky-soaked oats. Another popular dessert is the **Tipsy Laird,** essentially the same as a trifle but with whisky or brandy and Scottish raspberries.

Lunch and Dinner on a Budget

Even in pricey cities, plenty of inexpensive choices are available.

I've found that portions are huge, and **sharing plates** is generally just fine. Ordering two drinks, a soup or side salad, and splitting a £10 meat pie can make a good, filling meal. If you're on a limited budget, share a main course in a more expensive place for a nicer eating experience.

Pub grub is the most atmospheric budget option. You'll usually get hearty lunches and dinners priced reasonably at £8-15 under ancient timbers (see "Pubs," later).

Classier restaurants have some affordable deals. Lunch is usually cheaper than dinner; a top-end, £30-for-dinner-type restaurant often serves the same quality two-course lunch deals for about half the price.

Many restaurants have **early-bird** or **pre-theater specials** of two or three courses, often for a significant savings.

They are usually available only before 18:30 or 19:00 (and sometimes on week-days only).

Ethnic restaurants add spice to Britain's cuisine scene. Eating Indian, Bangladeshi, Chinese, or Thai is cheap (even cheaper if you do takeout).

Fish-and-chips are a heavy, greasy, but tasty British classic. Every town has at least one "chippy" selling takeaway fish-and-chips in a cardboard box or (more traditionally) wrapped in paper for about £5-7.

Picnicking saves time and money. Fine park benches and polite pigeons abound in most towns and city neighborhoods.

Pubs

Pubs are a fundamental part of the British social scene, and whether you're a teetotaler or a beer guzzler, they should be a part of your travel here. Smart travelers use pubs to eat, drink, get out of the rain, watch sporting events, and make new friends.

Though hours vary, pubs generally serve beer daily from 11:00 to 23:00, though many are open later, particularly on Friday and Saturday. (Children are served food and soft drinks in pubs, but you must be 18 to order a beer.) As it nears closing time, you'll hear shouts of "Last orders." Then comes the 10-minute warning bell. Finally, they'll call "Time!" to pick up your glass, finished or not, when the pub closes.

A cup of darts is free for the asking. People go to a public house to be social. They want to talk. Get vocal with a local. The pub is the next best thing to having relatives in town. Cheers!

Pub Grub: For £8-15, you'll get a basic budget hot lunch or dinner in friendly surroundings. For something more refined, try a **gastropub,** which serves higher-quality meals for £12-20.) The *Good Pub Guide* is an excellent resource (www.thegoodpubguide.co.uk).

Pubs generally serve traditional dishes, such as fish-and-chips, roast beef with Yorkshire pudding (batter-baked in the oven), and assorted meat pies, such as steak-and-kidney pie or shepherd's pie (stewed lamb topped with mashed potatoes) with cooked vegetables. Side dishes include salads, vegetables, and—invariably—"chips" (French fries). "Crisps" are potato chips. A "jacket potato" (baked potato stuffed with fillings of your choice) can almost be a meal in itself. A "ploughman's lunch" is a traditional British meal of bread, cheese, and sweet pickles. These days, you'll likely find more pasta, curried dishes, and quiche on the menu than traditional fare.

Meals are usually served from 12:00 to 14:00 and again from 18:00 to 20:00—with a break in the middle (rather than serving straight through the day). There's generally no table service. Order at the bar, then take a seat. Either they'll bring the food when it's ready or you'll pick it up at the bar. Pay at the bar (sometimes when you order, sometimes after you eat). It's not necessary to tip unless it's a place with full table service. For details on ordering beer and other drinks, see the "Beverages" section, later.

Good Chain Restaurants

I know—you're going to Britain to enjoy characteristic little hole-in-the-wall pubs, so mass-produced food is the furthest thing from your mind. But several excellent chains with branches across the UK offer long hours, reasonable prices, reliable quality, and a nice break from pub grub. My favorites are Pret (a.k.a. Pret à Manger) and Eat; other dependable chains include Côte Brasserie, Wagamama Noodle Bar, Byron Hamburgers, Ask, Pizza Express, Jamie's Italian, and Yo!. Expect to see these familiar names wherever you go.

Carry-Out Chains: Major supermarket chains have smaller, offshoot branches that specialize in prepared foods to go. The most prevalent—and best—is **M&S Simply Food** (there's one in every major train station). **Sainsbury's Local** grocery stores also offer decent prepared food; **Tesco Express** and **Tesco Metro** run a distant third.

Indian Cuisine

Eating Indian food is "going local" in cosmopolitan, multiethnic Britain. You'll find Indian restaurants in most cities, and even in small towns. Take the opportunity to sample food from Britain's former colony. Indian cuisine is as varied as the country itself. In general, it uses more exotic spices than British or American cuisine—some hot, some sweet. Indian food is very vegetarian-friendly, offering many meatless dishes. An easy way to taste a variety of dishes is to order a *thali*—a sampler plate, generally served on a metal tray, with small servings of various specialties.

Afternoon Tea

While more of an English custom, afternoon tea is served in Scottish tearooms and generally includes a pot of tea, small finger foods (like sandwiches with the crusts cut off), homemade scones, jam, and thick clotted cream. A lighter "cream tea" gets you tea and a scone or two. Tearooms, which often serve appealing light meals, are usually open for lunch and close at about 17:00, just before dinner.

Desserts (Sweets)

To the British, the traditional word for dessert is "pudding," although it's also referred to as "sweets" these days.

Trifle is the best-known British concoction, consisting of sponge cake soaked in brandy or sherry (or orange juice for children), then covered with jam and/or fruit and custard cream. Whipped cream can sometimes put the final touch on this "light" treat.

The British version of **custard** is a smooth, yellow liquid. Cream tops most everything that custard does not. There's single cream for coffee. Double cream is really thick. Whipped cream is familiar,

and clotted cream is the consistency of whipped butter.

Fool is a dessert with sweetened pureed fruit (such as rhubarb, gooseberries, or black currants) mixed with cream or custard and chilled.

Flapjacks here aren't pancakes, but are dense, sweet oatmeal cakes (a little like a cross between a granola bar and a brownie). They come with toppings such as toffee and chocolate.

Beverages

Beer: The British take great pride in their beer. Many locals think that drinking beer cold and carbonated, as Americans do, ruins the taste. Most pubs will have **lagers** (cold, refreshing, American-style beer), **ales** (amber-colored, cellar-temperature beer), **bitters** (hop-flavored ale, perhaps the most typical British beer), and **stouts** (dark and somewhat bitter, like Guinness).

At pubs, long-handled pulls (or taps) are used to draw the traditional, rich-flavored "real ales" up from the cellar. Served straight from the brewer's cask at cellar temperature, real ales finish fermenting naturally and are not pasteurized or filtered, so they must be consumed within two or three days after the cask is tapped. Naturally carbonated, real ales vary from sweet to bitter, often with a hoppy or nutty flavor.

Short-handled pulls mean colder, fizzier, mass-produced, and less interesting keg beers. Mild beers are sweeter, with a creamy malt flavoring. Irish cream ale is a smooth, sweet experience. Try the draft cider (sweet or dry)...carefully.

Order your beer at the bar and pay as you go, with no need to tip. An average beer costs about £4. Part of the experience is standing before a line of hand pulls, and wondering which beer to choose.

As dictated by British law, draft beer and cider are served by the pint (20-ounce imperial size) or the half-pint (9.6 ounces). In 2011, the government sanctioned an in-between serving size—the

Whisky 101

Whisky is high on the experience list of most visitors to Scotland—even for teetotalers. Whether at a distillery, a shop, or a pub, be sure to try a few drams.

Types of Whisky: Scotch whiskies come in two broad types: "single malt," from a single batch made by a single distiller; and "blends," mixed and matched from various whiskies.

There are more than 100 distilleries in Scotland, each one proud of its unique qualities. The **Lowlands,** around Edinburgh, produce light and refreshing whiskies. Whiskies from the **Highlands** and **Islands** range from floral and sweet to smoky and robust. **Speyside,** southeast of Inverness, is home to half of all Scottish distilleries. Mellow and fruity, Speyside whiskies can be the most accessible for beginners. The **Isle of Islay** is just the opposite, specializing in the peatiest, smokiest whiskies. Only a few producers remain to distill the smoky and pungent **Campbeltown** whiskies in the southwest Highlands, near Islay.

Tasting Whisky: Tasting whisky is like tasting wine; you'll use all your senses. First, swirl the whisky in the glass and observe its color and "legs"—the trail left by the liquid as it runs back down the side of the glass. Then take a deep sniff—do you smell smoke and peat? And finally, taste it (sip!). Swish it around and let your gums taste it, too. Adding a few drops of water is said to "open up the taste"—look for a little glass of water with a dropper standing by, and try tasting your whisky before and after.

schooner, or two-thirds pint (it's become a popular size for higher alcohol-content craft beers). Proper English ladies like a **shandy** (half beer and half 7-Up).

Whisky: The easiest and perhaps best option for sampling Scotland's national drink is to find a local pub with a passion for whisky that's filled with locals who share that passion. Many pubs have dozens of whiskies available. For more about whisky, see the "Whisky 101" sidebar.

Nonalcoholic Drinks: Teetotalers can order from a wide variety of soft drinks—

both the predictable American sodas and other more interesting bottled drinks, such as ginger beer (similar to ginger ale but with more bite), root beers, or other flavors (Fentimans brews some unusual options that are stocked in many pubs). The uniquely Scottish soft drink called Irn-Bru (pronounced "Iron Brew") is bright orange and tastes like bubble gum. Note that in Britain, "lemonade" is lemon-lime soda (like 7-Up).

SLEEPING

I favor hotels and restaurants that are handy to your sightseeing activities. In Britain, small bed-and-breakfast places (B&Bs) generally provide the best value, though I also include some bigger hotels.

Book your accommodations as soon as your itinerary is set, especially if you want to stay at one of my top listings or if you'll be traveling during busy times. See page 283 for a list of major holidays and festivals; for tips on making reservations, see page 263.

Rates and Deals

I've categorized my recommended accommodations based on price, indicated with a dollar-sign rating (see sidebar). The price ranges suggest an estimated cost for a one-night stay in a typical double room with a private toilet and shower in high season, and assume you're booking directly with the hotel.

While B&B prices tend to be fairly predictable, room rates are especially volatile at larger hotels that use "dynamic pricing" to set rates. Once your dates are set, check the specific price for your preferred stay at several hotels by comparing prices on Hotels.com or Booking.com, or by checking the hotels' own websites.

Staying in B&Bs and small hotels can save money over sleeping in big hotels. Chain hotels can be even cheaper, but they don't include breakfast. When comparing prices between chain hotels and B&Bs, remember you're getting two breakfasts (about a £25 value) for each double room at a B&B.

Types of Accommodations
Hotels

In cities, you'll find big, Old-World elegant hotels with modern amenities, as well as familiar-feeling business-class and boutique hotels no different from what you might experience at home. But you'll also find hotels that are more uniquely European.

An "en suite" room has a bathroom

Sleep Code

Hotels in this book are categorized according to the average price of a typical en suite double room with breakfast in high season.

$$$$ **Splurge:** Most rooms over £160
$$$ **Pricier:** £120-160
$$ **Midrange:** £80-120
$ **Budget:** £40-80
¢ **Backpacker:** Under £40
RS% Rick Steves discount

Unless otherwise noted, credit cards are accepted and free Wi-Fi is available. Comparison-shop by checking prices at several hotels (on each hotel's own website, on a booking site, or by email). For the best deal, always book directly with the hotel. Ask for a discount if paying in cash; if the listing includes RS%, request a Rick Steves discount.

(toilet and shower/tub) attached to the room; a room with a "private bathroom" can mean that the bathroom is all yours, but it's across the hall. If you want your own bathroom inside the room, request "en suite." If money's tight, ask about a room with a shared bathroom. You'll almost always have a sink in your room, and as more rooms go en suite, the hallway bathroom is shared with fewer guests.

Modern Hotel Chains: Chain hotels—common in bigger cities all over Great Britain—can be a great value (£60-100, depending on location and season). These hotels are about as cozy as a Motel 6, but they come with private showers/WCs, elevators, good security, and often an attached restaurant. Branches are often located near the train station, on major highways, or outside the city center.

Making Hotel Reservations

Requesting a Reservation: For family-run hotels, it's generally cheaper to book your room direct via email or a phone call. For business-class hotels, or if you'd rather book online, reserve directly through the hotel's official website (not a booking agency's site). For complicated requests, send an email.

Here's what the hotelier wants to know:
- type(s) of rooms and size of your party
- number of nights you'll stay
- your arrival and departure dates, written European-style as day/month/year
- special requests (such as en suite bathroom vs. down the hall, cheapest room, twin beds vs. double bed, quiet room)
- applicable discounts (such as a Rick Steves reader discount, cash discount, or promotional rate)

Confirming a Reservation: Most places will request a credit-card number to hold your room. If you're using an online reservation form, look for the https or a lock icon at the top of your browser. If you book direct, you can email, call, or fax this information.

Canceling a Reservation: If you must cancel, it's courteous—and smart—to do so with as much notice as possible, especially for smaller family-run places (which describes many of the hotels I list). Cancellation policies can be strict; read the fine print or ask about these before you book. Many discount deals require pre-payment, with no cancellation refunds.

Reconfirming a Reservation: Always call or email to reconfirm your room reservation a few days in advance. For B&Bs or very small hotels, I call again on my day of arrival to tell my host what time to expect me (especially important if arriving late—after 17:00).

Phoning: For tips on calling hotels overseas, see page 268.

This option is especially worth considering for families, as kids often stay for free. While most of these hotels have 24-hour reception and elevators, breakfast and Wi-Fi generally cost extra, and the service lacks a personal touch (at some, you'll check in at a self-service kiosk).

Room rates change from day to day with volume and vary depending on how far ahead you book. The best deals generally must be prepaid a few weeks ahead and may not be refundable—read the fine print carefully. The biggest chains are **Premier Inn** (www.premierinn.com) and **Travelodge** (www.travelodge.co.uk). Both have attractive deals for prepaid or advance bookings. Other chains operating in Britain include the Irish **Jurys Inn** (www.jurysinns.com) and the French-owned **Ibis** (www.ibishotel.com). Couples can consider **Holiday Inn Express,** which generally allow only two people per room (make sure Express is part of the name or you'll be paying more for a regular Holiday Inn, www.hiexpress.co.uk).

Arrival and Check-In: Many of my recommended hotels have three or more floors of rooms and steep stairs. Older

properties often do not have elevators. If stairs are an issue, ask for a ground-floor room or choose a hotel with a lift (elevator). Air-conditioning isn't a given (I've noted which of my listings have it), but most places have fans. On hot summer nights, you'll want your window open—and in a big city, street noise is a fact of life. Bring earplugs or request a room on the back side. If you suspect night noise will be a problem (if, for instance, your room is over a noisy pub), ask for a quieter room on an upper floor.

In Your Room: Note that all of Britain's accommodations are nonsmoking. Electrical outlets may have switches that turn the current on or off; if your appliance isn't working, flip the switch at the outlet.

To guard against theft in your room, keep valuables out of sight. Some rooms come with a safe, and other hotels have safes at the front desk. I've never bothered using one and in a lifetime of travel, I've never had anything stolen from my room.

Breakfast: Your room cost usually includes a traditional full cooked breakfast (fry-up) or a lighter, healthier continental breakfast.

Checking Out: While it's customary to pay for your room upon departure, it can be a good idea to settle your bill the day before, when you're not in a hurry and while the manager's there. That way you'll have time to discuss and address any points of contention.

Hotelier Help: Hoteliers can be a good source of advice. Most know their city well, and can assist you with everything from public transit and airport connections to finding a good restaurant, the nearest launderette, or a late-night pharmacy.

Hotel Hassles: Even at the best places, mechanical breakdowns occur. Report your concerns clearly and calmly at the front desk. For more complicated problems, don't expect instant results. Above all, keep a positive attitude. Remember, you're on vacation. If your hotel is a disappointment, spend more time out enjoying the place you came to see.

B&Bs and Small Hotels

B&Bs and small hotels are generally family-run places with fewer amenities but more character than a conventional hotel. They range from large inns with 15-20 rooms to small homes renting out a spare bedroom. Places named "guesthouse" or "B&B" typically have eight or fewer rooms. The philosophy of the management determines the character of a place more than its size and amenities.

B&B proprietors are selective about the guests they invite in for the night. Many do not welcome children. If you'll be staying for more than one night, you are a "desirable." In popular weekend-getaway spots, you're unlikely to find a place to take you for Saturday night only. If my listings are full, ask for guidance. Mentioning this book can help. Owners usually work together and can call up an ally to land you a bed. Many B&B owners are also pet owners. If you're allergic, ask about resident pets when you reserve.

Rules and Etiquette: B&Bs and small hotels come with their own etiquette and quirks. Keep in mind that owners are at the whim of their guests—if you're getting up early, so are they; if you check in late,

The Good and Bad of Online Reviews

User-generated review sites and apps such as Yelp and Booking.com can give you a consensus of opinions about everything from hotels and restaurants to sights and nightlife. If you scan reviews of a hotel and see several complaints about noise or a rotten location, it tells you something important that you'd never learn from the hotel's own website.

But as a guidebook writer, my sense is that there is a big difference between the uncurated information on a review site and a guidebook. A user-generated review is based on the experience of one person, who likely stayed at one hotel in a given city and ate at a few restaurants there (and who doesn't have much of a basis for comparison). A guidebook is the work of a trained researcher who, year after year, visits many alternatives to assess their relative value. I recently checked out some top-rated user-reviewed hotel and restaurant listings in various towns; when stacked up against their competitors, some were gems, while just as many were duds.

Both types of information have their place, and in many ways, they're complementary. If something is well-reviewed in a guidebook, and also gets good ratings on one of these sites, it's likely a winner.

they'll wait up for you. Most B&Bs have set check-in times (usually in the late afternoon). If arriving outside that time, they will want to know when to expect you (call or email ahead). Most will let you check in earlier if the room is available (or they'll at least let you drop off your bag).

Most B&Bs and guesthouses serve a hearty cooked breakfast of eggs and much more (for details on breakfast, see the Eating section, earlier). Because the owner is often also the cook, breakfast hours are usually abbreviated. It's an unwritten rule that guests shouldn't show up at the very end of the breakfast period and expect a full cooked breakfast.

B&Bs and small hotels often come with thin walls and doors, and sometimes creaky floorboards, which can make for a noisy night. If you're a light sleeper, bring earplugs. And please be quiet in the halls and in your rooms at night...those of us getting up early will thank you for it.

In the Room: Every B&B offers "tea service" in the room—an electric kettle, cups, tea bags, coffee packets, and a pack of biscuits.

Your bedroom probably won't include a phone, but nearly every B&B has free Wi-Fi. However, the signal may not reach all rooms; you may need to sit in the lounge to access it.

You're likely to encounter unusual bathroom fixtures. The "pump toilet" has a flushing handle or button that doesn't kick in unless you push it just right: too hard or too soft, and it won't go. (Be decisive but not ruthless.) Most B&B baths have an instant water heater. This looks like an electronic box under the showerhead with dials and buttons: One control adjusts the heat, while another turns the flow off and on (let the water run for a bit to moderate the temperature before you hop in). If the hot water doesn't work, you may need to flip a red switch (often located just outside the bathroom). If the shower looks mysterious, ask your B&B host for help...*before* you take your clothes off.

Paying: Many B&Bs take credit cards, but may add the card service fee to your bill (about 3 percent). If you do need to pay cash for your room, plan ahead to have enough on hand when you check out.

Short-Term Rentals

A short-term rental—whether an apartment (or "flat"), house, or room in a local's

PRACTICALITIES
SLEEPING

home—is an increasingly popular alternative, especially if you plan to settle in one location for several nights. For stays longer than a few days, you can usually find a rental that's comparable to—and even cheaper than—a hotel room with similar amenities.

Many places require a minimum night stay, and compared to hotels, rentals usually have less flexible cancellation policies.

Finding Accommodations: Aggregator websites such as Airbnb, FlipKey, Booking.com, and the HomeAway family of sites (HomeAway, VRBO, and VacationRentals) let you browse properties and correspond directly with European property owners or managers. If you prefer to work from a curated list of accommodations, consider using a rental agency such as InterhomeUSA.com or RentaVilla.com. Agency-represented apartments typically cost more, but this method often offers more help and safeguards than booking direct.

Confirming and Paying: Many places require you to pay the entire balance before your trip. It's easiest and safest to pay through the site where you found the listing. Be wary of owners who want to take your transaction offline to avoid fees; this gives you no recourse if things go awry. Never agree to wire money (a key indicator of a fraudulent transaction).

Hostels

A hostel provides cheap beds in dorms where you sleep alongside strangers for about £20-30 per night. Travelers of any age are welcome if they don't mind dorm-style accommodations and meeting other travelers. Most hostels offer kitchen facilities, guest computers, Wi-Fi, and a self-service laundry. Hostels almost always provide bedding, but not the towel (though you can usually rent one for a small fee). Family and private rooms are often available.

Independent hostels tend to be easygoing, colorful, and informal (no mem-

bership required; www.hostelworld.com). You may pay slightly less by booking direct with the hostel. A few chains have multiple locations around Scotland, including **MacBackpackers** (www.scotlandstophostels. com); others are listed on the **Scottish Independent Hostels** website, with a fun variety of well-established places (www. hostel-scotland.co.uk).

Official hostels are part of Hostelling International (HI) and share an online booking site (www.hihostels.com). In Scotland, these official hostels are run by the Scottish Youth Hostel Association (SYHA, also known as Hostelling Scotland, www.syha.org.uk). HI hostels typically require that you be a member or pay extra per night.

STAYING CONNECTED

One of the most common questions I hear from travelers is, "How can I stay connected in Europe?" The short answer is: more easily and cheaply than you might think.

The simplest solution is to bring your own device—mobile phone, tablet, or laptop—and use it just as you would at home (following the tips below, such as connecting to free Wi-Fi whenever possible). Another option is to buy a European SIM card for your mobile phone—either your US phone or one you buy in Europe. Or you can use European landlines and computers to connect. Each of these options is described below, and more details are at www.ricksteves.com/phoning. For a very practical one-hour talk covering tech issues for travelers, see www.ricksteves.com/mobile-travel-skills.

Using a Mobile Phone in Europe

Here are some budget tips and options.

Sign up for an international plan. Using your cellular network in Europe on a pay-as-you-go basis can add up. To stay connected at a lower cost, sign up for an international

Tips on Internet Security

Make sure that your device is running the latest versions of its operating system, security software, and apps. Next, ensure that your device and key programs (like email) are password- or passcode-protected. On the road, use only secure, password-protected Wi-Fi hotspots. Ask the hotel or café staff for the specific name of their Wi-Fi network, and make sure you log on to that exact one.

If you must access your financial info online, use a banking app rather than accessing your account via a browser. A cellular connection is more secure than Wi-Fi. Avoid logging onto personal finance sites on a public computer.

Never share your credit-card number (or any other sensitive information) online unless you know that the site is secure. A secure site displays a little padlock icon, and the URL begins with *https* (instead of the usual *http*).

service plan through your carrier. Most providers offer a simple bundle that includes calling, messaging, and data. Your normal plan may already include international coverage (T-Mobile's does).

Before your trip, call your provider or check online to confirm that your phone will work in Europe, and research your provider's international rates. Activate the plan a day or two before you leave, then remember to cancel it when your trip's over.

Use free Wi-Fi whenever possible. Unless you have an unlimited-data plan, you're best off saving most of your online tasks for Wi-Fi. You can access the Internet, send texts, and even make voice calls over Wi-Fi.

Most accommodations in Europe offer free Wi-Fi, but some—especially expensive hotels—charge a fee. Many cafés (including Starbucks and McDonald's) have free hotspots for customers; look for signs offering it and ask for the Wi-Fi password when you buy something. You'll also often find Wi-Fi at TIs, city squares, major museums, public-transit hubs, airports, and aboard trains and buses.

Minimize the use of your cellular network. Even with an international data plan, wait until you're on Wi-Fi to Skype, download apps, stream videos, or do other megabyte-greedy tasks. Using a

navigation app such as Google Maps over a cellular network can take lots of data, so do this sparingly or use it offline.

Limit automatic updates. By default, your device constantly checks for a data connection and updates apps. It's smart to disable these features so your apps will only update when you're on Wi-Fi.

Use Wi-Fi calling and messaging apps. Skype, Viber, FaceTime, and Google+ Hangouts are great for making free or low-cost voice and video calls over Wi-Fi. With an app installed on your phone, tablet, or laptop, you can log on to a Wi-Fi network and contact friends or family members who use the same service. If you buy credit in advance, with some of these services you can call any mobile phone or landline worldwide for just pennies per minute.

Many of these apps also allow you to send messages over Wi-Fi to any other person using that app.

Using a European SIM Card

With a European SIM card, you get a European mobile number and access to cheaper rates than you'll get through your US carrier. This option works well for those who want to make a lot of voice calls or needing faster connection speeds than their US carrier provides. Fit the SIM card into a cheap

How to Dial

International Calls

Whether phoning from a US landline or mobile phone, or from a number in another European country, here's how to make an international call. I've used one of my recommended London hotels as an example (tel. 020/7730-8191).

Initial Zero: Drop the initial zero from international phone numbers—except when calling Italy.

Mobile Tip: If using a mobile phone, the "+" sign can replace the international access code (for a "+" sign, press and hold "0").

US/Canada to Europe

Dial 011 (US/Canada international access code), country code (44 for Britain), and phone number.

▶ To call the London hotel from home, dial 011-44-20/7730-8191.

Country to Country Within Europe

Dial 00 (Europe international access code), country code, and phone number.

▶ To call the London hotel from Spain, dial 00-44-20/7730-8191.

Europe to the US/Canada

Dial 00, country code (1 for US/Canada), and phone number.

▶ To call from Europe to my office in Edmonds, Washington, dial 00-1-425-771-8303.

Domestic Calls

To call within Britain (from one British landline or mobile phone to another), simply dial the phone number, including the initial 0 if there is one.

▶ To call the London hotel from Edinburgh, dial 020/7730-8191.

More Dialing Tips

British Phone Numbers: Numbers beginning with 071 through 079 are mobile numbers, which are more expensive to call than a landline.

phone you buy in Europe, or swap out the SIM card in an "unlocked" US phone.

SIM cards are sold at mobile-phone shops, department-store electronics counters, some newsstands, and vending machines. Costing about $5-10, they usually include prepaid calling/messaging credit, with no contract and no commitment. Expect to pay $20-40 more for a SIM card with a gigabyte of data. If you travel with this card to other countries in the European Union, there may be extra roaming fees.

Public Phones and Computers

Most **hotels** charge a fee for placing calls—ask for rates before you dial. You

Toll and Toll-Free Calls: Numbers starting with 0800 and 0808 are toll-free. Those beginning with 084, 087, and 03 are generally inexpensive toll numbers (£0.15/minute from a landline, £0.20-.40/minute from a mobile). Numbers beginning with 09 are pricey toll lines. If you have questions about a prefix, call 100 for free help. International rates apply to US toll-free numbers dialed from Britain—they're not free.

More Phoning Help: See www.howtocallabroad.com.

European Country Codes		Ireland & N. Ireland	353 / 44
Austria	43	Italy	39
Belgium	32	Latvia	371
Bosnia-Herzegovina	387	Montenegro	382
Croatia	385	Morocco	212
Czech Republic	420	Netherlands	31
Denmark	45	Norway	47
Estonia	372	Poland	48
Finland	358	Portugal	351
France	33	Russia	7
Germany	49	Slovakia	421
Gibraltar	350	Slovenia	386
Great Britain	44	Spain	34
Greece	30	Sweden	46
Hungary	36	Switzerland	41
Iceland	354	Turkey	90

can use a prepaid international phone card (available at post offices, newsstands, street kiosks, tobacco shops, and train stations) to call out from your hotel.

Public pay phones are hard to find in Britain, and they're expensive. To use one, you'll pay with a major credit card (minimum charge-£1.20) or coins (minimum charge-£0.60).

Most hotels have **public computers** in their lobbies for guests to use; otherwise you may find them at Internet cafés or public libraries.

Mail

You can mail one package per day to yourself worth up to $200 duty-free from Europe to the US (mark it "personal purchases").

The Language Barrier?

Yes, Scots speak English, but with a thick brogue. They're proud of their old Celtic language, Gaelic, though it thrives only in the remotest corners of the Scottish Highlands and the Hebrides. Scotland has another language of its own, called Scots. Aye, you're likely already a wee bit familiar with a few Scots words, ye lads and lassies. Here are some Scots words that may come in handy during your travels:

Scottish	English
auld	old
aye	yes
bairn, wean	child
blether	talk
bonnie	beautiful, handsome, good
braw	good, fine
cairn	pile of stones
close (rhymes with "dose")	an alley leading to a courtyard or square
ken	to know
kirk	church
nae	no (as in "nae bother"—you're welcome)
neeps	turnips
pend	arched gateway
ree	king, royal ("righ" in Gaelic)
tattie	potato
wee	small
wynd	tight, winding lane connecting major streets

If you're sending a gift to someone, mark it "unsolicited gift." For details, visit www.cbp.gov, select "Travel," and search for "Know Before You Go."

The British postal service works fine, but for quick transatlantic delivery (in either direction), consider services such as DHL (www.dhl.com). For postcards, get stamps at the neighborhood post office, newsstands within fancy hotels, and some mini-marts and card shops.

TRANSPORTATION

In Scotland, I connect big cities (Edinburgh and Glasgow) by train or bus; but to explore rural areas (including most of the Highlands), I prefer to stay footloose and fancy-free with a rental car.

Trains

Regular tickets on Britain's great train system (15,000 departures from 2,400 stations daily) are the most expensive

Many Scots (or Gaelic) words relate to geography, and turn up often in place names:

Scottish	English
aber	confluence or mouth of a river
bal	town
ben	mountain
blair	clearing
brae	slope, hill
burn	creek or stream
crag or craig	cliff, rocky ground, sea rock
dun or dum	hill fort
eilean	island
fell	hill
firth	estuary
glen	narrow valley
innis or inch	island
inver	confluence or mouth of a river
kyle	strait
loch	lake
sea loch	inlet
strath	wide valley

per mile in all of Europe. For the greatest savings, book online in advance and leave after rush hour (after 9:30 weekdays).

Since Britain's railways have been privatized, a single train route can be operated by multiple companies. However, one website covers all train lines (www.nationalrail.co.uk), and another covers all bus and train routes (www.traveline.org.uk for information, not ticket sales). Another good resource, which also has schedules for trains throughout Europe, is German Rail's timetable (www.bahn.com).

While not required, reservations are free and can normally be made well in advance. They are an especially good idea for long journeys or for travel on Sundays or holidays. Make reservations at any train station, by phone, or online when you buy your ticket. With a point-to-point ticket, you can reserve as late as two hours before train time, but rail-pass holders should book seats at least 24 hours in advance.

Rail Passes

A **BritRail Pass** lets you travel by train in Scotland, England, and Wales for three to eight days within a one-month period, 15 days within two months, or for continuous periods of up to one month. In addition, BritRail sells three different regional Scotland passes that are good for three to eight days of train travel within three, eight, or 15-day periods. Discounted rates are offered for children, youths, seniors, or for three or more people traveling together.

BritRail passes are best purchased outside Europe (through travel agents or Rick Steves' Europe). For more on the ins and outs of rail passes, including prices, download my **free guide to Eurail Passes** (www.ricksteves.com/rail-guide) or go to www.ricksteves.com/rail.

If you're taking just a couple of train rides, individual **point-to-point train tickets** may save you money over a pass. Use this map to add up approximate pay-as-you-go fares for your itinerary, and compare that to the price of a rail pass. Keep in mind that significant discounts on point-to-point tickets may be available with advance purchase.

Map shows approximate costs, in US$, for one-way, second-class tickets at off-peak rates.

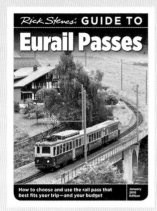

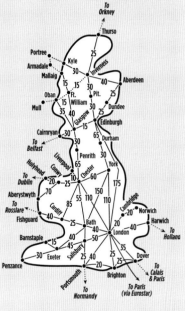

Rail Passes: There are three different Scotland-only passes: Spirit of Scotland (covers most trains in Scotland), Central Scotland (Edinburgh/Glasgow area), and Scottish Highlands (Glasgow and points north). But for a Scotland-only itinerary, these probably won't save you money over point-to-point tickets (particularly if you buy tickets in advance or use a discount Railcard—see later).

Especially if you travel between London and Scotland, consider the BritRail Pass (covers England, Scotland, and Wales). A rail pass offers hop-on flexibility and no need to lock in reservations, except for overnight sleeper cars.

Public Transportation Routes in Scotland

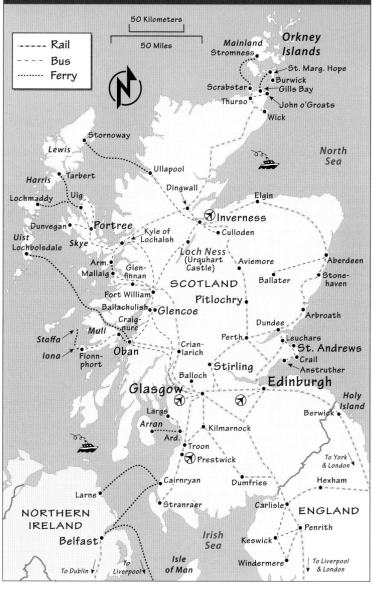

Rail
Bus
Ferry

50 Kilometers
50 Miles

Orkney Islands
Mainland
Stromness
St. Marg. Hope
Burwick
Scrabster
Gills Bay
Thurso
John o'Groats
Wick

Stornoway
Lewis
Tarbert
Harris
Ullapool
Lochmaddy
Uig
Dingwall
Elgin
Dunvegan
Portree
Inverness
Uist
Skye
Kyle of
Lochalsh
Culloden
Lochbolsdale
Loch Ness
(Urquhart Castle)
Aviemore
Aberdeen
Arm.
Mallaig
Glen-
finnan
SCOTLAND
Ballater
Stone-
haven
Fort William
Pitlochry
Ballachulish
Glencoe
Craig-
nure
Dundee
Arbroath
Staffa
Mull
Crian-
larich
Perth
Leuchars
Iona
Fionn-
phort
Oban
St. Andrews
Stirling
Crail
Balloch
Anstruther
Glasgow
Edinburgh
Largs
Holy
Island
Arran
Berwick
Ard.
Kilmarnock
Troon
Prestwick
To York
& London
Cairnryan
Dumfries
Hexham
Larne
Stranraer
Carlisle
ENGLAND
NORTHERN
IRELAND
Penrith
Belfast
Irish
Sea
Keswick
To Dublin
To
Liverpool
Isle
of Man
Windermere
To Liverpool
& London

North
Sea

BritRail passes cannot be purchased locally; buy your pass through an agent before leaving the US. Make sleeper reservations in advance; you can also make optional, free seat reservations (recommended for busy weekends) at staffed train stations. For specifics, see www.ricksteves.com/rail.

Buying Train Tickets in Advance: The best fares go to those who book their trips well in advance of their journey. To book ahead, go in person to any station, book online at www.nationalrail.co.uk, or call 0345-748-4950 (from the US, dial 011-44-20-7278-5240, phone answered 24 hours) to find out the schedule and best fare for your journey; you'll then be referred to the appropriate vendor—depending on the particular rail company—to book your ticket. You'll pick up your ticket at the station, or you may be able to print it at home.

Buying Train Tickets as You Travel: If you'd rather have the flexibility of booking tickets as you go, you can save a few pounds by buying a round-trip ticket, called a "return ticket" (a same-day round-trip, called a "day return," is particularly cheap); buying before 18:00 the day before you depart; traveling after the morning rush hour (this usually means after 9:30 Mon-Fri); and going standard class instead of first class. Preview your options at www.nationalrail.co.uk.

Senior, Youth, Partner, and Family Deals: To get a third off the price of most point-to-point rail tickets, seniors can buy a Senior Railcard (ages 60 and up), younger travelers can buy a 16-25 Railcard (ages 16-25, or full-time students 26 and older), and two people traveling together can buy a Two Together Railcard (ages 16 and over). A Family and Friends Railcard gives adults about 33 percent off for most trips and 60 percent off for their kids ages 5 to 15 (maximum 4 adults and 4 kids). Each Railcard costs £30; see www.railcard.co.uk.

Buses

Most long-haul domestic routes in Scotland are operated by **Scottish Citylink.** In peak season, it's worth booking your seat on popular routes at least a few days in advance (at the bus station or TI, online at www.citylink.co.uk, or by calling 0871-266-3333). At slower times, you can just hop on the bus and pay the driver. If you're taking lots of buses, consider Citylink's Explorer pass (£49/3 days in 5-day period, £74/5 days in 10-day period, £99/8 days in 16-day period).

Some regional routes are operated by Citylink's **Stagecoach** service (www.stagecoachbus.com). If a Stagecoach bus runs the same route as a Citylink one—such as between Glencoe and Fort William—it's likely cheaper (and maybe slower).

Longer-distance routes (especially those to England) are operated by **National Express** (tel. 0871-781-8181, www.nationalexpress.com) or **Megabus** (book far ahead for best discounts, toll tel. 0900-160-0900, www.megabus.com).

Renting a Car

Rental companies in Britain require you to be at least 21 years old and to have held your license for one year. Drivers under the age of 25 may incur a young-driver surcharge, and some rental companies will not rent to anyone 75 or older.

Figure on paying roughly $250 for a one-week rental. Allow extra for supplemental insurance, fuel, tolls, and parking. Most of the major US rental agencies (including Avis, Budget, Enterprise, Hertz, and Thrifty) have offices throughout Europe. Also consider the two major Europe-based agencies, Europcar and Sixt. It can be cheaper to use a consolidator, such as Auto Europe/Kemwel (www.autoeurope.com—or the often cheaper www.autoeurope.eu).

Always read the fine print or query the agent carefully for add-on charges—such as one-way drop-off fees, airport surcharges, or mandatory insurance

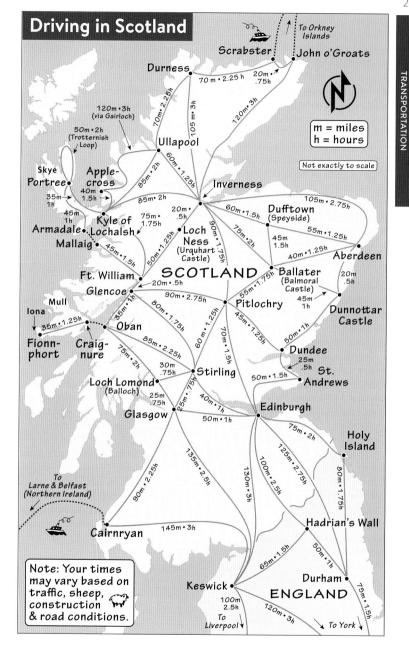

Driving in Scotland

To Orkney Islands

Scrabster

John o'Groats

Durness

70 m • 2.25 h

20m • .75h

120m • 3h (via Gairloch)

50m • 2h (Trotternish Loop)

70m • 2.25h

105m • 3h

120m • 3h

m = miles
h = hours

Not exactly to scale

Ullapool

60m • 1.25h

Skye

85m • 2h

Inverness

Apple-cross

Portree

105m • 2.75h

40m

85m • 2h

60m • 1.5h

Dufftown (Speyside)

35m 1h

45m 1h

20m • .5h

90m • 1.75h

75m • 2h

55m • 1.25h

Kyle of Lochalsh

75m • 1.75h

45m 1.5h

40m • 1.25h

Armadale

50m • 1.25h

Loch Ness (Urquhart Castle)

Aberdeen

Mallaig

45m • 1.5h

SCOTLAND

Ballater (Balmoral Castle)

20m .5h

Ft. William

20m • .5h

55m • 1.75h

45m 1h

Glencoe

90m • 2.75h

Pitlochry

Dunnottar Castle

Mull

35m • 1h

80m • 1.75h

45m • 1.25h

50m • 1h

Iona

Oban

85m • 2.25h

60m • 1.25h

70m • 1.5h

Dundee

35m • 1.25h

Fionn-phort

Craig-nure

75m • 2h

30m • .75h

25m .5h

St. Andrews

Stirling

50m • 1.5h

Loch Lomond (Balloch)

25m .75h

40m • 1h

Edinburgh

Glasgow

25m • .75h

50m • 1h

75m • 2h

Holy Island

To Larne & Belfast (Northern Ireland)

135m • 2.5h

125m • 2.75h

80m • 1.75h

90m • 2.25h

130m • 3h

100m • 2.5h

Hadrian's Wall

Cairnryan

145m • 3h

65m • 1.5h

50m • 1h

Note: Your times may vary based on traffic, sheep, construction & road conditions.

Keswick

Durham

ENGLAND

75m • 1.5h

100m 2.5h

120m • 3h

To Liverpool

To York

policies—that aren't included in the "total price."

For the best deal, rent by the week with unlimited mileage. I normally rent the smallest, least expensive model with a stick shift (generally cheaper than automatic). Almost all rentals are manual by default, so if you need an automatic, request one in advance. An automatic makes sense for most American drivers: With a manual transmission in Britain, you'll be sitting on the right side of the car, and shifting with your left hand...while driving on the left side of the road. When selecting a car, don't be tempted by a larger model, as it won't be as maneuverable on narrow, winding roads.

Picking Up Your Car: If you pick up your car in a smaller city or at an airport (rather than downtown), you'll more likely survive your first day on the road. Be aware that Brits call it "hiring a car," and directional signs at airports and train stations will read *Car Hire*.

Compare pickup costs (downtown can be less expensive than the airport) and explore drop-off options. Always check the hours of the location you choose: Many rental offices close from midday Saturday until Monday morning and, in smaller towns, at lunchtime.

When you pick up the rental car, check it thoroughly and make sure any damage is noted on your rental agreement. Rental agencies in Europe tend to charge for even minor damage, so be sure to mark everything. Before driving off, find out how your car's lights, turn signals, wipers, radio, and fuel cap function, and know what kind of fuel the car takes (diesel vs. unleaded). When you return the car, make sure the agent verifies its condition with you. Some drivers take pictures of the returned vehicle as proof of its condition.

The AA: The services of Britain's Automobile Association are included with most rentals (www.theaa.com), but check for this when booking to be sure you understand its towing and emergency road-service benefits.

Car Insurance Options

When you rent a car, you are liable for a very high deductible, sometimes equal to the entire value of the car. Limit your financial risk with one of these three options: Buy Collision Damage Waiver (CDW) coverage with a low or zero deductible from the car-rental company, get coverage through your credit card (free, if your card automatically includes zero-deductible coverage), or get collision insurance as part of a larger travel-insurance policy.

Basic **CDW** includes a very high deductible (typically $1,000-1,500), costs $15-30 a day (figure roughly 30-40 percent extra) and reduces your liability, but does not eliminate it. When you reserve or pick up the car, you'll be offered the chance to "buy down" the basic deductible to zero (for an additional $10-30/day; this is sometimes called "super CDW" or "zero-deductible coverage").

If you opt for **credit-card coverage,** you'll technically have to decline all coverage offered by the car-rental company, which means they can place a hold on your card (which can be up to the full value of the car). In case of damage, it can be time-consuming to resolve the charges with your credit-card company. Before you decide on this option, quiz your credit-card company about how it works.

For more on car-rental insurance, see www.ricksteves.com/cdw.

Navigation Options

If you'll be navigating using your phone or a GPS unit from home, remember to bring a car charger and device mount.

Mobile Phone: The mapping app on your mobile phone works fine for navigation in Europe, but for real-time turn-by-turn directions, alternate routes, and traffic updates, you'll need mobile data access. And driving all day can burn

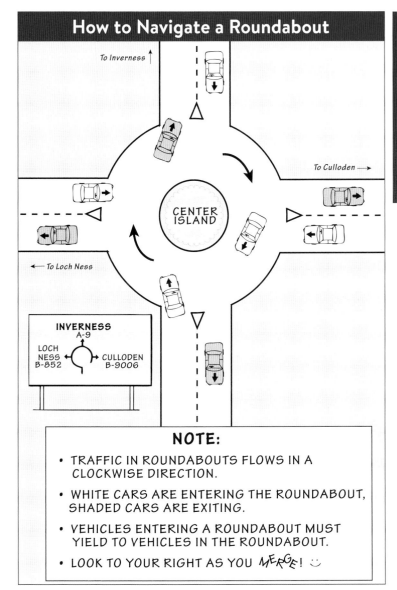

How to Navigate a Roundabout

NOTE:

- TRAFFIC IN ROUNDABOUTS FLOWS IN A CLOCKWISE DIRECTION.
- WHITE CARS ARE ENTERING THE ROUNDABOUT, SHADED CARS ARE EXITING.
- VEHICLES ENTERING A ROUNDABOUT MUST YIELD TO VEHICLES IN THE ROUNDABOUT.
- LOOK TO YOUR RIGHT AS YOU MERGE! ☺

through a lot of very expensive data. The economical workaround is to take your maps offline. By downloading in advance from Google Maps, Here WeGo, or Navmii, you can still have turn-by-turn voice directions and maps that recalibrate even though they're offline.

Download your map before you head out—it's smart to select a large region. Then turn off your data connection so you're not charged for roaming. Call up the map, enter your destination, and you're on your way. View maps in standard view (not satellite view) to limit data demands.

GPS Devices: If you prefer the convenience of a dedicated GPS unit, known as a "satnav" in Britain, consider renting one with your car ($10-30/day). These units offer real-time turn-by-turn directions and traffic without the data requirements of an app. Note that the unit may only come loaded with maps for its home country; if you need additional maps, ask.

A less expensive option is to bring a GPS device from home. Be aware that you'll need to buy and download European maps before your trip.

Maps and Atlases: Even when navigating primarily with a mobile app or GPS, I always make it a point to have a paper map. It's invaluable for getting the big picture, understanding alternate routes, and filling in when my phone runs out of juice. Several good road atlases cover all of Scotland. Ordnance Survey, Collins, AA, and Bartholomew editions are all available at tourist information offices, gas stations, and bookstores.

Driving in Scotland

Driving here is basically wonderful—once you remember to stay on the left and after you've mastered the roundabouts. Every year, however, I get a few notes from traveling readers advising me that, for them, trying to drive in Britain was a nerve-racking and regrettable mistake.

Many Yankee drivers find the hardest part isn't driving on the left, but steering from the right. Your instinct is to put yourself on the left side of your lane, which means you may spend your first day or two constantly drifting into the left shoulder. It can help to remember that the driver always stays close to the center line.

Road Rules: Be aware of Britain's rules

Sheep have the right of way.

of the road. Seat belts are mandatory for all, and kids under age 12 (or less than about 4.5 feet tall) must ride in an appropriate child-safety seat. It's illegal to use a mobile phone while driving. In Britain, you're not allowed to turn left on a red light unless a sign or signal specifically authorizes it. For more information about driving in Britain, ask your car-rental company or check the US State Department website (www.travel.state.gov, click on "International Travel," then specify your country of choice and click "Traffic Safety and Road Conditions").

Speed Limits: Speed limits are in miles per hour: 30 mph in town, 70 mph on the motorways, and 60 or 70 mph elsewhere. The national sign for the maximum speed is a white circle with a black slash. Motorways have electronic speed limit signs; posted speeds can change depending on traffic or the weather.

Note that road-surveillance cameras strictly enforce speed limits. Any driver (including foreigners renting cars) photographed speeding will get a nasty bill in the mail. Signs (an image of an old-fashioned camera) alert you when you're

entering a zone that may be monitored by these "camera cops." Heed them.

Roundabouts: Don't let a roundabout spook you. After all, you routinely merge into much faster traffic on American highways back home. Traffic flows clockwise, and cars already in the roundabout have the right-of-way; entering traffic yields (look to your right as you merge). You'll probably encounter "double-round-abouts"—figure-eights where you'll sling-shot from one roundabout directly into another. Just go with the flow and track signs carefully. When approaching an especially complex roundabout, you'll first pass a diagram showing the layout and the various exits. And in many cases, the pavement is painted to indicate the lane you should be in for a particular road or town.

Freeways (Motorways): The shortest distance between any two points is usually the motorway (what we'd call a "freeway"). In Britain, the smaller the number, the bigger the road. For example, the M-8 is a freeway, while the B-8000 is a country road.

Motorway road signs can be confusing, too few, and too late. Miss a motorway exit and you can lose 30 minutes. Study your map before taking off. Know the cities you'll be lacing together, since road numbers are inconsistent. British road signs are rarely marked with compass directions (e.g., *A-9 North*); instead, you need to know what major town or city you're heading for *(A-9 Inverness)*.

Unless you're passing, always drive in the "slow" lane on motorways (the lane farthest to the left). Remember to pass on the right, not the left.

Rest areas are called "services" and often have a number of amenities, such as restaurants, cafeterias, gas stations, shops, and motels.

Fuel: Gas (petrol) costs about $5.50 per gallon and is self-serve. Pump first and then pay. Diesel costs about the same. Diesel rental cars are common; make sure you know what kind of fuel your car takes before you fill up. Unleaded pumps are usually green.

Driving in Cities: Whenever possible, avoid driving in cities. Most cities have modern ring roads to skirt the congestion. Follow signs to the parking lots outside the city core—most are a 5- to 10-minute walk to the center—and avoid what can be an unpleasant grid of one-way streets or roads that are restricted to public transportation during the day.

Driving in Rural Areas: Outside the big cities and except for the motorways, British roads tend to be narrow. Adjust your perceptions of personal space: It's not "my side of the road" or "your side of the road," it's just "the road"—and it's shared as a cooperative adventure. If the road's wide enough, traffic in both directions can pass parked cars simultaneously, but frequently you'll have to take turns—follow the locals' lead and drive defensively.

Narrow country lanes are often lined with stone walls or woody hedges—and no shoulders. Some are barely wide enough for one car. Go slowly, and if you encounter an oncoming car, look for the nearest pullout (or "passing place")—the driver who's closest to one is expected to use it, even if it means backing up to reach

it. If another car pulls over and blinks its headlights, that means, "Go ahead; I'll wait to let you pass."

Parking: Pay attention to pavement markings to figure out where to park. One yellow line marked on the pavement means no parking Monday through Saturday during work hours. Double yellow lines mean no parking at any time. Broken yellow lines mean short stops are OK, but you should always look for explicit signs or ask a passerby. White lines mean you're free to park.

In towns, rather than look for street parking, I generally just pull into the most central and handy pay-and-display parking lot I can find. To pay and display, feed change into a machine, receive a timed ticket, and display it on the dashboard or stick it to the driver's-side window. Most machines in larger towns accept credit cards with a chip, but it's smart to keep coins handy for machines and parking meters that don't.

In some municipalities, drivers will see signs for "disc zone" parking. This is free, time-limited parking. But to use it, you must obtain a clock parking disc from a shop and display it on the dashboard (set the clock to show your time of arrival). Return within the signed time limit to avoid being ticketed.

Some parking garages (a.k.a. car parks) are totally automated and record your license plate with a camera when you enter. The Brits call a license plate a "number plate" or just "vehicle registration." The payment machine will use these terms when you pay before exiting.

Flights

The best comparison search engine for both international and intra-European flights is Kayak.com. An alternative is Google Flights, which has an easy-to-use system to track prices. For inexpensive flights within Europe, try Skyscanner.com.

Flying to Europe: Start looking for international flights about four to six

Haggis fans can fly home with Scotland's organ-meat specialty.

months before your trip, especially for peak-season travel. Off-season tickets can usually be purchased a month or so in advance. Depending on your itinerary, it can be efficient to fly into one city and out of another.

Flying Within Europe: Several cheap, no-frills airlines affordably connect Scotland with other destinations in the British Isles and throughout Europe. If you're considering a train ride that's more than five hours long, a flight may save you both time and money. When comparing your options, factor in the time it takes to get to the airport and how early you'll need to arrive to check in.

Well-known cheapo airlines that serve Scotland (primarily Edinburgh, Glasgow, and Inverness) include EasyJet, Ryanair, TUI, and Flybe.

But be aware of the potential drawbacks of flying with a discount airline: nonrefundable and nonchangeable tickets, minimal or nonexistent customer service, pricey and time-consuming treks to secondary airports, and stingy baggage allowances with steep overage fees. To avoid unpleasant surprises, read the small print before you book. These days you can also fly within Europe on major airlines affordably—and without all the aggressive restrictions—for around $100 a flight.

Resources from Rick Steves

Begin Your Trip at www.RickSteves.com

My mobile-friendly **website** is *the* place to explore Europe. You'll find thousands of fun articles, videos, photos, and radio interviews; a wealth of money-saving tips for planning your dream trip; my travel talks and blog; and guidebook updates (www.ricksteves.com/update).

Our **Travel Forum** is an immense collection of message boards, where our travel-savvy community answers questions and shares personal travel experiences—and our well-traveled staff chimes in when they can help.

Our **online Travel Store** offers bags and accessories designed to help you travel smarter and lighter. These include my popular bags (which I live out of four months a year), money belts, totes, toiletries kits, adapters, guidebooks, planning maps, and more.

Choosing the right rail pass for your trip can drive you nutty. Our website will help you find the perfect fit for your itinerary and your budget: We offer easy, one-stop shopping for rail passes, seat reservations, and point-to-point tickets.

Guidebooks, TV Shows, Audio Europe, and Tours

Books: *Rick Steves Best of Scotland* is just one of many books in my series on European travel, which includes country and city guidebooks, Snapshot guides (excerpted chapters from my country guides), Pocket Guides (full-color little books on big cities), and my budget-travel skills handbook, *Rick Steves Europe Through the Back Door.* My phrase books are practical and budget-oriented. A more complete list of my titles appears near the end of this book.

TV Shows: My public television series, *Rick Steves' Europe,* covers Europe from top to bottom with more than 100 half-hour episodes. To watch full episodes online for free, see www.ricksteves.com/tv. Or to raise your travel I.Q. with video versions of our popular classes (including my talks on travel skills, packing smart, most European countries, and European art), see www.ricksteves.com/travel-talks.

Audio: My weekly public radio show, *Travel with Rick Steves,* features interviews with travel experts from around the world. A complete archive is available at www.soundcloud.com/rick-steves, and much of this audio content is available, along with my audio tours of Europe's (and Spain's) top sights, through my free Rick Steves Audio Europe app (see page 29).

Small-Group Tours: Want to travel with greater efficiency and less stress? We offer tours with more than 40 itineraries reaching the best destinations in this book...and beyond. You'll find European adventures to fit every vacation length, and you'll enjoy great guides and a fun but small group of travel partners. For all the details, and to get our tour catalog, visit www.ricksteves.com or call us at 425/608-4217.

HOLIDAYS AND FESTIVALS

This list includes selected Scottish festivals plus national holidays observed throughout Scotland (and Great Britain). Many sights and banks close on national holidays—keep this in mind when planning your itinerary. Before planning a trip around a festival, verify the dates with the festival website, the Visit Scotland website (www.visitscotland.com), or my "Upcoming Holidays and Festivals in Scotland" webpage (www.ricksteves.com/europe/scotland/festivals).

Jan 25	Burns Night (poetry readings, haggis)
Early May	Early May Bank Holiday (first Mon)
Late May	Spring Bank Holiday (last Mon)
June	Edinburgh International Film Festival (www.royalhighlandshow.org)
Mid-June	Royal Highland Show, Edinburgh (www.royalhighlandshow.org)
July	Edinburgh Jazz and Blues Festival (www.edinburghjazzfestival.com)
Early Aug	Summer Bank Holiday (first Mon)
Aug	Edinburgh Military Tattoo (www.edintattoo.co.uk)
Aug	Edinburgh Fringe Festival (www.edfringe.com)
Aug	Edinburgh International Festival (www.eif.co.uk)
Late Aug	Cowal Highland Gathering, west of Glasgow in Dunoon
Early Sept	Braemar Gathering, north of Pitlochry (first Sat)
Oct	Royal National Mòd (http://ancomun.co.uk)
Nov 5	Guy Fawkes Night (fireworks, bonfires, effigy-burning)
Nov 30	St. Andrew's Day (dancing and cultural events) and Bank Holiday (closest Monday)
Dec 24-26	Christmas holidays
Dec 31-Jan 2	Hogmanay (music, street theater, carnival, www.hogmanay.net)

CONVERSIONS AND CLIMATE

Numbers and Stumblers
- In Europe, dates appear as day/month/year, so Christmas 2019 is 25/12/19.
- What Americans call the second floor of a building is the first floor in Scotland.
- On escalators and moving sidewalks, Scots keep the left "lane" open for passing. Keep to the right.
- To avoid the Scottish version of giving someone "the finger," don't hold up the first two fingers of your hand with your palm facing you. (It looks like a reversed victory sign.)
- And please...don't call your waist pack a "fanny" pack.

Weights and Measures
Scotland uses the metric system for nearly everything. Weight and volume are typically calculated in metric: A kilogram is 2.2 pounds, and one liter is about a quart (almost four to a gallon). Temperatures are generally given in Celsius, although some newspapers also list them in Fahrenheit. Driving distances and speed limits are measured in miles. Beer is sold as pints, and a person's weight is measured in stone.

1 stone = 14 pounds
1 Scottish pint = 1.2 US pints
1 schooner = 2/3 pint
1 imperial gallon = 1.2 US gallons or about 4.5 liters

Clothing Sizes
When shopping for clothing, use these US-to-UK comparisons as general guidelines.

Women: For pants and dresses, add 4 (US 10 = UK 14). For blouses and sweaters, add 2. For shoes, subtract 2½ (US size 8 = UK size 5½)

Men: For clothing, US and UK sizes are the same. For shoes, subtract about ½ (US size 9 = UK size 8½)

Scotland's Climate
First line, average daily high; second line, average daily low; third line, average days without rain. For more detailed weather statistics for destinations in this book (as well as the rest of the world), check www.wunderground.com.

Edinburgh

J	F	M	A	M	J	J	A	S	O	N	D
42°	43°	46°	51°	56°	62°	65°	64°	60°	54°	48°	44°
34°	34°	36°	39°	43°	49°	52°	52°	49°	44°	39°	36°
14	13	16	16	17	15	14	15	14	14	13	13

Packing Checklist

Whether you're traveling for five days or five weeks, you won't need more than this. Pack light to enjoy the sweet freedom of true mobility.

Clothing

- ❑ 5 shirts: long- & short-sleeve
- ❑ 2 pairs pants (or shirts/capris)
- ❑ 1 pair shorts
- ❑ 5 pairs underwear & socks
- ❑ 1 pair walking shoes
- ❑ Sweater or warm layer
- ❑ Rainproof jacket with hood
- ❑ Tie, scarf, belt, and/or hat
- ❑ Swimsuit
- ❑ Sleepwear/loungewear

Money

- ❑ Debit card(s)
- ❑ Credit card(s)
- ❑ Hard cash (US $100-200)
- ❑ Money belt

Documents & Travel Info

- ❑ Passport
- ❑ Ticket & confirmations: flights, hotels, trains, rail pass, car rental, sight entries
- ❑ Driver's license
- ❑ Student ID, hostel card, etc.
- ❑ Photocopies of important documents
- ❑ Insurance details
- ❑ Guidebooks & maps

Toiletries Kit

- ❑ Basics: soap, shampoo, toothbrush, toothpaste, floss, deodorant, sunscreen, brush/comb, etc.
- ❑ Medicines & vitamins
- ❑ First-aid kit
- ❑ Glasses/contacts/sunglasses (with prescriptions)
- ❑ Sewing kit
- ❑ Packet of tissues (for WC)
- ❑ Earplugs

Electronics

- ❑ Mobile phone
- ❑ Camera & related gear
- ❑ Tablet/ebook reader/laptop
- ❑ Headphones/earbuds
- ❑ Chargers & batteries
- ❑ Phone car charger & mount (or GPS device)
- ❑ Plug adapters

Miscellaneous

- ❑ Daypack
- ❑ Sealable plastic baggies
- ❑ Laundry supplies: soap, laundry bag, clothesline, spot remover
- ❑ Small umbrella
- ❑ Travel alarm/watch
- ❑ Notepad & pen
- ❑ Journal

Optional Extras

- ❑ Second pair of shoes (flip-flops, sandals, tennis shoes, boots)
- ❑ Travel hairdryer
- ❑ Picnic supplies
- ❑ Water bottle
- ❑ Fold-up tote bag
- ❑ Small flashlight
- ❑ Mini binoculars
- ❑ Small towel or washcloth
- ❑ Inflatable pillow/neck rest
- ❑ Tiny lock
- ❑ Address list (to mail postcards)
- ❑ Extra passport photos

INDEX

MAP INDEX

Start your trip at

Our website enhances this book and turns

Explore Europe

At ricksteves.com you can browse through thousands of articles, videos, photos and radio interviews, plus find a wealth of money-saving travel tips for planning your dream trip. And with our mobile-friendly website, you can easily

access all this great travel information anywhere you go.

TV Shows

Preview the places you'll visit by watching entire half-hour episodes of Rick Steves' Europe (choose from all 100 shows) on-demand, for free.

ricksteves.com

your travel dreams into affordable reality

Radio Interviews

Enjoy ready access to Rick's vast library of radio interviews covering travel tips and cultural insights that relate specifically to your Europe travel plans.

Travel Forums

Learn, ask, share! Our online community of savvy travelers is a great resource for first-time travelers to Europe, as well as seasoned pros. You'll find forums on each country, plus travel tips and restaurant/hotel reviews. You can even ask one of our well-traveled staff to chime in with an opinion.

Travel News

Subscribe to our free Travel News e-newsletter, and get monthly updates from Rick on what's happening in Europe.

Audio Europe™

Rick's Free Travel App

Get your FREE Rick Steves Audio Europe™ app to enjoy…

- Dozens of self-guided tours of Europe's top museums, sights and historic walks
- Hundreds of tracks filled with cultural insights and sightseeing tips from Rick's radio interviews
- All organized into handy geographic playlists
- For Apple and Android

With Rick whispering in your ear, Europe gets even better.

Find out more at ricksteves.com

Pack Light and Right

Gear up for your next adventure at ricksteves.com

Light Luggage

Pack light and right with Rick Steves' affordable, custom-designed rolling carry-on bags, backpacks, day packs and shoulder bags.

Accessories

From packing cubes to moneybelts and beyond, Rick has personally selected the travel goodies that will help your trip go smoother.

Shop at ricksteves.com

Rick Steves has

Experience maximum Europe

Save time and energy

This guidebook is your independent-travel toolkit. But for all it delivers, it's still up to you to devote the time and energy it takes to manage the preparation and logistics that are essential for a happy trip. If that's a hassle, there's a solution.

Rick Steves Tours

A Rick Steves tour takes you to Europe's most

great tours, too!

with minimum stress

interesting places with great guides and small groups of 28 or less. We follow Rick's favorite itineraries, ride in comfy buses, stay in family-run hotels, and bring you intimately close to the Europe you've traveled so far to see. Most importantly, we take away the logistical headaches so you can focus on the fun.

travelers—nearly half of them repeat customers—along with us on four dozen different itineraries, from Ireland to Italy to Athens.

Is a Rick Steves tour the right fit for your travel dreams? Find out at ricksteves.com, where you can also request Rick's latest tour catalog.

Europe is best experienced with happy travel partners. We hope you can join us.

Join the fun

This year we'll take thousands of free-spirited

See our itineraries at ricksteves.com

A Guide for Every Trip

BEST OF GUIDES

Full-color easy-to-scan format, focusing on Europe's most popular destinations and sights.

Best of England
Best of Europe
Best of France
Best of Germany
Best of Ireland
Best of Italy
Best of Spain

COMPREHENSIVE GUIDES

City, country, and regional guides with detailed coverage for a multi-week trip exploring the most iconic sights and venturing off the beaten track.

Amsterdam & the Netherlands
Barcelona
Belgium: Bruges, Brussels, Antwerp & Ghent
Berlin
Budapest
Croatia & Slovenia
Eastern Europe
England
Florence & Tuscany
France
Germany
Great Britain
Greece: Athens & the Peloponnese
Iceland
Ireland
Istanbul
Italy
London
Paris
Portugal
Prague & the Czech Republic
Provence & the French Riviera
Rome
Scandinavia
Scotland
Spain
Switzerland
Venice
Vienna, Salzburg & Tirol

THE BEST OF ROME

ome, Italy's capital, is studded with
oman remnants and floodlit-fountain
uares. From the Vatican to the Colos-
um, with crazy traffic in between, Rome
onderful, huge, and exhausting. The
wds, the heat, and the weighty history

of the Eternal City where Caesars walked
can make tourists wilt. Recharge by taking siestas, gelato breaks, and after-dark
walks, strolling from one atmospheric
square to another in the refreshing evening air.

fired **Pantheon**—which
gest dome until the
arly 2,000 years old
day over 1,500).

l of Athens in the **Vat-**
odies the humanistic
ance

, gladiators fought
another, entertaining
0.

is Rome **ristorante.**
rds at **St. Peter's**
t spring.

Rick Steves guidebooks are published by Avalon Travel, an imprint of Perseus Books, a Hachette Book Group company.

POCKET GUIDES

Compact, full-color city guides with the essentials for shorter trips.

Amsterdam
Athens
Barcelona
Florence
Italy's Cinque Terre
London
Munich & Salzburg
Paris
Prague
Rome
Venice
Vienna

SNAPSHOT GUIDES

Focused single-destination coverage.

Basque Country: Spain & France
Copenhagen & the Best of Denmark
Dublin
Dubrovnik
Edinburgh
Hill Towns of Central Italy
Krakow, Warsaw & Gdansk
Lisbon
Loire Valley
Madrid & Toledo
Milan & the Italian Lakes District
Naples & the Amalfi Coast
Normandy
Northern Ireland
Norway
Reykjavik
Sevilla, Granada & Southern Spain
St. Petersburg, Helsinki & Tallinn
Stockholm

Rick Steves books are available
from your favorite bookseller.
Many guides are available as ebooks.

CRUISE PORTS GUIDES

Reference for cruise ports of call.

Mediterranean Cruise Ports
Scandinavian & Northern European
Cruise Ports

Complete your library with...

TRAVEL SKILLS & CULTURE

Study up on travel skills before visiting "Europe through the back door" or gain insight on European history and culture.

Europe 101
European Christmas
European Easter
European Festivals
Europe Through the Back Door
Postcards from Europe
Travel as a Political Act

PHRASE BOOKS & DICTIONARIES

French
French, Italian & German
German
Italian
Portuguese
Spanish

PLANNING MAPS

Britain, Ireland & London
Europe
France & Paris
Germany, Austria & Switzerland
Ireland
Italy
Spain & Portugal

Be creative! Yo
"Two, please
"Please, whe
any language, espe
want, such as the
please).

HELLOS

Pleasantri

Hello.
Do you speak
English?
Yes. / No.
I don't spe
French.
I'm sorry.
Please.
Thank yo
much).
Excuse
attenti
Excuse
OK?
OK. (
say
Goo
Ve

PHOTO CREDITS

Avalon Travel
Hachette Book Group
1700 Fourth Street
Berkeley, CA 94710

Printed in China by RR Donnelley

First printing October 2018

ISBN 978-1-64171-165-4
First Edition

For the latest on Rick's talks, guidebooks, tours, public television series, and public radio show, contact Rick Steves' Europe, 130 Fourth Avenue North, Edmonds, WA 98020, 425/771-8303, www.ricksteves.com, rick@ricksteves.com.

RICK STEVES' EUROPE
Special Publications Manager: Risa Laib
Managing Editor: Jennifer Madison Davis
Project Editor: Suzanne Kotz
Editorial & Production Assistant: Jessica Shaw
Graphic Content Director: Sandra Hundacker
Maps & Graphics: David C. Hoerlein, Lauren Mills, Mary Rostad

AVALON TRAVEL
Senior Editor and Series Manager: Maddy McPrasher
Editor: Jamie Andrade
Editor: Sierra Machado
Copy Editor: Kelly Lydick
Proofreader: Elizabeth Jang
Indexer: Stephen Callahan
Cover Design: Kimberly Glyder Design
Interior Design: McGuire Barber Design
Production and Typesetting: Krista Anderson, Tabitha Lahr, Rue Flaherty
Maps & Graphics: Kat Bennett, Lohnes & Wright

Let's Keep on Travelin'

Your trip doesn't need to end.

Follow Rick on social media!